MW00461427

Equity & Cultural Responsiveness in the Middle Grades

A volume in
The Handbook of Research in Middle Level Education
Steven B. Mertens and Micki M. Caskey, *Series Editors*

THE HANDBOOK OF RESEARCH IN MIDDLE LEVEL EDUCATION SERIES

Vincent A. Anfara, Jr., *Series Editor*

The Handbook of Research in Middle Level Education (2001)
edited by Vincent A. Anfara, Jr.

Middle School Curriculum, Instruction, and Assessment (2002)
edited by Vincent A. Anfara, Jr. and Sandra L. Stacki

*Leaders for a Movement: Professional Preparation and Development
of Middle Level Teachers and Administrators* (2003)
edited by P. Gayle Andrews and Vincent A. Anfara, Jr.

Reforming Middle Level Education: Considerations for Policymakers (2004)
edited by Sue C. Thompson

Making a Difference: Action Research in Middle Level Education (2005)
edited by Micki M. Caskey

The Young Adolescent and the Middle School (2007)
edited by Steven B. Mertens, Vincent A. Anfara, Jr.,
and Micki M. Caskey

An International Look at Young Adolescents (2009)
edited by Steven B. Mertens, Vincent A. Anfara, Jr.,
and Kathleen Roney

*Voices from the Middle: Narrative Inquiry By, For, and About
the Middle Level Community* (2010)
edited by Kathleen F. Malu

*Common Planning Time in Middle Level Schools: Research Studies
from the MLER SIG's National Project* (2013)
edited by Steven B. Mertens, Vincent A. Anfara, Jr.,
Micki M. Caskey, & Nancy Flowers

Steven B. Mertens and Micki M. Caskey, *Series Editors*

*Research on Teaching and Learning with the Literacies
of Young Adolescents* (2015)
edited by Kathleen F. Malu & Mary Beth Schaefer

*Preparing Middle Level Educators for 21st Century Schools: Enduring
Beliefs, Changing Times, Evolving Practices* (2018)
edited by Penny B. Howell, Shawn A. Faulkner, Jeannine Jones,
and Jan Carpenter

Equity & Cultural Responsiveness in the Middle Grades

edited by

Kathleen Brinegar
Northern Vermont University

Lisa Harrison
Ohio University

Ellis Hurd
Illinois State University

INFORMATION AGE PUBLISHING, INC.
Charlotte, NC • www.infoagepub.com

Library of Congress Cataloging-in-Publication Data

A CIP record for this book is available from the Library of Congress
http://www.loc.gov

ISBN: 978-1-64113-673-0 (Paperback)
       978-1-64113-674-7 (Hardcover)
       978-1-64113-675-4 (ebook)

Printed in the United States of America

To the many young adolescents who demonstrate resilience within systems that marginalize them for who they are and who they dare to be.

MIDDLE LEVEL EDUCATION RESEARCH
SPECIAL INTEREST GROUP

The Handbook of Research in Middle Level Education is endorsed
by the Middle Level Education Research Special Interest Group,
an affiliate of the American Educational Research Association.

As stated in the organization's Constitution, the purpose of MLER
is to improve, promote, and disseminate educational research
reflecting early adolescence and middle level education.

CONTENTS

SECTION III

BUILDING EQUITABLE SPACES THROUGH THE IMPLEMENTATION OF CULTURALLY RESPONSIVE PRACTICES

SECTION IV

EMPOWERING MIDDLE LEVEL EDUCATORS TO WORK WITH YOUTH WITH MARGINALIZED IDENTITIES

FOREWORD

The pursuit of equity in academic outcomes and in educational opportunity is now the central focus of many school districts throughout the country. For those who have been working on equity issues for many years this is a welcomed development, but of course, it is also reasonable to ask what took so long? Challenges related to equity, which typically are manifest in the difficulties schools experience in reducing racial and socio-economic disparities in student achievement, are not new, particularly in the middle grades.

Today, more than 50% of the students served in our nation's public schools are from racial minority backgrounds (Gollnick & Chinn, 2017), and more than 50% of students qualify for free or reduced-price lunch (National Center for Education Statistics, 2018). We have known for many years that the most disadvantaged children generally do the least well in school and that the well-being of children as it pertains to health, nutrition, and other aspects of social, psychological, and emotional development, has an impact on academic performance. We also have a substantial body of evidence that schools serving the most disadvantaged children frequently struggle to meet the academic and social needs of the children they serve. Furthermore, throughout the United States, even schools with substantial resources and a track record for serving affluent White and Asian students well, often have difficulty in educating English learners, students with learning disabilities, and Black, Latinx, and Native American students, and low-income students generally.

Perhaps we have arrived at the "equity moment" because other approaches to reform, particularly those that focused exclusively on raising academic standards and holding schools and educators accountable, have proven to be inadequate at moving education forward. This Handbook provides solid advice to educators working with students in the middle grades, on how to address their academic and developmental needs. It also provides research that can help inform practices for teacher educators, researchers, and other constituents who work with marginalized and minoritized youth. The release of this volume could not be more timely. For many years, research has explained the failure of schools, particularly those in poor communities, as a byproduct of families who come from a culture of poverty. More recently, this same type of research has cited "bad teaching" and poor leadership as the most frequent factors contributing to school failure. Policymakers have responded to chronic failure and under-performance in schools largely with scrutiny, pressure, and even the threat of takeover. All of the available evidence shows that these approaches have not worked.

This Handbook takes us in a new direction with concrete strategies and ideas that can help schools to improve. By addressing equity challenges that frequently arise at the classroom level and describing the kinds of research and support that must be in place for teachers and teacher educators to be effective in addressing the academic needs of students, this volume will fill a critical need. It shifts the focus of educators from closing the so-called "achievement gap," to a new equity-based focus that responds to the needs of children of color by addressing the glaring "opportunity gaps" that are pervasive in American education. For those seeking guidance and practical suggestions or research on how to advance equity, this volume will be a breath of fresh air.

—**Pedro A. Noguera, PhD**
University of California, Los Angeles

REFERENCES

Gollnick, D. M., & Chinn, P. C. (2017). *Multicultural education in a pluralistic society* (10th ed.). Boston, MA: Pearson.

National Center for Education Statistics (2018). *Digest of education statistics: Number and percentage of public school students eligible for free or reduced-price lunch, by state: Selected years, 2000–01 through 2015–16* (Table 204.10). Retrieved from https://nces.ed.gov/programs/digest/d17/tables/dt17_204.10.asp?current=yes

ACKNOWLEDGMENTS

We would like to thank the many educators, researchers, and theorist whose life's work has been dedicated to creating equitable education practices for young adolescents whose voices and experiences remain silenced, stereotyped, and misrepresented in an unjust education system. Your work has inspired us, pushed our thinking, and informed our own scholarship and sense of human agency. This book only exists as an extension of the foundation of equity work that you have laid before us.

This book could not be possible without the authors. Your collaboration, support, and responsiveness to email requests made the daunting process of editing a book for the first time much easier. Thank you for contributing such thoughtful and important chapters to this book and for your work more broadly in the field of education. We are fortunate to have colleagues who are just as passionate and devoted to supporting culturally and linguistically diverse young adolescents. Thank you for making a difference.

Steve and Micki, thank you for your willingness to include this book in the *Handbook of Research in Middle Level Education* series and for your guidance throughout the process. Within this book we and other authors critique the field of middle level education for not attending to issues of diversity. Given this, sometimes it is hard not to feel like misfits, so we would be remiss not to acknowledge and thank you for supporting this work and allowing us a space to center this conversation within the field.

Finally, we would like to thank our family, friends, mentors, and other influential individuals who have shaped and supported our growth. Thank you for believing in us in spite of our faults, guiding us when we need direction, and encouraging us to achieve goals beyond our own foresight.

SECTION I

UNPACKING THE FAILURES OF RELYING ON DEVELOPMENTALISM AT THE MIDDLE LEVEL

CHAPTER 1

EXPLORING THE CONVERGENCE OF DEVELOPMENTALISM AND CULTURAL RESPONSIVENESS

Lisa M. Harrison
Ohio University

Ellis Hurd
Illinois State University

Kathleen M. Brinegar
Northern Vermont University

The field of middle level education is largely based on supporting the developmental needs of young adolescents. Scales (2010) defined *early adolescence* as the developmental period between the ages of 10 and 15, as he believed this age range reflected a distinctive set of physical, socioemotional, psychological, moral, and cognitive changes. Outside of infancy, early

Equity & Cultural Responsiveness in the Middle Grades, pages 3–21
Copyright © 2019 by Information Age Publishing

adolescence marks the time that a person will go through the most developmental change (Jackson & Davis, 2000). These changes are associated with distinct traits used to make meaning of and shape the experiences of young adolescents (Lesko, 2001).

Although developmentalism has been beneficial in bringing awareness to the needs of young adolescents, there is a growing critique that middle level education does not consider the needs of young adolescents from diverse backgrounds due to the over emphasis of developmentalism in the field (Hurd, Harrison, Brinegar, & Kennedy, 2018; Kennedy, Brinegar, Hurd, & Harrison, 2016; Vagle, 2012). Gay (1994) argued that when foundational middle level education texts include ethnicity or cultural diversity, they often do so superficially, include deficit perspectives, lack context, and are void of specific applications of tangible classroom practices. Furthermore, in critiquing the use of developmentalism in middle grades education, Burns and Hall (2012) stated that designing curriculum around developmentalism is dangerous because teachers are likely to respond negatively to young adolescents whose "racial, cultural, socio-economic, and gender identities" do not conform to developmental norms (p. 177). This creates a context where researchers who have been committed to the middle school movement often need to look outside of the field for theories and best practices that specifically addresses educational inequities for young adolescents from marginalized backgrounds.

Unfortunately, the middle school concept has not centered on supporting the educational experiences of minoritized youth (Hurd et al., 2018). However, there are other educational disciplines such as multicultural education (Banks, 1997; Brown & Kysilka, 2009; Nieto & Bode, 2012) and English as a Second Language (ESL) education (Rodriguez, 2011; Zimmerman, 2000) that have placed the educational equity of youth of color at the forefront of their research agendas. What cuts across these disciplines and what regrettably the field of middle level education largely left out of conversations is the role that culture plays in the educational experiences of students. This neglect has led to our frustration as researchers who value middle level education's commitment to advocacy for young adolescents, but whose work is about supporting young adolescents whose voices and experiences have largely been absent from the field of middle level education (Brinegar, 2015; Harrison, 2017; Hurd, 2012). It is from this duality that we conceptualized this book. Within this introductory chapter, we first provide an overview of developmentalism in the middle grades, explore culturally relevant frameworks that have been instrumental in supporting youth with marginalized identities, theoretically discuss what taking a cultural lens to developmentalism might look like, and finally we end with a set of implications for moving the field of middle level education forward in supporting every young adolescent.

SITUATING AND CRITIQUING DEVELOPMENTALISM IN THE MIDDLE GRADES

We cannot discuss young adolescents without mentioning G. Stanley Hall, who many consider the father of adolescence. As a pioneer in developmental psychology, his work has had a profound influence on how people think of adolescents today. Hall's (1904) two volume groundbreaking book *Adolescence: Its Psychology and Its Relations to Physiology, Anthropology, Sociology, Sex, Crime, Religion and Education* was instrumental in mainstreaming the developmental stage of adolescence (Harrison, 2016). Hall drew upon Darwin's evolutionary theory and expanded it into a psychological theory of recapitulation (Muss, 1962). In essence, Hall believed that as humans moved through different developmental stages they psychologically followed human evolutionary stages.

According to Hall's recapitulation theory, it was during what we now consider early adolescence that humans transitioned from their savage state to civilized state and therefore he took great interest in this developmental stage. It is important to note Hall focused much of his energy on White boys (Lesko, 2001). It was his belief that only White adolescents had the ability to recapitulate to a civilized state of being, while non-White races stayed in a primitive state. Therefore, he considered non-White races, such as those of African descent, "adolescent races" as they could not reach an adult stage and where subjugated to their savage state. Though the racial inferiority of minorities was already an accepted norm, it is evident that Hall's recapitulation theory only served to confirm and perpetuate this racial untruth.

While Hall was not the first person of his era to utilize recapitulation theory, and his research is scientifically inaccurate, racist, sexist, and imperialistic (Lesko, 2001), the way he applied it to adolescent development was groundbreaking and long-lasting. One abiding impact of Hall's work was the emphasis of using developmental characteristics to make meaning of adolescence. Expounding on this point, Hughes (2012) stated:

> Hall's original notions of how youth moved through certain developmental stages (of course, with his added belief that some [white boys] would move up the 'chain of being' faster than others [white girls], while others [children of color] could *never* reach 'true' civility) were taken up by psychologists, sociologists, and education theorists over the past 100 years, leaving little room to think about *adolescence* as a social, historical, and cultural construction. (p. 95)

This is especially true in the field of middle level education. While developmentalism historically has gone unchallenged, within the last two decades there have been several critiques of the prominence of the developmental perspective in middle level education because it does not attend to issues of power, privilege, and equity and thereby does not inherently serve the interest of all young adolescents (Beane, 2005; Brown, 2005; Lee & Vagle, 2010). For example, Vagle (2012) argued:

> Although stage developmentalism has brought attention to the needs of young adolescents in the name of developmental responsiveness, it also has proceeded without careful enough consideration of critical theoretical perspectives regarding issues related to power, interest, agency, gender, race, class, culture and so on. (p. 1)

When you examine developmentalism from an historical lens, it is no surprise that these critiques of it and of the field of middle level education exist. Despite the groundbreaking impact of Hall's work on adolescence, the harsh reality is that Hall never designed his conceptualization of adolescence to advocate for non-White boys. This created a context where it is not astonishing to understand why scholars have criticized a middle school movement that grounded its agenda in developmentalism, even a century and a half after Hall's work, for addressing the needs of some young adolescents while not adequately serving the needs of all young adolescents (Brinegar, 2015). More so, as the population in the United States becomes even more diverse, the needs and challenges of the past decade, and even this past sociopolitical year, have proven the traditional use of developmentalism to be largely outdated and out-of-touch with the ever-changing needs of adolescents.

FROM CULTURALLY RELEVANT TO CULTURALLY SUSTAINING PEDAGOGY

There are several pedagogical approaches that emphasize the importance of honoring students' cultural identity and making curricular choices grounded in their cultural norms. Some include cultural compatible education (Jordan, 1985), culturally congruent instruction (Au & Kawakami, 1994), and funds of knowledge (González, Moll, & Amanti, 2005). Paris (2012) termed these approaches as resource pedagogies in the ways that they:

> Repositioned the linguistic, cultural, and literate practices of poor communities—particularly poor communities of color—as resources to honor, explore, and extend in accessing Dominate American English (DAE) language and literacy skills and other White, middle-class dominate cultural norms of acting and being that are demanded in schools. (p. 94)

Paris stated that during the mid-1990s, a critical mass of research around resource pedagogies was generated but culturally relevant pedagogy (Ladson-Billings, 1995), and to a lesser extent, Gay's (2000) culturally responsive pedagogy have been taken up the most in educational research and practice.

According to Ladson-Billings (1995), there are three main outcomes of culturally relevant pedagogy, including student achievement, cultural competency, and an ability to engage in critical critique. As Ladson-Billings pointed out, it is important that we should not define student achievement solely by performance on standardized tests, but rather on overall intellectual growth. Cultural competency refers to a student's ability to develop a deeper understanding and appreciation of their own cultural heritage while also learning about a different culture. Cultural critique requires teachers to help students to develop the necessary skills to "recognize, understand, and critique current social inequities" (p. 476).

While culturally relevant pedagogy has made a significant contribution to the educational landscape, Ladson-Billings (2017) has brought attention to the fact that often scholars and educators misappropriate her work and reduce it to overly simplistic and static views of culture, omitting the emphasis on developing critical consciousness. Gorski and Swalwell's (2015) critique of multiculturalism reflected the way in which educators have taken up culturally relevant pedagogy inappropriately. They argued that work that centers on culture is often void of issues of equity and call for a move towards an equity literacy framework (Gorski, 2013) where educators recognize, respond to, and redress biases and inequities while creating an unbiased and equitable learning space.

While it is evident that equity is at the core of culturally relevant pedagogy, Ladson-Billings (2014) has called for a "remix" or updated version of culturally relevant pedagogy. She has argued that it is natural and inevitable that scholars would and should create new versions, building on the work of culturally relevant pedagogy. We see this in Emdin's (2011, 2016) reality pedagogy where teachers build on the cultural understanding and experiences of their students. Ladson-Billings (2017) stated that additionally we can see this "remix" in the work on culturally sustaining pedagogy (Paris, 2012; Paris & Alim, 2017). It aims to push past being culturally relevant or culturally responsive but rather sustain the cultural and linguistic competences of youth while also teaching them about dominate cultural and linguistic competences.

Even though educators and researchers have applied these frameworks largely to Black and Brown students, these also provide insight into thinking about how identities such as race and ethnicity and by extension sexuality and socioeconomic status influence the lived experiences of young adolescents. At their core, these are elements that have been largely void in the field of middle level education yet have so much to offer in helping the field stay relevant in supporting the needs of all young adolescents.

MOVING TOWARDS CONVERGING

Though we provide a critique of developmentalism within this chapter, instead of arguing for an outright dismantling of it, we call for a convergence of it with culturally responsive and equity-based practices. While we acknowledge that, historically, developmentalism has been rooted in White, heterosexual, male supremacy, the lens of developmentalism has also served a positive purpose in helping to formulate ways to think about young adolescents. In the same ways that Lesko (2001) situated developmentalism and young adolescents within a reductionist paradigm, scholars within the middle school movement have used it to advocate for young adolescents and to support their needs (Smith & McEwin, 2011). However, building a movement around stage-development, which at its foundation was exclusionary at best, but more likely racist, homophobic, classist, and sexist at worst, has grand implications for young adolescents who fit on the margins of "mainstream" society. We cannot escape that the "forefathers" of the middle school movement were also largely White, middle class, men. While we can give them the benefit of the doubt that their neglect to speak to the needs of students with backgrounds different from theirs was not based on malice intents, we can state that their writings, though progressive, reflected that there was at least a naiveté and colorblind approach used when laying the foundation for the middle school movement. Consequently, it created an essentialized young adolescent without acknowledging or realizing that culture matters.

To be developmentally responsive to young adolescents from marginalized backgrounds, one must be culturally responsive as well. The middle level literature currently presents developmental responsiveness so broadly and universally that it is limiting in its ability to support all young adolescents, particularly students with diverse backgrounds. Manning and Bucher (2012) stated, "Although developmental characteristics can be listed with considerable certainty, any objective discussion of young adolescents must emphasize that change is a constant and that diversity is the hallmark characteristic of young adolescents" (p. 28). Likewise, Caskey and Anfara (2014) warned that when exploring the developmental characteristics of young adolescents, it is important to realize that "race, ethnicity, gender, culture, family, community, environment and the like" (para. 3) can influence development. While these middle level experts spoke to the limitations of using developmental characteristics as the sole means of making meaning of young adolescents, these warnings still remain largely nothing more than a cautionary tale within the field of middle level education. Converging developmentalism and culturally responsiveness promotes a nuanced understanding of the experiences of all students.

Taking up three major developmental characteristics—physical, cognitive, and socioemotional—we explore how the literature has traditionally discussed these characteristics. We then discuss how the traditional developmental lens can be limiting for particular young adolescents and how applying a cultural lens to the traditional development characteristics can be beneficial in supporting a complex understanding of young adolescents.

Physical Development

Physical development refers to the changes that occur within the body. Physical developmental characteristics typically associated with early adolescence include improved gross and fine motor skills, hormonal changes, growth spurts, and the development of the sexual reproductive system (Powell, 2014; Scales, 2010). With these changes comes an increased self-awareness of young adolescents' physical appearance. Developmentally appropriate practices often taught based on these changes include creating lessons that are hands-on and incorporate movement, ensuring students have snacks to satiate hunger between meals, integrating health education within the curriculum to allow students to develop an understanding of the changes within their bodies, and educating parents about the importance of appropriate rest (Kellough & Kellough, 2008).

While these practices are important, from a cultural lens, there are several implications and limitations that should be part of the discourse on physical development when trying to support young adolescents from varied backgrounds. These include standards of beauty, gender identity formation, and homelessness. For example, notions of standards of beauty have implications for both young adolescents and those working with them. If from a physical development perspective, young adolescents have an increased awareness of their appearance then it is important to critique and understand what the traditional standards of beauty young adolescents might be comparing themselves to, especially for youth that might not be representative of "mainstream" culture. Normalized Eurocentric standards of beauty prioritize White skin, blond hair and blue eyes over browner skin tones, kinky hair, and brown eyes (Thompson, 2009). A review of recent news headlines highlights that schools with controversial policies that ban natural hairstyles such as dreadlocks and braids traditionally worn by Black girls reinforce these notions of beauty (Macon, 2015). Such policies devalue the natural state of Black girls' hair and reinforce White ideals of physical beauty. It takes applying a cultural lens to physical development to understand that we cannot inherently consider such policies developmentally responsive as degrading innate physical traits is damaging to Black young adolescents' self-concept.

Likewise, the discourse around sexual identity and gender identity with relation to physical development is also problematic in the way that it reinforces heteronormative beliefs. Warner (1991) defined heteronormativity as the use of heterosexuality as the norm for understanding gender and sexuality. While there are physical developmental differences that take place during early adolescence, the way that the middle level literature discusses gender often reinforces a gender binary of boys and girls (see Hart, 2016; Kommer, 2006; Weilbacher & Lanier, 2012; Zittleman, 2007). This inherently erases the experience of young adolescents who are intersex. Johnson, Mimiaga, and Bradford (2008) defined intersex as a person who is born with atypical genital or reproductive anatomy. Therefore, an intersex person may not fit into the typical definition of male nor female. Furthermore, the gender binary discourse does not allow a space to affirm young adolescents who might consider themselves gender-fluid, transgender, questioning, transitioning, or other non-cisgender identity (Rands, 2009). One could argue that understanding how to be responsive to physical developmental changes is even more important for young adolescents whose developing physical bodies do not reflect the people they are inside. This misalignment can cause transgendered youth to feel ashamed of their changing sexual characteristics (Burgess, 1999).

Conversations related to physical development also seem eerily silent when considering youth homelessness. Although a familiar and recognized social phenomenon, conversations surrounding youth homelessness and its impact on adolescents' physical development—directly related to economic living conditions—seem rather silent. Yet the impact of youth homelessness and its negative consequences on youth physical development cannot fall on deaf ears.

> Skyrocketing foreclosures and job layoffs have pulled the rug out from under many families, particularly those living in low-income communities. Deepening poverty is inextricably linked with rising levels of homelessness and food insecurity/hunger for many Americans and children are particularly affected by these conditions. (American Psychological Association, 2018)

The fact that homelessness "occurs disproportionately among people of color" (APA, 2018, para. 2), and "is linked to poor physical health for children including low birth weight, malnutrition, ear infections, exposure to environmental toxins and chronic illness (e.g., asthma)" (APA, 2018, para. 23), only intensifies the difficulty many youth face in undergoing physical development. These discussions and implications of homelessness on physical development for youth rarely occur in relation to one another.

These are only three examples that highlight how traditional discussions of physical development miss the complexity of young adolescents' realities. While conversations about growth spurts and fine and gross motor skills are important to have, simply confining physical development to biological factors limits the utility of using physical characteristics to understand young adolescents. Conversely, taking a culturally responsive lens requires educators to explore critically how young adolescents' identities impact the meaning that they and the world make of their physical development.

Cognitive Development

Cognitive development refers to a change in mental abilities such as reasoning and thinking. Cognitive developmental characteristics typically described during early adolescence include an increasing ability to think abstractly, favoring active rather than passive learning, and a growing curiosity about themselves and the world (Scales, 2010). Young adolescents also present a broad range of individual cognitive abilities during this stage, including their ability to engage in metacognitive and independent thought (Caskey & Anfara, 2014). Powell (2014), in addition, because of young adolescents' wide and varied range of interests and curiosities, described them as being very eager to learn about things that they deem interesting or see as useful.

Based on these cognitive characteristics, developmentally appropriate practices promoted in middle level education include using varied instructional strategies to hold young adolescents' attention and including both concrete and abstract concepts that challenge the thinking of young adolescent learners (Manning & Bucher, 2012). In addition, teachers should also provide opportunities for discussion about real-life concepts and curriculum that is relevant to young adolescent lives (Kellough & Kellough, 2008; Manning & Bucher, 2012).

Again, fundamentally there is nothing glaringly wrong with what the literature promotes about cognitive development. The problem is in the vagueness of the description and the exclusion of directly discussing how culture shapes the recommended pedagogical approaches. For example, if making curriculum relevant is a response to supporting the cognitive needs of young adolescents, as articulated in *This We Believe* (National Middle School Association, 2010), the vision statement of the Association for Middle Level Education, then culturally responsive practices should be a central focus of middle level education. However, Kennedy et al. (2016) found that culturally responsive pedagogies largely have been absent from middle level literature or loosely connected to middle level practices. Likewise, in Busey's (2017) critical race discourse analysis of *This We Believe,* he found that while the text included some culturally responsive practices, they were not situated within culture, thus essentially sanitizing race from the conversation of culturally responsive practices.

Educators cannot ask important questions about cognitive development when we remove notions of race, language, nationality, ethnicity, and socio-economic status from the conversation. Educators can use such questions to investigate which students school systematically presume are unable to engage in complex thinking tasks and thus schools do not give them the opportunity to develop critical thinking skills. Taking a culturally responsive look at cognitive development requires educators to be sensitive to the varied backgrounds of young adolescents, especially those from minoritized backgrounds.

We can see the neglect of practicing cultural responsiveness in language-omission. The (mis)handling of culture and the absence of rich language education, as a reflection of culture or background itself, is unfortunately prevalent in middle grades classrooms today. Sociolinguists such as Baker (2001), Brisk (2006), Collier (1995), and Krashen (1997) have long established the cognitive benefits of bilingualism over monolingualism and the advantages of having at least two sets of schemas from which to draw. Yet their research continues to show that the United States lags behind the rest of the world in thought and practice concerning the language education of American youth. Outside of a few innovative schools, academies, and districts sprinkled across the nation, most public educational institutions make use of monolingual practices that force culturally and linguistically diverse students toward rather monolithic experiences and oppressed identities and cultures. As Hurd (2012) established in his research, many teachers claim to treat all students the same regardless of backgrounds or races. But the problem with these claims is that it ultimately perpetuates White privilege and creates a failure to recognize the existence of racial and cultural diversity and racial inequities in schools.

When it comes to exploring academics, we can see these racial inequities in the overrepresentation of culturally and linguistically diverse students in special education (Connor, 2017; Ford & Russo, 2016; Sullivan, 2011) and their underrepresentation in gifted education (Wright, Ford, & Young, 2017). Simply framing the conversation about young adolescent development in terms of cognitive development does not consider the context in which cognitive development occurs. Therefore, instead of focusing on the fact that teachers receive limited training or professional development on how to support the cognitive development of linguistically diverse students (Menken & Antunez, 2001; Reeves, 2006), the solution becomes funneling students largely into special education versus providing necessary professional development for teachers. Solely focusing on a biological view of cognitive development promotes the myth of meritocracy (Milner, 2012), which states that one's success is simply based on their hard work, skills, and ability. Taking a culturally responsive look at cognitive developmental not only allows teachers to examine how they can use students' culture and identities as assets to support learning but also how some educational approaches and policies are harmful to the cognitive development of young adolescents.

Social-Emotional

Social-emotional development refers to a person's interactions with people around them and the ways in which they regulate their own emotions and behaviors. A large part of how society views young adolescents comes from the ways the literature describes their social-emotional development. This includes young adolescents experiencing a variety of unpredictable and extreme emotions in a short span of time. Powell (2014) claimed that a very prominent emotion of young adolescents is worry. She described how many young adolescents tie their emotions to their physical characteristics and, as a result, their self-esteem can suffer during this developmental stage. Scales (2010) mentioned how young adolescents are concerned about what other people think of them and therefore they focus increasingly on peer acceptance. He described how during this stage, young adolescents have a stronger sense of belonging and while peer membership is important, their need for independence and decision-making increases.

As a result of these social-emotional characteristics, best practices with young adolescents typically include recognizing the importance of peer relationships and providing students time to engage in constructive talk through activities such as argumentation or debate. In addition, experts encourage strategies like socio-drama and role play because they allow students to act out their emotions and promote self-reflection. There is also an emphasis on teachers modeling the behaviors they want students to adopt, which includes the avoidance of sarcasm (Kellough & Kellough, 2008; Manning & Bucher, 2012).

Again, we need a nuanced understanding of social-emotional development that takes young adolescents' multiple identities into consideration. Cultural identity inherently influences notions of belonging. Research indicated that children become aware of ethnicity as early as the age of three (Holmes, 1995). By the time students reach early adolescence they understand the social implications of ethnicity such as an awareness of social class differences between ethnic groups. Phinney (2008) stated:

> [E]xposure to a wider world during adolescence leads to an increased awareness of group stereotypes, as well as of differences among groups in terms of power and privilege and the implications of such difference. These experiences lead to questions and uncertainty that are at the basis of identity exploration. (p. 100)

While young adolescents are becoming aware of their identities and the stereotypes associated with those identities, research indicates that White teachers, which make up 82% of all public school teachers (U.S. Department of Education, 2016), often take a colorblind approach to teaching (Johnson, 2002). This is extremely problematic. It becomes impossible to help young adolescents, particularly those from culturally and linguistically diverse backgrounds, develop a strong sense of self when the teacher is blind to differences. Ullucci and Battey (2011) explained that "color blindness relegates racism to a historical artifact, refusing to recognize how it operates today. This mistakenly places individuals as existing outside the influence of privilege, oppression, and power" (p. 1202). To have conversations about supporting positive self-esteem and creating a sense of belonging that are void of discourses about racism, xenophobia, classism, homophobia, religious discrimination, and sexism is neglectful and impossible.

Shifting from neutral discussions of socio-emotional development to a culturally responsive one allows and requires teachers to reflect on how young adolescents' identities impact their social-emotional well-being, with the understanding that identities are socially and historically situated and consistently in flux (Saltman, 2005). Furthermore, it allows teachers to reflect on how to create affirming spaces for students with historically devalued identities that society continues to marginalize. Robinson and Espelage (2011) found that lesbian, gay, bisexual, transgender, and queer (LGBTQ) youth are disproportionately the victims of bullying. They also found that LGBTQ youth reported lower levels of belongingness compared to their peers. Likewise, research has indicated that schools are hostile spaces for Black students particularly with the influx of zero tolerance policies (Howard, 2016). Taking a culturally responsive lens to socio-emotional development allows schools to examine critically how they function as sites that damage the well-being of students with diverse backgrounds while also working towards supporting young adolescents who are coping with traumatic experiences that stem from society at large marginalizing them.

IMPLICATIONS FOR MIDDLE LEVEL EDUCATORS

Middle level educators must realize that culture and identity often matter more than age in shaping the experiences of young adolescents. Researchers indicate that people often assume that Black girls and boys are older than what they are and less innocent than their White peers (see Epstein, Blake, & González, 2017; Goff, Jackson, Di Leone, Culotta, & DiTomasso, 2014). The mere fact that they are of a certain race positions them as being more "adult like." The harsh reality is that the world often makes meaning of young adolescents based on their socially constructed identities despite their actual biological age or developmental stage. Therefore, it is not solely enough for middle level educators to understand different developmental characteristics without looking through the lens of identity to make meaning of development. Hall (1996) stated that "precisely because identities are constructed within, not outside, discourse, we need to understand them as produced in specific historical and institutional sites within specific discursive formations and practices, by specific enunciative strategies" (p. 4). Consequently, it is necessary to understand the socio-historical contexts that impact identity construction.

Middle level educators must also disrupt an essentialized view of young adolescents. Young adolescents are not monolithic but rather are dynamic beings who possess various identities. Instead of taking a monolithic view of early adolescence, the field should embrace an intersectionality lens, as age alone does not determine the experiences of young adolescents. Rather, age represents one of young adolescents' many identities. Shields (2008), writing on intersectionality, asserted that different social identities such as race, class, and gender weave together in a way that each identity cannot exist separately and that we must define each through its intersection with other identities. Intersectionality theory, which finds its roots in Black feminist scholarship (Collins, 1990; Combahee River Collective, 1977; hooks, 1984; Spelman, 1988) and critical legal studies scholarship (Crenshaw, 1989, 1991) has been beneficial in helping illuminate social inequities within and between groups of people who might share similar identities. Harrison (2017) asserted, "Intersectionality theory could be used as a way to advocate for marginalized youth...An intersectionality lens of adolescence could inform educators how certain policies, curriculum, and pedagogies might benefit one group while harming or ignoring another" (p. 1036). Intersectionality theory disrupts the concept of an essentialized womanhood, a concept that neglects how race and other axes of oppression affect experiences of Black women. In the same way, intersectionality theory can be a powerful tool in disrupting the singular and fixed view of young adolescence pervasive in middle level education, thereby helping to illuminate the complexity of what it means to be a culturally and linguistically diverse young adolescent within schools and society at large.

Finally, the field of middle level education needs to examine current middle level practices that are sacred to the middle level movement. Lesko (2001) argued that because the way society constructs adolescence "is so democratized, so commonsensical, and so trivialized, we often cannot see its regulation and containment of youth" (p. 10). This argument can hold true for components of the middle school concept, such as advisory programs, interdisciplinary curriculum, common planning time, and teaming. Within middle level education we operate with the notion that a middle school philosophy and the middle school concepts are the best way to support all young adolescents. Few middle level scholars have offered critiques about these practices. It is not to say that these components are not relevant or meaningful today, but the field needs to be open to examining whether the concepts promoted at the start of the middle school movement are still relevant to the ever-changing demographics of young adolescents. Harrison, Brinegar, and Hurd (2018) argued for a shift from generically discussing middle level practices to situating them within a larger social, cultural, historical, and political context. Perhaps the fields need to develop new practices that consider the needs of young adolescents from diverse backgrounds. As Ladson-Billings (2014) stated, "A literature that tells us what works for middle-class, advantaged students typically fails to reveal the social and cultural advantages that make their success possible" (p. 67). What would it look if we created practices that supported the needs of the most marginalized young adolescents instead of the most privileged?

CONCLUSION

This We Believe: Keys to Educating Young Adolescents (NMSA, 2010) outlined four essential attributes and 16 vital characteristics of successful schools for young adolescents. One of the strengths of this document and other foundational texts used to conceptualize middle grades education philosophy is its advocacy for young adolescents. At the core of this advocacy is creating a school culture and curriculum that caters to the developmental needs and characteristics of young adolescents. While developmental responsiveness may be a deserving emphasis of middle grades education, this emphasis has often been to the detriment of focusing on the cultural needs of young adolescents.

Because middle school philosophy largely centers on young adolescents as a collective group, the focus on developmentalism across all students has great implications for young adolescents, including but not limited to those with culturally and linguistically diverse backgrounds, LGBTQ youth, and those living in poverty. If middle level educators claim to advocate for young adolescents, we need to mainstream conversations about supporting every young adolescent, including those with marginalized identities. It empowers researchers, educators, and even young adolescents to examine critically and understand the intersectionality of identities that historically influenced (and continue to affect) young adolescents and why educators might perceive marginalized youth in certain ways.

It is for these reasons that researchers, teachers, administrators, and other key constituents involved in the education of young adolescents must devote themselves to the critical examination and understanding of the historical and current socio-cultural factors affecting all young adolescents. As much of this work has occurred outside of the field of middle grades education, the chapters in this handbook present research related to equitable and culturally responsive practices for working with young adolescents. These chapters serve to open an intentional and explicit space for providing a critical lens on early adolescence; a lens that understands that we need to emphasize both the developmental and cultural needs of young adolescents to create learning environments that support every young adolescent learner.

REFERENCES

American Psychological Association. (2018). *Effects of poverty, hunger and homelessness on children and youth* (Homelessness section). Washington, DC: Author. Retrieved from http://www.apa.org/pi/families/poverty.aspx

Au, K. H., & Kawakami, A. J. (1994). Cultural congruence in instruction. In E. R. Hollins, J. E. King, & W. C. Hayman (Eds.), *Teaching diverse populations: Formulating a knowledge base* (pp. 5–23). Albany: State University of New York Press.

Baker, C. (2001). *Foundations of bilingual education and bilingualism* (3rd ed.). Clevedon, England: Multilingual Matters Ltd. Retrieved from https://crianca bilingue.files.wordpress.com/2013/10/colin-baker-foundations-of-bilingual -education-and-bilingualism-bilingual-education-and-bilingualism-27-2001.pdf

Banks, J. A. (1997). Approaches to multicultural curriculum reform. In J. A. Banks & C. A. Banks (Eds.), *Multicultural education: Issues and perspectives* (3rd ed., pp. 229–250). Boston, MA: Allyn and Bacon.

Beane, J. A. (2005). Foreword. In E. R. Brown & K. J. Saltman (Eds.), *The critical middle school reader* (pp. xi-xv). New York, NY: Routledge.

Brinegar, K. (2015). A content analysis of four peer-reviewed middle grades publications: Are we really paying attention to every young adolescent? *Middle Grades Review, 1*(1), 1–8. Retrieved from https://files.eric.ed.gov/fulltext/ EJ1154860.pdf

Brisk, M. E. (2006). *Bilingual education: From compensatory to quality schooling*. Mahwah, NJ: Erlbaum.

Brown, E. R. (2005). Introduction. In E. R. Brown & K. J. Saltman (Eds.), *The critical middle school reader* (pp. 1–14). New York, NY: Routledge.

Brown, S. C., & Kysilka, M. (2009). *What every teacher should know about multicultural and global education*. Boston, MA: Pearson.

Burgess, C. (1999). Internal and external stress factors associated with the identity development of transgendered youth. *Journal of Gay & Lesbian Social Services, 10*(3–4), 35–47.

Burns, L. D., & Hall, L. A. (2012). Using students' funds of knowledge to enhance middle grades education: Responding to adolescen(TS). In M. Vagle (Ed.), *Not a stage! A critical reconceptualization of young adolescent education* (pp. 175–190). New York, NY: Peter Lang.

Busey, C. (2017, April). *This who believes? A critical race discourse analysis of the Association for Middle Level Education's This We Believe*. Paper presented at the meeting of the American Educational Research Association, San Antonio, TX.

Caskey, M. M., & Anfara, Jr., V. A. (2014). *Research summary: Developmental characteristics of young adolescents.* Retrieved from http://www.amle.org/Browseby-Topic/WhatsNew/WNDet.aspx?ArtMID=888&ArticleID=455

Collier, V. (1995). Acquiring a second language for school. *National Clearinghouse for Bilingual Education, 1*(4). Retrieved from http://www.thomasandcollier.com/assets/1995-v1-n4_ncela_acquiring_a_second_language__.pdf

Collins, P. H. (1990). *Black feminist thought: Knowledge, consciousness, and the politics of empowerment.* New York, NY: Routledge.

Combahee River Collective. (1977). *Combahee River Collective statement.* Retrieved from https://americanstudies.yale.edu/sites/default/files/files/Keyword%20Coalition_Readings.pdf

Connor, D. J. (2017). Who is responsible for the racialized practices evident within (special) education and what can be done to change them? *Theory Into Practice, 56*(3), 226–233.

Crenshaw, K. (1989). Demarginalizing the intersection of race and sex: A black feminist critique of antidiscrimination doctrine, feminist theory, and antiracist politics. *University of Chicago Legal Forum, 1,*139–167. Retrieved from https://chicagounbound.uchicago.edu/cgi/viewcontent.cgi?article=1052&context=uclf

Crenshaw, K. (1991). Mapping the margins: Intersectionality, identity politics, and violence against women of color. *Stanford Law Review, 43*(6), 1241–1279.

Ford, D. Y., & Russo, C. J. (2016). Historical and legal overview of special education overrepresentation: Access and equity denied. *Multiple Voices for Ethnically Diverse Exceptional Learners, 16*(1), 50–57.

Emdin, C. (2011). Moving beyond the boat without a paddle: Reality pedagogy, Black youth, and urban science education. *Journal of Negro Education, 80*(3), 284–295.

Emdin, C. (2016). *For White folks who teach in the hood . . . and the rest of Y'all too: Reality pedagogy in urban education.* Boston, MA: Beacon Press.

Epstein, R., Blake, J. J., & González, T. (2017). *Girlhood interrupted: The erasure of Black girls' childhood.* Georgetown Law Center on Poverty and Inequality. Retrieved from http://www.law.georgetown.edu/academics/centers-institutes/povertyinequality/upload/girlhood-interrupted.pdf

Gay, G. (1994). Coming of age ethnically: Teaching young adolescents of color. *Theory Into Practice, 33*(3), 149–155.

Gay, G. (2000). *Culturally responsive teaching: Theory, research, and practice.* New York, NY: Teachers College Press.

Goff, P. A., Jackson, M. C., Di Leone, B. A., Culotta, C. M., & DiTomasso, N. A. (2014). The essence of innocence: Consequences of dehumanizing Black children. *Journal of Personality and Social Psychology, 106*(4), 526–545.

González, N., Moll, L., & Amanti, C. (2005). *Funds of knowledge: Theorizing practices in households, communities, and classrooms.* Mahwah, NJ: Erlbaum.

Gorski, P. C. (2013). *Reaching and teaching students in poverty: Strategies for erasing the opportunity gap.* New York, NY: Teachers College Press.

Gorski, P., & Swalwell, K. (2015). Equity literacy for all. *Educational Leadership, 72*(6), 34–40.

Hall, G. S. (1904). *Adolescence: Its psychology and its relations to physiology, anthropology, sociology, sex, crime, religion and education.* New York, NY: D. Appleton.

Hall, S. (1996). Who needs 'identity'? In S. Hall & P. du Gay (Eds.), *Questions of cultural identity* (pp. 1–17). Thousand Oaks, CA: SAGE.

Harrison, L. M. (2016). G. Stanley Hall. In S. B. Mertens, M. M. Caskey, & N. Flowers (Eds.), *Encyclopedia of middle grades education* (2nd ed., pp. 187–188). Charlotte, NC: Information Age.

Harrison, L. M. (2017). Redefining intersectionality theory through the lens of African American young adolescent girls' racialized experiences. *Journal of Youth & Society, 49*(8), 1023–1039.

Harrison, L. M, Brinegar, K., & Hurd, E., (2018). Engagement for whom? *Middle School Journal, 49*(1), 2–3.

Hart, L. C. (2016). When "separate" may be better: Exploring single-sex learning as a remedy for social anxieties in female middle school students. *Middle School Journal, 47*(2), 32–40.

Holmes, R. (1995). *How young children perceive race.* Thousand Oaks, CA: SAGE.

Hooks, B. (1984). *From margin to center.* Boston, MA: South End Press.

Howard, T. C. (2016). Why Black lives (and minds) matter: Race, freedom schools & the quest for educational equity. *The Journal of Negro Education, 85*(2), 101–113.

Hughes, H. (2012). Always becoming never enough: Middle school girls talk back. In M. Vagle (Ed.), *Not a stage! A critical reconceptualization of young adolescent education* (pp. 93–118). New York, NY: Peter Lang.

Hurd, E., Harrison, L., Brinegar, K., & Kennedy, B. L. (2018). Cultural responsiveness in the middle grades: A literature review. In S. B. Mertens & M. M. Caskey (Eds.), *Literature reviews in support of the Middle Level Education Research Agenda* (pp. 25–51). Charlotte, NC: Information Age.

Hurd, E. (2012). A framework for understanding multicultural identities: An investigation of a middle level student's French-Canadian Honduran-American (Mestizo) identity. *Middle Grades Research Journal, 7*(2), 111–127.

Jackson, A. W., & Davis, G. A. (2000). *Turning Points 2000: Educating adolescents in the 21st century.* New York, NY: Teachers College Press.

Johnson, C., Mimiaga, M., & Bradford, J. (2008). Health care issues among lesbian, gay, bisexual, transgender and intersex (LGBTI) populations in the United States: Introduction. *Journal of Homosexuality, 54*(3), 213–224.

Johnson, L. (2002). "My eyes have been opened": White teachers and racial awareness. *Journal of Teacher Education, 53*(2), 153–167.

Jordan, C. (1985). Translating culture: From ethnographic information to educational program. *Anthropology and Education Quarterly, 16*(2), 105–123.

Kellough, R. D., & Kellough, N. G. (2008). *Teaching young adolescents: Methods and resources for middle grades teaching* (5th ed.). Upper Saddle River, NJ: Pearson Merrill Prentice Hall.

Kennedy, B. L., Brinegar, K., Hurd, E., & Harrison, L. (2016). Synthesizing middle grades research on cultural responsiveness: The importance of a shared conceptual framework. *Middle Grades Review, 2*(3), 1–20. Retrieved from http://scholarworks.uvm.edu/mgreview/vol2/iss3/2

Kommer, D. (2006). Considerations for gender-friendly classrooms. *Middle School Journal, 38*(2), 43–49.

Krashen, S. (1997). *Why bilingual education?* Charleston, WV: ERIC Clearinghouse on Rural Education and Small Schools (ERIC Document Reproduction Service No. ED403101). Retrieved from https://files.eric.ed.gov/fulltext/ED403101.pdf

Ladson-Billings, G. (1995). Toward a theory of culturally relevant pedagogy. *American Educational Research Journal, 32*(3), 465–491.

Ladson-Billings, G. (2014). Culturally relevant pedagogy 2.0: A.K.A. the remix. *Harvard Educational Review, 84*(1), 74–84.

Ladson-Billings, G. (2017). The (r)evolution will not be standardized: Teacher education, hip hop pedagogy, and culturally relevant pedagogy 2.0. In D. Paris & S. Alim (Eds.), *Culturally sustaining pedagogies: Teaching and learning for justice in a changing world* (pp. 141–156). New York, NY: Teachers College Press.

Lee, K., & Vagle, M.D. (2010). General introduction: Developmentalism and the need for critical conversations within and across the fields. In K. Lee & M.D. Vagle (Eds.), *Developmentalism in early childhood and middle grades education: Critical conversations on readiness and responsiveness* (pp. 1–9). New York, NY: Palgrave Macmillan.

Lesko, N. (2001). *Act your age: A cultural construction of adolescence.* New York, NY: Routledge.

Macon, A. L. F. (2015). Hair's the thing: Trait discrimination and forced performance of race through racially conscious public school hairstyle prohibitions. *Journal of Constitutional Law, 17*(4), 1255–1281.

Manning, M. L., & Bucher, K. T. (2012). *Teaching in the middle school* (4th ed.). New York, NY: Pearson.

Menken, K., & Antunez, B. (2001). *An overview of the preparation and certification of teachers working with limited English proficient students.* Washington, DC: National Clearinghouse of Bilingual Education. Retrieved from https://files.eric.ed.gov/fulltext/ED455231.pdf

Milner, H. R. (2012). Beyond a test score: Explaining opportunity gaps in educational practice. *Journal of Black Studies, 43*(6), 643–718.

Muss, R. E. (1962). *Theories of adolescence.* New York, NY: Random House.

National Middle School Association. (2010). *This we believe: Keys to educating young adolescents.* Westerville, OH: Author.

Nieto, S., & Bode, P. (2012). *Affirming diversity: The sociopolitical context of multicultural education* (6th ed.). Boston, MA: Pearson.

Paris, D. (2012). Culturally sustaining pedagogy: A needed change in stance, terminology, and practice. *Educational Researcher, 41*(3), 93–97.

Paris, D., & Alim, H. S. (Eds.). (2017). *Culturally sustaining pedagogies: Teaching and learning for justice in a changing world.* New York, NY: Teachers College Press.

Phinney, J. S. (2008). Bridging identities and disciplines: Advances and challenges in understanding multiple identities. *New Directions for Child and Adolescent Development, 2008*(120), 97–109.

Powell, S. D. (2014). *Introduction to middle school* (3rd ed.). Upper Saddle River, NJ: Pearson.

Rands, K. E. (2009). Considering transgender people in education: A gender-complex approach. *Journal of Teacher Education, 60*(4), 419–431.

Reeves, J. (2006). Secondary teacher attitudes toward including English-language learners in mainstream classrooms. *The Journal of Educational Research, 99*(3), 131–142.

Robinson, J. P., & Espelage, D. L. (2011). Inequities in educational and psychological outcomes between LGBTQ and straight students in middle and high school. *Educational Researcher, 40*(7), 315–330.

Rodriguez, D. (2011). Silence as speech: Meanings of silence for students of color in predominantly White classrooms. *International Review of Qualitative Research, 4*(1), 111–144.

Saltman, K. J. (2005). The construction of identity. In E. R. Brown & K. J. Saltman (Eds.), *The critical middle school reader* (pp. 237–234). New York, NY: Routledge.

Scales, P. C. (2010). Characteristics of young adolescents. In *This we believe: Keys to Educating young adolescents* (pp. 53–62). Westerville, OH: National Middle School Association.

Shields, S. (2008). Gender: An intersectionality perspective. *Sex Roles, 59*(5), 301–311.

Smith, T., & McEwin, K. (2011). *The legacy of middle school leaders in their own words.* Charlotte, NC: Information Age.

Spelman, E. V. (1988). *Inessential woman: Problems of exclusion in feminist thought.* Boston, MA: Beacon.

Sullivan, A. (2011). Disproportionality in special education identification and placement of English language learners. *Exceptional Children, 77*(3), 317–334.

Thompson, C. (2009). Black women, beauty, and hair as a matter of being. *Women's Studies, 38*(8), 831–856. doi:10.1080/00497870903238463

Ulluci, K., & Battey, D. (2011). Exposing color blindness/grounding color consciousness: Challenges for teacher education. *Urban Education, 46*(6), 1195–1225.

U.S. Department of Education. (2016). *The state of racial diversity in the educator workforce.* Washington, DC: Author. Retrieved from https://www2.ed.gov/rschstat/eval/highered/racial-diversity/state-racial-diversity-workforce.pdf

Vagle, M. D. (2012). Introduction: Being a bit disruptive. In M. D. Vagle (Ed.), *Not a stage! A critical re-conception of young adolescent education* (p. 1–9). New York, NY: Peter Lang.

Warner, M. (1991). Introduction: Fear of a queer planet. *Social Text, 29,* 3–17.

Weilbacher, G., & Lanier, J. (2012). An examination of a gender-separate advisory program. *Middle Grades Research Journal, 7*(1), 17–35.

Wright, B. L., Ford, D. Y., & Young, J. L. (2017). Ignorance or indifference? Seeking excellence and equity for under-represented students of color in gifted education. *Global Education Review, 4*(1), 45–60.

Zimmerman, L. W. (2000). Bilingual education as a manifestation of an ethic of caring. *Educational Horizons, 78*(2), 72–76.

Zittleman, K. R. (2007). Gender perceptions of middle schoolers: The good and the bad. *Middle Grades Research Journal, 2*(2), 65–97.

CHAPTER 2

MISSED OPPORTUNITIES, NO MORE

Mark D. Vagle
University of Minnesota

Tracy M. Hamel
University of Minnesota

ABSTRACT

Responding to the research question: Why is the middle school concept not more widely explored as a means of supporting marginalized students, we make three interrelated arguments. First, the middle school concept has missed many opportunities for insurrection. Second, the middle school concept has yet to embrace and respond fully and explicitly to the fluid, multiple, and intersectional nature of human experience. Third, it may just be important to focus less on the middle school concept writ large and focus more on what can be learned directly from young adolescents and adults who live and/or work in communities comprised primarily of marginalized students.

In this chapter, we respond to one of the guiding questions of this handbook, which focuses on why the middle school concept (e.g., Carnegie Council on Adolescent Development, 1989; Jackson & Davis, 2000; National

Equity & Cultural Responsiveness in the Middle Grades, pages 23–43
Copyright © 2019 by Information Age Publishing

Middle School Association, 2010) is not more widely explored as a means of supporting marginalized students through three interrelated arguments. It is important to note that our arguments are not the result of a data-based study. Rather they are the result of our theoretical and reflective analysis as scholars and pedagogues. Further, we describe our third argument as a "narrative of narratives" for two reasons. First, the tone of our writing turns from more traditional academic prose to more narrative writing. Second, this argument contains a few smaller narratives that we stitched together, for our purposes here, in unique and particular ways as a broader narrative. Our first argument is entitled *missed opportunities for insurrection*. In this section, we situate our argument, theoretically, by pointing to some central assertions Vagle (first author) makes in his article, *Reviving Theoretical Insurrection in Middle Grades Education* (Vagle, 2015). We suggest that the middle school concept, as it currently stands, may not be all that well-suited to respond to opportunities for insurrection as young adolescents witness schools driven by late stage neo-liberalism; communities speaking out for racial justice to seemingly deaf ears; the worst income and wealth gap since the Great Depression; and arguably one of the most divisive presidential elections in the history of the United States.

Our second argument is entitled, *not responding enough to the fluidities, multiplicities, and intersectionalities of the human experience*. In this section, we explore how the middle school concept does not appear to call explicitly for or fully utilize *intersectionality* (e.g., Crenshaw, 1991; hooks, 2000; Lorde, 1983)—and it could be a useful addition.

Our third argument, and the conclusion to the chapter, is entitled, *learning less from a concept to learn more from both young adolescents and adults who work with young adolescents about positionality, power, and relationship*. We write this section as a "narrative of narratives" based on Hamel's (second author) early teaching experiences and her current work with young adolescent youth in a low-income community of color. We purposefully have chosen not to write a traditional conclusion. Rather, we try to weave our "conclusion-like" food for thought throughout the first two sections and then let the narrative of narratives speak more for itself.

MISSED OPPORTUNITIES FOR INSURRECTION

According to the online Free Dictionary (n.d.), *insurrection* is "the act or an instance of open revolt against civil authority..." Working from *MSNBC* political commentator Chris Hayes' (2012) call for the need for *insurrectionist movements*, Vagle (2015) argued for an insurrectionist-oriented movement in middle grades education. He has suggested that the roots of the middle school movement (1970s), and what ultimately grew into a concept (1980s and 1990s), could be read as somewhat insurrectionist in nature—given how the movement and concept fundamentally changed grade configurations, teaching practices, curricula, home-school relationships, teaming structures, and master schedules on a large-scale throughout the United States and internationally. An organized, persistent, courageous, and passionate middle school movement made these accomplishments, and numerous more, possible. Many young adolescents benefited from it. However, Vagle also argued that since the turn of the century, he started to question the middle grades concept a bit, especially the foundational commitment to developmentalism and the missed opportunity to re-imagine itself contextually over time, and continue its insurrectionist ways. Contextually speaking, much changed in the early 2000s. The accountability movement hijacked the standards movement of the 1980s and 1990s (Ravitch, 2010). Standardized tests used for curricular planning and adjustments became high-stakes measures of student, teacher, principal, school, and school system success or failure (Nichols & Berliner, 2007). Education slowly and deliberately shifted from state purview to federal purview under No Child Left Behind (2001)—and over at least the last 25 years neo-liberal economic principles slowly and insidiously seeped into education, in the name of "reform." At the same time, the overall financial health of the country reached its lowest point since the Great Depression; the nation's income inequality was at its worst since World War II (Reardon, 2011); and racial upheaval in, for example, Ferguson, Missouri reminded us that explicit and institutionalized racism had by no means been eradicated as some would want us to believe.

Hayes (2012) argued that the decade, 2000–2010, should be referred to as the *fail decade.* A time in which all major institutions that our country depends on to care for its citizens (e.g., government, education, big business, organized religion) failed. He felt that to undo the damage of the fail decade we need another insurrectionist movement, much like the fight for civil rights in the 1960s. He thought the *Occupy Wall Street* movement had the makings of insurrection, but it did not quite take hold deeply enough.

Around the same time (1990s into the early 2000s), the middle grades movement did not appear to respond to its own "opportunity for insurrection," following Lesko's (2001) convincing call for a less prescriptive focus on developmental responsiveness. The movement often (wittingly or unwittingly) positions young adolescents in deficit-oriented ways, in favor of a more particularized responsiveness that honors young adolescents in the present and that begins to be more responsive, instead, for example, to the ethnic and cultural diversity of young adolescents (Gay, 1994).

Re-Imagining the Middle School Concept to Explicitly Support Marginalized Students

As mentioned prior, the far-reaching influence of the accountability movement (Ravitch, 2010) appears to have further calcified the very normative educational policies and practices Lesko (2001) aimed to disrupt. Developmental responsiveness is still an important (if not the most) pillar of middle grades education (NMSA, 2010). While being responsive to a developmental stage seems commonsensical to middle grades advocates, as Lesko and others have helped us think about, a developmental conception of growth and change can be read as "freezing" young adolescents in whatever characteristics are used to describe the developmental stage of early adolescence, unintentionally stripping them of the very agency advocates of developmental responsiveness desire.

Vagle (2012) suggested that it would be better to take up Lesko's (2001) call for a contingent (profoundly contextual and dependent), recursive (occurring over and over again, in and over time) conception of growth and change. This sort of theoretical move could *de-stabilize* growth and change as something inextricably linked to the innumerable situations and micro-contexts that young adolescents experience.

At the close of her book, *Act Your Age! A Cultural Construction of Adolescence*, Lesko (2001) called for alternative (to developmentalism and socialization) conceptions of growth and change. She wrote:

> I think that if we assumed that growth and change are *contingent*, we would need to specify the contingencies and that would lead us to examine and document multiple micro-contexts. I also think that a conception of growth and change as *recursive*, as occurring over and over as we move into new situations, would reorient us. Rather than the assumption of cumulative and one-way development that is now in place in both science and popular culture, a recursive view of growth and change directs us to look at local contexts and specific actions of young people, without the inherent evaluation of steps, stages, and socialization. (pp. 195–196)

Lesko's (2001) call is based on a set of critical theoretical assumptions about knowledge production. First, she pressed us to try to locate and then work to break from a dominant discourse, stage developmentalism in this case. This involves a careful examination of both the larger social matters that constrain some things and make other things possible. Second, such an approach requires that we actively and persistently seek to illuminate who ends up privileged and who ends up marginalized by the theories and practices we use. Third, and related, we must examine the social conditions that made (and continue to make) privilege and marginalization happen.

It has been three years since Vagle published these ideas (Vagle, 2015) and it is difficult for us to assess the degree to which this call to revive theoretical insurrection has been engaged. What is even less difficult to assess is the growing need for insurrection of the middle school concept. The last two years have once again demonstrated that tinkering around the edges of issues, concerns, and problems is not enough. Too much is at stake.

When we first communicated with the Handbook editors about our idea for this chapter back in 2016, we were certainly aware that the United States was experiencing arguably the most divisive political campaign in history (see Vagle, Stutelberg, Gast, Leitl, & Clements, 2017). We were aware, given the racial violence and resulting protests over the past three years that we were very likely finding ourselves in the midst of insurrection. However, like many perhaps, we did not anticipate how divisive the political landscape had become, until it came into full relief on election night. Although we have spent time trying to think, write, live, move, and theorize our way in, through, and against institutionalized "-isms" (race, class, and gender in particular) and the normalizations of assumptions about race, class, and gender that perpetuate these -isms, we were not entirely prepared for the more explicit normalization of -isms on display.

If Hayes (2012) thought 2000–2010 should be deemed the fail decade, how might we start to write *this* decade—now that we find ourselves in its eighth year? Perhaps our institutions have more than just "failed," perhaps they have violated, demonized, and divided. It is not just that our social institutions have not been "doing their job" in service to people, they could be read as actively working against their own purposes. Perhaps this decade could be called the *divisive decade?* —not only because issues are dividing the country's people, but also because the institutions themselves do plenty of dividing.

Opportunities for Insurrection

As teacher educators and scholars committed to equity-based education for young adolescents, we are wrestling with how we might not only be responsive to these social and political contexts, but also be active agents within institutions that divide. Part of being active agents in the institution of education involves an honest appraisal about ourselves and the institutions in which we participate. The middle school concept is also such an institution.

For Vagle, this means spending much less time turning to the middle school concept for guidance (conceptually, theoretically, pedagogically, practically) on how to act, and much more time trusting that educators committed to equity-based education for young adolescents can see, think, perceive, feel the contingent nature of things (i.e., Lesko, 2001). Continuing to work hard at getting better working in and through contingencies should be of primary concern.

Can the Middle School Concept Move Contingently and Recursively?

One reason why the middle school concept is not more widely explored to support students from marginalized backgrounds may be that it is not set up well to move contingently and recursively. Perhaps this a problem for any concept that gets institutionalized. It becomes difficult to move, change, shift, and re-make itself. This is all the more reason we think less time should be spent on using the concept as it currently stands and more time paying attention to situations—day-to-day, moment-to-moment—that we may have some degree of control over, no matter how small. Although we expand upon this point more substantively in our third argument later in the chapter, we close this section with a concrete example of something Vagle is trying to do.

To provide some context, Vagle found the incredibly divisive 2016 presidential election and the post-election analysis of voting within and across class and race lines concerning for any number of reasons. One reason stems from how the media described White, working-class people. As he experienced watching election coverage in real-time, CNN analysts' reference to voters "without a college degree," slowly morphed to reference these voters as "the uneducated." Of course, much of the post-election analysis centered on how the White "uneducated" made the election of Trump possible, with notably less attention paid to other groups of voters (e.g., the strong number of Republican party-line voters [likely spanning all levels of social class] who voted party-line, the large number of "pragmatic independents" who tipped from Obama/Biden to Trump/Pence).

However, the particulars of "how" the election turned out the way it did and who chose to vote for him, are not the most important takeaways. Rather, it is some of the things the election revealed. For instance, as a privileged White, heterosexual, male scholar and member of *the intellectual elite* who was born and raised in communities comprised predominately by "the uneducated," Vagle became particularly interested in examining how teacher education as an institution—led primarily by intellectual one-percenters—can challenge itself to use its collective privilege as an institution.

Vagle was on sabbatical in 2017–18 and planned to spend some time with working class White people and people of color who live and work in rural and diverse suburban spaces. He observed and, when permitted, participate in their labor—so he could more fully experience their skills, knowledge, experiences, values, goals, and desires in the spaces and places that shape their and their children's lives. The curriculum and pedagogies of U.S. schooling are steeped in White, middle class knowledge and assumptions of normality. In our outreach work in schools and communities, as well as our work with teacher candidates, working-class Whites and working-class people of color often report struggling to make sense of these school-based norms. They report often feeling like "their normal" is at best undervalued and misunderstood, and at times explicitly ignored and even publicly shunned. Oftentimes, the students and families, and the communities they come from, are blamed for their lack of achievement, rather than, for example, a social classed and raced system that marginalizes those not White and middle to upper-middle class (Berliner, 2006; Bourdieu, 1990; Jones & Vagle, 2013; Rothstein, 2004). To reframe this issue, it is crucial that research focus on the assets, understandings, knowledge, and discourses of working-class Whites and working-class people of color—and that teacher education courses, professional development experiences, and school curriculum incorporate the findings.

Nothing in the middle school concept that keeps an educator of young adolescents from studying the working-class labor of people of color and White people and in turn privileging knowledge and experience that schools often marginalize. However, the middle school concept, at this point, also does not feel like a resource for such efforts. Although it is important that the middle school concept emphasizes the need to listen to young adolescents' voices and respect their concerns, such an emphasis does not provide explicit direction and guidance about how to work against raced, classed, gendered systems of oppressions. This is a critically important part of supporting marginalized students.

NOT RESPONDING ADEQUATELY TO THE FLUIDITIES, MULTIPLICITIES, AND INTERSECTIONALITIES OF THE HUMAN EXPERIENCE

The middle school concept, at its foundation, seriously values the young adolescent learner and deeply cares about the holistic development (socially, psychologically, academically) of all young adolescents. This is good; though unfortunately, it is not enough.

If the middle school concept is to become more widely explored as a means of supporting marginalized students, we believe that it must focus more explicitly on the complicated fluidities, multiplicities, and intersectionalities of the human experience. We think that learning from Black feminist scholars such as Kimberly Crenshaw, bell hooks, and Audre Lorde—as well as critical theorists such as Paul Gorski, Stephanie Jones, and Hilary Hughes—about intersectionalities, fluidities, and multiplicities can provide us (and perhaps the middle school concept as well) with better insights and tools.

Emerging from Black feminist scholarship and activism, intersectionality theory posits that multiplicities of our identity matter, that they are inextricably connected and wrapped up with one another, simultaneously at work producing and shaping our lived experiences of the world and one another. As Gorski and Goodman (2011) noted,

> The notion of intersectionality holds that oppression rarely is about a single form of difference (Bell et al., 2007), that each of us embodies many intersecting identities simultaneously (Stirratt et al., 2007), and that these identities form a complex and fluid web rather than an additive list of single identities (Bowleg, 2008). (p. 470)

Further, Crenshaw's (1991) notion of intersectionality is a theoretical concept that inquires how identity and positionality produce particular realities and lived experiences. In her TED talk, "The Urgency of Intersectionality" Crenshaw (2016), a social justice lawyer, describes working on a case in which a Black woman faced race and gender discrimination when denied employment at a car plant. In this particular case, the employer provided evidence that they hired racially diverse men and women. The partial truth provided as evidence failed to provide a more nuanced depiction of employees hired, specifically the hiring practices in which Black employees were primarily men in industrial positions and women employees, were primarily White in secretarial positions. For Crenshaw, an intersection became an analogy and framing that allowed others to see what is often made invisible, layers of injustice experienced across multiplicities of identity. The frame the company used to employ workers and the frame the courts used to investigate race discrimination and gender discrimination were partial and incomplete; the frames prevented this particular Black woman from being seen at the intersection of race and gender discrimination.

Although Crenshaw (2016) is often credited for being the first to help others see intersectionality as a way to make sense of multiple identities (Hill Collins & Bilge, 2016; hooks, 2000), autobiographical work across the multiplicities of her identity is perhaps more recognizable in the field of education. In some of her work, hooks (1990, 2000) has called for ongoing collective public discourse that illuminates how race, class, and gender intersect and produce lived experiences of injustice, particularly situated within our nation's capitalist, White-supremacist, patriarchal systems and structures. The verb *produce* here is of particular significance, as it can help us see that lived experiences are not happening in a vacuum, nor are they static. Lived experiences are always, already produced by broader social and political forces that are much bigger than the individual and are difficult to get one's hands around. In this respect, it is not only important to listen to the voices of young adolescents, but it is also important to treat these voices as intersecting identities based on histories and presence of privilege and marginalization. This also means it is important to think systemically as well.

In her book, *Where We Stand: Class Matters*, hooks (2000) pointed to the way meritocratic ideology operates in the United States but also added important complex intersectional layering by describing how movements for social justice, civil rights, and women's liberation were leveraged against one another as they promoted "truth" in the narrative that anyone in America can make it. She stated:

> By the early eighties the idea that sexism and racism had been eradicated, coupled with the assumption that the existing white supremacist capitalist patriarchy could work for everybody, gained momentum and with it the notion that those groups for whom it did not work were at fault. (p. 66)

hooks (2000) maintained that the media's contribution has been to play "the central role as the propagandistic voice promoting the notion that this culture remains a place of endless opportunity, where those on the bottom can reach the top" (p. 65). According to U.S. census data in 2015, the poverty rate was 13.5%, totaling 43.1 million people living in poverty (U.S. Census Bureau, 2016). When one of the wealthiest countries in the world continues to create and maintain social conditions where individuals experience homelessness, malnutrition, and starvation, there is clear evidence of class warfare. In addition to its role perpetuating a mostly unquestioned belief in meritocracy, mass-media has also contributed to widely held narratives that denigrate poor and working-class people. hooks (2000) described the power of such narratives to cross race and gender lines while maintaining class interests.

> The denigration of the poor has been expressed most graphically by ongoing attacks on the welfare system and the plans to dismantle it without providing economic alternatives. Many greedy upper and middle class citizens share with their wealthy counterparts hatred and disdain for the poor that is so intense it borders on pathological hysteria. It has served their class interests to perpetuate the notion that the poor are mere parasites and predators. Of course, their greed has set up a situation where many people must act in a parasitic manner in order to meet basic needs—the need for food, clothing, and shelter. (p. 45)

hooks (2000) discussed how the U.S. capitalist economic system has produced a politics of greed. In what she named as a White-supremacist capitalist patriarchy, the politics of greed have worked to divide individuals across race and gender. She described how African Americans have been robbed continually of the capacity to function as citizens in community. This denial of socially acceptable participation (inadequate education, limited job opportunities) within society has created a context in which drug trafficking has become the sole economic enterprise that enables a poor person the same access to material possessions as the rich. She described how power dynamics operate to exploit the poor further and serve the elite.

> Unlike the legitimized beneficiaries of greedy capitalism, these profiteers lack the power to influence government spending or public policy. They function only as a fascist force that brings violence and devastation into what were once stable communities. They do the work of exploitation and genocide for the white supremacist capitalist patriarchal ruling class...This is class warfare. Yet the media deflects attention away from class politics and focuses instead on drug culture and youth violence as if no connection exists between this capitalist exploitation and the imperialist economies that are wreaking havoc on the planet. (pp. 67–68)

As well as serving to divide individuals across race, the politics of greed have also contributed to division within gender. hooks (2000) described reformist and revolutionary models within the feminist movement. In the reformist model of liberation, led primarily by White women, women were fighting for equal rights within the existing class structure. The revolutionary model, led primarily by women of color, was a call for radical change within the existing social structure. hooks argued that the reformist feminist movement bolstered the White-supremacist patriarchy because it prevented people of color from gaining equal access to economic power and privilege. People of color continue to be underrepresented in the elite class, however, media veils this reality by perpetuating the narrative that "anyone can make it here," where "success stories" permeate professional sports, pop culture, and even the oval office. Summarizing her analysis, hooks' (2000) made a powerful statement, "the only genuine hope for feminist liberation lies with a vision of social change that takes into consideration the ways interlocking systems of classism, racism, and sexism work to keep women exploited and oppressed" (p. 109).

Following hooks' (2000) lead in working to liberate those marginalized by gender, race, class, language, and sexuality is no simple task, for it is difficult to take action on multiple forms of oppression without privileging one over another. In fact, Lorde (1983) suggested that the notion that a single aspect of one's identity or form of oppression trumps another is itself oppressive. A "hierarchy of oppression' is dangerous because it silos identities and oppression. Bowleg (2008) poignantly and concisely articulated identity as intersectional, complex, and fluid in her title, *When Black + Woman + Lesbian ≠ Black Woman Lesbian*. Intersectionality theory insists that we understand individual identities and oppression as inextricably connected to one another.

Jones and Hughes (2016) problematized how a hierarchy of oppression in social justice-oriented teacher education contexts contributes to a hindrance of readily available story lines to educators and students. Similarly arguing against a hierarchy of oppression, Jones and Hughes sought to complicate the dominance of racialized story lines so that opportunities to see and interpret pedagogical interactions with students through multiple interlocking lenses can occur. They discussed the dominance of race, racism, and white privilege in teacher education and they connect their heightened awareness of race and racism to the narrow pattern of pedagogical responses they repeatedly utilized among different groups of aspiring educators over time. Jones and Hughes sought to interrogate their failure to engage feminist pedagogical responses. For example, when a student recalled the immense fear she experienced while riding the city bus, Jones and Hughes identified the student's remarks as emanating from a "fear-of-people-of-color story line" and were quick in responding with a readily available teacher educator story line, a social justice lesson on race and racism. As they reflected on the story lines students used, as well as the story lines they responded with, they observed race and racism story lines as readily available and misogyny story lines as more suppressed in teacher education. Situating themselves as antiracist and feminist scholars and pedagogues, Jones and Hughes wrote about the conundrum in which justice-oriented pedagogies bump up against racism and misogyny.

> Both of the first perpetrators of violence against each of us didn't find us on buses. They didn't have brown skin either. They were white, and they found us in much more intimate spaces. They changed us. We pay attention to where men are . . . what they are doing . . . if—or how—they are looking at us, surveying our bodies. We pay attention to where men are walking on the streets, how they are walking, and plan what we will do if we are approached . . . We are very astute readers of men. We don't however, characterize this as our fear of men and their potential as perpetrators. This is simply a fact of life; something that has become normalized in our own (and many others') lived experiences as a reflection of the naturalization of misogyny. (p. 175)

Jones and Hughes (2016) realized they were not recognizing their student's statement of fear as a suspicion toward men and her vulnerability as a woman in an unfamiliar public space. They suggested that failing to bring their feminist perspectives to bear was a substantive missed opportunity for teachers and students to work against misogyny. Jones and Hughes' analysis provides important insight into how lived experiences of fear by women in public spaces can become normalized, hegemonic story lines. These normalized, hegemonic story lines can obscure or limit the ability of teacher educators to recognize the individualized experiences of their students.

The middle school concept, as it stands, does not wade into these sorts of complexities, at least not explicitly. The focus is on, for example, helping "each young adolescent [in] becoming a fully functioning, self-actualized person" (Association for Middle Level Education, 2013, p. 4). Some questions to consider include:

What does it mean to be a fully functioning, self-actualized person?
What does this look like?
What must one do to demonstrate such an attainment?

Such a goal or vision could be read as treating identity and experience as singular and fixed—as an individual pursuit void of context, broader systems of oppression, power, privilege, marginalization, and histories.

What if the middle school concept instead focused more on supporting young adolescents to:

1. Explore their multiple and interlocking identities;
2. Analyze how systems of oppression privilege some and marginalize others;
3. Learn about intersectionality theories and how they can help people interpret the world around them; and
4. Pursue a state of "fully-functioning" that centers on a commitment to challenging oppression(s) around every corner.

LEARNING FROM YOUNG ADOLESCENTS AND YOUTH WORKERS ABOUT POSITIONALITY, POWER, AND RELATIONSHIP

To some degree, we think that the middle school concept should be used less and the experiences of young adolescents and adults who work with young people, who fundamentally believe the youth are the most knowledgeable about their lives, should be used more. To this end, we write this final section as a "narrative of narratives" based on some of Hamel's early teaching experiences and her current work with young adolescents in a low-income community of color. We let Hamel's narratives do most of the speaking here, instead of us doing much theorizing of her narratives. Our hope is that this "narrative of narratives" can serve as an appropriate closing, a contingent, recursive glimpse of one White, female teacher and youth worker's reflections on working with low-income young adolescents of color (in and over time), rather than a more theoretical tying together.

Background of Hamel's Narrative

A few years ago, I (Hamel) connected with a community-based organization serving middle and high school adolescents through after-school and
summer academic enrichment programming. Having recently entered a
doctoral program, I was searching for connection. I was very busy—busy
teaching graduate and undergraduate preservice educators, busy immersing myself in theory, philosophy, and methodology coursework, busy facilitating professional development workshops aimed at disrupting classism in
educational spaces and places.

I was busy *and* disconnected.

As a White middle-class, heterosexual, female, I felt disconnected from
young people. I felt disconnected from young people—experiencing a wide
spectrum of educational experiences situated precariously in the current
moment—that were central to the pursuit of my doctoral degree and to my
daily life. Having recently relocated for graduate school, I felt disconnected
from the community, uncertain of how my recent teaching experience half-
way across the country was/was not relevant here, now. The disconnection
was disruptive—while searching for knowledge about how social, political,
and economic systems produce particular lived realities for young people
in educational contexts, the distance between young people and myself was
growing. For me, teaching has always been about showing up for and with the
young people in front of you. As a graduate student and instructor, suddenly,
there were no young people. I wondered, what good is the acquisition of
knowledge if it is confined within my own psyche? Being a graduate student
is isolating, you spend a lot of time inside your head, siloed in the world of
academia. I longed for the time I spent working alongside young people; I
longed for the impassioned energy I experienced after a breakthrough learning moment; I longed for the relationships that both kept me up at night and
ignited me Monday-Friday mornings. I was searching for connection.

During the first two years of graduate school, I became disillusioned with
our educational system. For a time, hope disappeared. I was pretty sure that
if I was going to continue to learn from and with young people, it would have
to be outside the walls of a school building. As an introvert, it was difficult for
me to seek relationships outside my immediate circles; however, the feeling
of disconnection continued to grow with intensity. I began to move with more
intention and urgency as I sought connection. I began to tell my story.

My Story, My "Dream" Job

I was sure I landed my dream job my first year in the "real world." I moved
to a large metropolitan city and landed a third-grade teaching position at

a high performing/no excuses school. Having spent my entire life and teacher preparation in the Midwest, I was naive to the highly contested and combative political arena I eventually came to realize myself wrapped up in. What I did know was that this school had a surplus of resources for teachers and students, competitive salaries, and a commitment to serving under-resourced children. At the end of July, three weeks before students would begin their early-start academic year, I was immersed into teacher training. I learned the basic structure of every mini-lesson we would teach. We, novice and returning teachers, sat in small groups of about 10 rehearsing scripted lessons and receiving feedback from school leaders (principals, vice principals, deans, instructions coaches, veteran teachers). The next person up in the rotation was responsible for implementing the previously distributed feedback. A behavioral consultant coached me on classroom management that emphasized efficiency, silence, and "sweating the small stuff." School administration handed out packets, including a list of routines. As homework, school leaders asked us teachers to script verbal directions for each routine, to practice the actions based on a literal interpretation of our language use. The next day we returned to our small groups and implement our routines. We took turns playing the role of student and then providing feedback. When we played the role of a student, the facilitators distributed behavior cards. These cards described a more specific role "make noise, tap your pencil, talk to your neighbor, ignore all directions until you are redirected x times." The goal was to deliver our routine effectively, while managing "distracting, off-task, and defiant behaviors." The training was intense, but I was hopeful that these were the skills I would need to be set up for "success." My students deserved the best and I did not want to let them down. I did not realize that the high pressure, militaristic, perfectionist tactics used to train me would become the same tactics administrators expected us to employ with our students under the guise of "high expectations." Through our embodiment of the organization's "ethos," taken up as mastery, we subjected our students to an academic experience in which we demanded 100% compliance and 100% effort 100% of the time.

Losing Myself and Leaving the Classroom

I left the classroom when I no longer recognized myself as the educator I once aspired to become. Removed now, I am able to reflect on the kind of teacher I aspired to be compared to the kind of teacher I actually became.

My intentions were clear: accept and meet all children as they are and support each child growing and getting where they desire to be throughout the course of the school year. I nurtured relationships with children and their families; I poured my heart and soul into my career. My good intentions were not enough.

The fact that I was committed to building relationships and teaching with passion were not enough. I failed my students. I was complicit. I not only accepted the fixed, rigid, polarizing methods of an organization defining success through the narrow lens of test scores, I adopted these methods. I performed them exceptionally well—that is, I exerted my power and control over my students, all day, every day. I stripped the youth within the organization of their individual identities and agency by being complicit with the organization's narrow view of success (i.e., academic achievement in the form of standardized tests).

I did exactly what I was supposed to do. I did it really well. Yet, what I did was dangerous. I perpetuated the status quo and in doing so precariously positioned the young people I interacted with.

As a graduate student, I began to tell my story. Telling my story helped me to reflect on my teaching and the contexts producing my pedagogy critically. While painful, this was necessary to begin the process of healing and as a means of reclaiming my agency. A professor in the school of social work listened to my story. The professor watched as my eyes welled, as I quivered, fearful that he would respond with shock and judgment. The professor listened repeatedly as I shared more of my story.

The school held dress rehearsals leading up to the state math and ELA exams. The administration and teachers wanted their students to be familiar with the logistics, the expectations, and the rules. They wanted to build stamina and incentivize effort, growth, and high scores. The school coached instructional staff on how to stand and deliver nonverbal messages (ranging from the encouraging hand on the shoulder to the perch and glare conveying "sit up and pick up your pencil"). After consecutive half days of silent testing, most students went outside to play, celebrating their effort and determination. However, there were several youth diagnosed as "effort problems." They were young adolescents whose educators explained their subpar scores with the simple explanation of "a real lack of effort." After poor performance on a practice test earlier in the morning, a student raised their hand and requested to use the bathroom. The teacher looked down at the child's paper, no name, no date. The teacher stated, "You may use the restroom when you have begun your work" and walked away, not engaging with this student's excuse. The same child raised their hand a few minutes later. The teacher looked down at the student's paper again and stated, "As I previously stated, you may use the restroom when you've begun your work," and walked away again. A few moments later the student raised their hand again, this time the student informed the teacher, "I pissed my pants." There was a puddle beneath the child's chair.

This event was a defining moment early in my teaching career. It was a moment I can pinpoint when I was losing who I wanted to be as a teacher. This interaction was symbolic of power dynamics operating within classrooms and schools, among staff and students, between this child and myself. I learned that when students and teachers are entrenched in a system that promotes a limited outcome, everyone loses. At the end of every practice exam, the students listened as the teachers publicly announced their names and scores. They fell into four categories: (a) exceeding expectations, (b) meeting expectations, (c) approaching expectations, and (d) not meeting expectations. Students cheered when they fell into meeting and exceeding; they energetically made their way to the treasure chest and picked out their new book, new toy, and their reward. The students whose names educators read under approaching and not meeting, sunk in their chairs, waiting to be told just how much they failed by. It is important to acknowledge that it was common for students to pee their pants during these months. Perhaps peeing your pants, was letting go, perhaps it was even surrender. We may have broken that child and many others. The children collapsed in an environment that excessively promoted academic performance, at great cost.

Seeking and Finding Connection

After several meetings and after at least a month of continued processing of my story, the professor introduced me to the executive director at a local community-based organization. I told my story to the executive director who was searching for a licensed middle-grades teacher as a means to pursue a partnership with the public school system that would help provide additional resources for the program. The professor encouraged me to dare to teach again, and step into an opportunity where I could be authentically me, teaching in stark opposition to what I had learned in my initial teaching career. Upon meeting me, upon hearing my story, the executive director invited me into the space for the summer as a licensed teacher and as a mentor to the community-based experts that were already part of the team. I used the most recent literature from my courses to create a critical literacy curriculum for sixth-eighth grade students using digital cameras and storytelling. The summer was a test, though I did not know it then. At the end of summer, the executive director invited me to be the curriculum director for the organization, opening a pathway for connection to the local context that I had been searching for.

Our raced, classed, gendered bodies are positioned in and by the spaces that we find ourselves in. The multiplicity of our identities and the structural privileging and marginalization of these complex and fluid identities both produce and shape our lived experiences and our intentionalities.

As a White, middle-class, female, I am often privileged by existing societal structures and contexts. I move through spaces in which my regular body "fits." As a former K–12 student, elementary grades teacher, and current graduate student, I continually feel comfortable in varying schooling atmospheres where my embodied whiteness, middle-classness, and gender are represented overwhelmingly, and are often an unquestioned norm. I travel to school and to work conveniently, in a car that my parents passed down to me, on roads where people are likely to perceive my White female body and my black Jeep Liberty as safe and law-abiding. I go to doctor's appointments, swiping my debit card for $10 co-pays, assured my health insurance will likely cover the rest and that my doctors will ask and then listen to what brought me in. I shop for clothes and whether I am at the mall or a fancy boutique—people do not surveille my body. When the seasons change, my routine changes slightly. As the sun sets earlier and earlier, I hunt for the closest available parking spaces, willing to pay ridiculous meters for a slightly elevated peace of mind and a shortened amount of time spent alone, walking briskly through the dark.

The young adolescents in the community-based organization where I work do not look like me. The young adolescents do not self-identify as White or middle-class. The young adolescents self-identify as Black, poor, working-class, heterosexual, and gender and sexuality-fluid. I know very well that my own identities matter here, as well as the identities of my students. I know that my identities have collided to produce each of my lived experiences, just as my students, and that often these experiences are moments we find ourselves disconnected from rather than connected to one another.

The young adolescents I spend time with teach me every single day about the power they have and strive to acquire, about their positionality across and among the spaces they occupy, and about the relationships they hold dear to one another. Mostly, I show up ready to listen and learn from the young people in front of me. Sometimes, they might learn a thing or two from me, too. The wounds from my previous teaching experiences are beginning to close, I am healing here; and, I think the young people are too. A powerful moment from this work in the community based organization as illustrated below.

It was a typical Wednesday, the children rushed through the doors, greeted by Ms. Trinity, grabbing snack and shuffling down the stairs. We convened in the cafeteria, on pull-out chairs arranged in a circle. Breaking from a tradition of resistance, Amir volunteered to read the question of the day, "What TV show would you like to live in for a week?" Kamiya and the boy next to her did three rounds of rock, paper, scissors to compete to read the word of the day, "differentiate." Jaden begged to read the quote of the day, "Healing begins where the wound was made" by Alice Walker. Upon reading the quote, Jaden asked me questions about what it really meant, "you know, the deeper meaning." Corneal, a staff and community member, reminded the group about the importance of time, moving from homework and games to dinner on time, a skill that would be necessary in their future. After reading the word of the day, several young people offered up their interpretations of the definition, putting the word into a sentence. One young person shared, "I can differentiate between my cat and my brother's cat because we found his cat on the street," which received a chuckle from the majority of the group. Jaden read the quote of the day aloud for the group. Hands shot up, peers anxious to share their insights. Jaden offered his first, "I think this means... that when someone really hurts you, like not a cut or something like that, but with words, that you got to go to where it hurts and try to fix that." Diamond expanded, "I think it means like when people say mean things to you that those things last if you don't try and heal them. I also think it means don't sweat the small stuff," more scholars added. Corneal joked about the upcoming Super Bowl—how the Patriots are going to need to do some serious healing after they lose to the Falcons—the group laughed.

We swung from serious to humorous, heavy to light. I shared that sometimes I bury small things and eventually over time I am like a volcano waiting to erupt, that most of the time, for me, burying a bunch of small things often leads to an eruption—a breakdown. For me, the quote is a reminder that burying is not healing. Amir shared the question of the day, "What TV show would you like to live in for week?" and excitedly asked to go first. Was it Sponge Bob's world that Amir wanted to live in for a week? The young people were excited to respond to the question and there were a range of responses—*Empire, Bad Girls Club, Pretty Little Liars*, and many cartoons I had not heard of (note to self—we learn so much about our learners in these moments). We wrapped up the question of the day with another warm demand from Alex, his specialty. Corneal came down hard on the group about being quiet during the short designated mindfulness time at the end of free time and before homework. He talked about the need to center yourself during the day, the power of tuning out everything around you and checking in with yourself. I shared the research study our executive director sent over the weekend. I told the learners about the adults who had extreme adversity in their lives growing up, "the making it success stories" the media loves to tell, and how oftentimes these "successful" adults continue to suffer, from hypertension, diabetes, heart attack, cancer etc., due to the sustained level of stress they have endured their entire lives. I described that it might feel weird or unimportant now, but that slowing down and focusing on our minds, our bodies and our breath for a few minutes every day might just be lifesaving. Technically we were done with circle (and slightly overtime) but the young people were engaged, choosing to keep it going.

Then, something beautiful happened.

Anthony asked if he could share something with the group. He wanted to expand on the importance of breathing and centering ourselves. He told us about his mom. He described his mom's childhood as tough, that messed up family members had touched her inappropriately which led to her moving in and out of foster families. He talked about how now she is a single mom, she has children, and bills to pay, work, and no car. She has been diagnosed with cancer. Anthony's grandpa had cancer and beat it but his mom's cancer is back. Recently, doctors told her that she does not have much time to live.

The students said little, but everyone listened. I nodded silently communicating, "I hear you, we hear you, we are here for you." Nasir quietly said, "I'm praying for you man," it was so quiet that neither Anthony nor most of the circle had heard, but Jermaine—a staff and youth leadership and development graduate student—did. Jermaine chimed in, "Hey Anthony, I want you to know that when you finished sharing that Nasir said he was praying for you and I want you to know that there are kids here praying for you and that I am too," Anthony nodded. Nasir spoke, "Yeah. I just want you to know that I know what you're going through. My mom died of cancer when I was really young and my dad is dying of cancer right now," Jada raised her hand, "Did you all see Ms. Stacey (a teacher at the school) crying? She was crying and had to leave school because she found out her mom died of cancer today." I offered to set up a table with paper and markers for card decorating during free time. It was quiet. Another staff member asked the young people to bring their chairs to the tables as they left the circle for free time. The young people stood up and dispersed. The circle ended.

The community-based organization provides a safe space after school and during the summer for young people. It provides a warm meal that people do not take for granted in a community where food insecurity is very real. The adults show up for young people, welcoming each of them with compassion, curiosity, and respect. The young people come—on their own accord—for none, some, and all these reasons. The young people have power, here. Adults position young people as growing human beings, here. The young people form and invest in relationships with their peers, community members, and mentors, here. Young people are full of capacity to be agents of change in their lives and communities. The young people do not need adults to shape them, fix them, or change them. The young people need us to show up, as human beings, offering opportunities for connection. Connection that can foster our own and one another's capacity to live wholeheartedly, fully embracing the human experience.

REFERENCES

Association for Middle Level Education. (2013). *Study guide for this we believe: Keys to educating young adolescents.* Retrieved from https://www.amle.org/portals/0/pdf/twb/TWB_StudyGuide_Aug2013.pdf

Berliner, D. C. (2006). Our impoverished view of educational research. *Teachers College Record, 108*(6), 949–995. Retrieved from http://epsl.asu.edu/epru/documents/EPSL-0508-116-EPRU.pdf

Bourdieu, P. (1990). *The logic of practice.* Stanford, CA: Stanford University Press.

Bowleg, L. (2008). When Black+ lesbian+ woman≠ Black lesbian woman: The methodological challenges of qualitative and quantitative intersectionality research. *Sex Roles, 59*(5–6), 312–325.

Carnegie Council on Adolescent Development. (1989). *Turning points: Preparing American youth for the 21st century: The report of the task force on the education of young adolescents.* Washington, DC: Carnegie Council on Adolescent Development.

Crenshaw, K. (1991). Mapping the margins: Intersectionality, identity politics, and violence against women of color. *Stanford Law Review, 43*(6), 1241–1299. doi:10.2307/1229039.

Crenshaw, K. (2016, October). *The urgency of intersectionality.* [Video file]. Retrieved from https://www.ted.com/talks/kimberle_crenshaw_the_urgency_of_intersectionality.

Free Dictionary (n.d.). *The free dictionary.* Retrieved from http://www.thefreedictionary.com/

Gay, G. (1994). Coming of age ethnically: Teaching young adolescents of color. *Theory Into Practice, 33*(3), 149–155.

Gorski, P., & Goodman, R. D. (2011). Is there a "hierarchy of oppression" in U.S. multicultural teacher education coursework? *Action in Teacher Education, 33*(5–6), 455–475.

Hayes, C. (2012). *Twilight of the elites: America after meritocracy.* New York, NY: Crown.

Hill Collins, P., & Bilge, S. (2016). *Intersectionality.* Cambridge, England: Polity Press.

hooks, b. (1990). *Yearning: Race, gender, and cultural politics.* Boston, MA: South End Press.

hooks, b. (2000). *Where we stand: Class matters.* New York, NY: Routledge.

Jackson, A. W., & Davis, G. A. (2000). *Turning points 2000: Educating adolescents in the 21st century.* New York, NY: Teachers College Press.

Jones, S., & Hughes, H. (2016). Changing the place of teacher education: feminism, fear, and pedagogical paradoxes. *Harvard Educational Review, 86*(2), 161–182.

Jones, S., & Vagle, M. D. (2013). Living contradictions and working for change: Toward a theory of social class-sensitive pedagogy. *Educational Researcher, 42*(3), 129–141.

Lesko, N. (2001). *Act your age: A cultural construction of adolescence.* New York, NY: Routledge.

Lorde, A. (1983). There is no hierarchy of oppressions. *Bulletin: Homophobia and Education, 14*(3–4), 9.

National Middle School Association. (2010). *This we believe: Keys to educating young adolescents.* Westerville, OH: Author.

Nichols, S. L., & Berliner, D. (2007). *Collateral damage: How high-stakes testing corrupts America's schools.* Cambridge, MA: Harvard Education Press.

No Child Left Behind (NCLB) Act of 2001, Pub. L. No. 107-110, § 115, Stat. 1425 (2002).

Ravitch, D. (2010). *The death and life of the great American school system: How testing and choice are undermining education.* New York, NY: Basic Books.

Reardon, S. F. (2011). The widening achievement gap between the rich and the poor: New evidence and possible explanations. In G. Duncan & R. Murnane (Eds.), *Whither opportunity? Rising inequality, schools and children's life chances* (pp. 91–116). New York, NY: Russell Sage Foundation.

Rothstein, R. (2004). *Class and schools: Using social, economic, and educational reform to close the Black-white achievement gap.* Washington, DC: Economic Policy Institute.

U.S. Census Bureau. (2016). *Income and poverty in the United States: 2015.* Retrieved from https://www.census.gov/library/publications/2016/demo/p60-256.html

Vagle, M. D. (2012). *Not a stage! A critical re-conception of young adolescent education.* New York, NY: Peter Lang.

Vagle, M. D. (2015). Reviving theoretical insurrection in middle grades education, *Middle Grades Review, 1*(1), 1–8. Retrieved from http://scholarworks.uvm.edu/mgreview/vol1/iss1/2

Vagle, M. D., Stutelberg, E., Gast, K., Leitl, T., & Clements, C. (2017, April). *Pedagogical tensions in helping teacher candidates become social class-sensitive.* Paper presented at the Annual Meeting of the American Educational Research Association, San Antonio, TX.

CHAPTER 3

A FRAMEWORK FOR RESPONSIVE MIDDLE LEVEL MATHEMATICS TEACHING

Cheryl R. Ellerbrock
University of South Florida

Eugenia Vomvoridi-Ivanovic
University of South Florida

ABSTRACT

This chapter introduces an emerging conceptual framework for Responsive Middle Level Mathematics Teaching (RMLMT), defined as quality mathematics teaching for young adolescents that advances their mathematical thinking, promotes equity and social justice, and attends to their developmental characteristics, needs, and interests. The RMLMT framework fills a void in existing middle grades education and mathematics education literature by converging developmentalism and culturally responsive mathematics teaching to form a more comprehensive way of thinking about teaching middle level mathematics to young adolescent learners. In this chapter we describe the evolution of the RMLMT, discuss the frameworks that informed our thinking, speak to the need for a comprehensive approach for teaching middle level math-

Equity & Cultural Responsiveness in the Middle Grades, pages 45–65

ematics to young adolescent learners, introduce the RMLMT framework, and provide an example of a middle level mathematics lesson that illustrates the implementation of all RMLMT dimensions. We conclude with various calls to middle level teacher educators, subject-area specific teacher educators, and colleagues in the school district as well as present areas for future research.

To assist pre-service teachers (PSTs) in their understanding of culturally re-sponsive mathematics teaching (CRMT), Vomvoridi-Ivanovic, a mathemat-ics teacher educator and co-author of this chapter, regularly and explicitly modeled all six dimensions of CRMT (Aguirre, 2012) in her mathematics methods courses. Among other lessons, Vomvoridi-Ivanovic often selected grade level appropriate mathematics lessons that address a variety of social justice issues from the text, *Rethinking Mathematics: Teaching Social Justice by the Numbers* (Gutstein & Peterson, 2013). One of the lessons Vomvoridi-Ivanovic regularly used with her secondary (6–12) mathematics PSTs from this book is a lesson entitled, "Deconstructing Barbie: Math and Popular Culture." The lesson teaches mathematical concepts, such as averages and ratios. Part of the lesson asks students to form groups based on the gender they identify with, to determine the average size person in the group, and to draw this person's body contours on butcher paper to compare their body to the scaled-up version of Barbie (or a male equivalent superman doll). Often, this lesson generated great discussion about the impact of represen-tations in popular culture on body image, self-worth, and eating disorders. Other issues raised included the superficially "multicultural" nature of con-temporary Barbie (or Superman) and the sweatshop labor that produces the dolls. However, the first time Vomvoridi-Ivanovic modeled teaching this lesson to a group of middle level mathematics PSTs who are part of an innovative clinically-rich middle level (5–9) teacher preparation program, PSTs began asking questions she never received from her secondary (6–12) mathematics education PSTs, leaving her unprepared on how to respond. These questions specifically targeted the developmental appropriateness of the lesson. For example, "How can we ensure that our middle school students feel comfortable measuring parts of their bodies and sharing these measurements with the class when we know how conscious young adoles-cents feel about their bodies?"

All that Vomvoridi-Ivanovic could say in response to this, and other such questions, was that she implemented this lesson when she taught mathe-matics at the middle school level. It was in this moment that Vomvoridi-Iva-novic realized that she did not receive adequate preparation for teaching in developmentally appropriate ways for young adolescents in her second-ary mathematics teacher preparation program. She also recognized at this time that all of the readings and resources on CRMT focused on how to advance students' mathematical thinking and the promotion of equity and social justice in the mathematics classroom without explicitly addressing how to be responsive to the developmental needs of the age group she was teaching.

While aspects of this rather popular middle level mathematics lesson, found widely online as well as in mathematics education literature (e.g., Kitchen & Lear, 2000; Mukhopadhyay, 2013), may be viewed as responsive to young learners' needs (e.g., selection of gender one identified with, opportunity to talk about body image), without modifications, this lesson has the potential to be emotionally detrimental and could possibly marginalize students (e.g., students whose gender identities are outside of the gender binary of either girl or boy).

It was not until the PSTs in the above example questioned the developmental appropriateness of this lesson that we began to think critically about the role CRMT and developmentally responsive teaching must play in preparing middle level preservice mathematics teachers to be truly responsive to the needs of *all* young adolescent learners, inclusive of those of marginalized groups. We began to focus the main question of our research around whether CRMT alone is sufficient for middle level mathematics teaching and learning if it does not address young adolescents' developmental characteristics. In other words, is CRMT truly responsive to young adolescent mathematics learners' characteristics, needs and interests if the framework does not attend to developmental responsiveness? What does middle level mathematics teaching look like when developmental responsiveness, cultural responsiveness, and mathematical thinking hold equal status in instruction? How can we teach middle level mathematics to young adolescent learners in a way that is both responsive to their cultural needs and developmental characteristics, needs, and interests in a comprehensive fashion? Discovering answers for these types of questions to improve the preparation of middle level mathematics PSTs, mathematics teachers, and ultimately young adolescent mathematics learners is what motivated this work.

The purpose of this chapter is to introduce an emerging conceptual framework for teaching middle level mathematics to young adolescent learners called Responsive Middle Level Mathematics Teaching (RMLMT). We define RMLMT as quality mathematics teaching for *all* young adolescents that advances their mathematical thinking, promotes equity and social justice, and attends to their developmental characteristics, needs, and interests. We base our comprehensive manner of thinking about teaching young adolescent learners mathematics in both CRMT (e.g., Aguirre, 2012; Aguirre & Zavala, 2013; Turner et al., 2012) and developmentally responsive teaching (e.g., Association for Middle Level Education, 2010; Caskey & Anfara, 2014; Horowitz, Darling-Hammond, & Bransford, 2005; Jackson & Davis, 2000). While the tenets of CRMT and developmentally responsive teaching are valuable to the teaching of mathematics and the teaching of young adolescent learners, respectively, neither approach alone is comprehensive enough to address the evolving needs of young adolescents learning mathematics. RMLMT fills a void in the existing middle grades education and mathematics education literature by purposefully converging developmentalism and CRMT to form a more comprehensive way of thinking about teaching mathematics in a responsive way to young adolescent learners.

In this chapter, we describe the evolution of the RMLMT framework, discuss the frameworks that informed our thinking, speak to the need for a comprehensive approach for teaching middle level mathematics to young adolescent learners, introduce the RMLMT framework, and provide an example of a middle level mathematics lesson illustrating the integration of RMLMT dimensions. We conclude with various calls to middle level teacher educators, subject-area specific teacher educators, and colleagues in the school district along with areas for future research.

EVOLUTION OF RESPONSIVE MIDDLE LEVEL MATHEMATICS TEACHING

The RMLMT framework for teaching middle level mathematics to young adolescent learners originated during the planning and implementation of a science, technology, engineering, and math (STEM) middle level teacher preparation initiative that consisted of two parallel teacher preparation programs—one in middle grades mathematics and another in middle grades science—designed to attend to national standards and recommendations for teacher education, including an intense focus on the clinical preparation of middle level STEM teachers (for a detailed explanation of the Helios Middle School Residency program, see Ellerbrock, Kersaint, Smith, & Kaskeski, 2016). A planning and implementation grant from the Helios Education Foundation made this teacher preparation initiative possible. One goal of the middle level mathematics teacher preparation program was to develop responsive middle level mathematics teachers ready to enter middle school settings with high concentrations of poverty. We call this way of teaching RMLMT.

In the early years of implementing RMLMT in the middle level mathematics program, both of us were simply teaching our passions as they related to middle level teacher preparation to the students we shared with the hope that responsive teaching would be the byproduct of our efforts—Ellerbrock and her passion for developmentalism and Vomvoridi-Ivanovic and her commitment to cultural responsiveness. However, there were a few occasions when we combined our teaching passions and co-taught lessons for the PSTs in the middle level mathematics program. In one such lesson, we asked PSTs to analyze videos of a fifth grade social justice mathematics lesson through the lens of both CRMT and developmentally responsive teaching (The Learning Exchange, 2017). We asked the PSTs to respond to prompts such as, "How does the teacher create opportunities for students from various linguistic and ethnic backgrounds to discuss mathematics in meaningful and rigorous ways?," "Which equity/social justice issue are students asked to analyze?," and "How do they use mathematics as a tool to analyze this issue?" Additionally, we asked students to respond to questions such as, "Which characteristics of adolescent development are/are not being met in this lesson?," "What do teachers need to keep in mind, developmentally speaking, regarding adolescents and discourse?" and "What is the teacher's role in fostering equity and social justice at the middle level?" While this is one example of how we interwove developmentalism and cultural responsiveness through our co-teaching, for the most part, we taught developmentalism and cultural responsiveness in isolation of one another within our respective courses. It was not until we experienced incidents such as the one described in the opening example, along with our handful of co-taught lessons, that we realized responsive middle level mathematics teaching *must* simultaneously and intentionally attend to cultural responsiveness and developmentalism. It was then that we consciously began our quest to create the RMLMT framework.

Below, we discuss the existing frameworks that informed our thinking on RMLMT. We must note here, that with the RMLMT framework, we do not intend to minimize the importance of content knowledge and the role of content standards. The goal is to teach rigorous mathematics content and mathematical thinking while simultaneously valuing the role developmentalism and cultural responsiveness play in teaching mathematics to young adolescent learners. The result is what we believe to be a more holistic understanding of middle level mathematics teaching.

Culturally Responsive Mathematics Teaching

Over the past decades, scholars concerned with the mathematics education of ethnically and culturally diverse students have emphasized the need for mathematics teachers to: (a) build on students' cultural and linguistic funds of knowledge (e.g., Civil, 2007; Civil & Kahn, 2001); (b) help students understand the mathematical practices that are present in their communities and other familiar contexts (e.g., Díez-Palomar, Simic-Muller, & Varley, 2007; Turner, Varley Gutiérrez, Simic-Muller, & Díez-Palomar, 2009); and (c) on teaching mathematics in ways that help students understand power relationships and structures of social, economic, and civic issues within local, national, or global contexts (e.g., Gutiérrez, 2009; Gutstein, 2006; Mukhopadhyay & Greer, 2008; Tate, 1994). This literature base, along with that of culturally responsive pedagogy (Gay, 2010; Ladson-Billings, 1995; Nieto, 2000), informed the development of a framework for CRMT defined as "effective mathematics teaching that advances students' understanding of mathematics while affirming their intellectual, cultural, linguistic, political, and emotional contributions" (Aguirre, 2012, p. 1). Aguirre (2009) argued that, although elements from both literature bases related to pedagogical content knowledge and culturally responsive pedagogy contribute to effective mathematics teaching, neither alone offers a comprehensive focus on mathematics teaching and learning that privileges both equity and mathematics. Aguirre (2012), and later Aguirre and Zavala (2013), described how CRMT integrates important elements of both literature bases to create a more comprehensive context to support mathematics instruction.

The definition of CRMT and the development of a framework for CRMT has grown, in big part, through ongoing research and professional development experiences with K–8 pre-service and in-service mathematics teachers led by a group of mathematics education scholars as part of the *Teachers Empowered to Advance Change in Mathematics* (TEACH MATH) project (TEACH MATH, 2012b). Based on the CRMT framework developed by the TEACH MATH project (TEACH MATH, 2012a), the two main goals of CRMT are to develop students' mathematical thinking and to promote equity in mathematics education (Aguirre, 2012; Turner, et al., 2012). Aguirre (2012) identified the six dimensions of CRMT as: (a) cognitive demand; (b) depth of student knowledge and understanding; (c) mathematics discourse; (d) power and participation; (e) academic language support for English language learners (ELLs); and (f) cultural/community-based funds of knowledge/social justice.

According to Aguirre (2012), culturally responsive mathematics teachers regularly engage students in tasks that are of high cognitive demand, sustain the level of cognitive demand throughout lessons, and create ample opportunities for students to discuss mathematics in meaningful and rigorous ways. Further, culturally responsive mathematics teachers create a classroom environment where mathematical knowledge and authority is distributed among all classroom participants, value students' mathematics contributions, address status differences among students, provide academic language support for ELLs, help students connect mathematics with relevant and authentic situations in their lives, and support students' use of mathematics to understand, critique, and change inequities and social injustices that affect their lives and the lives of others.

In a later work, Aguirre and Zavala (2013) further refined the definition of CRMT. They stated, "CRMT involves a set of specific pedagogical knowledge, dispositions, and practices that privilege mathematical thinking, cultural and linguistic funds of knowledge, and issues of power and social justice in mathematics education" (p. 167). With this definition,

Aguirre and Zavala further elevated the importance of language, culture, and social justice in teaching mathematics through a culturally responsive lens. However, the overall goals and practices of CRMT remain the same as in previous work (e.g., Aguirre, 2012).

Developmentally Responsive Teaching

The literature notes early adolescence as both a transitional and distinctive period of human development that spans across ages 10 to 15 (Caskey & Anfara, 2014). This period of development generally correlates with the years young adolescents are in middle school. During this time, young adolescents experience remarkable developmental changes as their bodies and minds mature and they begin to have changing physical, cognitive-intellectual, psychological, social-emotional, and moral needs along with evolving interests (Brighton, 2007; Caskey & Anfara, 2014; National Middle School Association, 2010; Scales, 2010). Being able to understand and respond to the changing developmental characteristics, needs, and interests of young adolescent learners is one of four essential attributes outlined in *This We Believe: Keys to Educating Young Adolescents* (NMSA, 2010). In this document, the Association for Middle Level Education (AMLE) stated that an education for young adolescents must be developmentally responsive and it is the uniqueness of this age group that should drive all educational decisions. Ultimately, developmental responsiveness is "...the heart of middle level education" (NMSA, 2010, p. 5).

Middle level teachers must understand the characteristics, needs, and interests of young adolescent learners if they are to teach them well (Jackson & Davis, 2000). Horowitz et al. (2005) contended that educators must know where the child is developmentally to be able to create engaging and challenging tasks that are appropriate for the child. Therefore, when middle level teachers consider young adolescent development as paramount to making curricular decisions, instruction is more likely to support students' physical, cognitive-intellectual, psychological, social-emotional, and moral characteristics, needs, and interests, which can lead to student success (NMSA, 2010; Powell, 2014; Van Hoose, Strahan, & L'Esperance, 2009). It is important to note that many aspects of young adolescents' developmental characteristics vary, are not sequential, and are interrelated (Caskey & Anfara, 2014; NMSA, 2010; Scales, 2010; Smith et al., 2016). Additionally, the characteristics are often generalizations, may be restrictive, and may not always be representative of what each young adolescent is experiencing at any given time (Scales, 2010; Smith et al., 2016).

The Need for Responsive Middle Level Mathematics Teaching (RMLMT)

To be effective with today's young adolescent learners, teaching that is both culturally responsive and developmentally responsive is crucial (AMLE, 2012; Gay, 2010), especially in mathematics (Greer, Mukhopadhyay, Powell, & Nelson-Barber, 2009). While the literature on teaching middle level mathematics content is plentiful (Lester, 2007) and there is a growing body of literature that highlights the importance of CRMT (e.g., Aguirre, 2012; Aguirre & Zavala, 2013) as well as teaching that is developmentally responsive to young adolescents (e.g., AMLE, 2012; Caskey & Anfara, 2014; NMSA, 2010; Scales, 2010; Steinberg, 2014), little is known about how to teach mathematics to young adolescents in a way that is both responsive to their cultural needs *and* developmental characteristics, needs, and interests in a comprehensive manner.

As noted previously, two primary literature bases informed our definition of RMLMT: CRMT and developmentally responsive teaching. Independently, important elements from both literature bases contribute to what we think of as quality teaching for young adolescents. However, neither alone offers a comprehensive focus on teaching mathematics to young adolescent learners that is simultaneously culturally *and* developmentally responsive. While CRMT points to what teaching practices should be present in a mathematics classroom where both equity and mathematics are privileged, we argue that the cultural and mathematical needs of the students as well as the developmental needs of young adolescents should inform how educators implement these teaching practices. Yet, the CRMT framework does not address developmentalism. Conversely, while developmentally responsive teaching supports the characteristics, needs, and interests of young adolescent learners, it does not provide detailed and explicit connections to the teaching of mathematics to young adolescents or to the cultural and linguistic needs of this age group.

In *Turning Points 2000,* Jackson and Davis (2000) stated that middle level teachers must possess an understanding of developmentalism and culture, "Teachers should know about how developmental realities play out against a backdrop of race, ethnicity, religion, gender, socioeconomic status, family, and community" (p. 100). From our experience, few practicing middle level mathematics teachers and middle level mathematics PSTs place a strong emphasis on cultural responsiveness and developmentalism in their teaching. Educators who teach with an emphasis on CRMT or developmental responsiveness alone are missing a prime opportunity to meet the cultural and developmental needs of their young adolescent learners. Unfortunately, teacher educators are not frequently trained on both CRMT and developmentalism, and, thus, they do not afford mathematics PSTs with the opportunity to learn about young adolescents' needs in a more systematic and comprehensive manner. RMLMT integrates important elements of both bodies of literature to create a more comprehensive way of thinking about middle level mathematics teaching for *all* adolescent learners, inclusive of young adolescents of marginalized identities.

RESPONSIVE MIDDLE LEVEL MATHEMATICS TEACHING

The RMLMT framework elevates cultural responsiveness and developmentalism in such a way that these topics hold as much importance as mathematical thinking. Cultural responsiveness and developmentalism work synergistically in the context of teaching mathematical content and operate in an integrated fashion, reflecting a more holistic understanding of the young adolescent and how best to teach and reach this age group. We represent our conceptual framework illustrating these relationships in Figure 3.1.

We arranged our RMLMT framework into 11 key dimensions organized around three goals (see Table 3.1). While Goals 1 and 2 are reflective of the CRMT framework, we expanded on each to include a specific focus on middle level teaching (see Table 3.1). We added a third goal with five dimensions that specifically focuses on the developmental characteristics, needs, and interests of young adolescent learners and teaching at the middle level (see Table 3.1). We believe that RMLMT takes into consideration not only young adolescents' mathematical thinking and equity/social justice needs, but also the myriad of changes associated with young adolescents' physical, cognitive-intellectual, psychological, social-emotional, and moral development.

It is important to note that each of these goals and dimensions are equally important; thus, this is not a hierarchical framework. For example, Goal 1 is no more important than Goal 3. It is also important to note that there is not one set of explicit instructional practices that are associated

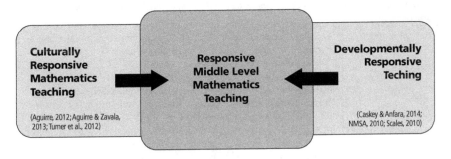

Figure 3.1 An emerging conceptual framework for Responsive Middle Level Mathematics Teaching (RMLMT).

TABLE 3.1 Responsive Middle Level Mathematics Teaching (RMLMT) Goals

Dimension	Explanation	Lesson Example
RMLMT Goal 1: Advance young adolescent learners' mathematical thinking		
1. Cognitive demand	Teaching that centers on high cognitive demand tasks appropriate for this age group. The teacher sustains the level of cognitive demand throughout the learning process so that young adolescent learners can closely explore and analyze middle level mathematics concepts, procedures, and reasoning strategies on a regular basis.	Tasks require complex, non-algorithmic thinking and require considerable cognitive effort. For example, students use their knowledge about multiplication, division, and percentages to interpret bullying statistics and solve relevant ratio problems.
2. Depth of knowledge & student understanding	Teaching that enables students' mathematical reasoning, explanations, and arguments to demonstrate fullness and complexity of understanding appropriate for this age group.	Students develop deep content knowledge by understanding connections among concepts (i.e., ratios, fractions, and percent) and procedures for solving problems that involve these ratios (e.g., finding the whole given the part and the percent). Students demonstrate their knowledge and explain their ideas through various means.
3. Mathematical discourse	Teaching that structures lessons in such ways so that all can participate in meaningful and rigorous mathematical discussions appropriate for this age group.	Students have the opportunity to contribute to the classroom, answering and posing questions, justifying claims with evidence, voicing conjectures, and communicating their reasoning process throughout the various parts of the lesson (e.g., whole class discussion, group work, gallery walk, stations).
RMLMT Goal 2: Promote equity in young adolescent learners' mathematics classroom learning experiences		
4. Power and participation	Teaching that promotes the distribution of mathematics knowledge authority among all classroom participants: teacher and young adolescent learners. The teacher explicitly addresses and minimizes status differences among classroom participants (teacher and young adolescent mathematics learners) by actively	The teacher positions students as valuable contributors, minimizes status issues, and fosters a shared authority of mathematics in the classroom by posing worthwhile tasks that tap into a wide range of knowledge, promote deep mathematical thinking, and have multiple entry points.

(continued)

TABLE 3.1 Responsive Middle Level Mathematics Teaching (RMLMT) Goals (continued)

Dimension	Explanation	Lesson Example
	eliciting all young adolescent learners' mathematics contributions and by ensuring classroom participants value and respect all mathematics contributions.	
5. Academic language support for English Learners (ELs)	Teaching that deliberately and continuously promotes language strategies that provide young adolescent ELs with academic language support as well as a focus on developing mathematical discourse and meaning making appropriate for this age group.	The teacher, in consultation with the ESL teacher, uses multiple strategies to support mathematics learning and academic language development. In all interactions with students, for example, the teacher regularly re-voices student ideas to model mathematical language use, affirms student's use of their home language to communicate mathematical ideas, and makes frequent use of physical and graphical objects to represent mathematical situations. Further, in preparation for this lesson, the language arts teacher helped students build background context knowledge and tackle linguistically demanding text.
6. Cultural/ community-based funds of knowledge	Teaching that promotes collective understandings of mathematics that involves intricate and relevant/authentic connections to community/cultural knowledge. The teacher builds lessons and units using authentic activities grounded in students' background knowledge and personal, family, and community experiences. Young adolescent learners analyze the mathematics within community contexts and examine ways the mathematics helps them understand these contexts. Further, young adolescent learners use mathematics deliberately as an analytical tool to understand issues that exist within their	Students use mathematics to explore a topic of great concern to them. Specifically, they use mathematics to make sense of bullying statistics and make estimates for how bullying affects students in their own school. Students also use the findings from their mathematical analysis of bullying statistics to create a poster and flyers that promote bullying awareness in their school.

(continued)

TABLE 3.1   Responsive Middle Level Mathematics Teaching (RMLMT) Goals (continued)

Dimension	Explanation	Lesson Example
	local community and beyond (i.e., state, national, global), formulate mathematically based arguments to address issues, and provide substantive pathways to change/transform the issues in ways that are appropriate for this age group.	
RMLMT Goal 3: Attend to young adolescent learners' characteristics, needs, and interests		
7. Physical characteristics	Teaching that attends to the varying bodily changes and physical maturity rates of young adolescents, including their physical growth, hormonal changes and development of secondary sex characteristics associated with puberty, substantial neurological changes in the brain especially in the prefrontal cortex, and their need for nutritious food, water, and physical activity.	Students engage in teaching activities that involve movement (i.e., gallery walk). Students also investigate bullying of students who others bully due to their physical characteristics (e.g., early/late maturers).
8. Cognitive-intellectual characteristics	Teaching that attends to the range of intellectual development of young adolescent learners associated with their increased ability to understand and reason. This involves helping young adolescent learners shift from concrete to abstract thinking, enhancing their metacognitive and independent thinking skills, and capitalizing on their ability to build on prior knowledge and experiences, their heightened level of curiosity about the world and self, and their interest in collaborating with peers on active learning tasks that have real-life application.	Students are developing a detailed understanding of the world around them and how groups of students who are bullied are mistreated. For the majority of the lesson, students are intentionally collaborating with specifically assigned peers on active learning tasks with a final product that has real-life application (bullying awareness).
9. Psychological characteristics	Teaching that attends to young adolescents' fixation with self, search for personal identity, quest for independence, passion for and commitment to an interest/hobby, varying and	

(continued)

TABLE 3.1 Responsive Middle Level Mathematics Teaching (RMLMT) Goals (continued)

Dimension	Explanation	Lesson Example
	fluctuating levels of self-esteem, self-conscious nature, increased propensity toward sex role identification, sensitivity toward critique, psychological vulnerability, potential decline in self-competence in athletics/academics/ other creative pursuits, and belief that their problems/experiences/ feelings are exclusive to only themselves.	Students are seeking to understand and value others and, in turn, can learn a great deal about themselves. This lesson helps students understand the large percent of young adolescents who are bullied and may help those who are victims of bullying understand that other adolescents share their experiences and feelings. Further, this lesson brings to the forefront timely issues for young adolescents such sex role identification.
10. Social-emotional characteristics	Teaching that attends to young adolescents' intense quest for approval, need for peer acceptance, desire for a sense of connectedness/belongingness to a group, search for social position within a group, need for family-like teacher-student and student-student relationships, overreaction to minor situations, emotional instability, embarrassment/ridicule/ rejection that results from negative experiences, quest to make independent decisions but dependency on the beliefs/values of parents and other adults, need for an non-familial adult others/ adult advocate, feeling sexual/ romantic attraction to others that may result in romantic relationships and/or sexual behaviors, and social vulnerability.	Students create a list of recommendations for promoting tolerance and acceptance of all students at their school. Through promoting awareness, tolerance, and acceptance, this lesson supports students' needs for approval, acceptance, and desire for a sense of connectedness and belongingness.
11. Moral characteristics	Teaching that attends to the moral reasoning of young adolescent learners. This includes helping young adolescents shift from accepting adult moral judgments to developing their own values, transitioning from self-centered moral reasoning to that of taking into consideration others'	Students research bullying of a particular group of adolescents and learn the statistics of bullying. The purpose is to increase awareness and promote acceptance and tolerance. Because students at this stage of development are developing their own values, beginning to take into

(continued)

TABLE 3.1   Responsive Middle Level Mathematics Teaching (RMLMT) Goals (continued)

Dimension	Explanation	Lesson Example
	perspectives, their capability of assessing complex moral issues, compassionate nature for others who experience struggles, idealistic understanding of the world and worldly issues, quest for asking complex and/or broad ethical and moral questions, impatience with the rate of social change, lack of acceptance of inconsistencies in adult behavior, quest for adult role models, and interest in exploring spirituality.	consideration others perspectives, and are understanding of rather complex moral issues, this lesson is timely in the development of these moral characteristics.

with RMLMT; rather, RMLMT can include multiple best instructional practices and responsive tasks designed to address the various dimensions of RMLMT directly. Lastly, similar to what Aguirre (2012) and her colleagues suggested (TEACH MATH, 2012a) regarding CRMT and the CRMT-TM Lesson Analysis Tool, it is not necessary for every single lesson to meet every single dimension in each goal. Instead, educators should think of RMLMT as *a way of teaching* and part of one's belief/philosophy of what quality mathematics teaching for young adolescents should include. The RMLMT goals and dimensions help make explicit the practices that should be consistently evident over time in middle level mathematics teaching.

This way of thinking about responsive mathematics teaching at the middle level is timely. It addresses questions posed by the middle grades research community as it pertains to ways successful middle level educators address adolescent development in their instruction (Smith et al., 2016) along with the need for middle level educators to be more equity focused (Kennedy, Brinegar, Hurd, & Harrison, 2016). The framework is also timely in mathematics education, a field that is increasingly interested in issues of equity and social justice (Diversity in Mathematics Education, Center for Learning and Teaching, 2007; Gutiérrez, 2013). To help actualize the framework, in the next section we provide a lesson example grounded in the dimensions of the RMLMT.

Responsive Middle Level Mathematics Teaching Lesson Example

This lesson example serves as a pragmatic application of how the dimensions of CRMT and developmentally responsive teaching come together to create a more comprehensive framework on responsive middle level mathematics teaching that we call RMLMT. This lesson example addresses many of the RMLMT dimensions multiple times. Table 3.1 includes a column that provided an example of how we represent each dimension in the lesson. However, this is not meant to be an exhaustive list of all the ways the lesson described addresses each dimension.

The lesson example is a multi-day sixth grade mathematics lesson entitled, "Using Mathematics to Unpack Bullying." This lesson centers on ratio and rate, one of the four critical areas of mathematics instruction for sixth grade as described in the Common Core State Standards for Mathematics (National Governors Association Center for Best Practices, Council of Chief State School Officers, 2010). Specifically, the standard calls for "connecting ratio and rate to whole number multiplication and division and using concepts of ratio and rate to solve problems" (p. 42). Students deepen their knowledge of percent and apply their understanding of the concept of ratio to make sense of statistics on bullying. Further, students use ratio language to describe statistics on bullying and to raise community awareness of bullying on young adolescents.

Prior to the lesson, the sixth grade teacher team asked their students to identify issues at school and in their life that concerned them. Specifically, students responded anonymously in writing to the following questions: "What do you think are the top three issues students face at your school?" and "When you think about your life right now, what at are your top three concerns?" Based on the information gathered, bullying was the most popular issue identified. As a result, the mathematics and language arts teachers on the sixth grade team decided to co-plan a multi-day interdisciplinary language arts and mathematics lesson on bullying. Once complete, they shared the plan with their students during a whole-class discussion and asked for input. Students seemed interested in this upcoming lesson but were not sure how they would be using mathematics to better understand bullying.

Following Henkin's (2005) suggestions, the language arts teacher used critical literacy as a vehicle to have students think about bullying. Specifically, students read children's literature, such as *Wonder* (2012) by R. J. Palacio (2012), *Twerp* (2013) by Mark Goldblatt, and *Inside Out & Back Again* (2013) by Thanhha Lai. Students also read statements on bullying statistics found on PACER's (2016) webpage (for more information see http://www.pacer.org/bullying/resources/stats.asp). The language arts teacher helped students make meaning of statements of high linguistic complexity, especially for ELLs, such as "Students with specific learning disabilities, autism spectrum disorder, emotional and behavior disorders, other health impairments, and speech or language impairments report greater rates of victimization than their peers without disabilities longitudinally and their victimization remains consistent over time." Students then wrote about and engage in class discussions on the effects of bullying from multiple perspectives (e.g., students, parents, teachers, school system).

In mathematics, the teacher built upon the bullying research introduced in language arts. The focus was on making sense of the statistics provided using ratio and ratio language. Because the student population included English learners, the team collaborated with an English as a second language (ESL) teacher to plan their lessons in ways that supported the learning of content and academic language development of all students. Below, we elaborate on the math portion of this interdisciplinary lesson.

The first part of the math lesson began with a whole class guided mathematical analysis of statements on bullying statistics found on PACER's (2016) webpage. The teacher told the students that she would model the type of mathematical analysis she expected them to conduct with their tablemates. For example, the teacher read the statement, *"More than one out of every five (20.8%) students report being bullied"* and asked students to discuss its meaning. To help students unpack the statement and determine its validity, she asked questions found in Table 3.2.

The teacher then read aloud another statement from the web page, *"64% of children who were bullied did not report it; only 36% reported the bullying."* The teacher asked students to work with their shoulder partner (person who they were sitting directly next to) to determine the validity of this statement and to use this information along with the information from the previous statement to estimate the ratio of students who have experienced bullying to those who have not. Important to note, the teacher heterogeneously arranged students into groups of four based on their pre-assessment scores

TABLE 3.2 Teacher Questions With Possible Student Responses During Whole Class Discussion

Teacher Question	Possible Response
How do the authors of this webpage determine that more than one out of every five students reported acts of bullying?	20.8% is just over 20% and 20% is the same as 1 out of 5.
How can we determine the exact ratio of students who report acts of bullying to that of those who do not report acts of bullying?	20.8 out of 100 is the same as $20.8 \times 5 = 104$ out of 500. This means that in every 500 students, 104 report acts of bullying. The ratio of students who report acts of bullying to those who do not report such acts is 104:396.
How do the authors know that 20.8% of students report being bullied? Where does that information come from?	The teacher clicks on the link right next to the statement and locates and highlights this percentage on page 5 of the document.
Does this mean that about one out of every five students experience bullying?	No more than about one of every five students report acts of bullying. There may be more students who experience bullying but do not report it.

using Kagan's team grouping structures (i.e., high, high medium, low medium, low). In this case, the high and low medium worked together and the high medium and low worked together. The teacher walked around, observed each pair as they worked on this task, and provided assistance as needed. The goal was for each student pair to draw the following conclusion: If only 36% of students who are bullied report it, then that means about 1 out of every 3 students who are bullied report it. Therefore, if about 1 out of every 5 students report being bullied, but only 1 out of every 3 students bullied actually reports the incident, then it is possible that 3 out of every 5 students actually experience bullying. This means the ratio of students who have experienced bullying to those who have not is 3:2.

If one student pair at the table finished before the other pair, the teacher instructed the students to move on to the next step and create a representation of these ratios using any medium desired. This could be a visual representation (e.g., drawing) or a physical representation (e.g., using manipulatives). Once both pairs completed both tasks, each pair shared their findings with their table partners and discussed any discrepancies until they reached a consensus. The teacher then prompted each table of four to engage in a discussion about what this ratio meant for bullying at their school and collaboratively use the ratio to estimate how many students in their school may have experienced bullying.

The second part of the lesson began by having each table of students conduct a mathematical analysis, similar to the one they did as a whole class, on bullying of select groups of young adolescent students (e.g., students with special needs; students who are early/late maturers; lesbian, gay, bisexual, transgender, and queer students; students who live in poverty; and students from different cultural backgrounds). Each student selected one aspect of their topic to research and teach to their table partners (e.g., detailed information on this group of students, statistics of bullying incidents involving this group of students, effects of bullying on this group of students, bullying prevention for this group of students). Together, each student group took the information learned on their topic and created a visual representation that displayed the results of their investigation along with a list of recommendations for promoting acceptance of all students at their school. Important to note, during this portion of the lesson students tended to bring up issues of bias (e.g., bias in statistics, personal bias, implicit bias); therefore, it was important to allocate time to talk about bias beforehand.

The last part of the lesson consisted of a gallery walk where half of the student groups presented their visual representation and explained the mathematical analysis to the other groups of students who took notes on their presentation. Notes contained information on each of the four categories, including group of students, statistics, effects, and prevention. Students rotated from group to group until they visited all presenting groups. Students then switched roles and repeated the process. Once the gallery walk was complete, students hung their visual representations around the school to educate the school community on bullying.

CONCLUSION

It is our intent that this chapter highlights the need for an intentional, laser-like focus on the convergence of developmentalism and cultural responsiveness in middle level mathematics teaching. Responsive middle level mathematics teaching (RMLMT) combined culturally responsive mathematics teaching (CRMT) and developmentally responsive teaching to create the emerging conceptual framework for RMLMT. While CRMT is not solely exclusive to middle level education, our thinking about the RMLMT framework is a direct result of our efforts to create a STEM middle level teacher preparation initiative that includes a middle level mathematics teacher preparation program. We do acknowledge that integrating culturally responsive teaching and developmentally responsive teaching together can occur in other disciplines besides mathematics and we encourage our middle level teacher educator colleagues, subject-area specific teacher educator colleagues, and colleagues in school districts to consider ways to integrate culturally and developmentally responsive teaching in other subject areas to support quality teaching.

Specific to middle level mathematics teaching, we call on practicing middle level mathematics teachers to consider the role of how developmentalism and cultural responsiveness, in an integrated fashion, plays out in their teaching practices. Likewise, we call on our teacher educator colleagues to consider the same as it pertains to their teaching in middle level mathematics teacher preparation programs. We need a better understanding of the ways in which middle level educators and mathematics teacher educators can work together to enact RMLMT. Further, we need tools and resources that help support the development of teachers' RMLMT competencies. We need future research studies that highlight RMLMT and its effects on middle level teacher preparation, middle level teaching, and young adolescent learners' mathematics thinking and learning. We especially call for studies that utilize this perspective in action such as case study examples of RMLMT applied to middle level mathematics teacher preparation and middle level mathematics teaching. It is also necessary to study the perspectives of students taught through the lens of RMLMT at both the collegiate and middle level.

REFERENCES

Aguirre, J. (2009). Privileging mathematics and equity in teacher education: Framework, counter-resistance strategies and reflections from a Latina mathematics educator. In B. Greer, S. Mukhopadhyay, S. Nelson-Barber, & A. Powell (Eds.), *Culturally responsive mathematics education* (pp. 295–319). New York, NY: Routledge.

Aguirre, J. M. (2012). Developing culturally responsive mathematics teaching. *News from TODOS: Mathematics For All, 8*(2), 1–4.

Aguirre, J. M., & Zavala, M. R. (2013). Making culturally responsive mathematics teaching explicit: A lesson analysis tool. *Pedagogies: An International Journal, 8*(2), 163–190.

Association for Middle Level Education. (2012). *Association for Middle Level Education Middle level teacher preparation standards with rubrics and supporting explanations.* Westerville, OH: Author. Retrieved from http://www.amle.org/AboutAMLE/ProfessionalPreparation/AMLEStandards.aspx

Brighton, K. (2007). *Coming of age: The education & development of young adolescents.* Westerville, OH: National Middle School Association.

Caskey, M. M., & Anfara, Jr., V. A. (2014). *Research summary: Developmental characteristics of young adolescents.* Retrieved from http://www.amle.org/Browseby-Topic/WhatsNew/WNDet.aspx?ArtMID=888&ArticleID=455

Civil, M. (2007). Building on community knowledge: An avenue to equity in mathematics education. In N. Nasir & P. Cobb (Eds.), *Improving access to mathematics: Diversity and equity in the classroom* (pp. 105–117). New York, NY: Teachers College Press.

Civil, M., & Kahn, L. (2001). Mathematics instruction developed from a garden theme. *Teaching Children Mathematics, 7*(7), 400–405.

Díez-Palomar, J., Simic-Muller, K., & Varley, M. (2007). El club de matemáticas. Una experiencia cultural de matemáticas de la vida cotidiana, para la diverisdad. *UNO. Revista de Didáctica de las Matemáticas, 45*, 99–106.

Diversity in Mathematics Education, Center for Learning and Teaching. (2007). Culture, race, power, and mathematics education. In F. K. Lester (Ed.), *Second handbook of research in mathematics teaching and learning* (pp. 405–433). Charlotte, NC: Information Age.

Ellerbrock, C. R., Kersaint, G., Smith, J. J., & Kaskeski, R. (2016). Transforming teacher preparation for the transition years: A partnership-based STEM residency program. In P. B. Howell, J. Carpenter, & J. Jones (Eds.), *Clinical preparation at the middle Level: practices and possibilities* (pp. 33–58). Charlotte, NC: Information Age.

Gay, G. (2010). *Culturally responsive teaching: Theory, research, and practice* (2nd ed.). New York, NY: Teachers College Press.

Greer, B., Mukhopadhay, S., Powell, A. B., & Nelson-Barber S. (2009). *Culturally responsive mathematics education.* New York, NY: Routledge.

Goldblatt, M. (2013). *Twerp.* New York, NY: Random House.

Gutiérrez, R. (2009). Helping students to play the game and change the game. *Teaching for Equity and Excellence in Mathematics, 1*(1), 4–8.

Gutiérrez, R. (2013). The sociopolitical turn in mathematics education. *Journal for Research in Mathematics Education, 44*(1), 37–68.

Gutstein, E. (2006). *Reading and writing the world with mathematics: Toward a pedagogy for social justice.* New York, NY: Routledge.

Gutstein, E., & Peterson, B. (Eds.) (2013). *Rethinking mathematics: Teaching social justice by the numbers* (2nd ed.). Milwaukee, WI: Rethinking Schools.

Henkin, R. (2005). *Confronting bullying: Literacy as a tool for character education.* Portsmouth, NH: Heinemann.

Horowitz, F. D., Darling-Hammond, L., & Bransford, J. (2005). Educating teachers for developmentally appropriate practice. In L. Darling Hammond, & J. Bransford (Eds.), *Preparing teacher for a changing world: What teachers should learn and be able to do* (pp. 88–125). San Francisco, CA: Jossey-Bass.

Jackson, A. W., & Davis, G. A. (2000). *Turning points 2000: Educating adolescents in the 21st century.* New York, NY: Teachers College Press.

Kennedy, B. L., Brinegar, K., Hurd, E., & Harrison, L. (2016). Synthesizing middle grades research on cultural responsiveness: The importance of a shared conceptual framework. *Middle Grades Review, 2*(3), 1–19. Retrieved from http://scholarworks.uvm.edu/cgi/viewcontent.cgi?article=1061&context=mgreview

Kitchen, R. S., & Lear, J. M. (2000). Mathematizing Barbie: Using measurement as a means for girls to analyze their sense of body image. In W. G. Secada (Ed.), *Changing the faces of mathematics* (pp. 67–73). Reston, VA: National Council of Teachers of Mathematics.

Ladson-Billings, G. (1995). But that's just good teaching! The case for culturally relevant pedagogy. *Theory Into Practice, 34*(3), 159–165.

Lai, T. (2013). *Inside out & back again.* Queensland, Australia: University of Queensland Press.

Learning Exchange, The. (2017). *Teaching mathematics through a social justice lens.* Retrieved from http://thelearningexchange.ca/projects/teaching-mathematics-through-a-social-justice-lens/?pcat=999&sess=3

Lester, F. K. (Ed.). (2007). *Second handbook of research on mathematics teaching and learning.* Charlotte, NC: Information Age.

Mukhopadhyay, S. (2013). Deconstructing Barbie: Math and popular culture. In E. Gutstein, & B. Peterson (Eds.), *Rethinking mathematics: Teaching social justice by the numbers* (pp. 200–201). Milwaukee, WI: Rethinking Schools Publications.

Mukhopadhyay, S., & Greer, B. (2008). How many deaths? Education for statistical empathy. In B. Sriraman (Ed.), *International perspectives on social justice in mathematics education* (pp.169–190). Charlotte, NC: Information Age.

National Governors Association Center for Best Practices, Council of Chief State School Officers. (2010). *Common Core State Standards Mathematics.* Washington, DC: Author.

National Middle School Association. (2010). *This we believe: Keys to educating young adolescents.* Westerville, OH: Author.

Nieto, S. (2000) *Affirming diversity: the sociopolitical context of multicultural education.* New York, NY: Longman.

PACER's National Bullying Prevention Center. (2016, December 8). *Bullying statistics.* Retrieved from http://www.pacer.org/bullying/resources/stats.asp

Palacio, R. J. (2012). *Wonder.* New York, NY: Alfred A. Knopf.

Powell, S. D. (2014). *Introduction to middle school* (3rd ed.). Upper Saddle River, NJ: Pearson.

Scales, P. C. (2010). Characteristics of young adolescents. In *This we believe: Keys to educating young adolescents* (pp. 53–62). Westerville, OH: National Middle School Association.

Smith, M., Strahan, D., Jones, J., Akos, P., Bouton, B., Cook, C., & McGaughey, N. (2016). Developmental aspects of young adolescents. In S. B. Mertens, M. M. Caskey, P. Bishop, N. Flowers, D. Strahan, D., G. Andrews, & L. Daniel (Eds.), *The MLER SIG research agenda* (pp. 1–3). Retrieved from http://mlersig.net/research/mler-sig-research-agenda/

Steinberg, L. (2014). *Age of opportunity: Lessons from the new science of adolescence.* Boston, MA: Houghton Mifflin Harcourt.

Tate, W. (1994). Race, retrenchment, and the reform of school mathematics. *The Phi Delta Kappan, 75*(6), 477–480.

TEACH MATH (2012a). *Culturally responsive mathematics teaching lesson analysis tool.* Unpublished instrument. Retrieved from http://www.mathconnect.hs.iastate.edu/documents/CRMTLessonAnalysisTool.pdf

TEACH MATH (2012b). *About: Teach math.* Retrieved from: http://www.mathconnect.hs.iastate.edu/index.html

Turner, E. E., Drake, C., Roth McDuffie, A., Aguirre, J., Bartell, T. G., & Foote, M. Q. (2012). Promoting equity in mathematics teacher preparation: A framework for advancing teacher learning of children's multiple mathematics knowledge bases. *Journal of Mathematics Teacher Education, 15*(1), 67–82. doi 10.1007/s10857-011-9196-6

Turner, E., Varley Gutiérrez, M., Simic-Muller, K., & Díez-Palomar, J. (2009). "Everything is math in the whole world": Integrating critical and community knowledge in authentic mathematical investigations with elementary Latina/o students. *Mathematical Thinking and Learning, 11*(3), 136–157.

Van Hoose, J., Strahan, D., & L'Esperance, M. (2009). *Promoting harmony: Young adolescent development and classroom practices.* Westerville, OH: National Middle School Association.

SECTION II

SUPPORTING YOUNG ADOLESCENTS
WITH MARGINALIZED IDENTITIES

CHAPTER 4

THE (UN)MUTED VOICES OF MIDDLE GRADES YOUTH EXPERIENCING HOMELESSNESS

Matthew J. Moulton
Indiana State University

ABSTRACT

Homelessness is a well-documented social phenomenon in popular culture and the media and, when discussed, often conjures negative thoughts of those experiencing it. Youth homelessness, on the other hand, challenges these dominant societal narratives; yet individuals in positions of power rarely provide opportunities for students experiencing homelessness to share their voices. This qualitative research study utilized the participatory method of map-making to document the in-and-out of school experiences of one youth identified as experiencing homelessness. Analysis of participant created maps and semi-structured interview transcripts through a frame influenced by *This We Believe* (NMSA, 2010) revealed how the participant's middle school both meets his needs and could better do so.

Equity & Cultural Responsiveness in the Middle Grades, pages 69–91
Copyright © 2019 by Information Age Publishing
All rights of reproduction in any form reserved.

It was probably close to 2:45 pm that Kyrie (all names are pseudonyms) and I found our way to a booth in this fast-food restaurant in this small city in the Southeastern United States. Kyrie, a seventh grader at Riverside Middle School who fits the federal government's definition of experiencing homelessness due to his lack of "a fixed, regular, and adequate nighttime residence" (McKinney Vento Homeless Education Assistance Improvements Act, 2001), should have been in school but administrators suspended him "for his own safety" to curb possibilities of a fight. Our food arrived, we chatted and ate, sketched pictures, and drew maps. After Kyrie finished his map, I asked him to walk me through his day, a typical Riverside Middle School day for him. He started in the front office and said, "I usually come in through the front office and then head into the cafeteria. Well, actually I walk in from the school bus entrance through the old gym and into the cafeteria." Seemed typical enough, but I knew that his current living situation in a home with anywhere from two to three households represented did not include access to a car (Hallett [2012] defined a household as "a family unit [e.g., mother and children]," p. 377). I asked him, "If you do come in the front entrance how do you get to school?" With a mouth full of soda and a chicken sandwich, he responded:

> I take the city bus. First thing I have to do is wait for the 12. It comes every 30 minutes or so. Once I am on the 12, it takes me to the transfer station where I wait for the 33 to take me out to Riverside. That could be at most a 30-minute wait, then a 30-minute ride. It takes so long because it has to circle all the way out past Wal-Mart and then circle past the high school. By the time I get to school I have already missed about an hour, maybe more, but that is just ELT (extended learning time). The thing that sucks the most is missing breakfast; but I can either get a snack from the cafeteria, if they have anything left, or I can drink lots of water to curb the hunger pains.

I let all that soak in. There is a lot to unpack from this bag of experiences that Kyrie brings with him on a daily basis to his seventh-grade classroom. I start at the beginning, "How often do you have to take the city bus to get to school?"

"Maybe once every other week. So, one out of every ten days."

"What does the school do for you on those days?" I ask while thinking about him exercising personal agency and putting school as a priority.

Kyrie takes a big slurp of his soda, seeming to make it more dramatic intentionally, "They give me a tardy."

The above exchange took place between me and a participant in a pilot study seeking to document the middle school experiences of youth identified as homeless. While reviewing the literature about homelessness, I noticed a lack of research studies that present the point of view of youth experiencing homelessness. Though brief, the narrative above about Kyrie's experiences in school provides a powerful glimpse into his life and how he interacts with the world and how the world impacts him.

Homelessness is a well-documented social phenomenon in popular culture and the media and, when discussed, often conjures negative thoughts of those experiencing it (Kim, 2013). Youth homelessness, on the other hand, challenges these dominant societal narratives. Kim (2013) described the discourse surrounding homelessness as dominated by beliefs that those experiencing it are male adults with mental health issues. The 1990s brought with it a huge increase in the population of families experiencing homelessness (Biggar, 2001). As a result, about 50% of individuals experiencing homelessness are under the age of 18 (Kim, 2013). Dominant narratives still picture adult males while, in reality, the faces are much younger and represented in classrooms across the United States. The education of youth experiencing homelessness is beginning to play a more influential role in the media and educational policy. During the 2015–2016 school year, public schools in the United States enrolled an estimated 1.3 million students experiencing homelessness (U.S. Department of Education, 2016). With the recent adoption of the Every Student Succeeds Act (2015), and the amendment of the McKinney-Vento Homeless Assistance Act (1987), public schools "must ensure that homeless children and youths have equal access to the same free, appropriate public education, including a public preschool education, as provided to other children and youths" (King, 2016, para. 2). Often youth experiencing homelessness are marginalized or absent from literature. Operating from this marginalized and underrepresented space, conversations about homelessness must include the voiced and lived-experiences and desires of students experiencing homelessness. To illuminate inequities in classroom environments and school structures, the Association for Middle Level Education's *This We Believe* (National Middle School Association, 2010), specifically the four essential attributes of successful middle level education, state that an education for young adolescents must be (a) developmentally responsive, (b) challenging, (c) empowering, and (d) equitable; and these essential attributes guided this chapter's research. Utilizing the methodology of map-making (Burke, Greene, & McKenna, 2014; Clark, 2010, 2011a, 2011b), this chapter draws from data collected as part of an ongoing project working with young adolescent students who have experienced homelessness. Specifically, I use student created maps and narratives to share how their middle school meets or neglects to meet their needs.

DEFINING HOMELESSNESS

The overwhelming perception of homelessness in the United States is that those who experience homelessness are inept, lazy, and irresponsible (Kim, 2013). When tasked with picturing someone who experiences homelessness, "people easily think of... dirty, hungry, drunken, addicted, or psychotic male adults wandering the streets, begging with cardboard signs, or sleeping under bridges" (Kim, 2013, p. 294). If one were to perform an image search on Google using simply the word *homeless*, the results would appear to match Kim's assertions. The Oxford Dictionary defines "homeless" as (of a person) without a home, and therefore typically living on the streets (Homeless, n.d.). Marginalized groups, such as individuals who experience homelessness, are often grouped together and assumed to fit within dominant narratives.

Student homelessness is altogether different from, but already shaped by, the dominant narratives surrounding homelessness. For the purposes of this chapter, I used the McKinney-Vento Homeless Assistance Act (1987) definition of homeless because of its standardization across the country and prevalence in the literature regarding the education of students identified as homeless (Miller, 2012). Originally passed in 1987, and most recently re-amended with the enactment of the Every Student Succeeds Act (King, 2016), McKinney-Vento drastically increases the count of homeless individuals in the United States and includes typical definitions of homelessness as described above with some expansions. Homelessness, according to McKinney-Vento includes:

> Children and youths who are sharing the housing of others due to loss of housing, economic hardship, or a similar reason; who are living in motels, hotels, trailer parks, or camping grounds due to the lack of alternative adequate accommodations; who are living in emergency or transitional shelters; who are awaiting foster care placement; who have a primary night-time residence that is a public or private place not designed for or ordinarily used as a regular sleeping accommodation for human beings; or who are living in cars, parks, public spaces, abandoned buildings, substandard housing, bus, or train stations, or similar settings. (Mohan & Shields, 2014, p. 190)

Despite a clear and explicit definition of homelessness, issues of educating stakeholders, implementation, and consistency still arise due to the dominant narrative surrounding homelessness (Hallett, Low, & Skrla, 2015; Hallett, Skrla, & Low, 2015).

Our society has an antiquated and deeply troubling perception of homelessness and those who experience it. This perception simultaneously defines, restricts, and positions homelessness as existing in some other place, separate from where people who have access to stable housing congregate and hold conversations. Students experiencing homelessness are "cloaked in a deceptive, superficial normalcy" (Feuer, 2012, para. 6). They exist in classrooms where misunderstandings of their lived experiences run rampant and teachers and administrators ignore the societal conditions that have contributed to inadequate access to stable housing. When students fail to conform to society's stereotypical perception of *who is homeless* their presence in classrooms with teachers ill-prepared for addressing their need for equitable access to education results in perpetuated marginalization. Aviles de Bradley (2011) saw the potential that school communities possess, writing that, "Schools can become vital spaces for students experiencing homelessness, if school administrators, faculty and staff are aware of their needs and are prepared to provide the resources and support that enhance educational outcomes for this group of students" (p. 157). The increased needs for teacher understanding and the representation of students' voices necessitates the significance of research with and for students experiencing homelessness.

Throughout this chapter, I make all attempts to refer to students who fit the definition of homeless as students experiencing homelessness rather than homeless students. Students experiencing homelessness is an example of people-first language, which seeks to avoid the subtle dehumanization that takes place when referring to individuals with the condition first. Students experiencing homelessness describes a set of people (students) who are experiencing a condition (homelessness) rather than defining them first and foremost as lacking a fixed, regular, and adequate night-time residence (Canfield, 2015). Students experiencing homelessness have many other aspects to their being; therefore, they should not be dehumanized to the point of solely residing within one categorical box.

WORKING WITH AND FOR STUDENTS EXPERIENCING HOMELESSNESS ACROSS THE LITERATURE

Homelessness is not solely an issue located within the walls of public schools across the United States. Likewise, literature on homelessness covers a wide landscape and includes (not exclusively): behavioral sciences (Kennedy, 2007), education (Hallett, 2012), government policy (Abdul Rahman, Fidel Turner, & Elbedour, 2015), law (Crooke, 2015), nursing (Hudson & Nandy, 2012), pediatrics (Oliveira & Burke, 2009), public health (Fowler, Toro, & Miles, 2009), and social work (Canfield & Teasely, 2015). This section provides a broad description of work with and for students experiencing homelessness.

How youth find themselves identified as homeless are varied but most often are the result of a housing or personal crisis. For example, in a large-scale quantitative survey conducted across the United States that focused on the experiences of youth seeking homeless services, one third of the participants reported some sort of history in foster care (Bender, Yang, Ferguson, & Thompson, 2015). Likewise, Kennedy (2007) found that violence exposure exacerbates the likelihood of experiencing homelessness. Once falling into homelessness, finding an exit becomes difficult and extremely costly. With opportunities for formal work few and far between due to a lack of transportation, identification, and stable address coupled with employers' reluctance to hire unskilled workers, job prospects are difficult for older adolescents experiencing homelessness, and subsequently, so is finding stable housing (Karabanow, Hughes, Ticknor, Kidd, & Patterson, 2010).

Narratives confronting homelessness do not often contain youth voices. Acknowledging that many programs and policies exist to support youth experiencing homelessness, Aviles de Bradley (2011) shared, "Often these approaches exclude the insight of those most affected, the youth themselves. It is critical to include these perspectives in an effort to provide a more thorough understanding of homelessness among youth" (p. 156). Addressing this gap, Aviles de Bradley conducted interviews with six youth experiencing homelessness in Chicago, so that the youth themselves could "frame, interpret, and share meaning of their educational experiences" (p. 158) and contribute to the slim body of knowledge relating to youth who are homeless and their experiences. The interviews revealed the influence of caring adults and a lack of identification with the label *homeless*. Considering this, Aviles de Bradley suggested that, in conjunction with participants, there exists a "need to redefine and re-conceptualize what it means to be homeless" (p. 168).

Taking up Aviles de Bradley's (2011) call for a redefinition and reconstitution of what it means to be homeless, Ellis and Geller (2016) used the term 'housing insecurity' when working with and discussing the experiences of youth labeled homeless. Ellis and Geller used narrative inquiry and viewed their results through a critical race theory lens and further confirmed the importance of supportive adults and provided evidence to counter the false stereotypes described above by Kim (2013). Ellis and Geller (2016) found that the stories shared by youth provided counter-narratives of students experiencing homelessness, specifically in relation to their work ethic. Despite these counter-narratives, the students described structural barriers which, on occasion, made accomplishing educational tasks complicated and more challenging than for their peers with stable housing. It is these structural barriers that need addressing to cultivate and sustain positive environments for students experiencing homelessness.

Grineski (2014) also presented an alternative to the dominant, deficit laden, narrative surrounding homelessness. He used interviews with stakeholders and surveys completed by youth to pursue "a more holistic narrative that illustrates [children experiencing homelessness] who act on varied interests, gifts, and talents" (p. 203). The individual ethnographic cases presented displayed a resilient and against-the-norm description of who these children were and what their lives were like. This work addressed biases and preconceived notions of homelessness, combating beliefs and narratives of pity which can be truly detrimental to motivation and achievement in classrooms.

In neoliberal, capitalist, and standardized times, numbers are sexy. Quick fix neoliberal initiatives encourage educators in our nation's poorest schools to adopt free-market-influenced policies that treat students experiencing poverty as data points, chess pieces almost, in a push for the transfer of public dollars into private hands (Davies & Bransel, 2007; de Saxe, 2015; de Saxe & Smith, 2016; Laitsch, 2013). However, when we discuss young adolescents solely as data points, we lose their faces and identities. Mohan and Shields (2014), using the McKinney-Vento definition of homelessness, conducted interviews and assembled portraits of students written in first person for an added layer of humanity. Their findings demonstrated how the belief that individuals experiencing homelessness suffer from addiction is unfounded and the influence of school faculty and staff is significant.

Regardless of how an individual first experiences homelessness, finding an exit is difficult (Karabanow et al., 2010). Society's perception of their experiences impacts individuals lacking stable housing by impacting their job prospects in addition to their self-esteem (Aviles de Bradley, 2011). The voices of youth who are experiencing homelessness are largely absent from movements seeking to dismantle oppression and in research defining their lived experiences (Aviles de Bradley, 2011; Ellis & Geller, 2016; Grineski, 2014). Thus, work with and for students experiencing homelessness must take place.

THE MIDDLE SCHOOL'S CONNECTION TO HOMELESSNESS

This We Believe (NMSA, 2010) is one of the seminal texts which guides work with young adolescents in middle schools. The position paper stated that young adolescents, "deserve an education that will enhance their healthy growth as lifelong learners, ethical and democratic citizens, and increasingly competent, self-sufficient individuals who are optimistic about the future and prepared to succeed in our ever-changing world" (p. 3). *This We Believe* called for middle schools to be: developmentally responsive; challenging; empowering; and equitable (NMSA, 2010). DiCicco, Cook, and Faulkner (2016) shared that the essential attributes and 16 characteristics, "emphasize the importance of staffing classrooms with teachers specifically prepared to work with the age group" (p. 2). Jackson and Davis (2000) stated that teachers in the middle grades must locate their curriculum within the cultural, historical, and personal interests and needs of young adolescents. To accomplish these directives, teachers must actively seek an understanding of their students' voices and experiences.

Middle grades research has not accomplished this in an equitable manner. Brinegar (2015) found that of the 691 articles and book chapters published in four main middle grades specific texts from 2000–2013 there was:

> A dearth of published research in areas that are critical to developing systems and practices meant to support the needs of every young adolescent, including specific populations (e.g., males, African Americans, students with disabilities), diversity (e.g., broad topics related to equity, discrimination, social justice, multicultural education), motivation and engagement, student voice, leadership, and family/community connections. (p. 1)

For example, Brinegar (2015) illuminated the inequity of representation of publications related to rural middle schools. She stated that despite 20% of the US population residing in rural areas, only two of the 691 articles and book chapters addressed the experiences and needs of rural youth. Similarly, Brinegar found that only 1% of published items addressed students living in poverty versus 22% of the nation's population identified as experiencing poverty. Middle grades research, specifically research published in the main middle grades texts, must pursue, borrowing from *This We Believe* (NMSA, 2010), more empowering and equitable research.

METHODOLOGY

The qualitative research study reported on in this chapter is part of a larger research agenda focused on working with and for young adolescents experiencing homelessness. This specific pilot study was guided by two research questions.

1. What are the day-to-day experiences of students experiencing homelessness?
2. How are those experiences supported, if at all, by school structures and personnel?

Mode of Inquiry

"Maps," according to Pacheco and Vélez (2009), "are visual artifacts of how people see the world as mediated by their particular value systems and relationships of power" (p. 288). When researchers use maps with youth, the intention is not to produce a 100% accurate topographical map of a space but rather to document how individuals feel or experience different places (Clark, 2011b). Maps provide a very telling interpretation of the experiences of youth identified as homeless in their school settings. An interview conducted while crafting a map of Kyrie's middle school inspired the opening vignette.

Maps can be extremely wide or they can be very local. Graue and Walsh (1998) wrote that working with and for children must be an intensely local process. This intense locality requires navigating and dismantling the borders constructed between youth and adults. Utilizing maps and map-making serves as an attempt to gain intensely local insights about in and out of school experiences of youth who meet the McKinney-Vento definition of homeless. When participants create artifacts, specifically maps, "different modes of expression" (Clark, 2011a, p. 327) present themselves that often challenge societal narratives and other conventional, research-driven modes of inquiry.

Clark (2011b) stated that specifically naming the act map-making "emphasizes the active process of meaning-making which can occur as children assemble the maps rather than placing importance solely on the product, the map" (p. 315). Throughout the process of creating the maps and walking through the spaces documented by the maps, researchers can perform "informal interviews about the physical environment" (Clark, 2011a, p. 324) and elucidate participants' experiences of being in the spaces being mapped.

Maps, and the accompanying conversations that are born out of the process, help clarify the state of *This We Believe*'s (NMSA, 2010) essential attributes within the walls of Riverside Middle School. The maps provide a suitable measure of the needs of students experiencing homelessness and also illuminate areas of strength. Participant-crafted artifacts serve as a means by which to present student participants' experiences so that schools can align their policies and structures to respond to and address inequities.

Context and Participant

The research that influenced this chapter took place in a small-city urban middle school, Riverside Middle School (RMS), in the southeastern United States. Riverside exists within a community that "is one of the most impoverished communities per capita in the country and is nested within a small city with a history of generational poverty where the residue of Jim Crow perseveres" (Hughes, Moulton, Andrews, 2016, p. 3). RMS is located in North Fork School District (NFSD). Three quarters of NFSD's students qualify for free or reduced-price lunches. Falling below the district average, roughly 60% of RMS' students qualify for free or reduced-price meals, but, due to a grant received by the district, every student receives breakfast and lunch free of charge regardless of their financial situation. Official government documents identified just under five percent of NFSD's students as experiencing homelessness. NSFD's homeless liaison believes that the true percentage of students experiencing homelessness could easily double if every family that fits the federal definition were to self-identify themselves (personal communication, October 3, 2016).

I recruited the sole participant in the study through purposive sampling. As a researcher, gaining access to young adolescent participants experiencing homelessness proved to be a difficult endeavor. I had to approach recruitment through school faculty and staff to comply with the National School Lunch Act (1946). I first approached the district's homeless liaison who, though enthusiastic about the project, felt that approaching families for participation might put an unnecessary strain on relationships. I next approached the school social worker who was simultaneously responsible for providing services to students at Riverside and one of its feeder elementary schools. This process led to two months of interactions between the school social worker and families experiencing homelessness before one student, Kyrie, and his mother Elizabeth, agreed to participate. At the time of the study, Kyrie was in the seventh grade. Including RMS, Kyrie had attended seven different schools and schools held him back twice due to absences. He was an above average student who loved science, art, and basketball. He was a constant performer and had a sly smile and sharp sense of humor.

Data Collection and Analysis

I collected data in multiple forms over the course of five meetings. Two meetings took place in Kyrie's residence and were not audio recorded. Semi-structured interviews lasted between 45 to 90 minutes and I conducted them at RMS and a local fast food restaurant three times over the course of two months. Each of these interviews was audio recorded and transcribed. I collected field notes during all five of the meetings so that I could capture information that would not be available in an audio recording including sensory details, facial expressions, body language, and my personal interpretations. Drawings and maps served as a source of data in their own right and as an elicitation device for semi-structured interviews (see Appendix for the semi-structured interview protocol). I began data analysis by reading all the data holistically. Following this holistic reading, I read the data through a frame influenced by *This We Believe* (NMSA, 2010). This frame asked "Was [key moment from data] developmentally responsive? Was it challenging? Was it empowering? Was it equitable? If so, how? If not, how not?" This frame allowed the participant's lived experience and expertise to display how Riverside addresses his needs as a young adolescent.

FINDINGS

Kyrie used two pieces of paper to draw a map of Riverside Middle School. For an example of the maps, see Figure 4.1. I used the maps as an elicitation device with the intention of uncovering stories and experiences from Kyrie's perspective of his time spent at school. After reviewing the transcripts, field notes, and Kyrie's maps, four themes became apparent. These four themes were: (a) the importance of caring adults, (b) food insecurity, (c) funds of knowledge, and (d) lack of inclusion of personal interests. These themes are described below.

The Importance of Caring Adults

Kyrie's maps documented locations in RMS where he had relationships with caring adults. After stopping by the cafeteria, Kyrie visited with the assistant principal, Mr. Jam, to check in. Kyrie shared that Mr. Jam was a positive presence in RMS and that the relationship that the two of them shared provided comfort. In describing his daily routine, the following exchange took place:

> **Kyrie:** I go down to Mr. Jam's office. What I do? Oh, let him know if I am ok or not. Because, you know, he knows about my mom.

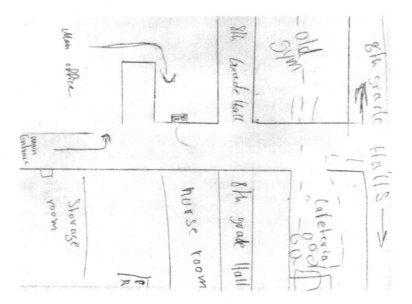

Figure 4.1 Example map created by Kyrie with his route represented.

Matt: Yeah. He checks in on you every day? Would you say that's, like, a good part about the school?

Kyrie: Yeah, just in case something bad happen. He would probably know because I check in with him, you know?

Matt: And does that help throughout the course of the day?

Kyrie: It lets me know that someone cares. He's like a mentor.

From our conversations, it is apparent that Kyrie believes that Mr. Jam is invested in his success at more than just an academic level.

As alluded to in the opening vignette, Kyrie and I were able to spend time with each other during a school day because the school suspended him, according to Kyrie, "for his own safety." What started as a verbal argument between he and another student nearly devolved into a physical altercation. One administrator suggested suspending both Kyrie and the other boy for multiple days but Mr. Jam, understanding what Kyrie was working through due to their daily check-ins, suggested that the school only suspend Kyrie for one day, which would not remain on his record. This simultaneously demonstrated Mr. Jam's role as a caring adult advocate and someone with the ability to remove a student with transience issues from a classroom.

Food Insecurity

According to the U.S. Department of Agriculture Economic Research Service (USDAERS, 2016), food insecurity consists of two different levels. The first, low food security, describes settings of "reduced quality, variety, or desirability of diet. Most report little or no reduction in food intake" (2016, para. 5). The second, very low food security, requires "multiple indications of disrupted eating patterns and reduced food intake" (2016, para. 5). Kyrie, his mother Elizabeth, and the other members of their combined household fluctuate between these two different levels of food insecurity. According to USDAERS' (2017a, 2017b) maps and data, the location of their residence is in a food desert, which the USDAERS (2017a) defined as an area that lacks access to healthy food sources. In addition to identification as a food desert, the USDAERS (2017b) also labels the location where Kyrie and Elizabeth resided as low-income and low-access because only 13% of residents have access to a vehicle and they are more than one mile from the nearest supermarket.

Food insecurity impacted the beginning of Kyrie's days and its effects rippled out across classes. As relayed in the opening vignette, on some occasions Kyrie arrived to school late, which impacted numerous parts of his day. Along with missing portions of the school day, Kyrie also missed out on eating the free breakfast provided by RMS. Missing breakfast meant a few different things for Kyrie. By missing breakfast, he not only missed out on food, he lost one of the only opportunities to interact with friends and classmates in an unstructured and less-governed time of the school day.

Riverside Middle recognized the impact that food insecurity has on students and developed a system to put food into hungry students' hands. Students and staff deposit leftover food (e.g., uneaten fruit, packaged items, and unopened drinks) into a clean and accessible container in the cafeteria. Should students feel hungry throughout the day, they can visit the cafeteria and find a snack. Kyrie, on days that he was late to school, made use of this resource before heading to class. This is an unstructured, unfunded, and unreliable means to acquire food, but it does meet the needs of students experiencing food insecurity.

Some days there were not any snacks available in the cafeteria and Kyrie began his day hungry. On these days he drank lots of water to soothe his hunger. Kyrie augmented his daily routine in response to food insecurity and hunger. After visiting with Mr. Jam, Kyrie used the restroom. Intentionally visiting the restroom is the result of a confrontation between Kyrie and a teacher, who he still respected and spoke highly of, who would not let him use the restroom during class on one of the days that Kyrie drank lots of water to calm his hunger pains. According to Kyrie, he asked politely and the teacher told him no. He asked again in a few minutes to the same result. He asked a third time and explained that it was an emergency only for the teacher to sternly rebuke hum and an argument ensued. Kyrie's food insecurity had a disciplinary consequence.

Funds of Knowledge

Kyrie's maps and stories challenge dominant narratives surrounding homelessness, specifically that those experiencing homelessness are unintelligent and lazy. The opening narrative which described Kyrie's journey from home to school on days that he missed the school bus provides an example of his determination and one of his funds of knowledge (Moll, Amanti, Neff, & Gonzalez, 1992). Moll and colleagues defined funds of knowledge as the facts, information, or skills that are "historically accumulated and culturally developed" (p. 133) through personal experiences. Kyrie has developed a level of literacy with the public transit system that demonstrates a thorough knowledge of not just how to navigate the system but how to utilize it to achieve his personal goals. He relayed a story of the days where he missed the school bus and still, despite narratives surrounding young adolescents (Beane, 1991) and homelessness (Kim, 2013), leveraged his personal funds of knowledge to set school attendance as a priority.

Not only is this fund of knowledge not honored or valued but the school greeted it with discipline.

Lack of Inclusion of Personal Interests

Some of the most telling findings presented themselves by reviewing what Kyrie did not include on his map. Figure 4.2 is an aerial photograph of RMS taken as a screenshot from Google Maps. Kyrie's has well-developed personal interests that are large parts of his life but he did not include them on the map. Three of these interests were: basketball, art, and friends.

Basketball

On the first day that I met Kyrie, he was wearing a basketball jersey for a team of which he was a member. Basketball was a large part of his life and was one of the most constant things in a school-aged life marked with

Figure 4.2 Aerial photograph of Riverside Middle School with dashed-line box overlaid. Kyrie included everything inside the dashed-line box on his map. He excluded everything outside that box.

transience. Despite his love for basketball and even membership on the school's team, Kyrie did not include the basketball gym in the map that he drew of school. Our interviews did not discuss basketball within the context of his school day but often our interactions concluded with me driving him to different courts to play with friends.

Art

Kyrie is an avid artist. His drawings, in addition to the maps, of RMS display a strong grasp on being able to relay depth and texture. Although I used drawing and map-making as elicitation devices in the interviews, Kyrie made no mention of art throughout the course of his day. In fact, the location of the art room in RMS falls in the space between his first and second map.

Friends

Kyrie's map of RMS does not include any mention of spaces for friends to congregate outside of when he arrives to school on time to sit down for breakfast. RMS has very few spaces for students to congregate. The school limited socialization in between classes. Kyrie stated that if he wants to interact with friends it must be before or after school, outside and possibly off school grounds.

DISCUSSION

The research literature has rarely included the experiences of students identified as homeless (Canfield, 2015; Hallett, 2012; Mohan & Shields, 2014). Kyrie's maps and interviews provide just a snapshot of his day-to-day life within the walls of RMS. He described, both with positive and negative examples, the importance of relationships with caring adults. On a regular basis, food insecurity influences his day. He carries with him funds of knowledge that RMS may not value and the maps of his school failed to include personal interests. His experiences, though singular, bear witness to areas that RMS could better meet the needs of students experiencing homelessness and places where the school is already supporting their success.

This We Believe (NMSA, 2010) called for the education of young adolescents to be, among other attributes, empowering and equitable. The position statement described an empowering education as "providing all students with the knowledge and skills they need to take responsibility for their lives, to address life's challenges, to function successfully at all levels of society, and to be creators of knowledge" (p. 13). Kyrie's experiences at RMS simultaneously display an environment that empowers and restricts. Similar to the findings of Aviles de Bradley (2011) concerning positive relationships with adults, relationships with caring adults, and a cafeteria staff who recognizes the impact that hunger has on a student's day empowered Kyrie. The lack of opportunities to engage with his classmates and friends in safe spaces and less than empowering relationships with some teachers restricted him. Speaking specifically on the motivation and empowerment of students experiencing homelessness that is borne from positive relationships with caring adults, Ellis and Geller (2016) wrote, "The stories the youth shared described their desire to do the work; however, structural barriers made work completion challenging and sometimes impossible. Furthermore, the lack of assistance from teachers discouraged these young people from trying" (p. 599). It is these structural barriers that need addressing to cultivate and sustain positive environments for students experiencing homelessness.

The lack of spaces for students to congregate could lead to the belief that school is not for socialization. *This We Believe* (NMSA, 2010) stated that "Young people's desire for peer acceptance and the need to belong to particular social groups are often intense and sometimes lead to shifting allegiance from adults to peers" (p. 7) and that young adolescents need to "develop the interpersonal and social skills needed to learn, work, and play with others harmoniously and confidently" (p. 12). The text seems to imply that empowerment and personal interest are born out of collaboration and interaction with peers. Collaboration and interaction manifest themselves in environments designed specifically with individuals in mind. Administrators and stakeholders must physically design middle schools to meet the needs of their students as opposed to a building they use to hold students in between elementary and high school. Additionally, students experiencing homelessness can find strength in relationships with others. If stakeholders do not view school as a place for students to interact with each other then it simply becomes another location of transience for students experiencing homelessness.

Middle schools must, according to *This We Believe* (NMSA, 2010), "advocat[e] for and ensur[e] every student's right to learn and provid[e] appropriately challenging and relevant learning opportunities for every student" (p. 13). Gorski (2016) described equity literate educators as individuals who can recognize even the subtlest forms of inequity and bias in school environments. He called for educators to ask of themselves:

> Do I understand the challenges students experiencing poverty face outside school well enough that I recognize even the subtlest ways in which those challenges are reproduced within schools? Am I capable of recognizing stereotypical depictions of people experiencing poverty when I flip through a textbook under consideration for adoption in my school district? (p. 17)

The young adolescents who populate the halls and classrooms of middle schools across the United States must have teachers who actively seek equity.

These teachers must understand that they should seek equity continuously in order to provide the most equitable environment for students.

Riverside Middle School recognizes the impact that hunger has on its students and seeks to provide an equitable opportunity to address that need. Many of RMS' students reside in food deserts and have inadequate access to fresh fruits and vegetables. The cafeteria's initiative to save food for students who need it eases the impact of that burden but does little, if anything, to remove the burden of hunger in the long term. In addition to providing food for hungry students, the cafeteria's unfunded resource encourages students to think more globally about issues of food waste and their potential role in contributing to seeking solutions.

The opening narrative demonstrated a fund of knowledge that Kyrie carried with him into school. His ability to navigate the public transit system is a skill that he can rely on outside of school but has little impact on the academic structure of his day. The city within which Kyrie resides recently increased access to public transit by removing all costs for youth under the age of 18. Kyrie makes use of public transit frequently, but this does not stop RMS faculty and staff from meeting his ability to navigate and utilize the system with discipline. By being late he receives a tardy. If he accrues enough tardies he receives a referral. Enough referrals and the school suspends him. His efforts to get to school result in him inching closer to removal from school. Exclusionary discipline impacts students' trajectory towards graduation (Marchbanks et al., 2015). Balfanz, Byrnes, and Fox (2015) found that "being suspended in middle or high school is the triggering event, which then leads to broader disengagement from schooling and eventually dropping out" (pp. 27–28). Yes, Kyrie needs to be in school, but the schools needs to consider his living situation and transportation issues.

Educators of young adolescents must value their experiences and interests (NMSA, 2010). Kyrie did not describe portions of his school day that aligned with his personal interests. Through omission, we can assume that Kyrie hold his personal interests separate from curriculum and school activities leading to a further gap between personal experiences and in school engagement.

This qualitative research study documented a small portion of the life of one student identified as experiencing homelessness. A popular critique of qualitative research is that its lack of generalizability limits its influence. Although the study was narrow, Myers (2000) reminded us that, "The ultimate aim of qualitative research is to offer a perspective of a situation and provide well-written research reports that reflect the researcher's ability to illustrate or describe the corresponding phenomenon" (p. 6). Kyrie is just one student from Riverside Middle School who has experienced homelessness, but he will not be the last. It is unlikely that he is the only student who makes use of school resources to meet his needs. It is unlikely that he is the only student who benefits from positive relationships with caring adults. It is unlikely that he is the only student who experiences a curriculum that excludes his funds of knowledge.

This We Believe (NMSA, 2010) seemed to serve as an adequate lens through which to filter Kyrie's experiences but elements of the position paper were constricting and limiting with regards to students experiencing homelessness. *This We Believe* described young adolescents as having a "heightened interest in personal grooming" (p. 6) while simultaneously making unhealthy nutritional choices. *This We Believe* does not even allude to the possibility that young adolescents may not have access to healthier options given the effects of poverty; it states, "Young adolescents also witness and experience the negative results of homelessness, racism, drug and alcohol abuse, crime, international terrorism, wars, domestic violence, and child abuse" (p. 9). This relegation to a position on a list does little to impact homelessness and the subsequent call for schools to "foster responsible, moral decision makers" (p. 9) almost seems to imply a lack of morality present within homelessness. I echo the call of Busey (2017) for the Association for Middle Level Education to work on developing more equitable and socially just positions for the benefit of young adolescents who do not fit a White and middle-class mold.

CONCLUSION

Kyrie, a middle school student identified as experiencing homelessness, used maps to document his day-to-day movements within Riverside Middle School. His maps and accompanying conversations demonstrated how RMS both helps and hinders students like himself. I analyzed maps and conversations through a lens influenced by *This We Believe* (NMSA, 2010) and revealed that RMS has some resources in place that are both empowering and equitable for Kyrie, mainly caring adults and a cafeteria food saving program. Although empowering and equitable measures exist at RMS, there is still room for growth in meeting the needs of students experiencing homelessness. School staff who are unaware of the lived experiences of students, especially the specific needs of students experiencing homelessness, put a strain on students who are seeking academic stability and consistency. Failures to acknowledge and plan for the documented transportation issues of students experiencing homelessness could lead to further marginalization.

Addressing youth homelessness will require collaboration from numerous stakeholders. This collaboration must include the youth themselves. The public perception of homelessness excludes the voices of these most important stakeholders. Including youth perspectives is part of the work required by middle grades educators. A learning environment cannot be equitable if members of the classroom community do not have the privilege to contribute to the discourse.

Students experiencing homelessness are not a homogenous group (Hallett, 2012). In no way should we see this one student's experiences as such. That was the point. This was an "extremely local" (Graue & Walsh, 1998, p. 9) research study which sought to celebrate one school's successes and "bear witness to the negativity" (Apple, Au, & Gandin, 2009, p. 4) to enhance the school experience of all students, especially those experiencing homelessness. As researchers, educators, and advocates, we must engage in more work to document and share the experiences of students identified as homeless so that we can add their voices to vital conversations about education.

APPENDIX
Interview Protocols

Semi-Structured Interview Protocol

During Initial Meeting

1. Tell me about your experiences in school.
   a. What are some things that you like about the school?
   b. What are some things that you would change if you had the opportunity?

Map-Making Protocol

1. Draw a map of your school
   a. Label the map with the places that you go (classes, lunch, before/after school, places you hang out, etc.)
2. Identify people/places/things on the map that are strengths of HMS
3. Identify people/places/things on the map that you feel could be improved
4. Conversation taking place after creation of map:
   a. Describe what you included in your map
   b. What were the strengths you listed?
      i. What about them makes you consider them strengths?
   c. What were the things that could be improved?
      i. What about them makes you think they could be improved?

REFERENCES

Abdul Rahman, M., Fidel Turner, J., & Elbedour, S. (2015). The U.S. homeless student population: Homeless youth education, review of research classifications and typologies, and the U.S. federal legislative response. *Child Youth Care Forum, 44*, 687–709.

Apple, M. W., Au, W., & Gandin, L. A. (2009). Mapping critical education. In M. W. Apple, W. Au, & L. A. Gandin (Eds.), *The Routledge international handbook of critical education* (pp. 3–19). New York, NY: Routledge.

Aviles de Bradley, A. M. (2011). Unaccompanied homeless youth: Intersections of homelessness, school experiences and educational policy. *Child & Youth Services, 32*(2), 155–172.

Balfanz, R., Byrnes, V., & Fox, J. H. (2015). Sent home and put off track: The antecedents, disproportionalities, and consequences of being suspended in the 9th grade. In D. J. Losen (Ed.), *Closing the school discipline gap: Equitable remedies for excessive exclusion* (pp. 17–30). New York, NY: Teachers College Press.

Beane, J. (1991). The middle school: The natural home of integrated curriculum. *Educational Leadership, 49*(2), 9–13.

Bender, K., Yang, J., Ferguson, K., & Thompson, S. (2015). Experiences and needs of homeless youth with a history of foster care. *Children and Youth Services Review, 55*, 222–231.

Biggar, H. (2001). Homeless children and education: An evaluation of the Stewart B. McKinney Homeless Assistance Act. *Children and Youth Services Review, 23*(12), 941–969.

Brinegar, K. (2015). A content analysis of four peer-reviewed middle grades publications: Are we really paying attention to every young adolescent? *Middle Grades Review, 1*(1), 1–8. Retrieved from https://files.eric.ed.gov/fulltext/EJ1154860.pdf

Burke, K. J., Greene, S., & McKenna, M. K. (2014). A critical geographic approach to youth civic engagement: Reframing educational opportunity zones and the use of public spaces. *Urban Education, 51*(2), 143–169.

Busey, C. (2017, April). *This who believes? A critical race discourse analysis of the Association for Middle Level Education's This We Believe.* Paper presented at the meeting of the American Educational Research Association, San Antonio, TX.

Canfield, J. (2015). *School-based practice with children and youth experiencing homelessness.* New York, NY: Oxford University Press.

Canfield, J. P., & Teasley, M. L. (2015). The McKinney-Vento Homeless Assistance Act: School-based practitioners' place in shaping the policy's future. *Children & Schools, 37*(2), 67–70.

Clark, A. (2010). Young children as protagonists and the role of participatory, visual methods in engaging multiple perspectives. *American Journal of Community Psychology, 46*(1–2), 115–123.

Clark, A. (2011a). Breaking methodological boundaries? Exploring visual, participatory methods with adults and young children. *European Early Childhood Education Research Journal, 19*(3), 321–330.

Clark, A. (2011b). Multimodal map making with young children: Exploring ethnographic and participatory methods. *Qualitative Research, 11*(3), 311–330.

Crook, C. (2015). Educating America's homeless youth through reinforcement of the McKinney Vento Homeless Assistance Act. *Faulkner Law Review, 6*(2), 395–408.

Davies, B., & Bansel, P. (2007). Neoliberalism and education. *International Journal of Qualitative Studies in Education, 20*(3), 247–259.

de Saxe, J. (2015). A neoliberal critique: Conceptualizing the purposes of school. *Catalyst: A Social Justice Forum, 5*(1). Article 7.

de Saxe, J., & Smith, G. (2016). Introducing novice teachers to corporate and neoliberal educational reforms: Challenges and opportunities. *The SoJo Journal: Educational Foundations and Social Justice Education, 2*(1), 45–58.

DiCicco, M., Cook, C. M., & Faulkner, S. A. (2016). Teaching in the middle grades today: Examining teachers' beliefs about middle grades teaching. *Middle Grades Review, 2*(3), 1–17. Retrieved from https://files.eric.ed.gov/fulltext/EJ1154810.pdf

Ellis, A. L., & Geller, K. D. (2016). Unheard and unseen: How housing insecure African American adolescents experience the education system. *Education and Urban Society, 48*(6), 583–610.

Every Student Succeeds Act (ESSA) of 2015, Pub. L. No. 114-95 § 114 Stat. 1177 (2015–2016).

Feuer, A. (2012, February 3). Homeless families, cloaked in normality. *New York Times*. Retrieved from http://www.nytimes.com/2012/02/05/nyregion/ordinary-families-cloaked-in-a-veil-of-homelessness.html

Fowler, P. J., Toro, P. A., & Miles, B. W. (2009). Aging-out of foster care: Pathways to and from homelessness and associated psychosocial outcomes in young adulthood. *American Journal of Public Health, 99*(8), 1453–1458.

Gorski, P. C. (2016, May). Re-examining beliefs about students in poverty. *School Administrator, 5*(73), 17–20.

Graue, M. E., & Walsh, D. J. (1998). *Studying children in context: Theories, methods, and ethics.* Thousand Oaks, CA: SAGE.

Grineski, S. (2014). The multi-dimensional lives of children who are homeless. *Critical Questions in Education, 5*(3), 203–217.

Hallett, R. E. (2012). Living doubled-up: Influence of residential environment on educational participation. *Education and Urban Society, 44*(4), 371–391.

Hallett, R. E., Low, J. A., & Skrla, L. (2015). Beyond backpacks and bus tokens: Next steps for a district homeless student initiative. *International Journal of Qualitative Studies in Education, 28*(6), 693–713.

Hallett, R. E., Skrla, L., & Low, J. A. (2015). That is not what homeless is: A school district's journey toward serving homeless, doubled-up, and economically displaced children and youth. *International Journal of Qualitative Studies in Education, 28*(6), 671–692.

Homeless. (n.d.). In *Oxford online dictionaries*. Retrieved from https://en.oxforddictionaries.com/definition/homeless

Hudson, A., & Nandy, K. (2012). Comparisons of substance abuse, high-risk sexual behavior, and depressive symptoms among homeless youth with and without a history of foster care placement. *Contemporary Nurse, 42*(2), 178–186.

Hughes, H. E., Moulton, M. J., & Andrews, P. G. (2016). Learning through crisis and paradox in justice-oriented teacher education. *Middle Grades Review, 1*(3), Art. 4.

Jackson, A. W., & Davis, G. A. (2000). *Turning points 2000: Educating adolescents in the 21st century.* New York, NY: Teachers College Press.

Karabanow, J., Hughes, J., Ticknor, J., Kidd, S., & Patterson, D. (2010). The economics of being young and poor: How homeless youth survive in neo-liberal times. *Journal of Sociology & Social Welfare, 37*(4), 39–63.

Kennedy, A. C. (2007). Homelessness, violence exposure, and school participation among urban adolescent mothers. *Journal of Community Psychology, 35*(5), 639–654.

Kim, J. (2013). Against the unchallenged discourse of homelessness: Examining the views of early childhood preservice teachers. *Journal of Early Childhood Teacher Education, 34*(4), 291–307.

King, J. B., Jr. (2016, July 27). *Letter on educational rights of homeless children and youths under the McKinney-Vento Act.* Washington, DC: U.S. Department of Education. Retrieved from http://www2.ed.gov/policy/elsec/guid/secletter/160726.html

Laitisch, D. (2013). Smacked by the invisible hand: The wrong debate at the wrong time with the wrong people. *Journal of Curriculum Studies, 45*(1), 16–27.

Marchbanks III, M. P., Blake, J. J., Booth, E. A., Carmichael, D., Seibert, A. L., & Fabelo, T. (2015). The economic effects of exclusionary discipline on grade retention and high school dropout. In D. J. Losen (Ed.), *Closing the school discipline gap: Equi*table *remedies for excessive exclusion* (pp. 59–74). New York, NY: Teachers College Press.

McKinney–Vento Homeless Assistance Act of 1987, Pub. L. 100-77, July 22, 1987, 101 Stat. 482, 42 U.S.C. § 11301.

McKinney-Vento Homeless Education Assistance Improvements Act of 2001, Pub. L. 100-77, 42 U.S.C. §§ 11431-11435 (2001).

Miller, P. M. (2012). Educating (more and more) students experiencing homelessness: An analysis of recession-era policy and practice. *Educational Policy, 27*(5), 805–838.

Mohan, E., & Shields, C. M. (2014). The voices behind the numbers: Understanding the experiences of homeless students. *Critical Questions in Education, 5*(3), 189–202.

Moll, L. C., Amanti, C., Neff, D., & Gonzalez, N. (1992). Funds of knowledge for teaching: Using a qualitative approach to connect homes and classrooms. *Theory Into Practice, 31*(2), 132–141.

Myers, M. (2000). Qualitative research and the generalizability question: Standing firm with Proteus. *The Qualitative Report, 4*(3), Article 9.

National Middle School Association. (2010). *This we believe: Keys to educating young adolescents.* Westerville, OH: Author.

National School Lunch Act, Pub. L. 79–396, 60 Stat. 230 (1946).

Oliveira, J. O., & Burke, P. J. (2009). Lost in the shuffle: Culture of homeless adolescents. *Pediatric Nursing, 35*(3), 154–161.

Pacheco, D., & Vélez, V. N. (2009). Maps, mapmaking, and critical pedagogy: Exploring GIS and maps as a teaching tool for social change. *Seattle Journal for Social Justice, 8*(1), 273–302.

U.S. Department of Agriculture Economic Research Service. (2016). *Definitions of food security.* Retrieved from https://www.ers.usda.gov/amber-waves/2007/june/struggling-to-feed-the-family-what-does-it-mean-to-be-food-insecure/

U.S. Department of Agriculture Economic Research Service. (2017a). *Documentation.* Retrieved from https://www.ers.usda.gov/data-products/food-access-research-atlas/documentation/

U.S. Department of Agriculture Economic Research Service. (2017b). *Food access research atlas.* Retrieved from https://www.ers.usda.gov/data-products/food-access-research-atlas/go-to-the-atlas/

U.S. Department of Education. (2016). *Supporting the success of homeless children and youth: Fact sheet.* Retrieved from http://www2.ed.gov/policy/elsec/leg/essa/160315ehcyfactsheet072716.pdf

CHAPTER 5

"SOUNDING FUNNY" AND MAKING SENSE

Multimodal Codemeshing as a Culturally Sustaining Pedagogy in an English-Centric Classroom

Mark B. Pacheco
University of Florida

Blaine E. Smith
University of Arizona

ABSTRACT

This comparative case study (Stake, 2006) examines the participation of two multilingual young adolescent students during a multimodal literature response project that encouraged students to leverage multiple modalities and multiple languages, or multimodal codemeshing. More specifically, this chapter examines the different ways in which the classroom context afforded and constrained two eighth grade students' use of Vietnamese and Spanish within their multimodal codemeshing processes and products. Findings showed how students found ways to engage with multiple audiences using text, oral lan-

Equity & Cultural Responsiveness in the Middle Grades, pages 93–112
Copyright © 2019 by Information Age Publishing
All rights of reproduction in any form reserved.

guage, and images, despite a marked view of their heritage languages within the English-centric context. The chapter concludes with implications for other culturally sustaining pedagogies that seek to recognize, leverage, and build on students' linguistic strengths in middle school classrooms.

As classrooms continue to grow in linguistic diversity (National Center for Education Statistics, 2016), recent scholarship has addressed the pressing need to include the full range of bilingual students' meaning-making resources to support their academic, linguistic, and social development (Garcia & Wei, 2013). In middle school literacy classrooms, integrating students' heritage languages—or the languages they might speak at home or in their communities—can be particularly powerful in supporting students as they make meaning in texts (Puzio, Keyes, & Jiménez, 2016), deepen vocabulary knowledge (Pacheco & Goodwin, 2013), and develop metalinguistic awareness (Martin-Beltrán, 2014). At the same time, including these languages can be challenging, especially in environments that adhere to monolingual language policies by practice and by law (Abiria, Early, & Kendrick, 2013; Pacheco, 2016).

This chapter explores how a culturally sustaining pedagogy (Paris, 2012) can address the needs and leverage the strengths of bilingual learners in English-centric classrooms. By eliciting and investigating the emic perspective of two bilingual eighth grade students—Sandra (all names in this chapter are pseudonyms), a student born in the United States who speaks English and Vietnamese, and Yuliana, a newcomer student born in El Salvador who speaks English and Spanish—this study seeks to understand their participation in a project that incorporates multimodal composition (Kress, 2010) and translanguaging (Garcia & Wei, 2013) to respond to a classroom text. In our analysis of design interviews (Dalton et al., 2015) with the two students and an analysis of their classroom participation in a four-week multimodal composition project, we sought to understand the ways in which the classroom context afforded and constrained their uses of heritage languages, and, in turn, how their participation with these languages shaped the "monolingual" classroom context.

We refer to these classrooms as *English-centric*, as English was the medium of instruction due to not only official language policy, but through the dominance of English as the language of verbal exchanges, the curriculum, instructional materials, and classroom resources (e.g., textbooks). We use English-centric rather than *English-only* with an understanding that students and teachers in these environments are often multilingual, and thus, the negotiated and constructed contexts in which they participate reflect aspects of this multilingualism (Pennycook, 2010). In this chapter, we hope to inform similar classroom pedagogies that attempt to incorporate aspects of students' cultural and linguistic identities into literacy instruction (Cummins et al., 2005). Next, we describe multimodal codemeshing as a culturally sustaining pedagogy, which we define and describe in greater detail. We then expand our theoretical framework for understanding both students' participation in the classroom project and how their participation relates to classroom contexts. We begin our findings by describing Sandra and Yuliana's experiences as a means to understand how other English-centric contexts can include culturally sustaining pedagogies that connect communities and classrooms with language and technology. We conclude our chapter with implications for both theory and practice.

MULTIMODAL CODEMESHING AS A CULTURALLY SUSTAINING PEDAGOGY

We describe multimodal codemeshing as the purposeful integration and leveraging of multiple languages and modalities in digital composition (Pacheco & Smith, 2015). We explore multimodal codemeshing as a culturally sustaining pedagogy (Paris, 2012), or classroom practice that "seeks to perpetuate and foster—to sustain—linguistic, literate, and cultural pluralism as part of the democratic project of schooling" (p. 95). Whereas understandings of culturally responsive pedagogy (Gay, 2002; Ladson-Billings, 1995) offer opportunities for teachers to recognize students' linguistic and cultural practices and structure instruction in ways that are relevant to these practices, culturally sustaining pedagogies offer educators opportunities to recognize, maintain, and expand these practices in instruction. As Paris (2012) argued, classroom instruction must be "more than responsive or relevant to the cultural experiences and practices of young people," and must sustain "the cultural and linguistic competence of [students'] communities while simultaneously offering access to dominant cultural competence" (p. 95).

In multimodal codemeshing, bilingual students have opportunities to draw on multiple semiotic resources in their heritage language and in English to negotiate meaning with multiple discourse communities (Smith, Pacheco, & de Almeida, 2017). As a student composes a message for a Spanish-speaking reader, for example, that student might leverage resources coded in Spanish to convey a concept. Within the same digital composition, that student might also draw on English-language resources to negotiate meaning with classmates or an English-speaking teacher (Durán, 2017).

There is extensive research that documents how students lose proficiency in their heritage language over time if educators are not explicit in encouraging them to use it in the classroom (see Cummins, 2000, for summary of research). As young adolescent students might have few opportunities to use languages other than English in classrooms where English is the medium of instruction (Daniel & Pacheco, 2016), multimodal codemeshing offers opportunities to leverage and possibly sustain aspects of students' heritage languages. At the same time, bilingual students participate in meaning-making practices, such as translation (Jiménez et al., 2015) and language brokering (Orellana & Reynolds, 2008) in their lives outside of school. Recognizing the cognitive, social, and linguistic demands of these rich practices, multimodal codemeshing offers students opportunities to mesh language, translate texts, and consider the affordances associated with different linguistic resources when communicating with an interlocutor.

Along with the explicit linguistic affordances associated with multimodal codemeshing, this composing practice offers opportunities for students to orchestrate multiple modes or modalities—including but not limited to text, sound, color, image, and movement—to communicate complex messages (Smith, 2016). A mode might carry a different semiotic affordance than another mode when used in composition (Kress & Van Leeuwen, 2001), and these modes' affordances might change as they interact with one another on the screen. Multimodal composition can be powerful for bilingual students to leverage cultural and social capital in response to texts (Bailey, 2009; Smith, 2014), to express identities in ways not typically afforded by written texts (Hull, Stornaiuolo, & Sahni, 2010), and to "braid" home literacy practices with school practices to craft and develop multilingual narratives (Zapata & Laman, 2016). At the same time research has demonstrated that a growing majority of youth compose multimodally outside of school to express themselves and connect with others (Ito et al., 2010; Rideout, Foehr, & Roberts, 2010).

Despite the seeming ease with which students access and use digital technologies, Van Leeuwen (2015) argued that instruction must still offer students "something that is not readily available elsewhere" (p. 584). As a culturally sustaining pedagogy, multimodal codemeshing attempts to build on and expand bilingual students' uses and understandings of language and technology. In this chapter, however, we also seek to uncover some of the challenges for including this type of pedagogy into a classroom context that is "English-only" by both policy and practice. Harman, Johnson, and Chagoya (2016) have reiterated in their research how bilingual learners might feel isolated or frightened in such classroom contexts, and Allexsaht-Snider, Buxton, and Harman (2013) pointed out specifically how local language policies can negatively affect the emotional well-being of adolescent bilingual students. Below, we describe the importance of such contexts in shaping multimodal codemeshing practices and then turn to the context of our study.

Multimodal Codemeshing and Classroom Context

Our framing of multimodal codemeshing builds from research in translanguaging pedagogies (Creese & Blackledge, 2010; Garcia, 2009) and translingual practice (Canagarajah, 2013). Theories of translanguaging suggest that individuals can draw on a holistic and integrated system of semiotic resources with varying degrees of awareness to negotiate meaning with an interlocutor. Translingual practice extends this work and explores how individuals might draw on divergent semiotic resources (i.e., an individual uses Spanish and another individual uses English) to negotiate meaning. Both of these framings of language use underscore the importance of language use as a practice—individuals strategically deploy semiotic resources in relation to goals, to other resources available in communication, and to the contexts in which they leverage these resources. As Palmer and Martinez (2016) argued in their work with multilingual students, language is not something that a student *has*, but a practice that a student *does*.

While goals and available semiotic resources are important for shaping the different ways that students might participate in different language practices in the classroom, Martinez-Roldan's (2015) work highlighted the importance of language ideologies and local language policies in shaping classroom translanguaging. When assessments are in English, educators explicitly value English as the language for participating in class activities, students' Spanish linguistic resources do not then share the same status as English in the classroom. Similarly, Daniel and Pacheco's (2016) work with bilingual middle school students showed how students began to view their heritage languages as not useful for their academic success if not explicitly encouraged to do so over time in their English-medium classrooms.

Echoing the findings in these studies and others, Canagarajah (2011) emphasized that language use is never fully "unbidden" (p. 405). As such, research must investigate students' participation in multimodal codemeshing in relation to the context in which students and teachers participate. This study seeks to understand the potential of multimodal codemeshing as a culturally sustaining pedagogy within a classroom where the teacher delivers instruction in English, students speak multiple heritage languages, and the teacher and students do not share proficiencies in these heritage languages. This chapter explores the following two questions:

1. How does the classroom context afford and constrain bilingual students' participation in multimodal codemeshing?
2. How does student participation in multimodal codemeshing shape the classroom context?

In the next section, we describe our methods for examining these questions before turning to our findings.

METHODOLOGY

To understand the dialogic relationship between students' multimodal codemeshing and the classroom context, we used comparative case methods (Stake, 2006)—which analyze similarities, differences, and patterns across cases—to understand two students' participation in a multimodal codemeshing project.

The Setting and Participants

We conducted this study in one eighth-grade English class at an urban school in a major city in the Southern United States, with 26% of the students at the school designated as English language learners (ELLs) and 96.1% receiving free or reduced-price lunch. In Ms. Lancaster's classroom (all names are pseudonyms), all of the 28 students were proficient in speaking languages other than English, which included Spanish, Mandarin, Pashto, Thai, Vietnamese, Arabic, Bahdini and Sorani (Kurdish languages), and Mushunguli (a Somalian language). All students in the class were either receiving ELL services or the school formerly designated them as ELLs.

We purposefully sampled two focal students for an in-depth analysis of their participation in a multimodal codemeshing project (Patton, 1991). We selected the two students based on conferrals with the teacher (Ms. Lancaster), initial researcher observations, and student interest surveys. We chose these two students for this analysis in that they represented two different populations of bilingual students—those that have lived in the United States for an extended period but still use and speak their heritage language alongside English, and those that are newcomers to the United States that are in the process of learning English as an additional language. The two students also varied in heritage languages, proficiencies in these languages, proficiencies in English, academic abilities (as reported by the teacher and state assessments), and experience with technology. We use the term *heritage language* to denote languages that students use with their families or communities that tie closely to their cultural heritage (Fishman, 2001). We emphasize that these languages were not necessarily a student's first or home language, or the language in which students were most proficient, as bilingual individuals often continue to develop multiple languages simultaneously. In the following, we provide background information for each focal student.

Yuliana

Born in El Salvador, Yuliana (15 years old) had only lived in the United States for two years at the time of the study. According to Yuliana, she has advanced proficiency in Spanish and state assessments showed she had limited proficiency in English. At home, she spoke English with her stepfather and Spanish with her mother—often serving as a language broker and translator (Orellana & Reynolds, 2008). At school, Yuliana spoke Spanish with her friends and usually acted reserved during class time. She was a dedicated student who was a deep thinker. Conscientious of her grades, Yuliana viewed "knowledge [as] power" and "never want[ed] to stop learning until the day [she] died." Yuliana had a computer at home but was "not allowed to touch it." As such, she exhibited limited technological proficiency. Important for this study, Yuliana expressed a strong desire to demonstrate her Spanish proficiency in the classroom space. She spoke of wanting to teach Ms. Lancaster, for example, and was eager to help her classmates and review their Spanish when working on the multimodal project.

Sandra

Born in the United States, Sandra (14 years old) lived with her Vietnamese mother and her older brother. She reported that she was intermediate at speaking Vietnamese, and advanced in English according to state assessments. At home, Sandra spoke Vietnamese with her mother and English with her brother. She expressed hesitation about speaking Vietnamese in school because "people laugh and generalize." Sandra strove to achieve in class and was well-liked among her peers. She shared that she had access to a computer at home; however, it did not have the same programs used in class (e.g., Microsoft PowerPoint). While usually outgoing in our observations of Sandra in Ms. Lancaster's class, Sandra reported that she was uncomfortable and shy to speak Vietnamese in front of her peers, and furthermore, could not recall a time in all her years of schooling when she had an opportunity to use her heritage language during class instruction.

"My Hero" Multimodal Project

Students participated in a four-week literature unit connected to the anchor text, *The Warrior's Heart* (Greitens, 2012), a memoir featuring stories of a U.S. Navy commander's humanitarian work across the world. The culminating project was a multimodal presentation where students chose a person in their life who they considered a personal hero. To begin the project, the class participated in a Scaffolded Digital Writer's Workshop (Dalton, 2013), which supported students in seeing themselves as "designers" and understanding how to use multiple modes for expression. This workshop model also focused on developing a supportive class community where students shared their work and relied on one another as resources.

Next, students conducted and recorded an interview with their hero—with many choosing to speak in their heritage languages. Students then used PowerPoint to create a multimodal presentation that provided background information of their hero, synthesis of their interview, connections to the novel, and personal reflections. According to Ms. Lancaster, there were several purposes for this assignment, including for students to: (a) make personal connections to the novel by telling the story of a hero in their life; (b) reflect on themes of heroism in the novel; (c) gain technical skills; and (d) learn to express themselves through multiple modes in digital environments. As many of the heroes students interviewed did not speak English, students chose to use other languages in their digital products. Ms. Lancaster encouraged students to use languages other than English in their digital products; however, she did not give direct instruction on how to integrate them, nor did she speak in languages other than English during class time.

Throughout the workshop, she provided students with explicit instruction on how to use PowerPoint and other technical skills (e.g., recording their voices, editing images). She showed them why and how to create a multimodal project and examined teacher-generated and real-world examples that made clear the various design decisions a composer could make. Students also had multiple opportunities to share their work, both in class (e.g., whole-class presentations, gallery walks, and peer workshops) and with a larger audience in a project showcase at the end of the unit that included their classmates, as well as students and teachers across their grade level.

As participant observers (Spradley, 1980), we collaborated with Ms. Lancaster to align the workshop model to her unit goals and helped develop curricular materials. Although we assisted with technical aspects and some student questions, our focus in the classroom was on collecting data. Ms. Lancaster remained the lead teacher of the class; however, her role often shifted to facilitator during in-class workshops. She constantly walked around to provide just-in-time support for individual students who had questions about the assignment or tools or wanted feedback on elements of their projects. Occasionally, she would provide a brief mini-lesson to the class if she noticed multiple students had a similar technical issue or question during work time.

Data Collection and Analysis

The findings presented in this chapter are part of a larger study that seeks to understand the processes and products involved in students' multimodal codemeshing. For the present analysis, we drew on three primary data sources that include students' digital products, screen capture of students' laptops during the composing process, and design interviews at the conclusion of the project.

In our analysis of students' digital products, we attended to instances where students used a language other than English in text or as a sound recording. We also identified instances where students included images and design choices that reflected their heritage languages or transnationalism, which we define as aspects of students' identities that suggest the bidirectional flow of information or goods across national borders (Portes, Guarnizo & Landolt, 1999). We then considered how the student meshed these languages with other modalities, such as the juxtaposition of an oral recording in Spanish and a text written in English.

To understand Sandra and Yuliana's composing process, we created time-stamped logs for each of their screen-capture videos, totaling seven videos for each student. Moving sequentially through the workshops, we recorded students' compositional actions, and instances of multimodal and heritage language use. We then used Smith's (2016) multimodal composing times-cape method to create fine-grained representations of each student's use of modes and languages. We developed *multimodal codemeshing timescapes* (see Smith, Pacheco, & de Almeida, 2017 for color versions of these timescapes), which served as an analytic tool and visual display for each student's process for each class workshop.

Lastly, we analyzed students' design interviews to understand their perspectives on using their heritage languages and multiple modes in the composing process. Students participated in a 45-minute semi-structured design interview (Dalton et al., 2015) after they completed their projects. The purpose of these interviews was to learn more about students' modal designs, heritage language use, and perspectives on their codemeshing processes. We showed students their multimodal products during the design interview on a laptop so they could point out specific elements of their work and reasoning behind design decisions. We analyzed these interviews using Gee's (2011) methods of discourse analysis that explore what is relevant or significant to the speaker, the practices that they enact, the social goods they value, and their relationships within a specific context. We concluded our comparative case analysis (Stake, 2006) by analyzing the individual themes and patterns for Sandra and Yuliana, such as heritage language decisions and attitudes, modal preferences, and perceived audiences. We then used axial coding (Strauss & Corbin, 1998) to generate overall themes across the two cases.

FINDINGS

We present our findings by describing how Sandra and Yuliana participated in the multimodal codemeshing project. We present three major themes that were evident in both students' participation. We conclude with a cross-case comparison that describes how students' multimodal codemeshing shaped and was shaped by the classroom context.

Sandra and Yuliana: "Sounding Funny" and Making Sense

Sandra chose to interview her mother in Vietnamese for her project. Sandra's multimodal composition explored her mother's experiences raising two children as a single mother in a new country. The composition included Sandra's feelings about her mother, as well as her perspective on her father leaving her family, her views of what it means to be a hero, and her analysis of heroism in Greitens' text. Yuliana also chose to interview her mother for this project, and as a result, conducted her interview entirely in Spanish. Figure 5.1 shares images from two of Sandra's slides that show the ways in which she orchestrated multiple modalities and languages to negotiate meaning with her reader.

"Sounding Funny" With Vietnamese and Spanish

To understand how the classroom context afforded and constrained Sandra and Yuliana's participation in multimodal codemeshing, we attend to different ways in which they described their feelings about using

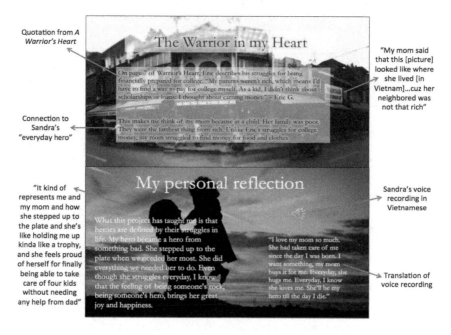

Figure 5.1 Two slides from Sandra's digital composition.

Vietnamese and Spanish within Ms. Lancaster's classroom. As this project afforded opportunities to use oral language in voice recordings, Sandra spoke of her hesitancy to do so, noting her lack of confidence in her abilities as well as the "funny" way that Vietnamese sounded in a classroom context dominated by English-participation norms. Sandra asked Ms. Lancaster if she could go to the "recording room"—a storage closet adjacent to the classroom—when recording in Vietnamese. She explained, "I had to practice because I kept getting nervous. I kept stuttering. I had to keep saying it over and over again, which made me even more nervous." She was also embarrassed for others to hear her mom's "funny" accent in the interview excerpts, see pictures of her "short" extended family members, or read her mother's first name on her introductory slide because the Vietnamese spelling ("Bich") was similar to an expletive in English.

Alternatively, Yuliana, though able to write in Spanish, was hesitant to record her voice in Spanish, as she had never done so before in the classroom. She wrote out what she wanted to say first and orally practiced numerous times before feeling comfortable enough to record. Using Spanish, however, did not seem to carry the same marked status in the classroom that Vietnamese did, perhaps due to the presence of other Spanish-speakers and perhaps due to Yuliana's comfort with the language. Whereas Sandra could not speak with her classmates in Vietnamese or write in Vietnamese script, Yuliana chatted with her classmates in Spanish, wrote messages to them on Google Chat, and wrote out her interview questions for her mother in Spanish.

Though Sandra first began her process by covertly using Vietnamese and switching her search engine to "Tieng Viet," she concluded her composing by recording her voice aloud in Vietnamese and sharing it with a classmate. She told us she "kinda wanted [her] mom to hear it as well because she can't read English." Sandra and Yuliana had opportunities to use their heritage languages in multiple parts of their projects; as they spoke and heard multiple languages in the composing process and as they considered how the official space of the classroom encouraged these languages, they increasingly incorporated these powerful tools into their digital compositions. At the same time, certain features of the compositional tool provided opportunities for students to explore these relationship and challenge some of the linguistic norms within the classroom. Students had opportunities to use these languages in oral and in written modalities, as well as in more private or covert uses such as searching for and accessing information online. These varied uses of heritage languages within the composing process supported students in not only creating multilingual and multimodal texts, but in creating a multilingual classroom space

Making Sense With Vietnamese, Spanish, and English

Despite Sandra's nervousness in using Vietnamese, she chose to use this language alongside English as it afforded her opportunities to negotiate meanings with readers with varying linguistic proficiencies. For example, she included her mother's Vietnamese speech, but also controlled how an English-speaking audience received this message by editing out repetitions and run-on sentences when translating this speech for an English-speaking audience. She told us, "My mom doesn't really use the proper grammar when she talks, and so her sentences are really short and they kinda say the same thing over and over again. I just like mashed those [sentences] together, but yet to make it exactly what she says." Rather than providing a word for word translation, Sandra preserved the sense of her mother's Vietnamese while considering which uses of syntax and vocabulary an English-speaking reader would best understand. Figure 5.2 shows Sandra's mother's Vietnamese, a direct translation of this Vietnamese, and then Sandra's paraphrasing on her digital composition.

Sandra also used Vietnamese to engage her mother as a potential reader. This included sending an oral message alongside a text in English. Sandra included an English written translation of her Vietnamese narration that

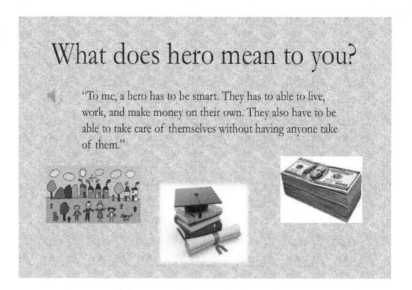

Figure 5.2 A slide from Sandra's composition using Vietnamese recordings and English text. Oral Recording: Cái người anh hung đó phải giỏi. Phải sống một mình. Từ đi làm, từ kiếm tiền. Không ai "take care" hết. Từ mình "take care" bản thân của mình thôi. (English translation: This person hero has to be good, has to live by themselves, independently goes to work, independently looks for money. No one "take care" [of them] at all. They "take care" of themselves by themselves.)

she recorded in class. Whereas she directly addressed her mother in the Vietnamese oral recording (*Con thu'o'ng me. nhiê´u la˘m*)—meaning "I love you very much,"—her English text speaks about her mother in the third person (*I love my mom so much*). This last phrase suggests that she intends this message to be for her mother and a broader audience simultaneously. Sandra explained, "I kinda want my mom to hear it as well because she can't read English. I wanted her to hear what I thought."

Similarly, Yuliana included a recorded Spanish oral commentary about why she believed her mother was her hero "so my mom understands, like she doesn't really know English, but a little bit, I just want her to know what I'm saying." She orally recorded the following message in PowerPoint, which she then paraphrased into English text: *Yo escogí esta fotografía por que se conecta al trabajo de mi mamá. Ella trabaja en un restaurante donde ella nos provee con los recursos necesarios. Ella trabaja muy duro y por esa razón yo la quiero mucho.*

Interestingly, the Spanish oral translation differed from the English text (Figure 5.3). In Spanish, she stated she loves her mother (*yo la quiero mucho*), wherein in English, she wrote, "I appreciate her hard work." Her Spanish message conveyed affection directly toward her mother, a possible audience for this recording, wherein her English text conveyed a more general description of her feelings toward her mother's work, possibly to English-speaking classmates, whom she identified as "other people."

For both Sandra and Yuliana, the multimodal codemeshing project offered the opportunity to engage with audiences outside the walls of the classroom, and moreover, challenge their own and their classmates' perspectives

My mom has worked hard to get me where I am now. She's a hard worker. Also, she works at a restaurant where she provides us with necessary supplies. My mom has and is working hard for me to get to college and for that reason I appreciate her hard work.

Figure 5.3 Yuliana using a Spanish oral recording and English text to engage multiple audiences.

on their heritage languages in this English-centric space. Sandra's decisions to use Vietnamese were no longer bound by the interlocutors or potential readers within the physical space of the classroom but extended across time and space to include her mother.

CONCLUSIONS ACROSS CASES

When comparing across cases to consider how the classroom context shaped Yuliana and Sandra's participation in the multimodal codemeshing project, we note three important similarities that have implications for including culturally sustaining pedagogies in similar classroom contexts. We include Table 5.1 that shows the different ways that Yuliana and Sandra used Spanish and Vietnamese before exploring these common themes.

First, though the language of the classroom was officially English, there were speakers of multiple languages that had opportunities to use these languages when composing. Yuliana was able to collaborate with other Spanish speakers in the workshop and leveraged her own Spanish literacy expertise when editing other classmates' digital products. She explained she was excited that her mother and classmates would understand sections written and spoken in Spanish, and in retrospect she wished she could have even "written more things" using Spanish. Sandra, however, did not have any classmates that spoke Vietnamese and even voiced discomfort about "sounding funny" in front of her peers. In one exchange with her

TABLE 5.1 Yuliana and Sandra's Use of Heritage Languages When Composing		
Use of heritage language while composing	Yuliana (Spanish)	Sandra (Vietnamese)
Writing in "My Hero" project	•	•
Recording voice for project	•	•
Conducting interview	•	•
Using Internet keywords	•	•
Sharing work with peers	•	•
Listening & editing interview audio		•
Reading online	•	•
Speaking to peers	•	
Translating interview notes by hand	•	
Chatting online with peers	•	
Using online translator		
Including music in heritage language	•	

classmate, Jonul, a student who spoke Bahadini, he emphasized that her language was "cool." With multiple students using languages other than English, Vietnamese no longer marked Sandra as different or "funny," but "cool" within this multilingual space.

Second, both students participated in the scaffolded workshop prior to the "My Hero" project and had opportunities to explore and critique how they could use languages and modalities. While this might seem like "just good teaching" for writing instruction—i.e., using mentor texts and considering different rhetorical choices—we emphasize the importance of this focused instruction within the context of culturally sustaining pedagogies. While students spoke multiple languages and had some familiarity with using PowerPoint, we did not assume that they were fully aware of the different reasons they might use their heritage languages or the affordances of different modes within a composition. Similarly, Ms. Lancaster circulated through the classroom as students composed, not only providing on the spot assistance with technology, but asking students about their heritage languages and why they made certain decisions. We argue that teacher scaffolding that included direct instruction about multimodal and multilingual tools, as well as awareness-raising of when and how to leverage these tools, afforded Sandra and Yuliana's participation in this pedagogy

Lastly, both students participated in this project to learn more about their personal histories and to engage with an actual audience. For Sandra, this was a chance to explore aspects of a painful relationship with her father and to understand her mother's resiliency. For Yuliana, this was a chance to demonstrate pride in her heritage and show gratitude for her mother's hard work. While this project supported students' engagement with a grade-level, students were able to build on and explore parts of their identity. Similarly, Spanish and Vietnamese were not simply bridges to English or something that was "cool" or exotic in the classroom. Using these languages offered Yuliana and Sandra opportunities to not only demonstrate their linguistic dexterity, but to engage with important potential readers outside of the classroom space.

IMPLICATIONS AND CONCLUSIONS

From our examination of students' multimodal codemeshing, we emphasize three major takeaways from this work that are relevant to teachers and researchers working with young adolescent multilingual students. First, framing multimodal codemeshing as part of translanguaging underscores the need to find ways of including the wide range of semiotic resources available to students in their classroom composing, including multiple languages and multiple modalities. This multimodal codemeshing project shows just one productive avenue for including these resources into the classroom. Podcasting (Smythe & Neufeld, 2010), digital narratives created with mobile devices (Ehret & Hollett, 2013), and recording oral narratives (Miller, 2014) all hold great promise for developing a wide range of students' meaning-making resources, as well as for developing the productive and receptive language proficiencies for students learning English as an additional language.

Second, this study emphasizes the importance of projects that not only access aspects of students' language and culture in the classroom but offer opportunities for students to explore them as well. Our work echoes McGinnis' (2007) research with inquiry-based multimodal and multilingual projects that encouraged students to investigate their experiences in a new country. For culturally and linguistically diverse students, as well as those that might be new immigrants or refugees (Hos, 2016), we encourage the continued exploration of such pedagogies. Though not described in the current study, share outs of students' compositions can be a useful time for students to examine critically their design choices and use of language, and furthermore, share their cultural identities with their classmates (see Pacheco, Smith, & Carr, 2017). Consistent with other research with culturally and linguistically diverse young adolescents, instruction that investigates and makes visible aspects of students' language and culture can be helpful for creating a more inclusive classroom context.

Lastly, this project sheds light on aspects of the classroom context—including available technology, teacher receptiveness, and a flexible curriculum—that afford students' productive participation in this composing practice. As Jocius (2017) has argued, how students engage in multimodal composition relates not only to their own goals and preferences, but the "pedagogical structures [that] support and constrain students as they create, compose, and interact with digital, multimodal tools" (p. 15). In our study, we found that an important *structure* in Ms. Lancaster's instruction was her and her students' overwhelming positivity in praising, welcoming, and recognizing the use of languages other than English, which is not the norm in most English-centric classroom contexts (Lee & Oxelson, 2006). While students might have thought that they initially "sounded funny" when recording, we noted that they began to feel more comfortable as they participated in the project over time. It is important to note that this was one of the first times that students had opportunities to use these languages in the classroom. While our work shows promise, we would be excited to see the academic possibilities of including such a project into a classroom community where multilingualism is the norm, rather than the exception.

A major limitation to this current work was an exploration of students' possible resistance to the codemeshing project. Jocius (2017) pointed out that these same pedagogical structures which afford some students' participation might inadvertently constrain others. The current research, and future studies that examine multimodality and translanguaging, could explore the relationship between learning contexts and individual students' composing practices. Pirbhai-Illich (2010) emphasized that when culturally and linguistically diverse students are actively able to shape aspects of these contexts, such as what counts as legitimate participation and what topics they can explore, they are more likely to participate in the middle school classroom. We hope that this current work shows that students' composing processes and products are varied, and as such, the varied pedagogical structures and contexts that afford student participation need continued attention in the research.

Along with the many educators and researchers that have long argued for a strength-based perspective of students' linguistic and literacy practices in the classroom (Palmer & Martinez, 2016; Ruiz, 1984), we emphasize the importance of building on students' linguistic resources in the context of culturally sustaining pedagogies with young adolescent students. Whereas the use of a language other than English could mark students as not knowing English or a peripheral participant in the classroom (Miller & Zuengler, 2011), this study shows how students use of languages other than English can be signs of strength, despite an "English-only" classroom.

REFERENCES

Abiria, D. M., Early, M., & Kendrick, M. (2013). Plurilingual pedagogical practices in a policy-constrained context: A Northern Ugandan case study. *TESOL Quarterly, 47*(3), 567–590.

Allexsaht-Snider, M., Buxton, C. A., & Harman, R. (2013). Research and praxis on challenging anti-immigration discourses in school and community contexts. *Norteamérica, 8,* 191–217.

Bailey, N. M. (2009). "It makes it more real": Teaching new literacies in a secondary English classroom. *English Education, 41*(3), 207–234.

Canagarajah, S. (2011). Codemeshing in academic writing: Identifying teachable strategies of translanguaging. *The Modern Language Journal, 95*(3), 401–417.

Canagarajah, S. (2013). *Translingual practice: Global Englishes and cosmopolitan relations.* New York, NY: Routledge.

Creese, A., & Blackledge, A. (2010). Translanguaging in the bilingual classroom: A pedagogy for learning and teaching? *Modern Language Journal, 94*(1), 103–115.

Cummins, J. (2000). *Language, power, and pedagogy: Bilingual children in the crossfire* (vol. 23). Clevedon, United Kingdom: Multilingual Matters.

Cummins, J., Bismilla, V., Chow, P., Cohen, S., Giampapa, F., Leoni, L., . . . & Sastri, P. (2005). Affirming identity in multilingual classrooms. *Educational Leadership, 63*(1), 38–43.

Dalton, B. (2013). Multimodal composition and the Common Core Standards. *The Reading Teacher, 66*(4), 333–339.

Dalton, B., Robinson, K., Lavvorn, J., Smith, B. E., Alvey, T., Mo, E., . . . & Proctor, C. P. (2015). Fifth-grade students' digital retellings and the Common Core: Modal use and design intentionality. *The Elementary School Journal, 115*(4), 548–569.

Daniel, S. M., & Pacheco, M. B. (2016). Translanguaging practices and perspectives of four multilingual teens. *Journal of Adolescent & Adult Literacy, 59*(6), 653–663.

Durán, L. (2017). Audience and young bilingual writers: Building on strengths. *Journal of Literacy Research, 49*(1), 92–114.

Ehret, C., & Hollett, T. (2013). (Re) placing school: Middle school students' countermobilities while composing with iPods. *Journal of Adolescent & Adult Literacy, 57*(2), 110–119.

Fishman, J. A. (2001). 300-plus years of heritage language education in the United States. In J. K. Peyton, D. A. Ranard, & S. McGinnis (Eds.), *Heritage languages in America: Preserving a national resource* (pp. 81–97). Washington, DC: Center for Applied Linguistics/Delta Systems.

García, O. (2009). *Bilingual education in the 21st century: A global perspective*. Malden, MA: Wiley/Blackwell.

Garcia, O., & Wei, L. (2013). *Translanguaging: Language, bilingualism and education.* New York, NY: Palgrave Macmillan.

Gay, G. (2002). Preparing for culturally responsive teaching. *Journal of Teacher Education, 53*(2), 106–116.

Gee, J. P. (2011). *An Introduction to discourse analysis: Theory and method* (3rd ed.). New York, Ny: Routledge.

Greitens, E. (2012). *The warrior's heart: Becoming a man of compassion and courage.* New York, NY: Houghton Mifflin Harcourt.

Harman, R., Johnson, L. L., & Chagoya, E. E. (2016) Bilingual youth voices in middle school: Performance, storytelling and photography. In S. Greene, K. J. Burke, & M. K. McKenna (Eds.), *Youth voices, literacies, and civic engagement.* (pp. 210–234). New York, NY: Routledge.

Hos, R. (2016). The lives, aspirations, and needs of refugee and immigrant students with interrupted formal education (SIFE) in a secondary newcomer program. *Urban Education*, 1–24. doi: 10.1177/0042085916666932

Hull, G. A., Stornaiuolo, A., & Sahni, U. (2010). Cultural citizenship and cosmopolitan practice: Global youth communicate online. *English Education, 42*(4), 331–367.

Ito, M., Horst, H., Bittanti, M., Boyd, d., Herr-Stephenson, B., Lange, P., . . . & Robinson, L. (2010). *Hanging out, messing around and geeking out: Kids learning and living in new media.* Cambridge, MA: MIT Press.

Jiménez, R. T., David, S., Fagan, K., Risko, V. J., Pacheco, M., Pray, L., & Gonzales, M. (2015). Using translation to drive conceptual development for students becoming literate in English as an additional language. *Research in the Teaching of English, 49*(3), 248–271.

Jocius, R. (2017). Good student/bad student: Situated identities in the figured worlds of school and creative multimodal production. *Literacy Research: Theory, Method, and Practice, 66*(1), 198–214.

Kress, G. (2010). *Multimodality: A social semiotic approach to contemporary communication.* New York, NY: Routledge.

Kress, G., & Van Leeuwen, T. (2001). *Multimodal discourse: The modes and media for contemporary communication.* London, England: Edward Arnold.

Ladson-Billings, G. (1995). But that's just good teaching! The case for culturally relevant pedagogy. *Theory Into Practice, 34*(3), 159–165.

Lee, J. S., & Oxelson, E. (2006). "It's not my job": K–12 teacher attitudes toward students' heritage language maintenance. *Bilingual Research Journal, 30*(2), 453–477.

Martin-Beltrán, M. (2014). "What do you want to say?" How adolescents use translanguaging to expand learning opportunities. *International Multilingual Research Journal, 8*(3), 208–230.

Martínez-Roldán, C. M. (2015). Translanguaging practices as mobilization of linguistic resources in a Spanish/English bilingual after-school program: An analysis of contradictions. *International Multilingual Research Journal, 9*(1), 43–58.

McGinnis, T. A. (2007). Khmer Rap Boys, X-Men, Asia's fruits, and Dragonball Z: Creating multilingual and multimodal classroom contexts. *Journal of Adolescent & Adult Literacy, 50*(7), 570–579.

Miller, M. E. (2014). The power of conversation: Linking discussion of social justice to literacy standards. *Voices from the Middle, 22*(1), 36–42.

Miller, E. R., & Zuengler, J. (2011). Negotiating access to learning through resistance to classroom practice. *The Modern Language Journal, 95*(s1), 130–147.

Milner IV, H. R. (2010). *Start where you are, but don't stay there: Understanding diversity, opportunity gaps, and teaching in today's classrooms.* Cambridge, MA: Harvard Education Press.

National Center for Education Statistics. (2016). *The condition of education 2016: English language learners in public schools.* Retrieved from https://nces.ed.gov/programs/coe/pdf/Indicator_CGF/coe_cgf_2016_05.pdf

Orellana, M. F., & Reynolds, J. F. (2008). Cultural modeling: Leveraging bilingual skills for school paraphrasing tasks. *Reading Research Quarterly, 43*(1), 48–65.

Pacheco, M. B. (2016). *Translanguaging in the English-centric classroom: A communities of practice perspective* (Unpublished doctoral dissertation). Vanderbilt University, Nashville, Tennessee.

Pacheco, M. B., & Goodwin, A. P. (2013). Putting two and two together: Middle school students' morphological problem-solving strategies for unknown words. *Journal of Adolescent & Adult Literacy, 56*(7), 541–553.

Pacheco, M. B., & Smith, B. E. (2015). Across languages, modes, and identities: Bilingual adolescents' multimodal codemeshing in the literacy classroom. *Bilingual Research Journal, 38*(3), 292–312.

Pacheco, M. B., Smith, B. E., & Carr, S. (2017). Connecting classrooms and communities with language and technology: A multimodal code-meshing project. *Voices from the Middle, 24*(3), 63–69.

Palmer, D. K., & Martínez, R. A. (2016). Developing biliteracy: What do teachers really need to know about language? *Language Arts, 93*(5), 379–385.

Paris, D. (2012). Culturally sustaining pedagogy: A needed change in stance, terminology, and practice. *Educational Researcher, 41*(3), 93–97.

Patton, M. Q. (1991). *Qualitative evaluation and research methods* (2nd ed.). Newbury Park, CA: SAGE.

Pennycook, A. (2010). *Language as a local practice.* London, England: Routledge.

Pirbhai-Illich, F. (2010). Aboriginal students engaging and struggling with critical multiliteracies. *Journal of Adolescent & Adult Literacy, 54*(4), 257–266.

Portes, A., Guarnizo, L. E., & Landolt, P. (1999). The study of transnationalism: pitfalls and promise of an emergent research field. *Ethnic and racial studies, 22*(2), 217–237.

Puzio, K., Keyes, C. S., & Jiménez, R. T. (2016). It sounds more like a gangbanger: Using collaborative translation to understand literary concepts. *Language Arts, 93*(6), 444–456.

Rideout, V. J., Foehr, U. G., & Roberts, D. F. (2010). *Generation M2: Media in the lives of 8–18 year-olds.* Menlo Park, CA: Henry J. Kaiser Family Foundation. Retrieved from https://files.eric.ed.gov/fulltext/ED527859.pdf

Ruiz, R. (1984). Orientations in language planning. *NABE Journal, 8*(2), 15–34.

Smith, B. E. (2014). Beyond words: A review of research on adolescents and multimodal composition. In R. E. Ferdig & K. E. Pytash (Eds.). *Exploring multimodal composition and digital writing* (pp. 1–19). Hershey, PA: IGI Global.

Smith, B. E. (2016). Composing across modes: A comparative analysis of adolescents' multimodal composing processes. *Learning, Media & Technology, 42*(3), 259–278. doi:10.1080/17439884.2016.1182924

Smith, B. E., Pacheco, M. B., & de Almeida, C. R. (2017). Multimodal codemeshing: Bilingual adolescents' processes composing across modes and languages. *Journal of Second Language Writing, 36*, 6–22.

Smythe, S., & Neufeld, P. (2010). "Podcast time": Negotiating digital literacies and communities of learning in a middle years ELL classroom. *Journal of Adolescent & Adult Literacy, 53*(6), 488–496.

Spradley, J. P. (1980). *Participant observation.* New York, NY: Holt, Rinehart & Winston.

Stake, R. E. (2006). *Multiple case study analysis.* New York, NY: Guilford Press.

Strauss, A., & Corbin, J. (1998). *Basics of qualitative research. Techniques and procedures for developing grounded theory* (2nd ed.). Thousand Oaks, CA: SAGE.

Van Leeuwen, T. (2015). Multimodality in education: Some directions and some questions. *TESOL Quarterly, 49*(3), 582–589.

Zapata, A., & Laman, T. T. (2016). "I write to show how beautiful my languages are": Translingual writing instruction in English-dominant classrooms. *Language Arts, 93*(5), 366–378.

CHAPTER 6

MIDDLE (MIS)MANAGEMENT

Staff Sanctioned Victimization in the Middle Grades

Brendan Downing
Ohio University

ABSTRACT

This chapter is a critical review of literature focusing on the victimization of LGBTQ young adolescents and how this victimization can be staff sanctioned. It weaves the author's personal narratives into a review of relevant literature and statistics on youth victimization and the effects of victimization in the middle grades. The personal narrative vignettes focus on the author's experience with staff sanctioned victimization, peer victimization, and the impact of this victimization on the author. I posit that staff play a critical role in the victimization of youth, either directly through bullying students or indirectly through enforcing a hidden curriculum of heteronormativity. The chapter concludes with recommendations that schools can utilize to prevent victimization in the middle grades.

Equity & Cultural Responsiveness in the Middle Grades, pages 113–129

This was it. I was finally a middle schooler.

With a pull of a mechanical lever, the folding bus door opened with a squeal revealing a set of rubber-coated stairs cascading down towards my gravel driveway. Those stairs were the only thing standing between me and the start of seventh grade. I began climbing onto the bus greeted by the same familiar face I had seen every morning before school since moving here five years ago. Mrs. Alexander smiled her toothy grin as her thin brown hair settled into a windblown coif from the small window next to the driver's seat.

However, her smile suddenly transformed into a sneer. My stomach sank as Mrs. Alexander smirked; she asked, "What, are you gay now?" My face burned, and turned a fiery shade of red. I grasped for my left ear where she fixed her gaze. On that humid August morning, one small silver stud started what would be years of victimization from both teachers and peers.

In 1997, during my seventh-grade year, my victimization as a gay youth began. Over the course of the next six years, the bullying, belittling, harassment, and othering—also known as victimization—escalated to the point that I was ready to take my own life. Sadly, the staff at my school played a major role in the victimization I experienced. Decades after my victimization began, victimization continues to impact LGBTQ (lesbian, gay, bisexual, transgender, and queer/questioning) youth, and a smattering of reports point to the unspoken issue that at least some of this victimization is staff sanctioned. Throughout this critical review of literature, I weave my own personal narratives into relevant studies and research surrounding this topic (see Grant & Booth, 2009). Narrative helps us understand experience through a personal lens (Patton, 2015). Furthermore, narratives help connect us to and make sense of research by tapping into the social nature of the human experience (Glesne, 2015; Patton, 2015). Through integrating narrative and related literature, I explore what LGBTQ victimization is, how school staff are participating in, and sanctioning this victimization, and the impact of victimization on students. Finally, I conclude with recommendations to assist educators and school staff in ending the cycle of victimization and working toward becoming advocates and allies for LGBTQ young adolescents.

LGBTQ YOUTH VICTIMIZATION

As I drew closer I could see it. Scrawled in black Sharpie across locker 121 was the word, Faggot. I had been branded. I walked passed, hoping the crowd wouldn't realize the locker belonged to me. I went to the auditorium; no one would be there this time of day. I sat in the dark room, a sea of empty seats around me, waiting for the sounds of the class change to die down in the hall. When the tardy bell rang I walked out, found a custodian and fought back tears as I asked him to help clean my locker. He smirked and handed me a scour pad as he told me, "You take care of it yourself." He added, "You might just want to leave it; you know they'll just write it again."[1]

LGBTQ students experience victimization at higher rates than heterosexual youth (Daley, Newman, Solomon, & Mishna, 2008). Putting this into perspective, the 2015 National School Climate Survey published by the Gay Lesbian and Straight Education Network (GLSEN) showed that almost all middle school aged students who identify as LGBTQ have experienced some type of victimization (Kosciw, Greytak, Giga, Villenas, & Danischewski, 2016). GLSEN's (2009) special report on the experiences of LGBTQ youth in the middle grades found a prevalence of victimization among young adolescents. Victimization can come in direct forms, such as verbal or physical harassment, and physical assault. According to GLSEN's report, 91% of middle school aged LGTBQ students reported that someone in school called them a derogatory name such as "fag." In addition, 59% of middle school aged students who identified as LGBTQ reported someone physically harassing them in the form of tripping, pushing, or shoving. Furthermore, 39% of LGBTQ students in the middle grades experienced someone physically assault them, which included someone punching, kicking, or having a weapon used against them.

In addition to direct forms of victimization, LGBTQ students also experience indirect forms of victimization (Daley et al., 2008). Indirect victimization occurs when an individual influences the social networks of a victim in order to cause them harm. Indirect victimization is an issue that affects most LGBTQ students through gossip or social isolation (citation?). Due to the nature of this type of victimization, it often goes unchecked. Daley et al., (2008) reported that most students do not speak up about indirect forms of victimization, saying "indirect bullying of lesbian and gay youth may be overlooked or treated as less severe than instances of direct bullying" (p. 19). When educators and school staff do not acknowledge indirect victimization, and fail to intervene and report it to administration, no one can fully understand the magnitude of the problem. Thus, underreporting hinders the ability of LGBTQ youth to receive proper support.

Victimization of students occurs not only through direct and indirect peer victimization, but also through structural oppression. Structural oppression can impact LGBTQ students when school districts, schools, and teachers take part in homophobic and heteronormative practices and policies (citation?). Heterosexism is the belief that heterosexuality is the "norm" (Chesir-Teran & Hughes, 2009). By creating policies, practices, and curriculum where heterosexuality is the norm, school districts, schools, and teachers privilege heterosexual people, creating a culture of heteronormativity. Yep (2002) defined heteronormativity as the "presumption and assumption that all human experience is unquestionably and automatically heterosexual" (p. 168). By condoning heterosexism and heteronormativity, school systems create a system of inequality and oppression that victimizes LGBTQ students on a macro-level, while contributing to and opening doors for direct and indirect victimization.

STAFF SANCTIONED VICTIMIZATION

"Hey fag, don't you know you're not allowed to walk passed me?" he sneered as he stuck out his foot and pushed me over it. My books and homework cascaded across the faux brick floors in front of the gymnasium. My face burned with embarrassment as I heard them snicker and walk away. I looked up briefly as I scrambled to gather my things; my eyes caught my physical education teacher's glance, and she quickly looked the other way. It wasn't something that shocked me anymore. Most of them did it. They stayed silent as I was put through hell.

When members of a school staff participate in direct victimization, indirect victimization, and structural oppression, the victimization of students becomes staff sanctioned. Twemlow, Fonagy, Sacco, and Brethour, (2006) surveyed teachers to understand their perceptions of teachers bullying students. In that study only 12% of respondents said that teachers never bully students. Moreover, 18% of respondents said that teachers were frequently the source of bullying for students. Additionally, 40% of respondents said that they had bullied their own students at least once.

In a case at East Lee County High School, students came forward about bullying behavior. However, this is more common among high schoolers who have more access to resources and report bullying at higher rates (Kosciw et al., 2016). LGBTQ-related school resources, such as an adult advocate in the school, could help LGBTQ students feel more comfortable with reporting inappropriate behavior by teachers (Waters & Mashburn, 2017). The fact that the perpetrator of the bullying is an authority figure, or trusted adult, the exact person we tell students to report such behaviors to, compounds the reluctance to report incidents of bullying/victimization.

While most middle schools have anti-bullying policies for students, schools do not have policies or guidelines in place to handle staff victimizing or bullying of their students (Kolbert et al., 2015). Compounding this problem is that staff victimization of students often plays out in public such as in the classroom, but away from the view of other staff members. This dynamic creates a situation where staff can feel safe in perpetuating victimization while reducing the likelihood of student reporting (McEvoy, 2005).

The second form of staff sanctioned victimization, called indirect victimization, occurs when staff fail to respond to student victimization. Horn, Kosciw, and Russell (2009) found that middle school students reported that staff fail to respond to most student slurs or homophobic comments. Likewise, they reported that the middle school staff within their study failed to intervene in homophobic verbal harassment most of the time. Less than one fifth of middle school students reported that staff stepped in to address victimization frequently. Of the students who did report incidents of victimization, only 29% said that school staff responded in an effective manner.

School staff are more likely to intervene in situations of bullying toward non-LGBTQ students than toward LGBTQ students (Holmes & Cahill, 2004). This failure to respond legitimizes the harassment perpetuated by other students. Young adolescents have low confidence in reporting victimization to staff, this results in lower numbers of students reporting victimization (citation?). This might explain why in GLSEN's research brief on the experience of LGBTQ middle school students, only 57% of young adolescents told school authorities about incidents of victimization (Horn et al., 2009). It is also alarming that students report victimization to individuals outside of school at even lower rates. Kosciw et al. (2016) reported that only 50% of students tell their family (including parents) about incidents of victimization. This underreporting of victimization to the students' families could be the result of the student not being out to their families. Students who are out to their families are more likely to report victimization to a family member (Kosciw et al., 2016).

The failure of staff to intervene in harassment is not unique to the LGBTQ marginalized population. Historically students from all marginalized populations have faced victimization, and failure of staff to intervene in their victimization (citation?). In a 1985 interview, Melba Pattillo Beals, a member of the Little Rock Nine (the group of students of color who integrated Central High School in Little Rock, Arkansas) recalled the cruel treatment she received from school staff (Beals, 1985). While the case of the Little Rock Nine is a highly public example of discrimination faced by students of color, it is not the only example of racial discrimination perpetuated by educators and school staff. The mistreatment of students of color continues today through a colorblind ideology of pre-service and in-service teachers and school curriculum (Joseph, Viesca, & Bianco, 2016). Moreover, the multiple oppressions faced by LGBTQ students of color is alarming, especially as current bullying policies fail to see the intersectionality of the student when addressing bias motivated victimization (Dominski, 2016).

This perceived lack of support raises red flags about how middle schools address LGBTQ issues. Despite sexual identity development and the coming out age trending towards the middle grades, outdated notions persist that LGBTQ issues are not middle school issues (Horowitz & Itzkowitz, 2011). While educators discuss physical development and sexual reproduction with young adolescents, middle schools often overlook issues related to early adolescence and sexuality, especially when it comes to LGBTQ students. When middle grades educators bring up sexuality, they often frame it in a negative or problematic way (Clark, 2010). There is a "long-held belief by staff that homosexuality should not be addressed in any way in middle school," (Horowitz & Itzkowitz, 2011, p. 37).

Staff fear of intervening in victimization can help perpetuate an unsafe environment for students. Horowitz & Itzkowitz (2011) discussed the phenomena of teachers who do not report victimization of LGTBQ students. The failure of staff to report victimization is not always condemnation of LGBTQ individuals, but instead an issue of fear. This fear is rooted in a lack of visibility and a lack of understanding of appropriate and useful ways for staff to talk to middle school students about LGBTQ identities. Kolbert et al. (2015) reported that school staff are less comfortable talking about LGBTQ issues than they are about issues surrounding other marginalized populations. Whether or not staff are aware of bullying that is happening is also in question. Kolbert et al. found that heterosexual teachers perceive their schools as safer for LGBTQ students than homosexual teachers do. This may result from a lack of awareness of LGBTQ issues stemming from a lack of training during teacher preparation programs. There is no current standard for what teacher educators should include in multicultural or diversity education, so many teacher candidates come away with different preparation on how to support minority populations (Banks, 2004).

A final type of staff sanctioned victimization occurs through participation in the structural oppression of LGBTQ students. Structural inequality and systemic oppression for LGBTQ students is rooted in homophobia, heterosexism, and heteronormativity. Religious fundamentalists structuralize these ideals in K–12 education to try to keep sexual orientation out of schools or curriculums by preventing progressive policy and influencing local, state, and national legislation (Ryan & Rivers, 2003). These policies, often called "No Promo Homo" policies work to make LGBTQ individuals and narratives invisible in K–12 education (Chesir-Teran & Hughes, 2009). Structuralized homophobia creates a world where even the most well-intentioned educators can perpetuate inequality for LGBTQ students through participation in the system.

Compounding the problem of staff sanctioned victimization is teachers' lack of concern and training when it comes to bullying behaviors. In Waters and Mashburn's (2017) study of middle school teachers' perceptions of bullying, they reported that teachers rate bullying as either their lowest or second lowest concern in the classroom. Additionally, only 21% of the teachers surveyed felt they had adequate training to deal with bullying behavior. Moreover, teachers do not always agree on what constitutes bullying, which can easily lead to middle school staff sanctioning bullying behavior by failing to report it (Bush, 2011).

Aside from a few questions on the GLSEN National School Climate Survey (Kosciw et al., 2016), which point to teacher victimization of LGBTQ youth, research in the area of LGBTQ staff sanctioned victimization is almost non-existent. Most of the research focused on teachers' bullying of students involves researchers focused on primary and high school students (Twemlow et al., 2006), which leaves the experiences of gay middle school students invisible. While students and teachers both identify that there is a problem, researchers must examine LGBTQ staff sanctioned victimization to understand the full extent of the problem. Overall a lack of research on staff sanctioned victimization persists, and this area would benefit from additional research.

THE IMPACT OF VICTIMIZATION

I clicked the safety on the gun. My hands trembled as I pointed it towards my head. Memories poured over me. As I squeezed my eyes shut I could feel the cold metal against my temple and the tears running down my face.

I had gone to the porch that day. What I was planning to do was messy enough, no need to ruin the carpet or couch in the process. My peers and my society broke me; I saw no other way out of my pain. I was tired of feeling like I was bad, like I was dirty, like I was wrong. I would sit at night and plead with God to take the pain away, to just make me like everyone else, to make me straight. But it seemed like God wasn't listening, like he didn't care . . . like nobody cared.

In the United States, there are over nine million LGBTQ individuals (Gates, 2011). Despite civil rights progress for the overall community, LGBTQ youth victimization is still very real (Kosciw et al., 2016). Moreover, the impact from victimization plagues LGBTQ young adolescents who are not only struggling with typical pre- and teenager stressors (such as family, school, peers, and self-esteem), but also their sexual and/or gender identity (Russell & Fish, 2016). LGBTQ youth face physical and verbal harassment at higher rates than non-LGBTQ students (Muraco & Russell, 2011). This victimization has a detrimental impact on various spheres of students' lives, including their mental health, physical health, and academic achieve-ment (Daley et al., 2008).

In addition to the everyday stress experienced by heterosexual individu-als, LGBTQ individuals experience greater levels of stress based on their minority status. This additional stress is termed minority stress syndrome. Meyer (2003) described minority stress as "excess stress to which individu-als from stigmatized social categories are exposed as a result of their so-cial, often a minority, position," (p. 4). This additional stress can include, among other things, internalization of negative perceptions of the LGBTQ community (internalized homophobia), and a fractured sense of identity relating to the hiding of sexual orientation (Meyer, 1995).

The severity of the victimization affects the rate at which youth experi-ence mental health issues. LGBTQ students are two times more likely than their non-LGBTQ peers to report clinical depression (Muraco & Russell, 2011). Additionally, LGBTQ youth report lower levels of self-esteem, life satisfaction, and social integration than their peers (Kahn & Gorski, 2016). These lower levels of self-esteem, satisfaction, and integration can lead to depression, suicidal ideation, suicidal attempt, and suicide completion (Mustanski, Newcomb, & Garofalo, 2012). Suicide is one of the leading causes of death among adolescents; and LGBTQ adolescents are two times more likely to complete suicide (Kann, et al., 2016).

In addition to the impact victimization has on the mental and physical health of LGBTQ young adolescents, victimization can also lead to these in-dividuals entering the Preschool to Prison Pipeline (PPP). A study by Palm-er and Greytak (2017) found that victimization of LGBTQ students can lead to disproportionate school discipline, and the possibility of entry into the criminal justice system based on low level, nonviolent offenses. LGBTQ stu-dents who feel unsafe at school due to victimization are more likely to miss school, which can lead to truancy charges and entry into the PPP (Majd, Marksamear, & Reyes, 2009; Snapp, McGuire, Sinclair, Garbrion, & Russell, 2015). Additionally, students report low levels of confidence in school staff paying attention when they reach out for help when victimized (Holmes & Cahill, 2004). The improper handling of victimization by staff can lead to students taking matters into their own hands through fighting and physi-cal altercations with students who perpetuate victimization (Snapp et al., 2015). LGBTQ students who do not fight back when peers physically assault them can be subject to discipline due to zero tolerance policies resulting in administrators and staff often punishing all students involved in fights instead of just the perpetrator (Palmer & Greytak, 2017). Moreover, schools discipline same-sex students for violations to school policy in the form of public displays of affection at higher rates than public displays of affec-tion between heterosexual couples (Palmer & Greytak, 2017; Snapp et al., 2015). Not only do public displays of affection lead to school discipline, but they can also lead to schools outing students to unsupportive parents when reporting discipline issues home (Palmer & Greytak, 2017). Schools outing students to unsupportive family members can result in student homelessness either by families forcing them out or students choosing to leave home to escape unsupportive environments (Snapp et al., 2015). The criminalization of homelessness through arrests for soliciting, drug use, loitering, or truancy effects non-heterosexual youth at higher rates than their heterosexual peers, and further perpetuates the possibility of LGBTQ youth entering the PPP (Cochran, Stewart, Ginzler, & Cauce, 2002).

RECOMMENDATIONS

Educators and school staff also perpetuate victimization. To address the causes, impacts, and prevention of victimization there are several steps outlined in the following paragraphs that middle level educators and school staff can use to become allies and advocates for young adolescents. By no means is this list exhaustive—but it is a starting point providing both big ideas and small steps educators and school staff can implement today.

Be an Ally

School staff acting as allies to LGBTQ students is an essential means of creating supportive and safe spaces for LGBTQ students (Clark, 2010; Dinkins & Englert, 2015). Kolbert et al. (2015) showed that having supportive staff is a significant source of protection against students attempting suicide after victimization. The Association for Middle Level Education, stated in their position paper, *This We Believe* (NMSA, 2010), that adult advocates who look out for the academic and personal needs of children are essential. Furthermore, the 2015 GLSEN National School Climate Survey found that advocates and allies of LGBTQ students, as well as access to safe spaces, helped decrease victimization in schools (Kosciw et al., 2016). Additionally, simply having a GSA (Genders & Sexualities Alliance/Gay-Straight Alliance) in a school decreased victimization and suicidality among LGBTQ at-risk students (Russell & McGuire, 2008).

Therefore, the use of beacons to guide LGBTQ students to safe and supporting staff, and safe spaces and supportive staff are essential. Beacons are conspicuously placed identifiers. These can include anything from "Safe Zone" stickers, an LGBTQ flag, pictures of historical LGBTQ figures featured in the classroom, or even LGBTQ themed books in a classroom library. In addition to physical beacons, GSAs and similar clubs or groups can serve as a symbolic beacon to LGBTQ students in distress. GSAs create an environment for students to feel supported, discuss their feelings, and even report victimization (Kosciw et al., 2016).

Providing beacons to and advocates for LGBTQ young adolescents is a positive step towards ensuring support for students. To be advocates school staff must also ensure that the policies and practices in their classrooms and schools are in the best interest of students. Teachers should examine current classroom, school discipline, and reporting policies to ensure they protect their students' sexual and gender identities. Supportive policies such a comprehensive anti-bullying and anti-harassment plan, preferred name and pronoun policies, and a fair discipline policy, such as restorative justice instead of zero tolerance policies, can be positive steps for schools and educators to take in ending victimization. Though the coming out age is trending towards young adolescents, some students are not yet out to their parents or caregivers, which can lead to victimization at home due to gender identity or sexuality (Horowitz & Izkowitz, 2011). Students should be the only people to disclose their gender identity or sexuality to parents and caregivers, not school staff.

Queer the Curriculum

The availability of supportive literature (such as LGBTQ related materials in textbooks and in library resources) is woefully unavailable in most middle schools, perpetuating victimization by failing to expose students to the narratives of LGBTQ individuals (Horn et al. 2009). Only 22% of students in middle and high school reported that their curriculum is inclusive of LGBTQ identities (Kosciw et al., 2016). The invisibility of LGBTQ individuals and narratives in the curriculum is often due to homophobia, heterosexism, and heteronormativity. This exclusion contributes to LGBTQ youth victimization. The same homophobia, heterosexism, and heteronormativity that create invisibility of LGBTQ individuals at the structural level also perpetuate a strict adherence to traditional gender expression by students (Daley et al., 2008). This can lead to further victimization by students policing their schools and victimizing those who fall outside of the gender binary.

By including the narratives of LGBTQ individuals in, and queering the curriculum, educators can use their lessons to question and confront heteronormativity, thus combat victimization (Britzman, 1995). Kosciw et al. (2016) reported that school environments are safer and more welcoming to LGBTQ students when teachers enact an inclusive curriculum. Hanlon (2009) stated that teachers can incorporate LGBTQ themes into all disciplines. When including LGBTQ individuals in the curriculum, it is important to remember individuals are not a singular identity, but instead a group of individuals with their own stories, individuality, and intersecting identities. It is important for educators to remember the intersectionality of identities when creating an inclusive curriculum that prevents the normalizing of the LGBTQ experience to that of one narrative (Blackburn & Clark, 2011). While every teacher who integrates such a curriculum has an impact on the lives of LGBTQ students, once a "critical mass" of educators do so, schools will start to see improvement in the climate for LGBTQ students (Snapp et al., 2015, p. 590).

The curriculum often presents LGBTQ identities to students in problematic or negative ways, instead of reflecting the accomplishments of groundbreaking individuals within the community (Snapp et al., 2015). An effective means for tailoring an LGBTQ inclusive curriculum is through what Bishop (1990) called mirrors, windows, and sliding glass doors. Windows allow students who are not necessarily LGBTQ, or allies, to see lives different from their own, and explore the LGBTQ community; sliding glass doors allow for students to step into the lives of another and further their understanding of that individual/community; mirrors allow for students to see themselves reflected through the curriculum (Bishop, 1990; Botelho & Rudman, 2009; Dinkins & Englert, 2015). Educators can expand Bishop's windows, mirrors, and sliding glass doors, as a way for educators to think about their lessons and the content of those lessons by asking, "How can I best provide positive windows, mirrors and sliding glass doors to the LGBTQ community for my students?" Through providing these three ways to view LGBTQ inclusive lessons teachers can help support all students in understanding LGBTQ identities and help end victimization.

Recognize and Dismantle Structural Oppression

Ultimately, if homophobia, heteronormativity, and heterosexism remain, making our schools safe spaces will be a struggle, and our efforts will simply be stopgap. To end staff sanctioned victimization, as well as overall victimization, we must work to recognize and dismantle structural oppression that takes the form of homophobia, heteronormativity, and heterosexism in our schools. Starting with recognizing how a hidden curriculum normalizes and replicates heterosexuality in our schools, we can begin to work towards dismantling it (Applebaum, 2009; Blackburn & Clark, 2011; Butler, 1999). The work of dismantling structural oppression is a lofty goal, but there are small steps every educator can take.

Part of dismantling oppression can come through the timely and accurate reporting of LGBTQ victimization. Students and staff in middle schools should have a streamlined, reliable, and effective means of reporting victimization. This reporting system should ensure the anonymity of the reporting party, as well as guarantee that the school preserves the privacy of the individual who was victimized (Allen, 2009). When people report an incident, administrators should be explicit in communicating with the students and staff involved what the process will be for addressing the incident. Furthermore, schools must outline that all staff are responsible for reporting any victimization of which they become aware. Finally, schools should record and track all reports of victimization to provide administrators with data on trends that can help inform how to move forward with addressing victimization within the school. Most importantly, when students report victimization, school personnel need to make sure to listen without judgment, document what the student stays, and let the students know to whom they are reporting the information, and how to follow up after the adult makes the report.

Dismantling structural oppression also involves an honest and critical look at school discipline policies. Educators and school staff must engage in interrogating discipline data to ensure that policies are not targeting minority populations and perpetuating the Preschool to Prison Pipeline. Snapp et al. (2015) showed that zero tolerance policies are ineffective and target members of minority populations. Equity in school discipline is long overdue. To end staff sanctioned victimization, school discipline policies must change. Schools can use discipline policies such as restorative justice as an effective means to repair the harm of victimization for both perpetrators and victims. Restorative justice seeks to repair the harm caused, instead of causing additional harm through the means of punishment. Restorative justice works by pulling together the perpetrator, victim, and community in a conference to address the offending behavior and come to a resolution that focuses on reconciliation and repair (Payne & Welch, 2015).

Finally, to dismantle systems of oppression it is essential to not only examine larger structural oppression, but also to examine one's own sphere of influence, whether that is a classroom, office, or other space in the school that might perpetuate oppression. Confront bias, interrogate language choices, text selections, classroom lessons, assignments, assessments, and discipline policies to determine what groups they are privileging, and what groups they are ignoring, and why. Taking part in the work of dismantling structural oppression involves critical thinking for both teacher and student.

Enhance Pre-Service and In-Service Learning

Teacher education programs and in-service professional development programs need to ensure they provide essential information and the necessary support for educators to support the needs of the diverse student populations in our middle schools. Complicating the issue of bringing high quality diversity education is the lack of clear support from teacher education accreditation bodies. The now defunct teacher accreditation program, National Council of Accreditation of Teacher Education (NCATE) began the slow march towards the devaluing of diversity education for teachers with its removal of the term "social justice," as well as reference to LGBTQ from its standards in 2005 (Heybach, 2009). When NCATE merged with the Teacher Education Accreditation Council (TEAC) to form the Council for the Accreditation of Educator Preparation (CAEP) in 2013, they dropped diversity as a standard altogether; instead CAEP merged the contents of the diversity standard across their new set of standards (Popham, 2015). While, in theory, applying aspects of diversity across the standards of teacher preparation sounds positive, it also has the potential to undermine the education pre-service teachers receive related to LGBTQ students and other diverse populations and how best to meet the needs of marginalized populations (Clark, 2010). Only through meaningful diversity and social justice education, both across the curriculum and through explicit diversity courses, can pre-service educators learn the necessary skills to become anti-homophobia educators and allies for LGBTQ students (Blackburn & Clark, 2011; Clark, 2010). It is necessary for pre-service teachers to seek out opportunities to enhance their learning about diverse populations through additional coursework and field experiences that allow them to work with diverse populations.

Professional development for in-service educators and staff around LGBTQ issues is necessary for staff to access their current attitudes about LGBTQ individuals and work towards becoming anti-homophobia and LGBTQ allies (Horowitz & Hansen, 2008). Providing educators space to confront their own biases and conceptions of the LGBTQ community is the first step toward creating a school environment that is safe and inviting for all students (Hanlon, 2009). Through adequate professional development, schools can equip school staff with the tools they need to talk about LGBTQ topics and issues. Professional development such as Safe Zone trainings, where teachers learn how to work effectively with LGBTQ students, is a good starting point for professional development. Furthermore, professional development can help staff develop the skills necessary to confront victimization. It is important to note that all members of a school community need professional development on LGBTQ topics and issues. Schools should provide all personnel with training, as all staff witness and can address victimization of LGBTQ students. In-service teachers should seek out professional development opportunities that allow for additional learning related to diverse populations, including the LGBTQ community. Universities offer a variety of quality courses that can count for professional development credit on ground campuses and online.

CONCLUSION

LGBTQ students are becoming more of a presence in our middle schools as more young adolescents are out, or coming out (Horowitz & Itzkowitz, 2011). The middle grades are the epicenter of LGBTQ victimization. This age group is at the stage of development where young people begin to identify their sexual orientation. However, middle schools often withhold discussions about LGBTQ identities and topics. This lack of acknowledgement creates an environment of heteronormativity, which forces students into the regulation of gender norms, at the risk of facing victimization for expressing behavior that falls outside the norm (Daley et al., 2008). School staff are at least partially responsible for the toxic environment experienced by LGBTQ students. First, by allowing victimization to go unchecked and unreported, and second by actively participating in direct forms of victimization. Lastly, staff can take part in this victimization by supporting the heteronormative structures within the school and their classrooms.

While rarely addressed in depth, staff sanctioned victimization can have a major impact on the stress and mental wellbeing of LGBTQ middle school students. This review of literature, woven together with personal narratives, suggests changes that districts and schools should make for the safety and wellbeing of youth. By making such changes, schools can foster an environment that is supportive of LGBTQ middle school students. To save our students and our schools from victimization, and further victimization through entry into the preschool to prison pipeline, we must start by looking inward and seeing what we are doing to help. Through being a beacon to students, participating in professional development, aiding in the development of reporting systems, queering our curriculum, and recognition of the structural oppression of our schools we can works towards ending staff sanctioned victimization, while also creating a better middle school environment for LGBTQ students.

NOTE

1. I previously posted portions of this narrative anonymously on a blog accessible at https://medium.com/@conversationed/the-f-word-d97224eb16ab

REFERENCES

Allen, K. P. (2009). A bullying intervention system: Reducing risk and creating support for aggressive students. *Preventing School Failure: Alternative Education for Children and Youth, 54*(3), 199–209.

Applebaum, B. (2009). Is teaching for social justice a "liberal bias"? *Teachers College Record, 111*(2), 376–408.

Banks, J. (2004). Multicultural education: Historical development, dimensions, and practice. In J. Banks & C. A. McGee-Banks (Eds.), *Handbook of research on multicultural education* (pp. 3–29). San Francisco, CA: Jossey-Bass.

Beals, M. P. (1985, November 30). Interview by Blackside Inc. [Tape recording]. Eyes on the prize: America's civil rights years (1954–1965). Washington University Libraries, Film and Media Archive, Henry Hampton Collection, St. Louis: MO. Retrieved from http://digital.wustl.edu/e/eop/eopweb/bea0015 .0713.009melbapattillobeals.html

Bishop, R. S. (1990). Mirrors, windows, and sliding glass doors. *Perspectives: Choosing and Using Books for the Classroom, 6*(3), ix–xi.

Blackburn, M. V, & Clark, C. T. (2011). Analyzing talk in a long-term literature discussion group: Ways of operating within LGBT- inclusive and queer discourses. *Reading Research Quarterly, 46*(3), 222–248.

Botelho, M. J., & Rudman, M. K. (2009). *Critical multicultural analysis of children's literature: Mirrors, windows, doors.* New York, NY: Routledge.

Britzman, D. P. (1995). Is there a queer pedagogy? Or, stop reading straight. *Educational Theory, 45*(2), 151–165.

Bush, M. D. (2011). *A quantitative investigation of teachers' responses to bullying* (Unpublished doctoral dissertation). Indiana University of Pennsylvania, Indiana, PA.

Butler, J. P. (1999). *Gender trouble: Feminism and the subversion of identity.* New York, NY: Routledge.

Chesir-Teran, D., & Hughes, D. (2009). Heterosexism in high school and victimization among lesbian, gay, bisexual, and questioning students. *Journal of Youth & Adolescence, 38*(7), 963–975.

Clark, C. (2010). Preparing LGBTQ-allies and combating homophobia in a U.S. teacher education program. *Teaching and Teacher Education, 26*(3), 704–713.

Cochran, B., Stewart, A., Ginzler, J., & Cauce, A. (2002). Challenges faced by homeless sexual minorities: Comparison of gay, lesbian, bisexual, and transgender homeless adolescents with their heterosexual counterparts. *American Journal of Public Health, 92*(5), 773–777.

Daley, A., Newman, P. A., Solomon, S., & Mishna, F. (2008). Traversing the margins: Intersectionalities in the bullying of lesbian, gay, bisexual and transgender youth. *Journal of Gay and Lesbian Social Services, 19*(3–4), 9–29.

Dinkins, E., & Englert, P. (2015). LGBTQ literature in middle school classrooms: Possibilities for challenging heteronormative environments. *Sex Education, 15*(4), 392–405.

Dominski, E. H. (2016). Intersectional bullying, LGBT youth and the construction of power. *International Journal of Educational and Pedagogical Sciences, 20*(9), 3265–3269.

Gates, G. J. (2011). *How many people are lesbian, gay, bisexual, and transgender?* Los Angeles, CA: The Williams Institute. Retrieved from https://williamsinstitute.law .ucla.edu/wp-content/uploads/Gates-How-Many-People-LGBT-Apr-2011.pdf

Gay, Lesbian & Straight Education Network (GLSEN). (2009). *The experiences of lesbian, gay, bisexual and transgender middle school students (GLSEN Research Brief).* New York, NY: Gay, Lesbian, and Straight Education Network. Retrieved from

https://www.glsen.org/sites/default/files/Experiences%20of%20LGBT%20
Middle%20School%20Students.pdf

Glesne, C. (2015). *Becoming qualitative researchers: An introduction* (5th ed.). Boston, MA: Pearson.

Grant, M., & Booth, A. (2009). A typology of reviews: An analysis of 14 review types and associated methodologies. *Health Information and Libraries Journal, 26*(2), 91–108.

Hanlon, J. (2009). How educators can address homophobia in elementary schools. *Encounter, 22*(1), 32–45.

Heybach, J. (2009). Rescuing social justice in education: A critique of the NCATE controversy. *Philosophical Studies in Education, 40*(1), 234–245.

Holmes, S. E., & Cahill, S. (2004). School experiences of gay, lesbian, bisexual and transgender youth. *Journal of Gay & Lesbian Issues in Education, 1*(3), 53–66.

Horn, S. S., Kosciw, J. G., & Russell, S. T. (2009). Special issue introduction: New research on lesbian, gay, bisexual, and transgender youth: Studying lives in context. *Journal of Youth and Adolescence, 38*(7), 863–866.

Horowitz, A., & Hansen, A. (2008). Out for equity: School-based support for LG-BTQA youth. *Journal of LGBT Youth, 5*(2), 73–85.

Horowitz, A., & Itzkowitz, M. (2011). LGBTQ youth in American schools: Moving to the middle. *Middle School Journal, 42*(5), 32–38.

Joseph, N. M., Viesca, K. M., & Bianco, M. (2016). Black female adolescents and racism in schools: Experiences in a colorblind society. *High School Journal, 100*(1), 4–26.

Kahn, M., & Gorski, P. C. (2016). The gendered and heterosexist evolution of the teacher exemplar in the United States: Equity implications for LGBTQ and gender nonconforming teachers. *International Journal of Multicultural Education, 18*(2), 15–38.

Kann, L., O'Malley-Olsen, E., McManus, T., Harris, W., Shanklin, S., Flint, K., . . . Zaza, S. (2016). Sexual identity, sex of sexual contacts, and health-related behaviors among students in grades 9–12. *Morbidity and Mortality Weekly Report, 65*(9), 1–202.

Kolbert, J., Crothers, L., Bundick, M., Wells, D., Buzgon, J., Berbary, C., . . . Senko, K. (2015). Teachers' perceptions of bullying of lesbian, gay, bisexual, transgender, and questioning (LGBTQ) students in a southwestern Pennsylvania sample. *Behavioral Sciences, 5*(2), 247–263.

Kosciw, J. G., Greytak, E. A., Giga, N. M., Villenas, C., & Danischewski, D. J. (2016). *The 2015 National School Climate Survey: The experiences of lesbian, gay, bisexual, transgender, and queer youth in our nation's schools.* New York, NY: Gay Lesbian and Straight Education Network. Retrieved from https://www.glsen.org/sites/default/files/2015%20National%20GLSEN%202015%20National%20School%20Climate%20Survey%20%28NSCS%29%20-%20Full%20Report_0.pdf

Majd, K., Marksamear, J., & Reyes, C. (2009). *Hidden injustice: Lesbian, gay, bisexual, and transgender youth in juvenile courts.* Berkeley, CA: Autumn Press.

McEvoy, A. (2005, September). *Teachers who bully students: Patterns and policy implications.* Paper presented at Hamilton Fish Institute's Persistently Safe Schools Conference, Philadelphia, PA.

Meyer, I. H. (1995). Minority stress and mental health in gay men. *Journal of Health and Social Behavior, 36*(1), 38–56.

Meyer, I. (2003). Prejudice, social stress, and mental health in lesbian, gay, and bisexual populations: Conceptual issues and research evidence. *Psychology Bulletin, 129*(5), 265–275.

Muraco, J. A., & Russell, S. T. (2011). How school bullying impacts lesbian, gay, bisexual, and transgender (LGBT) young adults. Frances McClelland Institute for Children, Youth, and Families. *Research Link, 4*(1), 1–4. Retrieved from https://mcclellandinstitute.arizona.edu/sites/mcclellandinstitute.arizona.edu/files/ResearchLink_Vol.%204%20No.%201_Bullying.pdf

Mustanski, B., Newcomb, M., & Garofalo, R. (2012). Developmental resiliency perspective. *Journal of Gay & Lesbian Social Services, 23*(2), 1–19.

National Middle School Association. (2010). *This we believe: Keys to educating young adolescents.* Westerville, OH: Author.

Palmer, N. A., & Greytak, E. A. (2017). LGBTQ student victimization and its relationship to school discipline and justice system involvement. *Criminal Justice Review, 42*(2), 163–187.

Patton, M. (2015). *Qualitative research & evaluation methods: Integrating theory and practice* (4th ed.). Thousand Oaks: SAGE.

Payne, A. A., & Welch, K. (2015). Restorative justice in schools: The influence of race on restorative discipline. *Youth and Society, 47*(4), 539–564.

Popham, J. A. 2015. *Does CAEP have it right? An analysis of the impact of the diversity of field placements on elementary candidates' teacher performance assessments completed during student teaching* (Doctoral dissertation). Retrieved from ProQuest Dissertations and Theses Global. (1735446552)

Russell, S. T., & Fish, J. N. (2016). Mental health in lesbian, gay, bisexual, and transgender (LGBT) youth. *Annual Review of Clinical Psychology. 12*(1), 465–487.

Russell, S., & McGuire, J. (2008). The school climate for lesbian, gay, bisexual and transgender (LGBT) students. In M. Shinn & H. Yoshikawa (Eds.), *Toward positive youth development: Transforming schools and community programs.* (pp. 133–149). New York, NY: Oxford University Press.

Ryan, C., & Rivers, I. (2003). Lesbian, gay, bisexual and transgender youth: Victimization and its correlates in the USA and UK. *Culture, Health & Sexuality, 5*(2), 103–119.

Snapp, S. D., McGuire, J. K., Sinclair, K. O., Garbrion, K., & Russell, S. T. (2015). LGBTQ-inclusive curricula: Why supportive curricula matter. *Sex Education, 15*(6), 580–596.

Twemlow, S. W., Fonagy, P., Sacco, F. C., & Brethour, J. R. (2006). Teachers who bully students : A hidden trauma. *International Journal of Social Psychiatry, 52*(3), 187–198.

Waters, S., & Mashburn, N. (2017). An investigation of middle school teachers' perceptions on bullying. *Journal of Social Studies Education Research, 8*(1), 1–34.

Yep, G. A. (2002). From homophobia and heterosexism to heteronormativity. *Journal of Lesbian Studies, 6*(3–4), 163–176.

CHAPTER 7

ILLUMINATING THE POWER OF PERSONAL NARRATIVE WRITING TO AFFIRM THE LITERACIES AND LIVES OF BLACK YOUTH

ThedaMarie Gibbs Grey
Ohio University

ABSTRACT

Through this qualitative case-study, I delineate the powerful written personal narratives that ninth-grade Black youth created in a GEAR-UP, college preparatory summer writing course. Critical race theory provided a framework for honoring the voices and stories of Black youth participants whose voices schools and society often marginalized. Culturally relevant pedagogy framed discussions regarding the type of teaching and learning that supports the literacy development and expression of Black youth in the middle grades. The findings speak to the ways in which Black youth created personal statements that served as counternarratives and identity texts. Furthermore, the study's findings demonstrate how educators connect Black youth in the middle

Equity & Cultural Responsiveness in the Middle Grades, pages 131–156
Copyright © 2019 by Information Age Publishing

grades to powerful writing tools, useful for their academic success, and connected to their personal lives. This study has implications for strengthening teaching in the middle grades to affirm and foster the literacies and lives of Black youth while preparing them for academic success.

> I am somebody.
> My life has meaning.
> There is success in me.
> My creations are worthy.
> My words speak.
> My self is shared.
> And my story is heard.
> I can and I will, for I, am the future.
> —*Affirmational Mantra by GEAR-UP Student Leaders*

In an effort to create an affirming writing space for ninth-grade students, the instructors of a summer writing course created the eight lines of the affirmational mantra above. The mantra embodies the guiding philosophy of both the writing course and program that are the focus of this study, which is to remind Black youth of the importance of their lives, stories and spoken and written words.

While research on adolescent literacy has increased over the past few decades, we still need additional research that focuses on adolescents' engagement in the wide range of literacy practices (Conley, 2008). More specifically, research that focuses on the literacy advancement of youth of color and Black youth, the focus of this research, is very essential. In contextualizing the significance of educational spaces that support the writing development of Black students in the middle grades, it is important to draw upon the rich body of research that focuses on educational spaces that honor the written narratives of youth of color. This research draws our intention to the effective teaching and learning strategies that educators can and should adopt in spaces that advance the literacy development of youth of color.

In addition to focusing on the academic importance of personal statement writing, I illuminate the importance of identity exploration that Black youth can experience through narrative writing. This study seeks to add to and extend the body of scholarship that explores beyond school spaces that honor the written narratives of youth of color (Blackburn, 2002; Jocson, 2006; Kinloch, 2010; Mahiri, 2004) and the identity exploration that can occur through personal narrative writing. Scholars such as Kirkland (2009) explored the ways in which young Black men utilize multiple forms of literacy for self-expression and self-exploration. Muhammad's (2012) research also focused on forms of identity exploration that Black girls can experience when educators intentionally create spaces meant to affirm their identities through literacy. Similarly, Winn (2011) discussed the significance of writing in the lives of Black girls with marginalized voices and literacies. Haddix and Sealey-Ruiz (2012) highlighted the lifting up of Black and Latino young men through spaces that allow them to create empowering literacies utilizing digital tools. The previous research importantly focuses on the significance of supporting the overall writing development of Black youth.

Because this study focuses on a specific genre of writing, college application personal statements for Black youth who live and learn in urban spaces, it is also necessary to contextualize the significance of preparing Black youth for college attendance. In 1998, Chaka Fattah, a former United States Congressman authored the Gaining Early Awareness and Readiness for Undergraduate Programs (GEAR-UP) grant in response to the underrepresentation of first-generation students, students of color, and students from families with low-incomes in post-secondary education (Fields, 2001). GEAR-UP's overarching mission is to eliminate educational inequities based on race and socioeconomic status by increasing academic and social support for underrepresented students (U. S. Department of Education, 2018). While college attendance rates for first generation students and Black students have increased over the past 10 years, disparities persist based on race and class (Kena et al., 2016). Researchers committed to eliminating these disparities draw our attention to educational strategies for ensuring increased access to a college education (Harper, Patton & Wooden, 2009; Strayhorn, 2006).

Educational practitioners committed to providing increased access to college for Black students, encourage schools to adopt "college-going cultures" (Knight-Diop, 2010). Doing so requires that schools engage in practices such as providing rigorous curriculum that successfully prepares students to meet the academic demands of college (Swail & Perna, 2002). While successful college applications rely upon multiple factors, creating strong personal statements is an important element. However, many students struggle with successfully completing college applications, including writing personal statements. According to Early, Decosta-Smith and Valdespino (2010), "...schools must work to demystify gatekeeping writing forms for underrepresented populations, so these students can develop necessary writing skills to gain admissions to colleges and universities" (p. 209). In Christensen's (2000) pivotal research with youth of color, she found that many students understood personal statement writing for college applications as a boring activity that simply required them to list their accomplishments. In response, she created a writing course to transform students' knowledge of and experience with writing personal statements for college. Christensen's research and teaching reminds us of the importance of intentionally supporting youth of color as they share their important narratives through creating personal statements.

In this chapter, I focus on the ways that personal narrative writing for college applications can increase ninth-grade students' confidence in and ability to create strong college applications. Increasing our understanding of how educational spaces support Black youth as they engage in personal narrative writing for college is one of the major premises of this research study. I explore the personal narratives of students transitioning from ninth to tenth grade through their participation in GEAR-UP, a college preparatory program. In addition to focusing on the academic importance of personal statement writing, I highlight the importance of identity affirmation that Black youth can experience through narrative writing. Throughout this chapter, I focus on students' participation in a writing course offered through the GEAR-UP Summer Institute.

THEORETICAL FRAMEWORKS

Throughout the study I focus on the importance of lifting the voices of Black youth through their writing. My use of critical race theory (CRT) and culturally relevant pedagogy as theoretical frameworks is evidence of my intentionality in choosing a framework that provided the space to analyze the experiences of Black youth. By utilizing both frameworks, I advocate for re-casting dominant school and societal discourses about communities of color who, historically and contemporarily, are often described through deficit lenses and perceived deficiencies (Solorzano & Yosso, 2009). Consequently, utilizing theoretical frameworks that centered on race and were rooted in telling humanizing stories of people of color was necessary to counter the marginalizing narratives about students of color that schools and society often perpetuate. I further highlight the importance of countering such narratives through my usage of CRT and counternarratives in my theoretical framework.

Critical Race Theory

CRT emerged in the 1970s in the legal field as a response to the ongoing need for theories and frameworks designed to address and combat racism (Delgado & Stefancic, 2012). Scholars framed CRT by the following central tenets that: (a) acknowledge the existence and normalcy of racism, (b) reject race neutrality and colorblindness, (c) recognize how interest convergence operates, (d) value counternarratives of 'communities of color,' and (e) possess a firm commitment to social justice (Delgado & Stefancic, 2012; Taylor, 2009). Within the field of education, CRT is a useful theoretical framework for critiquing dominant school curricula and instruction that deem Black youth as deficient (Ladson-Billings, 2009). Within the scope of this chapter, I primarily focus on the significance of counternarratives that detail the experiences of Black youth. According to Solorzano and Yosso (2009), the counternarrative or counter-story is "a method of telling the stories of those people whose experiences are not often told (i.e., those on the margins of society) . . . and is a tool for exposing, analyzing, and challenging the majoritarian stories of racial privilege" (p. 138). Consequently, counternarratives in research are useful in illuminating the lived experiences of people of color whose voices are often absent in dominant discourses. Furthermore, counternarratives seek to dispel myths about people of color and marginalized communities that are often present in dominant, majoritarian narratives. As Ladson-Billings and Tate (1995) asserted, without listening to and including the very important voices that reveal the lived experiences of people of color, we are unable to understand accurately and effectively or discuss their educational experiences. Utilizing counternarratives to frame students' personal narratives, provided the space to affirm their humanity as Black youth and detail the importance of educational spaces that allowed them to speak about their lives on their own terms and from their own perspectives.

Culturally Relevant Pedagogy

When developing a curriculum for any student, particularly students of color, it is important to understand their unique needs and develop curricular strategies that meet those needs. Ladson-Billings (1995) advocated for the type of instruction that intentionally seeks to meet the needs of students of color, particularly Black students. She encourages educators to understand and adopt equity-based pedagogies such as culturally relevant pedagogy. Culturally relevant pedagogy as defined by Ladson-Billings rests on three tenets: "(a) students must experience academic success; (b) students must develop and/or maintain cultural competence; and (c) students must develop a critical consciousness through which they challenge the status quo of the current social order" (p. 160). These tenets ensure that educators embrace Black students in educational spaces committed to their educational success via curricula that honors their culture and identity and supports their development of critical consciousness. Thus, culturally relevant pedagogy provided a guiding framework for both the philosophy and operation of the GEAR-UP program, as well as the design and implementation of the writing course.

METHODOLOGY

The guiding research questions that frame the study are: (a) In what ways, if at all, does a summer personal statement writing course influence the writing development of ninth grade, young adolescent, Black youth? and (b) How do their personal narratives serve as identity texts and counternarratives of their lives? To effectively explore the guiding research questions, I employed a qualitative, case-study design (Stake, 2000). Employing a case study design is appropriate for this study since a key element of case study research involves a clearly defined bounded system or case (Stake, 2000). In my study, the bounded system, and the unit of analysis that I am studying is a GEAR-UP pre-college program, and more specifically a summer personal statement writing course. According to Merriam and Tisdell (2015), "qualitative researchers are interested in how people interpret their experiences, how they construct their worlds, and what meaning they attribute to their experiences" (p. 15). I conducted the larger study over the span of nine months and included five Jordan University (pseudonym) GEAR-UP programs located in the Midwest. The GEAR-UP program served as the major unit of analysis and students served as smaller units of analysis. In this specific study, I focused on understanding how ninth-grade students made sense of their experience in a personal statement writing course and what their writing revealed about their identities and lived experiences. Utilizing a case study design allowed for an in-depth exploration of the GEAR-UP program structure as well as students' experiences in the program.

Study Context

The GEAR-UP program is a federally-funded program that focuses on increasing the number of underrepresented students who pursue postsecondary education. At the time of the study, the Jordan University GEAR-UP program worked with approximately 1,000 students in primarily urban middle and high schools. Students began their participation in GEAR-UP during seventh grade and continued until their first year in post-secondary education. The Jordan University GEAR-UP hosted five major programs during the year, and data from the study focus on students' participation in one of these programs, the Knowledge is Power summer institute.

Through the summer institute, two cohorts of approximately 35–40 ninth-grade students spent a week on Jordan University's campus. During the program they participated in three major courses: an ACT preparation course, a restorative justice course, and a personal-statement writing course. In the context of this chapter I focus on the personal-statement writing course. In concert with the GEAR-UP staff, I created the personal statement course to strengthen the GEAR-UP students' confidence in and ability to write successful personal statements for their future college applications. Prior to serving as a researcher of the program, I worked for 10 years as a program coordinator for the GEAR-UP program. My commitment to supporting the academic success of Black youth in pre-college programs led to my later engagement in action-oriented research with the program.

The creation of the course was an explicit response to a steady trend of our GEAR-UP students' lack of confidence and anxiety toward successfully writing personal narratives for their college applications. The goals of the course were to: (a) increase students' understanding of the purpose and format of personal statements for college applications; (b) provide students with writing tools to write personal statements effectively; (c) strengthen students' confidence in writing personal statements for college; and (d) provide an affirming space for students to share important aspects of their lives through personal narrative writing. We utilized tenets of culturally relevant pedagogy in the design and implementation of the study. To affirm students' identities as Black writers, we introduced mentor texts and writing samples from Black writers such as Maya Angelou and Langston Hughes. The GEAR-UP curriculum developers not only highlighted the contributions of Black writers into the philosophy of the writing course, but also throughout the entire GEAR-UP program. The director and program staff embodied a philosophy of preparing students for college in ways that intentionally affirmed their identities as Black youth, future Black college students, and Black youth writers who come from an expanding lineage of Black writers.

Through participating in the writing course, students produced two major pieces of writing: a poem and a draft of their personal statement. We provided students with the following five essay prompts from the 2014 National Common Application system:

1. Recount an incident or time when you experienced failure. How did it affect you, and what lessons did you learn?
2. Reflect on a time when you challenged a belief or idea. What prompted you to act? Would you make the same decision again?
3. Describe a place or environment where you are perfectly content. What do you do or experience there, and why is it meaningful to you?
4. Discuss an accomplishment or event, formal or informal that marked your transition from childhood to adulthood within your culture, community, or family.
5. Some students have a background or story that is so central to their identity that they believe their application would be incomplete without it. If this sounds like you, then please share your story.

During the writing course, students created a warm-up poem, drafted outlines of their personal statements, and composed several working drafts of their personal statements for future college applications. To expose students to multiple genres of personal narratives and to Black writers, we integrated and analyzed Langston Hughes' poem, *I Dream a World* and Maya Angelou's poem, *Alone*. Students discussed their interpretations of the poems, identified themes and main ideas, and explored the rhetorical devices present in both poems. We utilized *I Dream a World* as a mentor poem and prompted students to create their own poetic narratives about their dreams on the first day of the workshop. This activity served as a warm-up activity and I intended for students to tap into their dreams about their futures as they transitioned into writing their personal narratives. The student leaders also introduced students to the significance of the Harlem Renaissance (African American Literature Book Club, 2018) for Black writers. This provided the space for students to engage in a discussion about writing genres and how writers can tell their personal stories across myriad genres of writing.

Data Collection

I collected multiple forms of data to develop a comprehensive understanding of the structure and function of the writing course, as well as students' written narratives and experiences as participants. Thus, data from the study included: (a) drafts of GEAR-UP students' personal statements, (b) student course evaluations, (c) curricula samples from the personal statement writing course, (d) 27 individual interviews with students and staff, and (e) field notes from program observations. I collected data specific to the writing course over the span of the two weeks of the summer program. I developed and administered a survey evaluation, inclusive of the six open-ended questions below, designed to capture students' experiences during the course:

1. What did you enjoy the most about the personal narrative workshop?
2. What did you enjoy the least about the personal narrative workshop?
3. Name at least two things you learned from the personal narrative workshop?
4. How can you use what you learned in school?
5. Did you learn new writing skills or strategies? If yes, what did you learn?
6. Do you feel better prepared to write your personal statement for college?

The students completed the survey anonymously to relieve any pressure in responding honestly to the questions. In total, I collected and analyzed drafts of 75 students' personal statements, 73 survey responses, and 63 students' warm-up writing activities. For this analysis, I selected and utilized excerpts from eight GEAR-UP students' draft personal statements to further illustrate the topics of their self-exploration. I utilized purposive sampling (Miles, Huberman & Saldana, 2014) to select the eight students. I chose students who either participated in individual interviews or whose narratives most comprehensively illuminated responses to the three prompts that most GEAR-UP students chose. Through these dominant responses, students focused on their transitions to adulthood, ability to overcome obstacles, and their descriptions of places that made them feel content or at peace with themselves. Additionally, because the GEAR-UP program is a co-educational program, I wanted to ensure balanced representation of narratives authored by participating young women and men.

Data Analysis

I applied narrative analysis techniques to analyze students' written personal statements for college. Utilizing narrative analysis was an appropriate analytical tool given its focus on autobiographical storytelling (Clandinin & Connelly, 2000). Through students' personal statements, they created rich autobiographical snapshots of important life experiences. According to Lieblich, Tuval-Mashiach and Zilber (1998), "One of the clearest channels for learning about the inner world is through verbal accounts and stories presented by individual narrators about their lives and their experienced reality" (p. 7). To make sense of the parts of students' lives written in their narratives, I read each personal statement and then categorized them according to the accompanying prompts. I then read each narrative, hand coding as I read and subsequently transferring the codes to an Excel codebook. The within-category codes allowed me to create subcategories for each of the themes of students' narratives. For example, one of the themes spoke to how students overcame obstacles, however some of the codes represented types of obstacles such as academic challenges, personal loss, and personal health concerns.

FINDINGS

Data analysis revealed how the spaces created in both programs helped students to make sense of and share their important life experiences through writing. Two central findings from the study speak to the ways in which participating in the GEAR-UP summer writing course: (a) fostered the creation of identity texts and counternarratives, and (b) provided students with writing tools to successfully create drafts of their personal statements for college. The majority of students wrote in response to the three prompts requiring them to describe a failure, a major event that marked their transition into young adulthood, or a place where they felt contentment. Students utilized these prompts to describe challenges they faced and how they overcame or were overcoming these challenges actively. Sub-themes across students' personal statements spoke to the salience of family, personal aspirations for academic and career success, and life transitions that contributed to identity development. Through narrative analysis researchers also focus on the form and style of writing (Riessman, 1993). Thus, I also discuss students' use of rhetorical devices such as metaphors and similes to describe their life experiences.

In the first findings section, I draw from students' survey responses and information they provided during the interview to discuss how the course strengthened their writing confidence and skills and allowed them the space to engage in self exploration and demonstration of their feelings and experiences.

Utilizing Writing to Foster Identity Exploration

Engaging in the course affirmed for students that their feelings and experiences mattered. Additionally, students reported that the course re-affirmed the existence of captive audiences willing to listen to their stories. The students' written responses to survey questions that focused on eliciting what they learned from and liked about the writing course illustrated this:

- It helped me let some feelings out that I really needed to;
- I enjoyed being able to write my feelings, as well as having people read my story; and
- I learned that it is acceptable to show your feelings, and that in general, people are understanding.

Through the first response, students spoke to the need for spaces and opportunities for Black students to channel their feelings and experiences. The second student's response further amplified this point, but also illuminated the importance of Black students' access to platforms where people are interested in reading about their experiences and lives. The third response illuminated the importance of having spaces where people are not only interested in reading their narratives but are also committed to understanding their stories.

Additionally, through the personal-statement writing course, students engaged in self-reflection of life events and experiences that contributed to their identity development. In this sense, I refer to students' personal narratives as what Paris (2009) referred to as *identity texts*. In the context of his specific research that focuses on the language and literacy practices of youth of color, Paris (2009) operationalized identity texts as "youth-space texts inscribing ethnic, linguistic, local and transnational affiliations on clothing, binders, backpacks, public spaces, rap lyrics, and electronic media" (p. 279). In this specific context, I focused on how Black students utilized personal statement writing to inscribe their identities through their relationships with themselves, their families, schools, and peers. Through these experiences, they demonstrated their ability to overcome obstacles, recover from failure, and persevere through major life transitions. In the discussion that follows, I illustrate the various forms of personal narrative identity texts students in the GEAR-UP program created.

Gaining Newfound Strength: Overcoming Life Obstacles

For many of the GEAR-UP students, writing about their ability to overcome various obstacles in their lives was salient. I begin with the narratives of two students: Jocelyn and Keisha (all names are pseudonyms) were both ambitious and dedicated GEAR-UP students. Their narratives revealed stories of young women who faced various obstacles in their lives yet were able to draw upon their commitments to their families and themselves to push successfully through these obstacles. Jocelyn chose to write about how she dealt with the obstacle of losing several family members in a short span of time. Below is an excerpt from her statement.

> Life is an ongoing rollercoaster. There's that slow buildup of thoughts, anticipation, and dreams but within that same minute, a plunging drop that makes you hold your breath...At the end of the ride though, once it's over, you catch your breath and find a newfound sense of strength, determination, and overall bravery and accomplishment. This rollercoaster may just be a metaphor, but at one point I felt like it was the story of my life. In the middle of October my mom's uncle died...Less than a month later my grandfather passed...About 2 months later my dad's aunt also passed...Eventually though I realized that I couldn't keep crying forever. I knew that life moved on that it would keep going whether or not I moved along with it. I got back up, dusted myself off, and decided to keep moving forward.

Through her use of metaphors and descriptive sensory details, Jocelyn vividly described a tremendously challenging time in her life where she and her family experienced the loss of several family members. During our interview Jocelyn expounded on why she chose to write about her family losses in her personal statement and why it was important for her to discuss, "So I felt it was a moment in my life where like if I wrote about that, it'd really like touch hearts and see like, kinda put an insight on me as a person more than like the rest of my application which was just grades and numbers and all that."

Jocelyn also contextualized the significance of her narrative and expressed her desire for admissions counselors to understand that any singular factor including her grade point average or any other demographic information included in her profile could not capture who she was. Most importantly, she wanted them to acknowledge her strength, and her story of enduring and recovering from the loss of family members. While this loss took a toll on her emotionally, she conveyed a message of her ability to find strength in the face of obstacles. She allowed herself to grieve, but she also drew upon her internal desire for academic success and the support of her family to remain focused on her academic goals.

Keisha also elected to write her personal statement about an obstacle that she successfully overcame. Her personal obstacle centered on the struggles she faced with academic success in her math class. Here is an excerpt from a draft of her personal statement entitled "Overcoming My Math Obstacle:"

> Overcoming obstacles is what makes you a stronger person. No one in life has it easy but, you can't let that one thing stop you from moving on in life... One failure I experienced was when I started to get bad grades in Algebra... My grades were slowly getting worse and I felt as if everything was just falling apart...However, when second semester came I developed a plan...I did my math homework first, took notes in class, and watched extra videos to refresh my mind. I used all my resources to help me get back on top...I got my results back and I had passed! I was proud of myself. I had overcome a failure and an obstacle...I had a failure but, I didn't let that stop me from moving on. Everyone will encounter failures and obstacles in their lives it's what makes us stronger.

Through her personal statement, Keisha explored her tenacity and commitment to succeeding in math. As she noted, she experienced significant obstacles in her life but her math obstacle was one of the most salient. Keisha expounds on why she chose to write about her math obstacle.

> In the educational area, like math is like my biggest problem that I have to overcome and I did and I'm so happy cause, like math is like, is a real big struggle for me...And I wanted to talk about something that I overcame.

As Keisha expressed in our interview, she chose to write about her obstacle in math because it afforded her the space to also discuss how she overcame this obstacle. Additionally, because of her unfamiliarity with writing personal statements for college, participating in the course increased her knowledge about the structure and purpose of a college personal statement. She chose to talk about her math obstacle not because she walked away feeling defeated, but because when she reflected on it, she felt accomplished in her ability to turn what she viewed as an academic failure into an academic success.

I Am a Man: Navigating the Transition From Boyhood to Manhood

Another significant pattern was the significance of young men writing about events signaling major transitions in their lives. While 15% of students wrote in response to the prompt focusing on events that signaled their transitions to young adulthood, young men wrote 80% of these narratives, detailing their transitions from boyhood to becoming young men. In this section, I detail three excerpts that speak to these transitions written by Khari, Joshua, and Mario. In his personal narrative, below, Khari vividly described how dealing with the loss of a close family member forced him to reflect on his life and make changes for his own personal improvement.

> In my life, I have noticed that there are many events where a boy is turned into a man. But in my personal experience, I have had many events that made me think "I am a man."... Recently, I was taught the hard way that nothing can test a man more than a death in the family. The day my aunt passed away was the toughest day of my life, and it was also the day it was time to stop being a child, and become an adult. Before that tragic event happened, I was merely a boy masquerading as an adult... After that day, I began to reflect. Reflecting on my decisions that I made as a boy, and how I should change them as man... The best way for me to do that is be myself... That was the day I was given the blueprint on how to be a man, and it's quite simple. In order to make the transition from being a child to an adult, you must be able to put your pride aside sometimes.

Khari very eloquently chose to write about losing someone very close to him, his aunt. In writing this very poignant story, Khari, like all the students in the program, allowed himself to be vulnerable and recount a very challenging and life altering time in his life. Losing his aunt prompted an intense self-reflective period of what manhood meant to him. His narrative is a manifestation of his self-reflection about decisions that he made and how they impacted him and other people in his life. Khari metaphorically characterized the life lessons he learned through dealing with this tremendous loss as "... the blueprint on how to be a man."

While a death in the family marked Khari's transition into manhood, Joshua's transition to manhood happened through a series of events surrounding his academic performance and his response to those events as detailed in the excerpt below:

> The transition from my childhood to become a young man was very difficult. The one I really will remember was 7th grade year the real beginning of my

middle school year. I went to the local school in my community with the boys that I grew up with . . . I was on a good start compared to my friends. Christmas break was over and I was back to school and I was excited to show off my stuff I got for Christmas. After that I got lots of respect and started to get out of out of control: skipping school with the local boys that I grew up with and getting suspended. . . . My G.P.A went from a 3.4 to a 2.9 then 2.5 . . . I felt dumb for the choices I made . . . I really understood education was very important. [Now] I only hang with my friends during the summer . . . I knew it was for a good cause and it changed me and set me in a path to become a better man, since males (in) my family didn't go to college.

Joshua ended his personal statement draft with a powerful statement "I knew it was for a good cause and it changed me and set me in a path to become a better man, since males (in) my family didn't get to go to college." As he mentioned briefly at the end of his narrative, many of the male members of his family did not have the opportunity to attend college. He viewed himself as a trailblazer in his family, which he demonstrated in his commitment to becoming one of the first men in his family to attend college. His narrative also disrupted dominant narratives that fail to acknowledge the academic aspirations and potential that young Black men possess, in spite of experiencing academic challenges.

Mario's transition into manhood occurred as he learned of his parents' divorce through a conversation. This conversation served as the central focus of Mario's personal narrative. Below is an excerpt from Mario's personal narrative:

. . . One day, on the way home from school I noticed a stoic look on my father's face. After parking the car he turned and looked at me . . . He drifted into a speech of his experiences becoming a man . . . Any bystander could have easily mistaken it for a sermon, due to his strong gestures and intensity when speaking . . . I could almost feel the passing of the torch, the fire getting closer and closer to my face. Now so deep in his words I failed to notice I was looking down into my lap, the conversation was now too strong for eye contact . . . As I now looked up for the first time as a man, the first thing I noticed was the time. The car's clock now read 10:25, three hours since our initial stop. My father and I were now both tired, him from talking, and me from learning . . . We walked up to the apartment, two men side by side.

Mario recounted a profound conversation with his father regarding the ways in which he understood his life changing. He remembered his feelings, his and his father's detailed actions and the exact time their conversation ended. He utilized writing his personal statement to explore and represent his feelings as he dealt with learning about his parents' divorce through an intense conversation with his father. Mario uses several profound and descriptive metaphors to describe what happened as a result of the conversation including that it marked his "evolution into manhood" and that he "... could almost feel the passing of the torch" of becoming the only man present in their house.

I Am at Peace With the World: Searching for Safe Spaces and Contentment

As with the GEAR-UP students' narratives about obstacles they overcame, students' personal narratives focusing on a place where they experienced contentment revealed significant information about their lives and their experiences. To illuminate further the significance of GEAR-UP students' writing about places where they felt content, I included excerpts from the narratives of three students: Lena, Etienne, and Michael. I begin with an excerpt of Lena's personal narrative. Lena was one of the most dedicated GEAR-UP students who participated in almost all the GEAR-UP programs since she was in seventh grade.

> There are mirrors on the wall, balancing beams, and ballet bars in the most peaceful room in life. As I step on the soft mats feeling free and relieved, the music surrounds me; I close my eyes and feel the beat while others are dancing...My time has finally come...I love dance as a hobby and as a way to express my feelings, emotions, and words that are unexplainable...Nobody knew I didn't have a vent to let out my steam, but dance became the vent. I also use to cry a lot because I felt like I didn't matter to the world. I felt like I didn't belong here which lead me to crying all the time. When dance came into my life I stop being angry because I had ways to express myself. I stopped crying because I found love with Dance and dance has showed me I am important to many others because of my gift. When I dance its [sic] like I leave the world for and enter a zone I feel the calmest and I'm at peace with world, not just the world but myself as well.

Throughout Lena's writing she, in different ways, acknowledged how she felt about the absence of a space for releasing her feelings. Within her personal statement she surpassed simply describing a place where she experienced comfort as the prompt asked her to do. Instead, Lena utilized personal statement writing as a means to talk about some of the challenges she grappled with in her life. She described the dance studio as a place where she mattered to the world and experienced a sense of belongingness. Dancing served as a means of validation and inner peace. She also expressed that people in her life were unaware that she had so many thoughts and feelings bottled up. Thus, Lena utilized her personal statement as a vehicle to share her voice with the world and process her emotions and experiences.

As Lena expressed, students not only utilized the prompt to talk about a place where they felt content, but also a place where they could be themselves. Etienne also chose to write in response to this same prompt.

A place where I'm perfectly content is at home. I feel this way at home because that is the main place where I can just be myself, relax, and excel the most. When I'm away from home, I worry about being judged or criticized. Also, this is a place where I get my inspiration and motivation to succeed and do well in life. . . . Writing is another comfort zone for me. When I pick up the pen and pencil my creative and talented side magically appears. This is where I feel I can finally be in my place and be able to write however I feel inside and just go deep into my mind. Another reason writing is a comfort zone for me is because it's one of my favorite things to do when I'm bored. Whenever I write, I experience a different amount of emotions and my sensitive side immediately comes into play.

For Etienne, the ability to write about a place where he felt perfectly content allowed him the space to discuss challenges that he faced. In his warm-up writing sample, he included a line referencing his dreams of being free from shyness. He returned to his experience with shyness in his personal statement, signaling how significant this was in his life. The places he described in his narrative, where he experienced contentment, protected him from "being judged and criticized" and provided him with "inspiration and motivation." Etienne also shared that the act of writing was comforting because it allowed him to express his creative energy and release many of his feelings.

Michael also utilized his writing time to describe a place that allowed him to showcase his creativity and talent. Below is an excerpt from Michael's personal narrative:

Thump! Thump! Thump! That's the sound my heart makes when I'm getting ready to go on stage and entertain boatloads of people . . . Sweat drips from my face like water off the leaves of a tree after it rains . . . I spoke my first line and everything took off, I felt a tickle of satisfaction in my belly, all my pains and sorrows began to evaporate. That's when I realized I was genuinely happy and there was nothing that could make me feel more alive . . . I strive to eventually change the world with my craft . . . It makes me proud to know that I can change someone's life and be someone's inspiration. That is what pushes me to keep going, knowing that there is someone out there that needs me.

During the writing course one of the writing strategies that student leaders reinforced to students centered on utilizing vivid words and imagery to engage their readership. Michael was quite successful in doing just that and drawing in his reader. He utilized his personal statement to tell an important story about his dreams of becoming a director. Michael also outlined his plans to use theater as a vehicle for becoming a change agent. For Michael, becoming a director would not only benefit him individually, but he also viewed it as a vehicle to impact positively the lives of other people.

DISCUSSION

As the students' writing revealed, the personal statement course allowed them to draft their personal statements for college while writing about significant lived experiences. Students were able to express themselves not through deficit lenses, but through asset-based lenses affirming that they matter. Their personal narratives revealed stories of Black youth who utilized their written words to express their dreams of academic success creatively, and of becoming college graduates, artists, and doctors. However, society often overlooks the dreams and talents of Black youth. This is evident in the number of Black students that schools over-identify for special education, under-identify for gifted and talented programs (Ford, 2010) and inequitably discipline, which can lead to negative academic outcomes (Raible & Irizarry, 2010; Skiba, Arredondo & Williams, 2014). To prevent the perpetuation of these negative educational and life outcomes for Black youth, it is important that as educators we commit to understanding who they are and allow them to tell life stories on their own terms. Schools must embrace Black youth by building and sustaining humanizing educational environments, inclusive of educators who care about their voices and lives. In the discussion that follows, I unpack the narratives of the focal students and detail how they served as counternarratives. Additionally, I offer recommendations for how educators in the middle grades can utilize and expand upon the space that GEAR-UP created to support the identity development and affirmation of Black middle school youth through writing.

Honoring the Voices and Written CounterNarratives of Black Youth

Winn (2011) reminded us that "rather than needing a "voice," most youth need a space, an opportunity, and an engaged audience so they can share their voices" (p. 20). These engaging audiences must include teachers and school classrooms designed to honor the voices of Black youth. GEAR-UP students shared their voices through their written narratives that spoke to their humanity. Their narratives encompassed universal themes many middle school students contend with such as living and growing as students who lost loved ones yet learned how to work through their pain (Yost & Vogel, 2012); experiencing academic failures and creating action plans to overcome failures; and successfully traversed the challenging terrain of transitioning from childhood to young adulthood. In this space, students were able to direct and create their own self-written narratives about their realities and possibilities for their futures. When teachers in the middle grades commit to learning about the realities of Black students, they are then able to create classrooms that invite students to utilize writing in ways that are meaningful to their lives (Montero, 2012).

For Mario, Joshua and Khari, the summer course offered an opportunity to discuss significant life events that marked their transitions into manhood. The mere act of writing narratives for their college applications sits in stark contrast to deficit narratives that claim Black boys lack an interest in their academic development (Harper & Davis, 2012; Howard, 2013). Although Joshua struggled academically in seventh grade, through his narrative he demonstrated his commitment to himself, and his family to become a first-generation college graduate. Mario's narrative affirmed his father's love and commitment to his son, which also counters the ways in which Black fathers are pathologized as absent and unconcerned about relationship building with their children. The prevalence of Black young men in the program writing about becoming young men was very significant and demonstrated their need to engage in an activity that allowed them to explore and express their feelings. Etienne's honest account of experiencing judgment and criticism and turning to writing for healing exemplified how Black boys utilize writing for relief and restoration. Scholars such as Kirkland (2013) reminded us that educational spaces often silence the lives and literacies of Black young men. Furthermore, Everett (2016) drew our attention to the lack of understanding focused on how writing positively impacts young Black men as well as the importance of acknowledging the potential and capabilities in Black male writers such as Etienne and Mario. Consequently, teachers must develop instructional strategies that honor the voices and experiences of Black male students in the middle grades. As Tatum (2005) posited, "curricula and educational plans have fallen short of addressing the academic, cultural, emotional, and social needs of Black males" (p. 15). The narratives presented here demonstrate the importance of spaces that allow Black students to talk about the challenges and triumphs they experienced academically, emotionally, and socially. More specifically, their narratives illuminated the need for spaces that support Black young men as they navigate challenging transitions.

Creating spaces that meet the same needs for Black young women are paramount to their academic success as well as their social, cultural, and emotional well-being. Keisha's commitment to improving her math content knowledge and skills was significant given the lack of narratives that centralize and illuminate Black girls' experiences and values regarding mathematics (Gholson, 2016). Her commitment to improving her math performance demonstrated the value she placed on academically succeeding in math. Jocelyn's narrative speaks to the need for Black girls to talk about the importance of family, commitment, academic success, loss, and healing. Through her narrative, Lena illustrates her search for spaces where the world could hear her voice and affirm her story. Spaces for Black girls to do so are especially important given the lack of school structures focused on supporting their developmental needs (Morris, 2016; Ricks, 2014). Too often schools silence Black girls from telling their stories and deem their voices as insignificant, loud, and aggressive (Koonce, 2012). Just as positive and empowering visual narratives of Black girls are largely absent in mainstream media (Lindsey, 2013), these same narratives in written form are missing from societal and classroom narratives. Therefore, Black girls also deserve spaces that affirm and support the healthy development of their self-esteem and self-worth.

Affirming the Writing Identities of Black Youth

The curricular design of the course was rooted in tenets of culturally relevant pedagogy to ensure that students understood the value in their stories, voices, and writing. Brinegar, Kennedy, Hurd, and Harrison (2016) presented a compelling list of questions that researchers should consider when foregrounding culturally responsive pedagogies in middle grades research. One of these important questions is "How can the middle school concept be used to enhance educators' culturally responsive practices for young adolescents from marginalized backgrounds?" (p. 4)

Utilizing curricular strategies rooted in cultural relevance that are meant to be identity-affirming are important in all settings, but particularly in the middle grades. During the middle school years students are developing, navigating, and negotiating their identities. They are shaping and forming identity constructions of how they see themselves, how the outside world sees them and how they want others to see them. At this stage, young people are also developing an understanding of societal constructions of race and forming their identities in relation to their race and ethnicity (Chavous et al., 2003; Ford, Harris & Scheurger, 1993). Consequently, educational spaces that support positive racial identity development are key. However, Akos and Ellis (2008) drew our attention to the lack of attention placed on supporting the racial identity development of students in the middle grades.

Supporting students' development of positive identities as Black youth necessarily means educators must deem Black culture and the stories of Black youth as worthy and valuable. Culturally relevant pedagogy also requires that Black students develop or maintain cultural competence or an understanding and awareness of the richness of their own cultures as well as others. In the context of the writing course, utilizing the narrative writing of Maya Angelou and Langston Hughes affirmed the powerful and eloquent writing contributions that Black authors have made and continue to make. We wanted students to strengthen their awareness of their connection to a rich lineage of Black writers who create personal narratives across various genres. These models of writing were meant to encourage students by demonstrating what is possible for their own writing. To be clear, these curricular choices were intentional as not every GEAR-UP program that engages with students of color necessarily adopts a culturally relevant curricula. Similarly, teachers must be intentional, critically conscious and prepared to integrate culturally relevant pedagogy effectively within their classrooms.

Equipping Black Youth With Writing Tools for Academic Success and Personal Reflection

In addition to connecting Black youth to the possibilities of what they can do with their writing, culturally relevant pedagogy draws educators' attention to ensuring that Black students receive quality instruction that propels their academic success forward. I provided students with the writing tools to experience academic success, relative to strengthening their ability to write successful personal statements that would enhance their future college applications. For many of the GEAR-UP students, the writing course demystified the purpose of the personal statement for college as well as the process for writing it. Through the course, instructors covered important elements related to structure, making sense of writing prompts and topics, effectively responding to writing prompts and questions, syntax, grammar, effectively utilizing rhetorical devices such as similes and metaphors, drafting, editing, and peer-workshopping. These writing tools were not only relevant for writing personal statements, but also for writing across genres and content areas. According to the National Council of Teachers of English (2016), "Students should become comfortable with prewriting techniques, multiple strategies for developing and organizing a message, a variety of strategies for revising and editing, and methods for preparing products for public audiences and deadlines" (pp. 6–7). We also valued the process of allowing students to experience writing beyond and in addition to meeting academic requirements. All students need to feel connected to their writing through understanding and valuing the significance of what they are writing and why they are writing. To ensure that students felt connected to their writing, the instructors dedicated time throughout the course to connect personal statement writing to lifelong personal reflection for personal growth.

While it is important for teachers and counselors to introduce students to personal statements early in high school, beginning earlier in middle school can provide a more solid foundation. GEAR-UP students' responses on the course evaluation highlighted their unfamiliarity with the purpose and process of writing personal statements for college, thus demonstrating their need for writing assistance. Ensuring that school districts adopt and integrate college preparatory curriculum beginning at the middle school level is key (Cowan-Pitre & Pitre, 2009; Reid & Moore, 2008). This is particularly important given the opportunity gaps that Black students inequitably experience as a result of sub-standard academic preparation (Chambers, 2009; Ladson-Billings, 2006; Milner, 2010). Educators responsible for the academic success of Black students in the middle grades must seek to eliminate such gaps in academic resources in all areas including writing and academic preparation for success in college. Through the course, I provided students with the tools to create a document, which in tandem with other factors played a significant role in preparing them to submit their college applications. The course was rooted in the belief that Black students are just as capable and deserving of an opportunity to excel in college as any other student. The course helped them to maneuver through the college application process and provided them with skills useful for navigating their paths to college. They were also able to acquire necessary tools for completing their personal statements, subsequently drafting their statements in preparation for their college applications, while simultaneously writing about their lives.

IMPLICATIONS

Through participating in the writing course, students were able to create powerfully candid and beautifully written drafts of their personal statements in a limited span of one week. Therefore, the possibilities are endless for the type of writing that can occur in sustained ways with additional time across the entire academic year. While the writing course took place in a beyond school setting over the summer, key elements regarding the design and implementation of the course are relevant for middle school classroom spaces and advisories. According to Jackson and Davis (2000):

> Small schools, teams, and advisories are the structures commonly associated with a successful middle grades school. Unfortunately, many middle grades schools go no further than creating these structures, never connecting them to improving teaching and learning so that every student can meet or exceed high academic standards. (p. 144)

Given the need to strengthen the ways in which advisories support students' academic and social development, the recommendations in this section focus on how teachers, advisors and counselors in the middle grades can support their students' ability to craft personal narratives successfully. Teachers and counselors should begin conversations about the requirements for college applications early in middle school. Introducing Black students in the middle grades to the purpose and format of personal statements for college can serve to relieve anxiety and build their confidence when they begin to construct their applications in their eleventh and twelfth grade years. Counselors in the middle grades and high school can also construct advisory sessions that connect students with current college students including Black college students who can share their wisdom and experience and provide mentor models of successful college personal statements. Inviting admissions counselors from local colleges and universities who can provide guidance and answer students' questions about their personal statements and the college application process is also valuable.

Additionally, educators in the middle grades must improve the ways in which they integrate and sustain culturally relevant teaching methods. This first requires that educators acknowledge the humanity and value in Black students and also the value in culturally relevant teaching methods. This in many ways is no easy task as it also requires teachers to reflect critically and contend with the biases and misconceptions about Black youth they may possess. It also calls upon school administrators to provide resources in the form of professional development and connecting teachers to experts who can model and connect teachers to effective culturally relevant teaching and learning tools. Teachers in the middle grades must continue to integrate models of Black excellence meaningfully in writing via the books, texts and authors highlighted in classroom curricula throughout the academic year. Black youth must understand the multiple ways that Black writers engage in personal narrativizing through poetry, essays, debates, short stories, and song lyrics. Connecting students in the middle grades to contemporary and historical Black writers as well as fostering their identities as valuable writers is essential to their academic and personal development.

Researchers can continue to engage in scholarship that demonstrates the ways in which educators in school and beyond school successfully develop curricula that connects to students' lives and support their successful academic and personal development. They must continue to create research studies that focus on highlighting the oral and written narratives of Black youth. Researchers have the power to reshape the ways in which schools and society position Black youth by critically highlighting the first-person accounts of youth who write about their humanity in reference to their identities as young adolescents, students, Black youth and all the other identities they embody. This type of research can continue to shift narrow narratives of Black youth that do not acknowledge and embrace their potential and excellence.

In moving forward, I return to the opening mantra guiding the summer course and this chapter. As we continue the necessary journey of crafting middle grades curriculum, teaching methods, research, and practice, we must do so intent on ensuring that Black youth know they are somebody, their lives are meaningful, their written words tell stories that we will honor, and that we will provide them with the academic tools to establish futures where they are destined for greatness via multiple career and educational pathways, including college.

REFERENCES

African American Literature Book Club. (2018). *The Harlem renaissance.* Retrieved from https://aalbc.com/content.php?title=The+Harlem+Renaissance

Akos, P., & Ellis, C. M. (2008). Racial identity development in middle school: A case for school counselor individual and systemic intervention. *Journal of Counseling & Development, 86*(1), 26–33.

Blackburn, M. V. (2002). Disrupting the (hetero) normative: Exploring literacy performances and identity work with queer youth. *Journal of Adolescent & Adult Literacy, 46*(4), 312–324.

Brinegar, K., Kennedy-Lewis, B., Harrison, L., & Hurd, E. (2016). Cultural responsiveness. In S. B. Mertens, M. M. Caskey, P. Bishop, N. Flowers, D. Strahan, D., G. Andrews, & L. Daniel (Eds.), *The MLER SIG research agenda* (pp. 4–6). Retrieved from http://mlersig.net/mler-sig-research-agenda-project/

Chambers, T. V. (2009). The" receivement gap": School tracking policies and the fallacy of the "Achievement Gap." *The Journal of Negro Education, 78*(4) 417–431.

Chavous, T. M., Bernat, D. H., Schmeelk-Cone, K., Caldwell, C. H., Kohn-Wood, L., & Zimmerman, M. A. (2003). Racial identity and academic attainment among African American adolescents. *Child Development, 74*(4), 1076–1090.

Christensen, L. (2000). *Reading, writing, and rising up: Teaching about social justice and the power of the written word.* Milwaukee, WI: Rethinking Schools.

Clandinin, F. M., & Connelly, D. J. (2000). *Narrative inquiry: Experience and story in qualitative research.* San Francisco, CA: Jossey-Bass.

Conley, M. W. (Ed.). (2008). *Meeting the challenge of adolescent literacy: Research we have, research we need.* New York, NY: Guilford Press.

Cowan-Pitre, C., & Pitre, P. (2009). Increasing underrepresented high school students' college transitions and achievements: TRIO educational opportunity programs. *NASSP Bulletin, 93*(2), 96–110.

Delgado, R., & Stefancic, J. (2012). *Critical race theory: An introduction.* New York, NY: New York University Press.

Early, J. S., DeCosta-Smith, M., & Valdespino, A. (2010). Write your ticket to college: A genre-based college admission essay workshop for ethnically diverse, underserved students. *Journal of Adolescent & Adult Literacy, 54*(3), 209–219.

Everett, S. (2016). "I just started writing:" Toward addressing invisibility, silence, and mortality among academically high-achieving Black male secondary students. *Literacy Research: Theory, Method, and Practice, 65*(1), 316–331.

Fields, C. D. (2001). Can TRIO and GEAR UP continue to co-exist? *Black Issues in Higher Education, 18*(21), 26–31.

Ford, D. (2010). *Reversing underachievement among gifted Black students.* (2nd ed.). Waco, TX: Prufrock Press.

Ford, D. Y., Harris, J. J., & Schuerger, J. M. (1993). Racial identity development among gifted Black students: Counseling issues and concerns. *Journal of Counseling & Development, 71*(4), 409–417.

Gholson, M. L. (2016). Clean corners and algebra: A critical examination of the constructed invisibility of Black girls and women in mathematics. *The Journal of Negro Education, 85*(3), 290–301.

Haddix, M., & Sealey-Ruiz, Y. (2012). Cultivating digital and popular literacies as empowering and emancipatory acts among urban youth. *Journal of Adolescent & Adult Literacy, 56*(3), 189–192.

Harper, S. R., & Davis III, C. H. (2012). They (don't) care about education: A counternarrative on Black male students' responses to inequitable schooling. *The Journal of Educational Foundations, 26*(1–2), 103–120.

Harper, S. R., Patton, L. D., & Wooden, O. S. (2009). Access and equity for African American students in higher education: A critical race historical analysis of policy efforts. *The Journal of Higher Education, 80*(4), 389–414.

Howard, T. C. (2013). How does it feel to be a problem? Black male students, schools, and learning in enhancing the knowledge base to disrupt deficit frameworks. *Review of Research in Education, 37*(1), 54–86.

Jackson, A. W., & Davis, G. A. (2000). *Turning points 2000: Educating adolescents in the 21st century*. New York, NY: Teachers College Press.

Jocson, K. M. (2006). "There's a better word": Urban youth rewriting their social worlds through poetry. *Journal of Adolescent & Adult Literacy, 49*(8), 700–707.

Kena, G., Hussar W., McFarland J., de Brey C., Musu-Gillette, L., Wang, X., ... Dunlop Velez, E. (2016). *The condition of education 2016* (NCES 2016-144). Washington, DC: U.S. Department of Education, National Center for Education Statistics. Retrieved from http://nces.ed.gov/pubsearch

Kinloch, V. (2010). *Harlem on our minds: Place, race, and the literacies of urban youth*. New York, NY: Teachers College Press.

Kirkland, D. E. (2009). The skin we ink: Tattoos, literacy, and a new English education. *English Education, 41*(4), 375–395.

Kirkland, D. E. (2013). *A search past silence: the literacy of young Black men*. New York, NY: Teachers College Press.

Knight-Diop, M. G. (2010). Closing the gap: Enacting care and facilitating Black students' educational access in the creation of a high school college-going culture. *Journal of Education for Students Placed at Risk, 15*(1–2), 158–172.

Koonce, J. B. (2012). "Oh, those loud Black girls!": A phenomenological study of Black girls talking with an attitude. *Journal of Language and Literacy Education, 8*(2), 26–46.

Ladson-Billings, G. (1995). But that's just good teaching! The case for culturally relevant pedagogy. *Theory Into Practice, 34*(3), 159–165.

Ladson-Billings, G. (2006). From the achievement gap to the education debt: Understanding achievement in U.S. schools. *Educational Researcher, 35*(7), 3–12.

Ladson-Billings, G. (2009). Just what is critical race theory and what's it doing in a nice field like education? In E. Taylor, D. Gillborn, & G. Ladson-Billings (Eds.), *Foundations of critical race theory in education* (pp. 17–36). New York, NY: Routledge.

Ladson-Billings, G., & Tate, W. (1995). Toward a critical race theory of education. *Teachers College Record, 97*(1), 47–67.

Lieblich, A., Tuval-Mashiach, R., & Zilber, T. B. (1998). *Narrative research: Reading, analysis and interpretation.* Thousand Oaks, CA: SAGE.

Lindsey, T. B. (2013). "One time for my girls": African-American girlhood, empowerment, and popular visual culture. *Journal of African American Studies, 17*(1), 22–34.

Mahiri, J. (2004). *What they don't learn in school: Literacy in the lives of urban youth.* New York, NY: Peter Lang.

Merriam, S. B., & Tisdell, E. J. (2015). *Qualitative research: A guide to design and implementation* (4th ed.). San Francisco, CA: John Wiley & Sons.

Miles, M. B., Huberman, A. M., & Saldana, J. (2014). *Qualitative data analysis: A methods sourcebook* (3rd ed.). Thousand Oaks, CA: SAGE.

Milner IV, H. R. (2010). *Start where you are, but don't stay there: Understanding diversity, opportunity gaps, and teaching in today's classrooms.* Cambridge, MA: Harvard Education Press.

Montero, M. K. (2012). Literary artistic spaces engage middle grades teachers and students in critical-multicultural dialogue: Urban students write about their lives in one-word poems and on traveling scrawled walls. *Middle School Journal, 44*(2), 30–38.

Morris, M. (2016). *Pushout: The criminalization of Black girls in schools.* New York, NY: The New Press.

Muhammad, G. (2012). Creating spaces for Black adolescent girls to "Write it out." *Journal of Adult and Adolescent Literacy, 56*(3), 203–211.

National Council of Teachers of English. (2016). *Professional knowledge for the teaching of writing.* Urbana, IL: Author. Retrieved from https://dpi.wi.gov/sites/default/files/imce/ela/resources/Professional%20Knowledge%20for%20the%20Teaching%20of%20Writing.pdf

Paris, D. (2009). Texting identities: Lessons for classrooms from multiethnic youth space. *English Education, 42*(3), 278–292.

Raible, J., & Irizarry, J. G. (2010). Redirecting the teacher's gaze: Teacher education, youth surveillance and the school-to-prison pipeline. *Teaching and Teacher Education, 26*(5), 1196–1203.

Reid, M. J., & Moore III, J. L. (2008). College readiness and academic preparation for postsecondary education: Oral histories of first-generation urban college students. *Urban Education, 43*(2), 240–261.

Ricks, S. A. (2014). Falling through the cracks: Black girls and education. *Interdisciplinary Journal of Teaching and Learning, 4*(1), 10–21.

Riessman, C. K. (1993). *Narrative analysis.* Newberry Park, CA: SAGE.

Solorzano, D. G, & Yosso, T. J. (2009). Critical race methodology: Counter-storytelling as an analytical framework for educational research. In E. Taylor, D. Gillborn, & G. Ladson-Billings. (Eds.), *Foundations of critical race theory in education* (pp. 131–147). New York, NY: Routledge.

Skiba, R. J., Arredondo, M. I., & Williams, N. T. (2014). More than a metaphor: The contribution of exclusionary discipline to a school-to-prison pipeline. *Equity & Excellence in Education, 47*(4), 546–564.

Stake, R. (2000). Case studies. In N. Denzin & Y. Lincoln (Eds.), *Handbook of qualitative research* (2nd ed., pp. 435–454). Thousand Oaks, CA: SAGE.

Strayhorn, T. L. (2006). Factors influencing the academic achievement of first-generation college students. *NASPA Journal, 43*(4), 82–111.

Swail, W. S., & Perna, L. W. (2002). Pre-college outreach programs. In W. G. Tierney & L. S. Hagedorn (Eds.), *Increasing access to college: Extending possibilities for all students* (pp. 15–34). Albany: State University of New York Press.

Tatum, A. W. (2005). *Teaching reading to Black adolescent males: Closing the achievement gap*. Portland, ME: Stenhouse.

Taylor, E. (2009). The foundations of critical race theory in education: An introduction. In E. Taylor, D. Gillborn, & G. Ladson-Billings (Eds.), *Foundations of critical race theory in education* (pp. 1–16). New York, NY: Routledge.

U.S. Department of Education. (2018). *Programs: Gaining Early Awareness and Readiness for Undergraduate Programs (GEAR UP)*. Washington, DC: Author. Retrieved from https://www2.ed.gov/programs/gearup/faq.html

Winn, M. T. (2011). *Girl time: Literacy, justice, and the school-to-prison pipeline*. New York, NY: Teachers College Press.

Yost, D. S., & Vogel, R. (2012). Writing matters to urban middle level students: The Writers Matter program motivates urban youth to write about their lives. *Middle School Journal, 43*(3), 40–48.

SECTION III

BUILDING EQUITABLE SPACES
THROUGH THE IMPLEMENTATION
OF CULTURALLY RESPONSIVE PRACTICES

CHAPTER 8

CREATING A SPACE FOR CULTURALLY SUSTAINING PEDAGOGY

James Nagle
Saint Michael's College

Will Andrews
Winooski High School

ABSTRACT

How does culturally sustaining pedagogy look in a personalized learning environment? We asked this question when examining the iLab academic program at Winooski Middle and High School in Vermont. While many may not think of Vermont as a mecca of diversity, Winooski is a pocket of diversity within the state. With more than 25 languages spoken and a large student population of new Americans, Winooski Middle and High School has an opportunity to address Vermont's recent educational policy reform of proficiency-based education and flexible pathways in a manner that honors diversity. In this chapter, we report on our investigation into the engagement and learning of students who are part of a project-based learning program centered on a personal learning framework and student voice. The findings suggest that

Equity & Cultural Responsiveness in the Middle Grades, pages 159–179
159

focusing on the personal learning framework of identity, growth and reflection, and transformation in a project-based learning environment can create a space for new American students to explore and strengthen their cultural identity while at the same time developing an understanding of how to interact in a new community.

In this chapter, we describe how the iLab academic program at Winooski Middle and High School affects students' understanding of their cultural identity when working through a personalized learning process that utilizes project-based learning pedagogies. The iLab is a technology-rich space in which students explore their own areas of interest, work with community experts, and take ownership of their learning. Students in Grades 6 through 12 can enroll in the iLab just like any other course in middle or high school; however, the curriculum is student-directed and project-based for students interested in investigating authentic real-world issues important to them. Projects include topics such as participating in a "Black Lives Matter" rally as a member of a local Peace and Justice Center and performing a Buddhist ceremony for family and friends.

Started in 2013, the Winooski Middle and High School created iLab to respond to decreasing student engagement and to address a recent Vermont educational policy reform at the time. *Act 77–Flexible Pathways Initiative: Dual Enrollment* encouraged expanded learning opportunities in and out of school through students' personal pathways leading to high school graduation and college and career readiness (Vermont Statutes Annotated Title 16, §§ 16, §§ 941-945). Bishop, Downes, and Nagle (2017) described the initiative as melding three pillars of personal learning—personal learning plans, flexible pathways, and proficiency-based assessment. Personal learning plans (PLPs) help students monitor their personalized educational programs related to their interests. Students develop PLPs with assistance from family members and teachers. Flexible pathways enable students to pursue a variety of learning activities, including project-based learning, mentorships, internships, online learning, and service learning, based on the goals outlined in their personal learning plans. The proficiency-based assessment system is a standards-based system of assessment and reporting in which students demonstrate competence or mastery in a specific skill, knowledge set, or concept usually through project-based learning.

Bishop et al. (2017) contended that when educators implement each pillar simultaneously, effective personal learning results. Likewise, the essential elements of personal learning—personal learning plans, flexible pathways, and proficiency-based assessment through a project-based curriculum was the genesis of the iLab's "Think it, Learn It, Make It, Share It" framework. In this framework, students do not take any tests, quizzes, or final examinations. Rather, iLab requires students to follow the process of

"Think it"—set goals for a semester-long project; "Learn it"—create an action plan to investigate and learn about the project; "Make it"—implement the action plan to create a final product; and "Share it"—write a paper about the learning process and present the product and the learning process to the community. Teachers in the iLab facilitate this learning process by ensuring that students are accountable for their designated goals and selected academic proficiencies.

The student participants in this research study started iLab in sixth grade with projects that tended to be very personal, but as they moved through the program, students began to investigate topics that addressed societal issues and involved community elements. For instance, when Kinaya was in sixth grade her project was about her native country—Kenya. By the time she was in eighth grade, she was working on a project called "Sisters in Sports" that depicted her involvement as a mentee in a basketball-mentoring program with a local college. This progression sparked our research questions: How does a personalized, project-based learning program affect the academic and social development of new American students? Would these authentic learning opportunities in the iLab reinforce students' identity in culturally sustaining and positive ways? Would there be an assimilation of traditional American culture and a loss of cultural family backgrounds? In thinking about this tension, we wondered if the iLab would extend Ladson-Billings' (1995) concept of culturally relevant pedagogy by supporting "young people in sustaining the cultural and linguistic competence of their communities while simultaneously offering access to dominant cultural competence" (Paris, 2012, p. 95). Educators initially intended for iLab to provide students with a personalized and alternative pathway toward high school graduation and beyond. We wondered whether it would also create a space for new Americans[1] to explore and strengthen their cultural identity while at the same time develop an understanding of how to interact in their new American community.

To examine this tension between cultural identity and access to the dominant culture, first we highlight three important areas of educational research to understand how the iLab may affect new Americans: personalized learning, project-based learning, and culturally sustaining pedagogy. The convergence of these three literature bases is where, we believe, teaching and learning at the iLab intersect for new American students at Winooski Middle and High School. Next, we describe the context of the iLab and explain the modes of inquiry into this personalized learning landscape. Finally, we present the findings and discuss implications for this type of learning environment for schools with significant populations of new Americans.

LITERATURE REVIEW

In some ways, the iLab is unique because it is set in a policy environment of Vermont in which flexible pathways, personalized learning, and proficiency-based assessment systems are becoming the norm for middle and high schools. These policies intersect with the project-based learning framework of the iLab ("Think it, Learn It, Make It, Share It"), and the student population of new Americans with their unique mix of cultural identities.

Personalized Learning

Models of personalized learning began in earnest in the early 2000s with Jenkins and Keefe's (2002) profile of two high schools and Levine's (2002) case study of the original Big Picture Learning School, the Metropolitan Regional Career and Technical Center, known as The Met. In both studies, the authors described six elements of personalized learning that include: (a) the role of the teacher as a facilitator of learning; (b) personalization of the curriculum based on the student's learning needs, interests, and strengths; (c) a collegial school culture to support personal relationships; (d) an interactive learning environment with a variety of instructional approaches; (e) flexible learning in and out of school; and (f) authentic assessments including presentations to community members.

Clarke (2013) provided a similarly detailed illustration of personalized learning in his case study of the Pathways program at Mount Abraham Union Middle/High School in Bristol, Vermont. He noted similar elements in the Pathways program such as its individualized and interest-based curriculum, emphasis on community-based learning, exhibitions of learning, and proficiency-based system of assessment as described by Jenkins and Keefe (2002) and Levine (2002). Clarke's contribution was his insight into how the academic structure and learning scaffolds, along with the primacy of teacher as facilitator, enhanced the personalized learning process.

When DiMartino and Clarke (2008) studied personalized learning, they noted how personalized learning placed students at the center of the learning experience and realized that relevance and flexibility were essential attributes in learning. Nagle and Taylor (2017) saw the shift from teacher-centered to student-centered learning as a process that both teachers and students could learn. They offered an iterative process in their "personal learning framework" that guided students through a series of stages: identity, growth, and reflection through goal setting and evidence collection, and transformation (Taylor & Nagle, 2015). In most of these studies (Clarke, 2013; DiMartino & Clarke, 2008; Nagle & Taylor, 2017), project-based learning played a prominent role in affording students autonomy over their learning by allowing them to have choice in selecting what they learn and voice in how they learn it (Bray & McClaskey, 2015).

Project-Based Learning

For personalized learning to be successful, in many instances it relies on a robust implementation of inquiry-based or project-based pedagogies. As mentioned previously, project-based learning allows for student voice and choice (i.e., autonomy) in their learning. Larmer (2015) noted four common criteria for project-based learning: (a) a driving question about a specific issue; (b) the development of specific and essential skills to complete the project successfully; (c) an appropriate amount of time to design, investigate, and complete the project; and (d) an understanding that the project drives the learning from start to finish.

As with personalized learning, there is a shift in teaching and learning roles. The teacher's role in a project-based learning environment is to support student learning by providing feedback, assisting in creating authentic learning opportunities within the classroom or with community members, and holding students accountable in authentic ways (Krajcik & Shin, 2014). The student role also changes; students become much more responsible for their learning. They choose their project topic, identify and develop essential skills needed to investigate driving questions, coordinate the gathering of information from multiple sources including community members, and present to authentic audiences (Krajcik & Shin, 2014). This shift in teaching and learning roles creates more engaged learners (Bradford, 2005; Lam, Cheng, & Ma, 2009). The question we consider is whether project-based learning in the iLab promotes engaged learning that supports exploration of cultural identity.

Culturally Sustaining Pedagogy

Starting with Ladson-Billings' seminal work on culturally relevant pedagogy, many educational researchers and commentators have discussed the importance of nurturing and supporting cultural competence and developing a critical consciousness about our educational system and American society (Gregory, Skiba & Noguera, 2010; Gutiérrez & Rogoff, 2003; Ladson-Billings, 1995; Villegas & Lucas, 2002). In his recent review of research about resource pedagogies, Paris (2012) offered a new stance that moves conceptually beyond culturally relevant and culturally responsive pedagogies toward culturally sustaining pedagogy. Paris' critique of cultural relevance and responsiveness is that these "do not guarantee in stance or meaning that one goal of an educational program is to maintain heritage ways and to value cultural and linguistic sharing across difference, to sustain and support bi- and multilingualism and bi- and multiculturalism" (Paris, 2012, p. 95). Paris stated explicitly:

> The term *culturally sustaining* requires that our pedagogies be more than responsive of or relevant to the cultural experiences and practices of young people—it requires that they support young people in sustaining the cultural and linguistic competence of their communities while simultaneously offering access to dominant cultural competence. Culturally sustaining pedagogy, then, has as its explicit goal supporting multilingualism and multiculturalism in practice and perspective for students and teachers. That is, culturally sustaining pedagogy seeks to perpetuate and foster—to sustain—linguistic, literate, and cultural pluralism as part of the democratic project of schooling. (p. 95)

In offering this new stance, Paris cited others who have examined cultural and linguistic practices and cautioned us not to make the link between certain cultural practices and cultural groups but rather look to how adolescents make those connections between and among cultures in the dominant society (Alim & Reyes, 2011; Irizarry, 2007; Kirkland, 2011). While these commentators have been critical of school structures in dampening cultural practices, there are instances in which school structures can alleviate the pressures on youth as they attempt to sustain their cultural practices while interacting with the dominant society. In investigating immigrant experiences in a middle school, Brinegar (2010) noted that the structure of teaming, both multiple-age and multiple-year, can enhance immigrant youths' perceptions of safety, belonging to a larger group, and developing their own voice and identity. In this chapter, we report how the structures and learning scaffolds of the iLab affect student engagement and their interaction with their own cultural identity.

CONTEXT AND PARTICIPANTS

The educational context of this study is both familiar and unusual. It is familiar because it takes place in a middle and high school in an urban setting with a diverse student population; but it is unusual in that Vermont has embraced a proficiency-based education system with flexible avenues for college and career readiness. While this policy context is not unheard of, it is new. Only 10 states, including Vermont, have comprehensive policies concerning personalized learning and flexible pathways in middle and high school (Patrick, Worthen, Frost, & Gentz, 2016). As stated previously, the Winooski School District created iLab, and the middle school version, jiLab, to address this policy context while also attempting to improve student engagement in learning.

Winooski Middle and High School is located in Winooski, Vermont; it is small in comparison to other secondary schools around the country. In the 2016–2017 academic year, the middle school, Grades 6 through 8, had 167 students, and the high school had 233 students. Of the students who attended Winooski Middle and High School, 76% were eligible for free and reduced-price lunch and 20% received learning services such as Individual Education Plans (IEPs). While 56% of students were White, the remainder represented more than 25 ethnic and cultural backgrounds—Somali, Sudanese, Nepalese, Iraqi, Afghani, and other ethnicities—of which, 42% received instruction as English language learners (ELLs). Students enrolled in the jiLab and iLab during the 2016–2017 academic year represented similar demographics.

The middle school version of iLab, named jiLab, is a course that middle school students take in Grades 6 through 8. The high school version, iLab, is an elective course that any high school student may take. In this study, we reviewed student work produced by two cohorts of students participating in jiLab and iLab. This investigation was part of a larger study that examined similar programs in two other secondary schools in Vermont. Both student cohorts at Winooski Middle and High School have experienced jiLab since the sixth grade when the school first implemented the program. The jiLab cohort consisted of 23 students who were in eighth grade and their third year of jiLab. The iLab cohort included 13 students who were in ninth grade and who had participated previously in jiLab for three years before enrolling in iLab in the high school.

MODE OF INQUIRY

While the purpose of the larger study was to investigate the implementation of personalized learning at three different secondary schools in Vermont, we felt it was important to extend the examination to Winooski Middle and High School to understand the unique cultural context of new Americans in the jiLab and iLab programs as they interacted with personalized learning. As an academic advisor, teacher, and coordinator of internships at jiLab and iLab (Andrews) and a professor in a teacher educator program at a local college (Nagle), we brought different perspectives to the study based on our own experiences. Andrews designed and currently works in the JiLab and iLab programs. Nagle brought an outsider's perspective during the investigation.

Together, we developed a theoretical framework and designed the methods for data collection. Our research design is a mix of a qualitative self-study and narrative ethnography. The project is a self-study of our work in the jiLab and iLab as it "is used in relation to teaching and researching practice in order to better understand: oneself; teaching; learning; and the development of knowledge about these" (Loughran, 2004, p. 9). We also followed the story of the jiLab and iLab as told through teachers and students over time. Interviews occurred in the 2016–2017 academic year, although the interview questions referenced work that students completed as far back as three or four years ago (See Appendix for Interview Items). In following these students, we had access to their electronic files that included all their work products saved on their Google Drive accounts for both jiLab and iLab. We interviewed all four teachers involved and eight students, four from jiLab and four from iLab, who represented specific cultural and academic characteristics from those cohorts during the 2016–2017 academic year. We also observed all students and teachers at work in the jiLab and iLab classrooms during the 2016–2017 academic year. The interviews of teachers focused on the changes made to the learning environment and academic program of jiLab and iLab since their inception, as well as how teachers conceived of their role as jiLab and iLab facilitators. We formally interviewed students during each semester during the 2016–17 academic year, first to discuss their academic, social, and family background, and then again, to delve deeply into the work that they produced during their time in the jiLab or iLab. Observations occurred monthly throughout the year and included all facets of the project progression ("Think it, Learn It, Make It, Share It"). Though we gathered data on all students in both cohorts, for the purposes of this chapter, we highlight the experiences of three eighth grade students in jiLab and three ninth grade students in iLab. We selected these students because their work files were the most complete on Google Drive.

We analyzed the data using a combination of narrative and thematic analysis. The data collected allowed us to look back in time to the first work that students created for their projects, reviewing the scaffolds that were in place at that time (see Table 8.1). While the interviews of these students and teachers occurred in the 2016–2017 academic year, the content of the interviews spanned the entire time that students participated in jiLab and iLab. In this sense, participants were involved in narrative ethnography, a method in which the interviews allow for students and teachers, with the assistance of their own work created in the past, to develop a narrative of how they see their work and learning evolve over time (Gubrium & Holstein, 2009).

Initially, as part of the larger study on student engagement and personalized learning in three alternative secondary school programs, we structured the interviews, observed classroom interactions, and reviewed student work based on preconceived themes. These preliminary themes included student engagement, scaffolds for student engagement, project topic, project

TABLE 8.1   Participant Projects and Driving Questions Over Time and by Cohort

jiLab Cohort	Projects (with driving question)		
Sang Vietnamese	San Francisco What makes San Francisco a cool city to visit?	Chinatown What are the parts of Chinatown that make it different from other neighborhoods?	Alcatraz What made Alcatraz such a hard prison to escape from?
Siara Dominican	Space What does it take to travel in space?	Cells What do cells do and how do they do it?	Autism Therapies How can people help students with Autism?
Kinaya Kenyan	Kenya What is it to live in Kenya?	Lisa Leslie What makes Lisa Leslie such a good basketball player?	Sisters in Sports How does the Sisters in Sports program help me to go to college?
iLab Cohort			
Aamino Somali	Colorism How does colorism affect my life?	Coloring as new Racism How is colorism the new racism and what can I do about it?	Racism in Criminal Justice System Why are there more black people in prison?
Alpana Nepalese	Indian War of Independence Why are there so many homeless in India?	African American History How does knowing African American history help me understand racism?	Black Lives Matter What is Black Lives Matter and how can I stop racism?
Milarepa Bhutanese	Buddhism What is Buddhism and am I a Buddhist?	Puja How can I share my Buddhist faith with friends and family?	Slavery What are the effects of slavery today?

completion, alignment with goals/proficiencies, and relationship to student interests/lives. As the study progressed, especially at Winooski Middle and High School, we followed a more conventional qualitative approach in collecting and analyzing data sources to gain a thick description of teaching and learning as it was occurring in jiLab and iLab. We collected and analyzed data on a continual basis and we used Corbin and Strauss's (2008) coding strategies to add to our preliminary coding scheme, which we refined over the course of the study. We noted the generation of themes in the data from interviews and review of student work that included the interaction of family/cultural identity and American culture. We explored these themes further by returning to the data generated by student interviews, observations of students, and student work products. Reviewing these data, we followed a selective coding process by creating broad categories developed in the analytical notes. We cross tabulated these initial categories with different sets of data to refine the categories. We used this process of developing codes and triangulating the categories with different sets of data (e.g., interviews, observations, review of Google Drive files), to establish validity and reliability among these qualitative data sets and generate the narratives (Gibbs, 2007).

FINDINGS

In this section, we discuss the findings at the program structural level and at the individual learning level. At the structural level, the jiLab and iLab programs underwent transformation over the course of the study to provide students with more flexibility in their choice of the types of topics and issues presented as well as in the way students shared these projects to the wider community. The teachers' development of structures that provided students with clear expectations and more specific and new responsibilities for the facilitators ironically resulted in more flexibility in learning. The intersection of the program's refinement over time and the experience that students generated as they matured into the new learning framework of "Think it, Learn It, Make It, Share It" may create opportunities for new Americans to examine their own cultural identity while exploring their new community.

Structure and Flexibility Affects Student Choice and Voice

In reviewing student work products over the past three to four years, we found that the structure of the jiLab and iLab programs changed dramatically as teachers realized the need for more structure around the process of the "Think it, Learn It, Make It, Share It" framework. Structure afforded students more flexibility around the type of projects they pursued and the way in which they presented their learning. Over the course of the experience, teachers, with input from students, developed a process with specific stages of project development, deadlines for work completed, and specific expectations for each stage. One iLab teacher described the process:

> Initially, we followed a more open approach to project development and allowed students to lead the process, but we didn't have specific expectations in play. Students were all over the map. So, after the first year we talked with students about their projects—successes and weaknesses—and created some non-negotiables for participation in the iLab.

The non-negotiables became the essential elements of project-based learning for the iLab and jiLab. The educators broke down each part of the "Think it, Learn It, Make It, Share It" framework into specific timeframes with deadlines based on prior student experiences. For instance, within two weeks of the start of the semester students need to complete their "Think it" stage—the stage in which they brainstorm their project ideas, create at least three learning goals, and map out an action plan that guides students toward completing the plan. Other essential components of the framework included weekly reflections and status reports detailing completion and the "next steps;" designing a "community connection" with teachers, family members, community-based experts, and/or community-based service; and a public presentation to an authentic audience with a reflection on the learning that the project afforded the student.

These non-negotiable aspects of the "Think it, Learn It, Make It, Share It" framework provided structure and flexibility for students to gain voice. One jiLab teacher described the process as a tension. They stated, "We create guardrails for our students to follow toward completing their project but still let them move in unexpected directions while working on the project. In some ways, we become these advance men—looking for opportunities for students to explore."

In one case, a student in jiLab, Siara, an eighth grader from the Dominican Republic, wanted to study autism; however, as she learned more about it she wanted to know how to support children who have autism. As part of the process, Siara's teacher acted more like a scout than a facilitator did in that her teacher found potential community members to interview. Siara, with the help of one of her teachers, selected an autism therapist to interview. Siara contacted the therapist via email and arranged to conduct an interview through Skype. During the interview, the therapist recommended that Siara contact a yoga instructor who does yoga therapy with students who have autism. Again, with the help of the teacher, Siara was able to visit the studio of the yoga therapist and learn some of the techniques used to help students with autism. In Siara's final presentation, a Google slideshow with audio voice over, she demonstrated the types of exercises that the yoga instructor taught her. Siara's case is representative of the types of structures and scaffolds that teachers put in place for students to follow through on their projects.

Developmentally Appropriate Investigations

There are some fundamental differences in the type of project and the sophistication of the project that arises among jiLab and iLab students. In one way, we can explain the primary difference through the level of social development seen in an eighth grader versus a ninth grader. Educators who do not regularly work with young adolescents between the ages 13 and 15 years of age, the age range of the participants in this study, may not think there is much of a difference in the level of social development that occurs in this three-year span. However, the literature (see Brighton, 2007) and the findings of this study show interesting changes in social development through the type of projects pursued in the jiLab versus the iLab.

Abstraction

The comparison of projects between the eighth-grade students in the jiLab and the ninth-grade students in the iLab demonstrated a continuum of abstraction in the types of topics investigated. Returning to Table 8.1, the representative student projects from the jiLab and iLab, showed a substantial change in the level of abstraction, depth of knowledge, and advocacy between eighth and ninth graders. The jiLab cohort projects, except for Siara's Autism Therapies project and Kinaya's Sisters in Sports project, were investigations that explored topics much like a traditional research report (see Table 8.1). They consisted of driving questions posed and answered through conventional resources of texts, videos, and websites; their investigations also included human sources such as interviews, surveys, or demonstrations. The driving questions of these projects as well as the description and explanations of topics were at the knowledge and comprehension levels of Bloom's (1956) taxonomy.

In the iLab projects, most students examined more abstract concepts or issues such as slavery, Buddhism, colorism, racism, and homelessness. Further, students chose such topics because in some way they wanted to take a stand. For instance, Aamino, a Somali ninth grader, chose colorism:

> ...because I am sick of people putting down dark skinned people. My goal is for people in our school to understand colorism and for comments like "Blacky" to stop. I want people to understand that colorism is a form of racism. And, if we want the Black community to be better we need to stop putting each other down.

Aamino went on to explore colorism in her native country, Somalia, through exploring its media, examining how American popular culture handles colorism in social media, and interviewing friends and family about their attitudes about colorism. After completing the project on colorism, Aamino reflected:

> The first way in getting rid of colorism is recognizing it exists which means educating people. We need more dark skin models so that dark skin girls don't grow up thinking they aren't pretty enough. Boycotting companies that sell skin bleaching creams, and most importantly educating the black community

about this issue. My hope by the end of my project is I educated some people in Winooski to understand colorism and how it can hurt.

In this narrative, Aamino is adopting a more sophisticated perspective about a topic—she is learning about the issue from multiple sources, both internationally and locally, and she is taking a stand on the issue and proposing action to address it. She is moving from Bloom's (1956) levels of knowledge and comprehension to application, analysis, and synthesis.

Scaffolding

While Aamino's involvement in her project may be attributable to her social development, the type of scaffolding that educators developed in iLab over the last number of years may have influenced it. Although jiLab and iLab pulled from the same framework, "Think it, Learn It, Make It, Share It." the way teachers' operationalized it differed. In jiLab much of the scaffolding focused on working through projects in a concrete way and usually individually. Teachers gave students a set of instructions to follow that were accessible through their Google Drives. These directions and documents provided a step-by-step guide for students to create driving questions, write a rationale for the project, set a procedure to gather resources, write a report of the evidence that answered the driving questions, and present the project to jiLab classmates. Once eighth grade students went through this process, they seemed to like the structure as long as they had choice in the topics for their projects. Most students preferred working on individual projects, though they conferred with classmates about resources and ideas for presenting their projects.

One major distinction in the "Think it, Learn It, Make It, Share It" framework between jiLab and iLab was the "Make It" step. In jiLab, teachers and students interpreted the "Make It" step as writing up information collected in the form of a research report. For students and teachers in iLab, "Make It" referred to a tangible product that was the outcome of the students' learning. Projects in jiLab were for the most part research reports that students presented using different presentation tools such as PowerPoint, Vimeo, or Google Slides. Even while Siara and Kinaya moved beyond the traditional sources for their projects on Autism Therapies and Sisters in Sports, respectively, their project products were still research report based.

In contrast, the "Make It" stage in iLab usually involved the community in some way. Milarepa became a practicing Buddhist and shared his new religion by leading a Puja with friends and family. Alpana studied the War of Independence in India to understand why there were so many homeless children when she returned to India on a family trip. While she learned about the consequences of British rule in India, her project entailed working with local Nepalese businesses to organize a charity to send money and clothes to India to help homeless children. For Aamino, learning about colorism was the beginning of a journey that ended with her joining a boycott of skin bleaching products and informing other students about colorism. These cases are representative of the types of project/advocacy of students in iLab.

We can partially explain students' movement toward more authentic and involved community projects by the developmental nature of a ninth grader versus an eighth grader; it may also be attributable to the scaffolds teachers put in place at iLab. iLab teachers do provide instructions and sample templates to walk students through projects. Starting in the 2016–2017 academic year, iLab also instituted weekly discussion sessions among the students in which they provided status reports and discussed progress and challenges to their projects and received feedback from their peers and teachers. One iLab teacher explained, "We wanted our students to see themselves as sources of information for each other, not just relying on websites, community experts or us as teachers, we wanted them to see they have important things to contribute to." To provide this opportunity, iLab teachers instituted mandatory discussion sessions at different points in the semester. They titled these sessions "This is what I want to do," "This what I am doing," and "This is what I have done." In each session, students shared their process and received feedback and ideas from the group. The final presentation culminated in a public evening presentation to members of the school, community, and families during Expo Week—JanPo for the January Exhibition and JunPo for the June Exhibition.

Iterative Process of Moving Between

Current ninth grade students in iLab moved through three years of the more structured jiLab to their first year in iLab while grappling with being a young adolescent in today's society—both globally and locally. For the new Americans profiled in this chapter, iLab and to some extent jiLab, allowed students to move between their own culture and American culture in informal and formal ways. The iLab "Think it, Learn It, Make It, Share It" framework in a personalized learning environment helped to provide students with the voice and choice about what and how they learn—allowing them to feel comfortable and acknowledged as they move between the worlds of culture, teaching and learning, and community engagement.

For instance, in her project on colorism, Aamino explored colorism in her native country—Somalia, and in her adopted country, the United States. She investigated the historical effects of colonialism, today's media, and stereotyping among the Black community as factors in attributing to colorism in her generation. This project allowed Aamino to look inward to understand her own identity and to look outward critically to understand our society's attitudes. As a prime example, she described in her written reflection how colorism appears in American popular culture:

> In 2013, when the song Poetic Justice by Kendrick Lamar and Drake came out, I was one of the girls that made their instagram bio "young east african girl." This had nothing to do with the fact that this quote was trending but everything to do with self love. Back then most of my friends were white, I straighten my hair everyday to fit into their beauty standards, and I hated admitting that I was foreign. Changing my instagram bio to "young East African girl" was a big step for me. This was when I first started accepting myself as who I really was an African girl.

As Aamino examined popular culture references and social media posts, she also interviewed Somali friends and college students to understand how colorism affected students like her emotionally and socially. Part of Aamino's revelation about herself came after interviewing a Somali college student. Aamino concluded, "Roda [college student] is one of hundreds of people that don't feel comfortable in the skin they were born in. Our society has normalized putting down dark skin people and we don't even realize that we are doing it." Aamino speaking with Roda about her discomfort with her "Blackness" until she attended college and lived with other Somali college students, allowed Aamino to acknowledge who she was as a Black person in Winooski, Vermont.

The iLab process also allowed Alpana to move between cultures in her projects and gain a critical understanding of the systemic consequences of British colonialism in India and slavery in the United States. Her first project examined homelessness in India. She recalled:

> When I was a kid, my family and I used to go see our family in India, it was a two-day trip to India from Nepal....I was on the bus looking through the window, many little kids were asking for money or food. I saw old people just sleeping on the street asking for money or food to eat.

This observation began a series of projects beginning with homelessness in India, understanding the effects of British rule in India, exploring the connection between African American history and racism, and culminating in a project investigating how she could prevent racism in her school. This latest investigation lead Alpana to propose a new project on racism in America; specifically, how the Black Lives Matter movement can affect change in America and how she can affect change in Winooski by joining the local Peace and Justice Center.

Like Aamino and Alpana, Milarepa's first project explored an issue that was close to him—his initial disinterest toward his family's religion—Buddhism. In discussing his selection of this topic, he stated:

My parents wanted me to learn about this religion my whole life. They kept wanting me to learn, but I never listen to them. They gave up trying to make me focus on our religion. But I was never interested, so I never focused on it.

In an ironic twist, he chose Buddhism as the topic for his first iLab project because "I didn't know much about this religion. It would be really nice if I got to learn more about the religion then my parents would be proud and be happy with my work." As he studied about the religion, his choice in learning about Buddhism led him to become a practicing Buddhist who leads Pujas, a Buddhism religious ceremony for his family. His interest in Buddhism also led him to examine intolerance in America, which in turn, led to his latest project on American slavery and the effects of it on today's society. In one of the mandatory discussion sessions, "This what I am doing," Milarepa and Alpana reported how they began to work together on researching the Black Lives Matter movement and how they could become part of the Peace and Justice Center to promote tolerance and restorative justice at their school.

IMPLICATIONS FOR EDUCATORS

While this qualitative study is limited in its scope and generalizability it to other middle and high school programs, teachers can explore some important insights to enhance the opportunities for new Americans to investigate their cultural identity as they participate in programs like iLab. The jiLab, and especially the iLab, allowed students to examine their identities in the context of their lived experiences, not through a perceived lens of others. In other words, these programs afforded the explicit opportunity of supporting cultural identity in the practices and perspectives of these students (Paris, 2012). While it was not the explicit purpose of iLab's "Think it, Learn It, Make It, Share It" framework to become a process for culturally sustaining pedagogy, it did lay the foundation for such learning. It gave students the opportunity to explore issues and topics that were important to them.

Recommendations for jiLab and iLab

Allowing students to examine their cultural identity is rare in a traditional secondary school setting. Even iLab educators can improve it within the iLab experience. The iLab program can be more intentional in structuring the "Think it, Learn It, Make It, Share It" process to allow students more opportunities to grapple with what it means to be a young adolescent in today's multicultural society. Based on the findings of this study, we make three recommendations. First, teachers should incorporate the mandatory discussion sessions from iLab into the jiLab experience. These sessions moved students forward on their projects and more importantly developed a sense of community and opportunities for collaboration while at the same time allowed students to see themselves as sources or funds of knowledge (Moll & Gonzalez, 1994). Also, teachers should raise the bar for presentations in the jiLab program. Just like in iLab, the final presentation culminates in a public forum to members of the school, community, and families.

Second, along with providing more opportunities for conversation and collaboration, teachers and students should develop a more robust integration of participation from community members. In each student case highlighted in this chapter, the level of student engagement in their project was greater when a community member was part of the project, either as an expert a student interviewed or as a liaison for student participation in a community-based organization. As these programs move forward in the future, development of a wider range of community organizations will become instrumental in expanding the civic participation of students in understanding who they are and who they want to be in today's society.

Third, mentorship between the jiLab and iLab learners could be used to foster greater understanding about the process and allow jiLab students to witness models of project-based learning that include an authentic community-based component. A mentoring program could also foster a more genuine community among students and ease the transition for middle school students as they move up to high school.

Recommendations for Creating Culturally Sustaining Spaces

While the "Think it, Learn It, Make It, Share It" framework is a good start for programs like jiLab and iLab, it is only a start. For teaching and learning to continue to provide more voice and choice in what and how new Americans learn, structures and spaces that allow for examination of cultural identity, exploration of issues important to students, and investigations with community members need to continue. These three types of learnings are rare in our current conventional middle and high school curricula. However, these spaces are essential for students to examine societal issues important to them while gaining the foundational skills needed to participate in our society. Personalized learning and project-based learning provide such spaces in programs like jiLab and iLab but also in individual classrooms. The essential elements for teachers interested in moving toward a more culturally sustaining pedagogy are threefold. First, create a learning environment in which teachers and students are co-learners about issues that are meaningful to students. Second, develop an inquiry-based process of learning like the "Think it, Learn It, Make It, Share It" framework. In such a framework, the role of students as learners changes—they become more engaged and responsible for their learning; the role of teachers also changes—they work as scouts and coaches to facilitate learning. Third, include the community as an active member in the learning process and as an authentic audience for the presentation of learning. These are the essential components of the "Think it, Learn It, Make It, Share It" framework that have allowed new Americans to pursue their learning in ways that honor their heritage and explore their new communities.

NOTE

1. "Immigrants are U.S. citizens and permanent residents who were born abroad to non-U.S. citizens; second-generation Americans are U.S. citizens with one or both parents born outside of the United States. Together, immigrants and second-generation Americans are 'New Americans'" (U.S. Department of Education, 2016. p. 1).

APPENDIX
Interview Items

Student Interviews

Phase 1—Academic, social, and family background
- Family background and immigration narrative
- Current friends and family
- Interests and academics over past (2–3 years)

Phase 2—Projects
- Past projects—review in Google Drive
  - Rationale, Successes/challenges, learning
- Current Project
  - Trajectory to this particular project
  - Rationale, successes/challenges, learnings
  - Collaborators—teachers, peers, community members

Teacher Interviews

Phase 1—Experience and Background
- Education and teacher experience
- Experiential trajectory to the jiLab/iLab position.
- Experience in the jiLab/iLab since start
- Current responsibilities—routines (daily, weekly, semester)
- Challenges and benefits of jiLab/iLab
- Changes in academic program of of jiLab/iLab since start
- Students and their projects–family background, academic achievement and social interests

Phase 2—Projects
- Scaffolding throughout semester—review and discuss curricular materials, calendars, Google Drive architecture
- Protocols for teacher–student, student–student, student–community member
- Successes/challenges over semester
- Changes to academic program during semester

REFERENCES

Alim, H. S., & Reyes, A. (2011). Complicating race: Articulating race across multiple social dimensions. *Discourse & Society, 22*(4), 379–384.

Bishop, P., Downes, J., & Nagle, J. (2017). How personal learning is working in Vermont. *Educational Leadership, 74*(6). [Online]. Retrieved from http://www.ascd.org/publications/educational-leadership/mar17/vol74/num06/How-Personal-Learning-Is-Working-in-Vermont.aspx

Bloom, B. (1956). *Taxonomy of educational objectives handbook 1: Cognitive domain.* White Plains, NY: Longman.

Bradford, M. (2005). Motivating students through project-based service learning. *T.H.E. Journal, 32*(6), 29–30.

Bray, B., & McClaskey, K. (2015). *Make learning personal: The what, who, wow, where, and why.* Thousand Oaks, CA: Corwin.

Brighton, K. (2007). *Coming of age: The education and development of young adolescents.* Westerville, OH: National Middle School Association.

Brinegar, K. (2010). I feel like I'm safe again: A discussion of middle grades organizational structures from the perspective of immigrant youth and their teachers. *Research in Middle Level Education Online, 33*(9), 1–14. doi: 10.1080/19404476.2010.11462072

Clarke, J. H. (2013). *Personalized learning: Student-designed pathways to high school graduation.* Thousand Oaks, CA: Corwin.

Corbin, J., & Strauss, A. (2008). *Basics of qualitative research: Techniques and procedures for developing grounded theory* (3rd ed.). Thousand Oaks, CA: SAGE.

DiMartino, J., & Clarke, J. H. (2008). *Personalizing the high school experience for each student.* Alexandria, VA: Association for Supervision and Curriculum Development.

Flexible Pathways Initiative: Dual Enrollment. Vermont Statutes Annotated Title 16, §§ 941–945.

Gibbs, G. R. (2007). *Analyzing qualitative data.* Thousand Oaks, CA: SAGE.

Gregory, A., Skiba, R. J., & Noguera, P. A. (2010). The achievement gap and the discipline gap: Two sides of the same coin? *Educational Researcher, 39*(1), 59–68.

Gubrium, J. F., & Holstein, J., A. (2009). *Analyzing narrative reality.* Thousand Oaks, CA: SAGE.

Gutiérrez, K., & Rogoff, B. (2003). Cultural ways of learning. *Educational Researcher, 35*(5), 19–25.

Irizarry, J. (2007). Ethnic and urban intersections in the classroom: Latino students, hybrid identities, and culturally responsive pedagogy. *Multicultural Perspectives, 9*(3), 21–28.

Jenkins, J. M., & Keefe, J. W. (2002). Two schools: Two approaches to personalized learning. *Phi Delta Kappan, 83*(6), 449–456.

Kirkland, D. (2011). Books like clothes: Engaging young Black men with reading. *Journal of Adolescent & Adult Literacy, 55*(3), 199–208.

Krajcik, J. S., & Shin, N. (2014). Project-based learning. In R. K. Sawyer (Ed.), *The Cambridge handbook of the learning sciences* (2nd ed., pp. 275–297). New York, NY: Cambridge University Press.

Ladson-Billings, G. (1995). Toward a theory of culturally relevant pedagogy. *American Educational Research Journal, 32*(3), 465–491.

Lam, S., Cheng, R. W., & Ma, W.Y. K. (2009). Teacher and student intrinsic motivation in Project-Based Learning. *Instructional Science: An International Journal of the Learning Sciences, 37*(6), 565–578.

Larmer, J. (2015). *Gold standard PBL: Essential project design elements.* Retrieved from https://www.pblworks.org/blog/gold-standard-pbl-essential-project-design -elements

Levine, E. (2002). *One kid at a time: Big lessons from a small school.* New York, NY: Teachers College Press.

Loughran, J. J. (2004). A history and context of self-study of teaching and teacher education practices. In J. J. Loughran, M. L. Hamilton, V. K. LaBoskey, & T. Russell (Eds.), *International handbook of self-study of teaching and teacher education practices* (pp. 7–39). Dordrecht, The Netherlands: Kluwer.

Moll, L., & Gonzalez, N. (1994). Lessons from research with language minority children. *Journal of Reading Behavior, 26*(4), 23–41.

Nagle, J., & Taylor, D. (2017). Using a personal learning framework to transform middle grades teacher practice. *Middle Grades Research Journal, 11*(1), 85–100.

Paris, D. (2012). Culturally sustaining pedagogy: A needed change in stance, terminology and practice. *Educational Researcher, 41*(3), 93–97. doi:10.3102/001318 9X12441244

Patrick, S., Worthen, M., Frost, D., & Gentz, S. (2016, May). *Promising state policies for personalized learning.* Vienna, VA: International Association for K–12 Online Learning (iNACOL). Retrieved from http://www.inacol.org/wp-content/ uploads/2016/05/iNACOL-Promising-State-Policies-for-Personalized-Learning .pdf

Taylor, D., & Nagle, J. (2015). Personal learning framework. *PLP Pathways.* U.S. Department of Education, Institute of Education Sciences, National Center for Education. Retrieved from https://sites.google.com/site/plppathways/ framework

U.S. Department of Education. (2016). *New American undergraduates enrollment trends and age at arrival of immigrant and second-generation students.* Washington, DC: Author. Retrieved from https://nces.ed.gov/pubs2017/2017414.pdf

Villegas, A. M., & Lucas, T. (2002). Preparing culturally responsive teachers: Rethinking the curriculum. *Journal of Teacher Education, 53*(1), 20–32.

CHAPTER 9

#NoDAPL

Collaboratively Designing
Culturally Responsive Curriculum

Becky Beucher
Illinois State University

Amy Smith
Illinois State University

ABSTRACT

We draw on Geneva Gay's and Paulo Freire's conceptual work related to culturally responsive liberatory pedagogy to conceptualize designing culturally responsive humanities middle school curriculum for a racially and culturally diverse group of students. The school community supports the Standing Rock Movement (represented on social media as #NoDAPL) and encourages culturally knowledgeable, globally competitive young adolescent leaders. We believe that creating culturally responsive curriculum requires curriculum designers to account for and deconstruct the systems of oppression that have constructed barriers to knowing and engaging in appropriate practices for culturally marginalized students. We begin this work by examining our own positionality in relation to systemic oppressions. Next, we explore how schol-

Equity & Cultural Responsiveness in the Middle Grades, pages 181–205
Copyright © 2019 by Information Age Publishing

arly and community resources can be leveraged to inform best practices for young adolescents in alignment with the school's mission. Finally, we consider how critical media analysis, coupled with digital storytelling, can position young adolescents as leaders adept at constructing powerful, action-oriented narratives about a current, culturally salient social justice movement.

> *Growing the intellectual and technical capacity of our tribal members,*
> *and especially our youth, is critical to building the economy of the future.*
> —Honor the Earth, 2009, p. 27

In fall 2016, members of Indigenous Tribes and allies of the Native American people travelled across the continent and around the globe to join in solidarity with the Sioux Nation at the Standing Rock Indian Reservation. The aim of this chapter is to share our initial thinking around designing culturally responsive humanities middle level curriculum (i.e., #NoDAPL curriculum) for Mní School, a school located in the Pacific Northwest that serves a racially and culturally diverse student body comprised of youth who identify as Native American, Latinx, White, of African descent, and Hmong.

The curriculum, #NoDAPL, draws its namesake from the social media hashtag specific to the Standing Rock Movement that went viral in late October 2016. In support of a long-standing resistance to the proposed building of an oil pipeline across native lands, hundreds of Native American people and non-native allies travelled from around the world to join water protectors[1] at the Standing Rock Indian Reservation. As the numbers of protectors increased, tensions mounted on the ground. Private security personnel, employed by pipeline developer Energy Transfer Partners, worked with local law enforcement often attacking water protectors and placing them under 24-hour drone surveillance. Local law enforcement arrested water protectors for trespassing and other charges and held people in dirty cages for extensive periods. Water protectors used the hashtag #NoDAPL to communicate with one another and to provide livestream photographic and written coverage with those following on social media. We use the hashtag because it represents the fundamental concepts informing both our methods curriculum—solidarity, critical representation, and digital, networked technology.

Mní School community members are invested deeply in supporting the Standing Rock Movement. According to Eagle,[2] a member of the tribe, "This topic touches on significant outcomes [that signify] disrespect of [ancestral] traditional and sacred lands. Lands and property that are recognized as sacred by Native Peoples." He continued, "...with the slightest error, the result will be devastation to water sources and rivers downstream" (interview, May 10, 2017). Several members of the Mní School community traveled to Standing Rock, and even as pipeline development began and we wrote this chapter, energized conversations continued among the Mní School community members. We wrote this curriculum in solidarity with the Standing Rock water protectors, the Mní School youth, and community members; we drew inspiration for this curriculum from the Standing Rock young adolescents who initiated this movement (Simon, 2017).

CHAPTER OVERVIEW

We begin the chapter with an introduction of how the project began, which includes a discussion of our research and curriculum design methods. Next, we discuss the alignment between the school vision and the #NoDAPL curriculum. A brief historical narrative follows this section. It captures the tensions between Eurocentric and Indigenous perspectives about education and sovereignty. This narrative underscores current calls for the purposeful integration of culturally responsive schooling in schools serving Native American students. As such, the critically conscious educator must integrate young adolescents' interests and orient them towards addressing current social dilemmas, particularly those directly affecting their lives. Next, focusing on young adolescents and culturally responsive educational practices, we continue with a brief discussion of Paulo Freire's (2000) and Geneva Gay's (2002) conceptualization of culturally responsive pedagogy. Their work underscores how forging meaningful and respectful relationships between youth, school, and community supports adolescents' academic achievement and leadership capacities.

The next section on critical media literacies and digital storytelling reflects on the role social and independent news media played in informing our concept of Standing Rock; it inspired the genesis of the #NoDAPL curriculum. In considering how young adolescents might engage Freire's (2000) problem-posing approach to reading with critical consciousness, our discussion draws on literature that recognizes a longstanding history of rampant essentialization and iconization of Native American people in mass media. We propose critical media analysis and digital storytelling as curricular avenues in which young adolescents may engage culturally relevant and critical literacies in creating their own narratives in solidarity with the Standing Rock water protection movement. Envisioning next steps in this project, we share our learning from community members in drawing from interview conversations with Eagle, Sebastian, and Kyle. Together, we collectively consider the utility of integrating critical media literacies (Kellner, 2011; Mirra, Morrell, & Filipiak, 2018; Morrell, 2012) and digital storytelling (Beucher, 2016; Hull & Katz, 2006) as a culturally responsive literacy practice with Mní middle school young adolescents. We end the chapter with a reflection on our initial research question, "What should educators consider in designing culturally responsive middle level curriculum related to Standing Rock and related events?"

CULTURALLY RESPONSIVE PRACTICE
AT THE MIDDLE LEVEL

A challenge for teachers designing culturally responsive middle level curriculum is the lack of agreement among educators about how to define culture and as well as how to teach in a culturally responsive manner. In a review of scholarly literature regarding middle school practices, Kennedy, Brinegar, Hurd, and Harrison (2016) found a need to define cultural responsiveness and effective practices for teachers to utilize with young adolescents due to the lack of recently published articles on the topic. While there are many important iterations of culturally responsive practice that address different facets of teaching with cultural awareness and critical consciousness, we look to Geneva Gay (2002) and Paulo Freire (2000) who both offered explicit planning steps to culturally responsive and liberatory curriculum design that we draw upon throughout this chapter.

Examining one's positionality is an important and necessary step in teaching in a culturally responsive manner. We identify as White, female, cisgender, able bodied, middle class, teacher educators, curriculum designers, secondary literacy education scholars, and activist education allies. Kyle,[3] the Water is Life Education Director, also identifies as able bodied, cisgender, White, and female, and works for one of the three Tribes that wrote the charter for Mní School. Kyle was our first introduction to Mní School. As family members, Kyle and Becky have been talking about Mní School since its genesis. As such, Kyle served as an initial liaison between Mní School community members and us.

As White allies working alongside Native American Tribal members, our approach to designing culturally responsive curriculum consciously accounted for the role formal education has played historically in erasing Indigenous knowledge and practices. Explaining the conditions for developing sustaining humanizing relationships through research partnerships, San Pedro and Kinloch (2017) explained, "When we ask questions and seek answers from others without consideration of our own identities, positionalities, and subjectivities, we deny the existence of multiple truths, which, we argue, materialize under specific spatial-temporal conditions" (p. 377S). Thus, to understand the values of the community with whom we work, we need to acknowledge first how our inherent values inform how we listen, ask questions, and draw conclusions. Herein, we outwardly acknowledge that our positionality as education experts directly follows from our White privilege. If we are to succeed in developing culturally responsive curriculum, we must be aware of our own cultural blind spots, lest we recreate the very systems we intend to disrupt. We must own that incomplete narratives have shaped our expertise. We intentionally describe the formal education context and process as one that must foster young adolescent thinking rather than solely teach them how, or what to think.

Continuing to under emphasize culturally responsive educational practices in teacher education programs creates normative schooling conditions where "too many teachers are inadequately prepared to teach ethnically diverse students" (Gay, 2002, p. 106). Gay (2002) asserted that teachers must acquire "explicit knowledge about cultural diversity" to "meet the needs of culturally diverse youth" (p. 106). According to Gay, a first step in culturally responsive education is "understanding the cultural characteristics and contributions of different ethnic groups" (p. 107). Culture is a complex, contested, and often misunderstood word. Determining young adolescents' cultural characteristics necessitates that educators engage the intellectual work necessary to attend to this complexity.

We understand ourselves as co-investigators in this work to define youth culture. Freire (2000) cautioned against viewing people as "objects of investigation," but rather, as "co-investigators" (p. 106). Furthermore, Gay (2002) continued by adding that "the second requirement for developing a knowledge base for culturally responsive teaching is acquiring detailed factual information about the cultural particularities of specific ethnic groups" (p. 107). The participants in the #NoDAPL curriculum design endeavor have begun to define collectively Mní School adolescent culture through conversations and scholarly research related to Native American education and young adolescent youth.

Much of the scholarship we discuss in the following sections stems from our sensitivity to the ways in which settler colonialist practices have constantly threatened Native American and Indigenous people's education sovereignty. Yet, the conversations and interviews we have had with Mní School community members, Eagle, Kyle, and Sebastian, counter deficit narratives that may follow in the wake of naming racial privilege and oppression. Sebastian, who identifies as half Indian and half Mexican, described people observing ancestral cultural practices at Standing Rock:

> An Eternal Fire burned 24 hours a day at the main campsite. People would address the elders of the hosting tribe, of North Dakota and say, "If it pleases the elders, may I speak or share this story?" and they would say "Yes," and then people would share. [There were] Native Americans [who] were still living a Native American way of life. They had the regalia and that protocol. I said, wow, it makes me want to be more Indian. This is what it was like 100–150 years ago. I was able to get a glimpse of how people were able to live off the land. What an honor to see my current ancestors. It was impactful. (interview, April 19, 2017)

Clearly, culturally responsive pedagogy must simultaneously attend to Indigenous people's power, resilience, resistance, and diversity.

MNÍ SCHOOL AND THE STANDING ROCK CURRICULUM INITIAL CONVERSATIONS

Becky held initial conversations with Mní School teacher, Frank, and Director, Jason, about the #NoDAPL curriculum. Following their enthusiastic approval of the idea, Kyle shared the proposal with Mní School Tribal board members, who also showed support and excitement about the curriculum. Kyle shared the idea with several Tribal Elders and community members, all of whom expressed approval, and offered various ideas for how they would volunteer to support middle level humanities curriculum related to educating youth about Standing Rock and its significance for the students.

We initially envisioned the project as one in which middle level students would critically analyze mainstream and social media coverage of the Standing Rock Water Protection movement using critical media literacies as a precursor to composing digital stories about those events. Ernest Morrell (2012) defined critical media literacy as the "decoding and analysis of texts produced across many genres" (p. 302). Decoding texts involves students reading for power and oppression in media narratives. We began by inviting students to examine stylistic elements of the text, which is typical of English language arts curriculum (e.g., What do you observe? What shapes do you see? What symbols do you see/recognize? Who is in the image? How are objects and people positioned in relation to one another? What colors are being used, where?). Next, we had students use analytical questioning to inquire, "Who do you think the audience is for this text? Is this image playing off a culturally or historically familiar idea (or trope?)." Finally, we invited a critical line of questioning, "Whose perspectives are represented? Whose voices are heard? Whose voices are left out? Who is the hero or heroes of this story? Who are the villains? Would you use this text to tell a story about DAPL? What might need to be modified to make it more accurate?" Critical literacies questions focus students' attention on power and inequity as the message is constructed within the text. Therefore, critical media literacies equip students with a socio-political lens that they can then bring to each media text.

As they read and interpret media, they consciously deconstruct how media utilizes cultural symbols, tropes, and signs to relay messages that empower and disempower people through promoting social and political agendas. Refining one's critical media literacies as a reader of text forms an important precursor to composing multimedia texts, like digital stories. To compose bold, powerful, and humanizing narratives about those involved in Standing Rock, students must first practice interpreting and deconstructing other's texts before bringing that same critical lens to their own work. If students miss this step, they risk reproducing inequity in their digital compositions.

However, while we can develop curriculum that would involve students in critically deconstructing theirs and others' texts using general sets of critical media analysis questions, our frames of reference for Standing Rock were shaped by and through mainstream and social media. Furthermore, we were not members of the Mní School community; we missed the opportunity to visit Standing Rock, and prior to Becky's visit in spring 2018, we did not have relationships with the students for whom we were designing the curriculum. Thus, we held significant blind spots regarding Mní School young adolescents' and community members' cultural practices and about the significance of Standing Rock for the Mní School community (which we are constantly challenged to understand as something we should refer to as significant for *all* people). Given that culturally responsive curriculum requires that the curriculum responds to students' cultural assets and knowledge, we sought out a methodological framework that would facilitate our development of a robust understanding of the students for whom we were designing this curriculum.

We looked to San Pedro and Kinloch's (2017) framework for Projects in Humanization (PiH henceforth) as a guiding framework for the research methods informing our approach to collaborative curriculum design. The bedrock for this framework involves researchers and participants who build and sustain relationships through collaborative storytelling. The scholars explained, "Theoretically and methodologically, PiH are enacted through the development of relationships, the process of listening and storying, and the dialogic engagements that occur during the telling and receiving of stories that have the potential to effect change" (San Pedro & Kinloch, 2017, p. 374S). Grounded in Indigenous research methodologies and humanizing research, PiH centers storytelling as the vehicle for building relationships and identifies these stories as the units of analysis. Furthermore, this process draws on grounded theory methods that involves ongoing and simultaneous data collection and analysis (see Charmaz, 2006). As we developed relationships with participants through dialogue and in collaborative planning, we researchers continuously reflected on how our positions and viewpoints were shifting and changing as a result of these ongoing conversations. We call attention to these shifts in thinking in this chapter.

San Pedro and Kinloch (2017) described the "storying interaction" as a sort of "dialogic spiral" where the speakers build and off one another's stories advancing toward a collective truth (p. 380S). In this way, PiH "[values] listening, knowledge co-construction, vulnerability, agency, and multiple perspectives" (Kinloch, 2015, p. 31, as cited in San Pedro & Kinloch, 2017,

p. 374S). Thus, this process invites differences of opinion and demands openness to hearing and working through these differences to reach shared understandings. Given the diversity of voices solicited for this project, we anticipated that ideological tensions might arise as we discussed the objectives, content, and orientation for the #NoDAPL curriculum. Rather than shy away from these tensions, through engaging PiH, we invited them through conversation and in opening opportunities for ongoing dialogue throughout the curriculum design process. This iterative process resulted in ongoing curriculum revision over the course of the semester.

While our hope was to spend the semester in weekly meetings with the entire group discussing the curriculum and reflecting upon our practice as we designed, distance and availability hindered this option. We lived thousands of miles away from the Mní School, and all parties involved worked demanding jobs and hours, some as community organizers, many are raising families, and some attend school themselves; thus, we were not able to speak at length as we had wished. However, we spoke with Sebastian and Eagle about curriculum design via phone interviews, and during summer 2017, we collaborated with Frank, the teacher of the #NoDAPL curriculum, about curriculum design. These collaborations continued through spring 2018. The continuation of these conversations highlights another key aspect of PiH. Over time, and through conversation, we developed and built sustained relationships that have continued even beyond the scope of this project.

Throughout the semester, we included the curriculum as a conversational point on the school board meeting agendas. In the subsequent meetings, board members expressed continued interest and excitement in the curriculum and offered to speak with us about curriculum design and community resources. Our conversations about the curriculum often included several community and board members.

Throughout this chapter, we include excerpts from the interviews that especially influenced the curriculum. This inclusion allows us to showcase the viewpoints members of the community expressed and which simultaneously reflects curricular content, as these individuals attended Frank's classes throughout the 2017–2018 school year to share stories that arose in conversation with Becky and Amy. We also discuss several points of tension, or varying viewpoints around the curriculum, that we resolved through ongoing discussion and collaborative storying. Furthermore, Kyle provided a written description of Mní School, and the following section is a modified version of her written words. As researchers committed to developing humanizing relationships:

> We listen not to extract; rather, we listen to build, develop, and share our own stories with those who have shared their stories with us. In so doing, we contextualize storying as research and knowledge production, which allows us to

forward social justice, educational equity, and positive social change through PiH. (San Pedro & Kinloch, 2017, p. 378S)

Mní School[4]

Mní School is located on historically tribal lands in a small town, Climbing Rock, located in the Northwestern region of the United States. The Water is Life Tribe, along with two other surrounding tribes opened Mní School in 2010, and as of spring 2017, served approximately 65 students across all grade levels (K–12). Mní School continues to grow in popularity, and grades often have a waitlist. In fall 2017, Mní School served 10 middle school students across 6–8 grades. Given the small class sizes at each individual grade level, teachers sometimes use multi-age grouping in class instruction. This grouping across grades aligns with culturally responsive pedagogy as students learn from peer mentors, who in turn understand their knowledge as valuable for the learning community. Specifically, through multi-age grouping, younger students learn socially relevant cultural practices and academic skills through mentorship from older classmates (Hoffman, 2002). Furthermore, multi-age grouping benefits older students reciprocally. In assuming authentic leadership positions, older students learn that their knowledge is legitimate and integral to the education of their younger peers (Brinegar, 2010).

The Mní School Vision Statement reads that all students will display good stewardship of the earth and have respect for the land, river, and all living things. The desire to deliver curriculum that places emphasis on community action projects, civil engagement, and culture has always been a central focus for Mní School stakeholders; the #NoDAPL curriculum forwards these efforts. Mní School bases their educational philosophy on long-standing cultural systems of teaching and learning that value passing intrinsic knowledge, culture, and skills intergenerationally. Traditional learning for Native adolescents involves community-wide educational systems uniquely designed to utilize every facet of learning relevant to one's life. For instance, the education of young adolescents began with grandmothers who educated children in relevant life-skills, customs, and taboos. Grandmothers guided young adolescents in successfully integrating and applying that knowledge through skills and practices that would benefit the well-being of the entire community. Depending upon gender, at puberty, the young adolescents moved to learning from tribal community experts. Much practice was involved in assisting young adolescents to hone their selected craft.

Most successful communities that work as a group so that all individuals thrive require that some of their members take on leadership roles. Mní School's founding members realized the need of the school to help develop future leaders and community organizers. Therefore, themes of Tribal governance, Tribal sovereignty, public policy, service learning, community action, and natural resource management constitute important curricular topics. Moreover, the Blended Learning Model (Ferdig, Cavanaugh, & Freidhoff, 2012) which is both problem and technology based, informs curriculum delivery at Mní School. Students have the freedom to choose different strategies and approaches to learning. Jason, the education director and Frank, the middle level teacher, viewed the #NoDAPL curriculum as a seamless fit with the Blended Learning Model. We have discussed how this curriculum can offer a generative avenue that promotes good stewardship, hard work, wise laws, and spiritual beliefs among students. Further, curriculum development will align with current curriculum goals and endeavors related to ensuring that the culture, traditions, and customs are the foundational sources for establishing curriculum. For these reason, the #NoDAPL curriculum aligns well with the Founding Members' vision for Mní School.

CULTURALLY RESPONSIVE SCHOOLING

Indigenous scholars and non-Native allies assert that cultural sovereignty is essential to political sovereignty.

—Amsterdam, 2013, p. 54

A Brief History: "Remarks Concerning the Savages of North America"

Native American people have been making a clear case for educational sovereignty as long as White people have attempted to interfere. In his 1784 report, "Remarks Concerning the Savages of North America," Benjamin Franklin reported on an exchange between the Virginia government and the Haudenosaunee[5] regarding the education of Indigenous youth. The government of Virginia established a fund to educate Native American tribal adolescents. Franklin relayed that "the Government would take Care that they should be well provided for, and instructed in all the Learning of the White People." The Six Nation, or Haudenosaunee, leadership responded in kind:

> But you who are wise must know, that different Nations have different Conceptions of Things, and you will therefore not take it amiss if our Ideas of this kind of Education happen not to be the same with yours. We are however not the less oblig'd by your kind Offer tho' we decline accepting it; and to show our grateful Sense of it, if the Gentlemen of Virginia will send us a Dozen of

their Sons, we will take great Care of their Education, instruct them in all we know, and make Men of them. (as cited in Brayboy, 2014, pp. 396–397)

While the scope of this chapter does not allow the room to discuss these events in depth, settler colonialist education programming drove sweeping efforts to eradicate Indigenous cultural knowledge systems often by forceful removal of Native American children from their homes and by placing the children in boarding schools (Piccard, 2013). Creators of these early schools designed them to "Americanize" adolescents by teaching them English and Eurocentric practices (Jewell, 1987, p. 87).

Today, Tribal communities adamantly call for culturally responsive schooling (CRS), or schooling "designed and practiced in ways that more closely match the cultures students bring with them from home" (Castagno & Brayboy, 2008, p. 946). Failure to engage CRS among Indigenous adolescents has led to "the most negative consequences for tribal communities" (Castagno & Brayboy, 2008, p. 945). CRS underscores that school leadership and teachers work with families to create porous boundaries between home and school thereby disrupting status quo notions of expert and learner.

The Critically Conscious Educator

Many political and educational plans have failed because their authors designed them according to their own person views of reality, never once taking into account the men-in-a-situation to whom their program was ostensibly directed.
—Freire, 2000, p. 94

A critically conscious educator must reject a banking concept of knowledge, which assumes that a teacher's role is to fill students with information (Freire, 2000). Kyle explained that Mní School's "educational philosophy is based on [ancestral] traditional systems of education where intrinsic knowledge, culture, and skills are passed from one generation to the next" (interview, May 11, 2017). Thus, culturally responsive education at Mní School must involve acknowledging and fostering relationships between young adolescents and their Elders.

Furthermore, young adolescents have interests that drive their activities out of school. Modern adolescents know a lot about the world beyond their local contexts, and they continuously expand their access through networked digital technology. We envision that the #NoDAPL curriculum will involve young adolescents in telling stories about Standing Rock using digital technology; students will engage critical media analysis to compare the different narratives circulating on social and news media about Standing Rock. Initially, we wondered what tensions may arise between ancestral storytelling practices and modern methods for learning and disseminating findings. Becky asked Eagle and Sebastian about these tensions.

Sebastian said that to withhold the Internet from young adolescents would be an injustice. He explained, "We can't ignore or be ignorant to technological advances. If we only stick to storytelling, we would quickly be left behind and in the dark ages. We need to pair the technology with cultural practices" (interview, April 19, 2017). Eagle shared that, rather than viewing the Internet and digital technologies as a form of "cultural sabotage," they should be viewed as avenues for "cultural preservation" (interview, May 10, 2017). Sebastian envisioned ways that young adolescents could access ancestral cultural practices through the Internet. He explained, "Now they [adolescents] can go to Indian sites and read things, not just the typical history book...they are able to stay connected. The Internet holds cultural knowledge that students can access" (interview, April 19, 2017).

The critically conscious educator must honor the dynamic ways in which young adolescents learn and culturally relevant classrooms must position youth as intellectuals capable of thinking about how to reconcile social injustices such as the building of the Dakota Access Pipeline. Gloria Ladson-Billings (2017) recently reiterated this imperative:

> [A] culturally relevant approach to teaching helps students understand that their learning can and should be connected to the everyday problems of living in a society that is deeply divided along racial, ethnic, linguistic, economic, environmental, social, political, and cultural lines. Students should be learning that education can and should alleviate problems and divisions. (21:00)

We recognize that young adolescents have historically and are presently leading social movements in which they are actively working to counter oppressive practices and policies. Strategic alignment between school and youth community activism can lead to generative academic and activist gains for youth (see Ginwright, Noguera, & Cammarota, 2006).

MIDDLE LEVEL CULTURALLY RESPONSIVE EDUCATION

Every Indigenous group has its own conceptualization for relating to one another based on the fundamental notion of respect.
—Shirley, 2017, p. 174

Relationships and Community Engagement

Every fall, millions of young adolescents walk into classrooms across the United States. Here, they develop ideas and beliefs about the person they are becoming. As Fine, Burns, Payne, and Torre (2004) noted, schools are ". . . intimate places where youths construct identities, build a sense of self, read how society views them, [and] develop the capacity to sustain relations and forge the skills to initiate change" (p. 2198). Middle schools are in the unique position to create connections that promote fulfillment during this time of social, cognitive, and physical changes (Ellerbrock & Kiefer, 2014) and can offer students a sense of belonging when they experience academic success (Covarrubias & Fryberg, 2015). *This We Believe: Keys to Educating Young Adolescents* (National Middle School Association, 2010) highlighted 16 components of schools that are responsive to the unique needs of middle school students. Culturally responsive pedagogy builds on successful relationships; therefore, we focus on the three components related to relationship building. First, educators must understand the needs of middle school young adolescents. Second, all members of a classroom benefit from collaborative, engaged, active, and purposeful learning. Third, school structures should foster positive relationships among in-school stakeholders and the out-of-school community.

When thinking about how middle schools relate to Native American adolescents, one must take into consideration that Indigenous families experience even more challenges within schools. These families must cope with decades of racial discrimination in the school system that utilized "residential schooling and assimilative practices that aimed to eliminate their culture" (Milne, 2016, p. 274) and has continued to enforce the knowledge and experiences of the White, middle class population. As Hare and Pidgeon (2011) wrote, "Indigenous youth struggle to find relevance in classrooms that make little or no efforts to represent their histories, values, perspectives, and worldviews" (p. 96). Therefore, teacher's pedagogical practices and dispositions, and school-community relationships need to shift in order to improve academic success for Native American adolescents (Brayboy & Castagno, 2009).

Critically Conscious Pedagogy

It is crucial that young adolescents experience an environment that nourishes their thoughts, allows voice, and promotes critical thinking. This critically conscious position rejects the "banking" method of education (Freire, 2000) where teachers assume to deposit knowledge into students whom they see as empty vessels. This predominant method of education reflects colonial assimilationist practices by valuing Eurocentric knowledge systems and devaluing adolescents' interests. Freire (2000) explained how banking is detrimental to efforts to support students viewing of the world in complex ways. For Freire, teacher-centered banking method suppresses students' creativity and critical consciousness; he explained, "The more students work at storing the deposits entrusted to them, the less they develop the critical consciousness which would result from their intervention of the world as a transformer of the world" (p. 54). Price and Menke (2013) explained, "When students become producers of knowledge and active transformers of society, they no longer become sedentary acceptors of dominant ideologies through the banking method" (p. 92). Thus, critical consciousness liberates young adolescents from being passive recipients of information. When educators incorporate the realities and perspectives of young adolescents within education, the collective empowerment of minoritized populations occurs (Ladson-Billings, 1995).

School systems must know their community in order to offer a learning environment that will honor young adolescents' tribal customs and beliefs that offer "American Indian students a sense of pride in their education" (Hudiberg, Mascher, Sagehorn, & Stidham, 2015, p. 138). As Gay (2010) wrote, "Using the culture and experiences of Native Americans.... facilitates their school success" (p. 15). This will assist in the production of young adolescents who are academically prepared, active within their communities, and knowledgeable about Native American contributions to society (Brayboy & Castagno, 2009). Critical consciousness as an organizing pedagogy is respective of youth by positioning them as intellectuals. The curriculum that we are designing intends to have students learn from community elders and members who visited Standing Rock and have knowledge of the cultural and ancestral practices that will acknowledge students' histories, perspectives, and viewpoints.

#NoDAPL: MEDIA COVERAGE AND CRITICAL STORYTELLING

Current media representations of American Indians are understandable only if seen as the legacy of a complex mesh of cultural elements, including formal history, literature, material artifacts, folklore, photography, cartoons, art, mass media, and anthropological discourse.

—Bird, 1999, p. 62

Representation and Media

Since September 2016, we have been following the #NoDAPL protection movement coverage on social media, namely Facebook. We have archived hundreds of static and video images composed by people on the ground covering the events unfolding at Standing Rock as well as news coverage disseminated on Facebook. We have diligently watched the on the ground coverage by nonprofit news outlet, Democracy Now! and have read and archived mainstream online news articles (e.g., CNN, Washington Post). Given the salience of social media and digital media in young adolescents' lives (Ito et al., 2010), as teacher educators and critical literacy scholars, we have spent a lot of time contemplating the importance of designing curriculum to support youth in critically navigating multimedia narratives circulating online.

Facebook is the most popular social media platform among adolescents (Lenhart, 2015). The Education Director, Jason, shared that most of the Mní School students use Facebook, some use Snapchat and Instagram, and students spend half of their days on computerized programs learning individualized curriculum; the students are immersed in digital technology. Over the months of following social media and news media coverage of the #NoDAPL movement, we wondered what conversations were happening at Mní among the students about the Standing Rock narrative and how media informed their thinking.

In February, Kyle sent us an email in which she reported the following:

> Gina, the school secretary, said the kids saw a short clip of the DAPL protest and got all excited when they saw the flags from the local Tribes flying. The clip was only a few seconds long so not too much exposure. (email, February, 28, 2017)

The students were celebrating their representation on the ground at Standing Rock. They were proud. This made us wonder how often images of Tribal flags were appearing in media coverage of Standing Rock and what themes one might discover through analysis. Given the profound influence media has on shaping people's beliefs and opinions about themselves and the world, culturally responsive teaching must include young adolescents engaged in critical media literacies.

Critical Media Literacies

Critical media literacies, as previously discussed, involves "decoding and analysis of texts produced across many genres" (Morrell, 2012, p. 302). When students engage this process of critically deconstructing text they are reading for power to challenge inequitable social structures and counter oppressive systems (Freire, 2000). In the #NoDAPL curriculum project, critical media literacies involves youth deconstructing the multimodal media narratives arising from social and news media coverage of the Standing Rock Water Protection Movement. Through close examination of the images, printed words and videos, students will ask questions like, "Whose interests does the media represent? Whose interests does the media neglect? How does the media depict people? What values does the media express? They would use these words to draw informed conclusions about media representations of people and events. The critical analysis of media narratives allows students to bring this same lens to their own media productions which decreases the risk of them reproducing stereotypes in their own media composition. Given the proliferation of misrepresentational imagery, reinforcing critical deconstruction of others' texts serves to reinforce the practice for student authors who can then apply this same approach to their own work.

Unfortunately, mainstream and entertainment media have little to offer Native American people in terms of respectful or dynamic forms of representation (Elliott, 1998; King, 2014; Leavitt, Covarrubias, Perez, & Fryberg, 2015). Lamenting the anachronistic iconization of a romanticized past, Elliott (1998) argued, "...Indians are the only minority group that the Indian lovers won't let out of the 19th century." Elliott continued, "They love Indians as long as they can picture them riding around on ponies wearing their beads and feathers, living in picturesque tipi villages and making long profound speeches" (Elliott, 1998, p. 14). We can trace offensive, homogenizing, essentializing representations of Native American people back to the earliest film and still image capture technologies (Deloria, 1998), people still dress as so-called Indians at Halloween, and *A People's History of the United States* (Zinn, 2003) that offers a more historically accurate narrative of European colonization, continues to be a censored book.

Sebastian shared the importance of youth reading the Standing Rock media coverage with *critical consciousness*. In our interview, one of Sebastian's comments about the diversity of Indian culture reflected at Standing Rock triggered my recollection of the lack of that representation reflected in much of the media imagery we had been archiving.

Becky: This makes me think about the media representation of Native American people pictured at Standing Rock. I remember seeing a mainstream news outlet article, I think CNN, there was this image of a dark-skinned male who was shirtless and had flowing long black hair, a headdress of feathers, and he was riding a horse, and I remember thinking about how this image, however benevolently conceived, reflected a stereotype.

Sebastian: Yes, relating back to that time; these are the savages who lived back then and when the English colonies expanded, this image of the male, with the long hair, on a horse is representative of the savages who were overcome. I wouldn't be surprised if it was meant in a positive light. The message ends up being, these are the savages opposing the pipeline, seems to be the message here, whether intentional or not.

Coupling storytelling with critical media analysis in a culturally responsive curriculum offers students' opportunities to compose affirming, culturally grounded, counter narratives.

Storytelling

The oral traditions and storytelling central to many tribal communities can and should serve as foundations for the written and text-based literacies required by and developed within schools.

—Brayboy & Castagno, 2009, p. 43

In the time leading up to our interviews with community members, we worked to educate ourselves on Indigenous forms of storytelling. We began to understand that documented examples of Indigenous storytelling are complex and, in many ways, radically different from dominant school storytelling practices. For instance, Stanton and Sutton (2012) argued, "Traditional storytelling promotes an interaction between the teller and the hearer" (p. 78). This form of storytelling differs significantly from school writing where teachers expect student authors to imagine their various audiences and are subsequently evaluated on their abilities to write for teacher-defined audiences. Advocating for the blending of ancestral and modern storytelling practices, Brayboy and Castagno (2009) wrote, "The oral traditions and storytelling central to many tribal communities can and should serve as foundations for the written and text-based literacies required by and developed within schools" (p. 43).

We often reached out to Kyle to discuss what we were learning and to express the noticeable gaps in our own knowledge about the Native American cultural practices. We had been reading ethnographies, scholarly studies, compiled readers, and online Native American news publications with the goal of trying to learn about the significance of water for the Water is Life Tribe. In emailing and speaking on the phone with Kyle, Becky expressed her discomfort in using this "scholarly" approach to determining reasons for Indigenous people's investments in protecting Standing Rock's natural elements. Kyle always turns to Tribal Members to learn. She responded with this email:

> Eagle just offered, if you like this idea, to tell the kids (not read but tell) the creation story and then sing the water song. He will use his deer toe rattle or clapper stick while singing. His voice is beautiful. (email communication, March 2, 2017)

Over the past several months, countless others who went to Standing Rock offered to share their experiences and photographs with Mni School young adolescents. We teachers often lament the challenges of getting young adolescents' guardians to show up for school activities; these examples illustrate the fluid ways in which relationship building may occur when schooling aligns with community interests.

Critical Digital Storytelling

Growing the intellectual and technical capacity of our tribal members, and especially our youth, is critical to building the economy of the future.

—Honor the Earth, 2009, p. 27

Digital storytelling is a form of multimodal composition wherein authors compose narratives with music, pictures, voice, written words, colors, styles, video, and movement. Middle school adolescents have used digital storytelling to teach their school community about themselves and their interests (Vasudevan, Shultz, & Bateman, 2010) and to engage professional journalistic literacies through composing news coverage media clips (Ranker, 2008). With regard to working with Native American students specifically, Iseke and Moore (2011) argued that digital storytelling "provides opportunities for Indigenous peoples to control the images and structures through self-representations that challenge the taken-for-granted and stereotypical representations along with the misrepresentations of Indigenous peoples in dominant society" (Iseke & Moore, 2011, p. 21). We envision the #NoDAPL curriculum involving young adolescents in critically composing digital stories with media imagery that they collect as they learn about social, news, and community constructed narratives about Standing Rock and related cultural events and stories.

With a heightened sensitivity to White America's penchant for appropriating and stereotyping Native American culture, we cautiously wondered how integrating digital technology into a culturally responsive curriculum might inadvertently perpetuate the systemic erasure of Native American people's diverse cultural practices. Becky spoke to Sebastian and Eagle about our concerns with integrating digital storytelling as a modern storytelling practice in a culturally responsive curriculum. We hoped that they could enlighten us to any tensions curriculum designers should be aware of when engaging young adolescents in storytelling. Yet, despite our reservations, both Sebastian and Eagle underscored the importance of integrating digital tools and technologies in school curriculum. Sebastian reflected:

Unfortunately, we have lost a lot of our Native traditions, including storytelling. In a community a few hours from here, where I used to live, there were more traditional practices, or at least people were trying to uphold traditional practices to start meetings by opening with a Native dance and prayer. But, a lot of that has slipped away and has not been passed along as it could have and should have been. There are very few native language speakers. Tying things together with YouTube and Vimeo, could encourage and spark action. Maybe we have story time and hold the story stick, and we talk, and then we can watch a video, and still have a storytelling session. It would be a modern day passing of traditions, at least acknowledging the traditional ways. It is okay to use technology and share the way that we are. This is where we are as a society. (interview, April 19, 2017)

Eagle explained, "I used the program Hyper-Studio in my classroom of third and fourth graders. I see "tensions" [as] being a lack of understanding modern techniques and a feeling of "cultural sabotage" rather than a way of cultural preservation" (interview, May 10, 2017).

Eagle and Sebastian's responses to our questions, "What should educators be aware of when having students tell stories with digital technology? How might this approach to storytelling conflict with traditional storytelling practices? Do you see a way for these tensions to be resolved?" enlightened us to our ignorance about Native American adolescents' literacy practices. Eagle pointed out that our assumption of asking about tensions implied that tensions existed. Rather, both Sebastian and Eagle underscored the imperative that educators integrate digital technologies into classroom practices to preserve and develop current Native American cultural practices, as well as to teach young adolescents about ancestral cultural practices that they may have little daily interaction with.

Before speaking with Sebastian and Eagle, we had not considered that a rich archive of diverse Native American cultural practices exists on networked, digital media platforms like YouTube and Vimeo. Clearly, leveraging the knowledge of community members like Sebastian and Eagle is integral to supporting educators in identifying cultural practices and resources for students to draw from when composing their digital narratives. Herein, we argue that coupling critical analysis with community identified culturally relevant texts positions young adolescents to participate in and shape cultural discourses through composing powerful digital narratives about issues that matter to them and to their communities.

WALKING THROUGH THE UNKNOWN IN SOLIDARITY

Celebrating the powerful beauty and hope harnessed through solidarity, Sebastian reflected on the significance of Standing Rock, "Whether this is recognized or not, this is an awakening. I believe we have just awoke [sic] a native giant; it is something larger" (Sebastian, April 19, 2017). We write this chapter on the heels of an especially contentious presidential election.

Shortly after taking office, President Trump signed an executive order to advance the building of the Dakota Access Pipeline along with the Keystone XL pipeline, thereby signaling the new administration's dismissal of Native American sovereignty regarding treaty granted land rights. As intergenerational cohorts of Native American people and their allies continue fighting for water and land rights, we believe that Sebastian's words should inspire educators to join us in inquiring, "What should educators consider in designing culturally responsive middle level curriculum related to Standing Rock and related events?"

Directing young adolescents' attention to the events, coverage, and community participation surrounding the Standing Rock water protection movement is our effort to recognize this historical moment in time, but also capitalize on the significance of what this means for student leadership. Such an approach begins through engaging the work of Paulo Freire, Geneva Gay, and others (see Kennedy, Brinegar, Hurd, & Harrison, 2016; Kirkland, 2013; Lankshear & Knobel, 2011) who have long decried the imperative for teaching culturally responsive and critical pedagogy in schools. Cultivating youth leadership begins with an understanding that youth and community members are intellectuals worthy of informing school curriculum. Educators can use culturally responsive pedagogy that values students' intellectualism for transformative social impact (Ladson-Billings, 2017).

Hence, rejecting a banking concept of education in order to engage culturally responsive practice requires that educators step into the space of unknowing with their students. This move is imperative for the learning community to learn collectively something new about one another and about how to work, walk, learn, and design in solidarity. Once we educators envision ourselves working in communion with others invested in education, we can relinquish a sense of responsibility for solving all the problems, and perhaps more importantly, realize that we cannot do this work in isolation.

In this regard, we encourage educators to work in collaboration with local community members, organizations, and active parents and guardians to design critical activist scholarship among young adolescents. Unlike the traditional banking concept of education that positions community members and students as only having something to learn from academics, collaborative co-design conceptualizes everyone as possessing knowledge imperative to the learning context. Local community members play an imperative role in supporting the design of curriculum that is responsive to the unique positioning of Native American adolescents. Such insight can ensure that students customs and beliefs are honored thereby fostering a sense of pride for youth, which is an important aspect for student success (Gay, 2010).

In preparation for this collaborative work, we advise educators to follow our process of using a critical framework to educate oneself about how the communities one works with have historically experienced schooling and how formal schooling has responded to the communities' cultural norms. This knowledge can ready one for understanding the tensions between formal schooling and culturally salient ways of knowing the world.

Finally, educators must maintain a complex view of culture that recognizes the diversity among people sharing identity group affiliations (see Gutierrez & Johnson, 2017). Consequently, educators should expect collaborative conversations to be messy and at times humbling. In reflecting on our early conversations with Sebastian and Eagle specifically, we realized how our White-gaze had skewed our assumptions about the water protectors' motivations, as well as what community members believed the middle level culturally responsive curriculum should include. Each conversation we have with Mní School community members, board members, school administration and teachers further challenges our thinking and deepens our understanding of the resonant and diverse cultural value systems reflected in the words of our interviewees. These varied responses serve as important reminders that culture, while shared, certainly not uniformly, reflect a homogeneous set of beliefs and values. An openness to learning from one's students and those students' school community members must always keep an open and flexible mind to the complexities that all humans possess. We also humbly realized that once we started asking questions, those questions were met with more questions than answers. We view designing collaborative culturally responsive activist curriculum as the start of a generative learning relationship that forms the basis for dialogue and collaborative learning. Change, after all, requires a willingness to step into the unknown and keep walking.

NOTES

1. Water Protector is the chosen name of the Native American people and allies who protested the building of the Dakota Access Pipeline. The focus of the allied group is to protect the water from pollution and contamination related to the pipeline construction and operations. The mantra for the movement is, Water is Life.
2. Names are pseudonyms depending on author preference, but we changed full names and locations to protect anonymity.
3. All names used are pseudonyms to protect participant anonymity. In solidarity with Standing Rock, the water protection movement inspired the pseudonyms.
4. This section is co-authored with Kyle (pseudonym). We made collective decision to not include Kyle as third author on this manuscript because her given name directly links via a Google search engine search to her place of work.

Including her name on the paper would jeopardize the anonymity of the other people involved on this project.

5. "The Iroquois… Haudenosaunee are a historically powerful northeast Native American confederacy" (Iroquois).

ACKNOWLEDGMENT

We graciously thank all members of the Mní School community who contributed to this project. We also thank the editors of this volume, Dr. Kathleen Brinegar, Dr. Lisa Harrison, and Dr. Ellis Hurd, for their editing suggestions and feedback on this chapter, and we thank Joe Durling for his careful edits on our final revisions.

REFERENCES

Amsterdam, L. (2013). All the eagles and the ravens in the house say yeah: (Ab) original hip-hop, heritage, and love. *American Indian Culture and Research Journal, 37*(2), 53–72.

Beucher, R. K. (2016). Speaking through digital storytelling: A case study of agency and the politics of identity formation in school. In S. Green, K. Burke, & M. McKenna (Eds.), *Youth voices, public spaces, and civic engagement* (pp. 62–79). New York, NY: Routledge.

Bird, S. E. (1999). Gendered construction of the American Indian in popular media. *Journal of Communication, 49*(3), 61–83.

Brayboy, B. (2014). Culture, place, and power: Engaging the histories and possibilities of American Indian education. *History of Education Quarterly, 54*(3), 395–402.

Brayboy, B., & Castagno, A. (2009). Self-determination through self-education: Culturally responsive schooling for Indigenous students in the USA. *Teaching Education, 22*(1), 31–53.

Brinegar, K. (2010). I feel like I'm safe again: A discussion of middle grades organizational structures from the perspective of immigrant youth and their teachers. *Research in Middle Level Education Online, 33*(9), 1–14.

Castagno, A., & Brayboy, B. (2008). Culturally responsive schooling for Indigenous youth: A review of the literature. *Review of Educational Research, 78*(4), 941–993.

Charmaz, K. (2006). *Constructing grounded theory: A practical guide through qualitative analysis.* Thousand Oaks, CA: SAGE.

Covarrubias, R., & Fryberg, S. (2015). The impact of self-relevant representations on school belonging for Native American Students. *Cultural Diversity and Ethnic Minority Psychology, 21*(1), 10–18.

Deloria, P. (1998). *Playing Indian.* New Haven, CT: Yale Historical Publications.

Ellerbrock, C., & Kiefer, S. (2014). Fostering an adolescent-centered community responsive to student needs: Lessons learned and suggestions for middle level educators. *The Clearing House, 87*(6), 229–235.

Elliott, J. (1998). America to Indians: Stay in the 19th century In B. Bigelow & B. Peterson (Eds.), *Rethinking Columbus: The next 500 years. Resources for teaching about the impact of the arrival of Columbus in the Americas* (2nd ed., pp. 14–15). Milwaukee, WI; Rethinking Schools.

Ferdig, R., Cavanaugh, C., & Freidhoff, J. (2012). *Lessons learned from blended programs: Experiences and recommendations from the field*. Vienna, VA: iNACOL.

Fine, M., Burns, A., Payne, Y., & Torre, M. E. (2004). Civics lessons: The color and class of betrayal. *Teachers College Record, 106*(11), 2193–2223.

Freire, P. (2000). *Pedagogy of the oppressed*. New York, NY: Continuum.

Gay, G. (2002). Preparing for culturally responsive teaching. *Journal of Teaching Education, 53*(2), 106–116.

Gay, G. (2010). *Culturally responsive teaching: Theory, research, and practice*. New York, NY: Teachers College Press.

Ginwright, S., Noguera, P., & Cammarota, J. (Eds.). (2006). *Beyond resistance: Youth activism and community change*. New York, NY: Routledge.

Gutierrez, K., & Johnson, P. (2017). Understanding identity sampling and cultural repertoires: Advancing a historicizing and syncretic system of teaching and learning in justice pedagogies. In D. Paris & S. Alim (Eds.), *Culturally sustaining pedagogies* (pp. 247–260). New York, NY: Teachers College Press.

Hare, J., & Pidgeon, M. (2011). The way of the warrior: Indigenous youth navigating the challenges of schooling. *Canadian Journal of Education, 34*(2), 93–111.

Hoffman, J. (2002). Flexible grouping strategies in the multiage classroom. *Theory Into Practice, 41*(1), 47–52.

Honor the Earth. (2009). *Sustainable tribal economies: A guide to restoring energy and food sovereignty in Native America*. Retrieved from http://d3n8a8pro7vhmx .cloudfront.net/themes/524d95ff9670a41eab000002/attachments/original/ 1388422349/Sustainable_Tribal_Economies_HTE.pdf?1388422349

Hudiberg, M., Mascher, E., Sagehorn, A., & Stidham, J. (2015). Moving toward a culturally competent model of education: Preliminary results of a study of culturally responsive teaching in an American Indian Community. *School Libraries Worldwide, 21*(1), 137–148.

Hull, G., & Katz, M. (2006). Crafting an agentive self: Case studies of digital storytelling. *Research in the Teaching of English, 41*(1), 43–81.

Iroquois. (n.d.). In *Wikipedia*. Retrieved from https://en.wikipedia.org/wiki/Iroquois

Iseke, J., & Moore, S. (2011). Community-based Indigenous digital storytelling with elders and youth. *American Indian Culture and Research Journal, 35*(4), 19–38.

Ito, M., Baumer, S., Bittanti, M., Boyd, D., Cody, R., Herr-Stephenson, B. H.,... Tripp, L. (2010). *Hanging out, messing around, and geeking out: Kids living and learning with new media*. Cambridge, MA: MIT press.

Jewell, D. P. (1987). *Indians of the Feather River: Tales and legends of the Concow Maidu of California*. Menlo Park, CA: Ballena Press.

Kellner, D. (2011). Cultural studies, multiculturalism, and media culture. In G. Dines & J. Humez (Eds.), *Gender, race, and class in media: A critical reader* (pp. 7–18). Thousand Oaks, CA: SAGE.

Kennedy, B., Brinegar, K., Hurd, E., & Harrison, L. (2016). Synthesizing middle grades research on cultural responsiveness: The importance of a shared conceptual framework. *Middle Grades Review, 2*(3), 1–19.

King, J. (2014). Change or no change: Native American representations of race in Disney. *Film Matters, 5*(2), 58–61.

Kinloch, V. (2015). Critically conscious teaching and instructional leadership as Projects in Humanization. *Education Review 4*(3), 29–35.

Kinloch, V., & San Pedro, T. (2014). The space between listening and story-ing: Foundations for projects in humanization. In D. Paris & M. Winn (Eds.), *Humanizing research: Decolonizing qualitative inquiry with youth and communities* (pp. 21–42). Thousand Oaks, CA: SAGE.

Kirkland, D. E. (2013). *A search past silence: The literacy of young Black men.* New York, NY: Teachers College Press.

Ladson-Billings, G. (1995). But that's just good teaching: The case for culturally relevant pedagogy. *Theory Into Practice, 34*(3), 159–165.

Ladson-Billings, G. (2017, April 5). *Hip hop, hip hope: Reinventing culturally relevant pedagogy* [Video file]. Retrieved from https://www.youtube.com/watch?v=oj4z6AQj9zA&t=1338s

Lankshear, C., & Knobel, M. (2011). *Literacies: Social, cultural and historical perspectives.* New York, NY: Peter Lang.

Leavitt, P., Covarrubias, R., Perez, Y., & Fryberg, S. (2015). Frozen in time: The impact of Native American media representations on identity and self-understanding. *Journal of Social Issues, 71*(1), 39–53.

Lenhart, A. (2015, April 9). *Teens, social media & technology overview 2015.* Retrieved from http://www.pewinternet.org/2015/04/09/teens-social-media-technology-2015/

Milne, E. (2016). I have the worst fear of teachers: Moments of inclusion and exclusion in family/school relationships among Indigenous families in Southern Ontario. *Canadian Review of Sociology, 53*(3), 270–289.

Mirra, N., Morrell, E., & Filipiak, D. (2018). From digital consumption to digital invention: Toward a new critical theory and practice of multiliteracies. *Theory Into Practice, 57*(1), 12–19.

Morrell, E. (2012). 21st-Century literacies, critical media pedagogies, and language arts. *Reading Teacher, 66*(4), 300–302.

National Middle School Association. (2010). *This we believe: Keys to educating young adolescents.* Westerville, OH: Author.

Piccard, A. (2013). Death by boarding school: The last acceptable racism and the United States genocide of Native Americans. *Gonzaga Law Review, 49*, 137–185.

Price, P., & Menke, P. (2013). Critical pedagogy and praxis with Native American youth: Cultivating change through participatory action research. *Educational Foundations, 27*(3), 85–103.

Ranker, J. (2008). Composing across multiple media: A case study of digital video production in a fifth grade classroom. *Written Communication, 25*(2), 196–234.

San Pedro, T., & Kinloch, V. (2017). Toward projects in humanization: Research on co-creating and sustaining dialogic relationships. *American Educational Research Journal, 54*(1S), 373S–394S.

Shirley, V. J. (2017). Indigenous social justice pedagogy: Teaching into the risks and cultivating the heart. *Critical Questions in Education, 8*(2), 163–177.

Simon, E. (2017, February 25). *Meet the youths at the heart of the Standing Rock protests against the Dakota Access pipeline.* Retrieved from http://abcnews.go.com/US/meet-youth-heart-standing-rock-protests-dakota-access/story?id=45719115

Stanton, C., & Sutton, K. (2012). I guess I do know a good story: Re-envisioning writing process with Native American students and communities. *The English Journal, 102*(2), 78–84.

Vasudevan, L., Schultz, K., & Bateman, J. (2010). Rethinking composing in a digital age: Authoring literate identities through multimodal storytelling. *Written Communication, 27*(4), 442–468.

Zinn, H. (2003). *A people's history of the United States: 1492-present.* New York, NY: Collins.

CHAPTER 10

MIDDLE LEVEL ADMINISTRATORS' PERSPECTIVES ON DISCIPLINARY CONSEQUENCES ASSIGNED TO AFRICAN AMERICAN FEMALE STUDENTS

Kriss Y. Kemp-Graham
Texas A&M University–Commerce

ABSTRACT

Nationwide, African American girls have the highest suspension rates among all racial and ethnic groups and are the most severely and disproportionately affected by school discipline policies and practices when compared to other girls (Smith & Harper, 2015). Despite these alarming statistics, limited empirical research exists to explain this phenomenon (Crenshaw, Ocen, & Nanda, 2015). Unfortunately, empirical researchers often leave out African American

Equity & Cultural Responsiveness in the Middle Grades, pages 207–238
Copyright © 2019 by Information Age Publishing
207

girls when they consider factors of race and gender, and they rarely capture and report the narratives and experiences of being African American and female, more directly, being "pushed out" of schools as compared to African American males (Blake, Butler, Lewis, & Darensbourg, 2011; George, 2015; M. Morris, 2012, 2016; Rollock, 2007; Wun, 2015). This chapter provides insight beyond the "discipline data" to tell the narratives of three middle school leaders curiously juxtaposed between working with adolescent African American girls and enforcing school discipline policies. It explores mitigating factors that may account for the disproportionality experienced by African American girls and school discipline from the perspectives of three African American male middle school leaders.

U.S. public school students lose approximately 18 million days of instruction in one year due to exclusionary discipline (Losen, Hodson, Keith, Morrison, & Belway, 2015). Nationally, 2.8 million students receive one or more out of school suspensions, including 1.2 million African American students (Smith & Harper, 2015; U.S. Department of Education Office for Civil Rights, 2016). African American students are 3.8 times more likely to receive an out of school suspension when compared to their White peers (U.S. Department of Education Office for Civil Rights, 2016). Moreover, African American girls represent 8% of enrolled students, but 13% of all out of school suspensions (U.S. Department of Education Office for Civil Rights, 2016). Often overlooked is the fact that African American girls have the highest suspension rates among all racial and ethnic groups and are the most severely and disproportionately affected by school discipline policies and practices when compared to other girls (Crenshaw, Ocen, & Nanda, 2015; Morris, 2014; Smith & Harper, 2015; U.S. Department of Education Office for Civil Rights, 2014, 2016).

Researchers who have highlighted the racial and gender disparities in discipline suggest that there is a relationship in how society views African American girls and the negative perceptions of them that teachers and school leaders hold (Archer-Banks & Behar-Horenstein, 2012; Farinde & Allen, 2013). For instance, society often stereotypes African American female students as sassy, hostile, angry (Cooper, 2015; Evans-Winters & Esposito, 2010; Morris, 2007), "loud, ghetto, aggressive, ratchet, confrontational, and unlady-like" (George, 2015, p. 101). Research suggests that these perceptions and biases may impact decision making in terms of the assignment of disciplinary consequences to African American girls by school leaders (Murphy, Acosta, & Kennedy-Lewis, 2013).

Compared to elementary and high school students, it is during the middle grades when schools suspend students the most (Arcia, 2007; Raffaele-Mendez, 2003). Suspensions during middle school may have long-term repercussions for students. Balfanz (2009) presented compelling evidence that communities can identify approximately 75% of students destined to drop out of school before they enter high school, particularly in high poverty neighborhoods. Spaulding et al. (2010) established a convincing case that student behaviors that result in disciplinary action during middle school are due to inappropriate behaviors directed at school personnel such as defiance and disruption when compared to high school, which are more tardiness and truancy related.

Middle school can be a challenging time for young adolescents, their parents, and their teachers. Correspondingly, the empirical research has identified the transition from elementary school to the middle school, with added freedoms and responsibilities, such as adjusting to multiple sets of behavioral and classroom rules, pressures to meet new academic demands, and making new friends as possible sources of stress for young adolescent students (Theriot & Dupper, 2010). Researchers have connected the transition to middle school with negative academic outcomes and declines in student motivation and attitudes towards school (Eccles et al., 1993; Elias, 2002; Parker, 2009; Theriot & Dupper, 2010). While boys and girls experience this transition differently, negative social and academic outcomes exist for both genders when transitioning is not successful. Boys tend to experience higher drops in academic achievement than girls do (Clark, Flower, Walton, & Oakley, 2008), and girls tend to experience higher levels of stress, low self-concept, and depression than boys do (Carter, Clark, Cushing, & Kennedy, 2005).

In addition to gender, research informs us that minority students may experience higher levels of difficulty in transitioning than their non-minority peers, particularly in urban school districts (Akos, Lineberry, & Queen, 2015; Bailey, Giles, & Rogers, 2015). Coupled with adjusting to new school structures and expectations, minority students must also contend with the social pressures of racism, discrimination, stereotypes, and prejudice (Gutman & Midgley, 2000).

Despite the grave disproportionality in the assignment of disciplinary consequences to African American girls when compared to their similarly gendered peers, limited empirical research exists to explain this phenomenon (Crenshaw et al., 2015). Given this gap in the empirical research base, the investigation of the intersectionality of race, gender, and disciplinary consequences for middle school African American girls guided this research. I explored the following research questions:

1. What are trends in the assignment of exclusionary disciplinary consequences to middle school African American girls in South School District?

2. What are the perceptions, beliefs, and attitudes of middle school principals in South School District that may contribute to the

disproportionality in the assignment of exclusionary disciplinary consequences to middle school African American girls?

INTERSECTIONALITY OF RACE, GENDER, AND EXCLUSIONARY DISCIPLINARY CONSEQUENCES

Research on school discipline and race has shown how the use of exclusionary discipline practices, which remove students from their normal instructional setting, have become primary classroom management strategies (Arcia, 2007). Frequently, teachers and school leaders remove students in response to *mis*behaviors that they deem inappropriate or contrary to the norms and expectations held by teachers and schools (Fenning & Rose, 2007; Gregory & Mosely, 2004; Monroe & Obidah, 2004). For example, teachers may refer students for disciplinary action because they *mis*interpret student behaviors as inappropriate due to a possible lack of cultural synchrony. Particularly for African American female students, their behaviors and actions may appear counterintuitive to White middle-class norms (Morris, 2014). As a result, some observed student behaviors might not conform to teacher beliefs of how African American female students should conduct themselves.

Even though teachers did not perceive African American girls as posing the "physical" threat that they often perceive African American boys to be (Blake, Butler, Lewis, & Darensbourg, 2011), teachers often labeled them as assertive, aggressive, and confrontational. Adults in school often interpret these stereotypical characterizations for many African American girls as "defiance," which results frequently in disciplinary action. Conversely, the very *qualities* school systems appear to criminalize African American girls for are qualities that successful African American women have identified as essential for success in combating both racism and sexism in society (George, 2015). Nevertheless, for White girls, standing up for oneself, making oneself heard, demonstrating confidence, and mastering critical thinking skills are qualities that society encourages development in and mastery of as they are essential to entering middle and upper-class occupations (Morris, 2007).

Blake, Butler, Lewis, and Darensbourg (2011) explored the differential treatment experienced by African American girls in public schools by their teachers and found that the teachers of African American girls cited and removed them from the classroom more frequently than their White and Latina peers. Notably schools sanctioned African American girls for behaviors that appear to defy traditional standards of femininity such as appearing to be angry, hostile, and hypersexual. Blake et al. found that teachers cited behaviors such as "defiance, use of profane language towards a peer, and physical aggression" (p. 100) as reasons for removal.

Often missed by teachers and administrators when interpreting inappropriate behaviors and assessing disciplinary consequences are cues, verbal or nonverbal, that signal to adults that African American girls are experiencing a crisis (Morris, 2012). Teachers and administrators are often insensitive or unaware of the needs of African American girls abused both physically and mentally, and as a result, teacher actions are often punitive and not empathetic (Smith-Evans, George, Graves, Kaufmann, & Frohlich, 2014). It is important to note that violence, physical, sexual, and emotional abuse disproportionately impacts African American girls who live in high concentrated areas of poverty and crime (Wun, 2015). Under these circumstances, African American girls may appear on the surface to be angry, belligerent, hostile, or defiant due to experiencing or having recently experienced a crisis and need in-school support and not exclusionary suspensions and further re-victimization.

As much as teachers and school leaders have relied on zero tolerance policies to address nonviolent minor infractions, it is those very systemic institutional practices that "push out" African American girls from schools directly into the school to prison pipeline (STPP), resulting in this demographic being the fastest growing segment of the juvenile justice system (Crenshaw et al., 2015; George, 2015; Morris, 2014). Researchers have documented for decades the failure of policies adopted to keep schools safe by managing student behaviors, such as zero tolerance (American Psychological Association Zero Tolerance Task Force, 2008). Additionally, school policies that result in the assignment of exclusionary disciplinary consequences are far too frequently overused, research has shown them to be ineffective, and often the consequences outweigh the benefits (American Academy of Pediatrics, 2003; Gregory, Skiba, & Noguera, 2010; Losen et al., 2015). The unintended consequences of these policies include students missing essential instructional time, students falling behind their peers, disengagement from peers and teachers, and ultimately disengagement from school (Kemp-Graham & Templeton, 2016; Wilson, 2014; Wun, 2015).

METHODOLOGY

Using a case study methodology (Yin, 2013), I sought to examine the assignment of exclusionary disciplinary consequences to middle school African American female students in a school district located in one of the 13 southern states (Smith & Harper, 2015) identified as having above the national average suspension rates for African American girls. I used a mixed methods sequential explanatory research design (Creswell, 2009) to analyze qualitative and quantitative data sources to identify factors such as school leader beliefs, school leader action, and institutional policies and practices that may contribute to the disproportionality in the assignment of disciplinary consequences to African American girls attending middle schools. The mixed-methods sequential explanatory design consists of two distinct data collection phases: quantitative followed by qualitative (Creswell, 2009). I collected and analyzed the quantitative data first to provide a general understanding of the research problem. Next, I collected and analyzed the qualitative data to explain the quantitative results by exploring participants' views more in depth (Ivankova, Creswell, & Stick, 2006).

More specifically, the mixed methods sequential explanatory approach enabled me to examine the issue of disproportionality in suspension rates of African American girls in middle schools more extensively than I could have explored using only qualitative or quantitative data. I collected and analyzed data for this research in two phases. The first phase consisted of examining quantitative data to explore trends in the assignment of disciplinary consequences to African American girls. The second phase consisted of the collection of qualitative data from interviews with middle school principals, which served to assist in the interpretation of the quantitative data. Additionally, I analyzed the school district code of conduct to identify policies and procedures that may contribute to the disproportionate assignment of disciplinary consequences to African American girls.

The discipline (quantitative) data alone provides only a numerical finding of the existence of disproportionality in the assignment of disciplinary consequences. However, expanding the research beyond the quantitative findings by including qualitative data sources such as interviews and review of policies provided for a richer understanding of factors, perceptions, attitudes, institutional practices, and policies that may contribute to this phenomenon. Figure 10.1 provides a visual model of the data collection process and analysis for this research.

The Setting—South School District

The three middle schools selected for this study were in South School District (a pseudonym), a suburban school district located in the Southwest

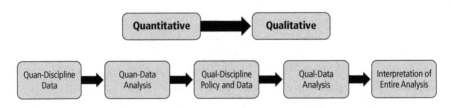

Figure 10.1 Sequential explanatory design for Black girls matters frontline research.

Region of the United States. African American male principals who had an average of 12.5 years leading middle schools led the three middle schools.

Researchers have found that schools with higher proportions of African American and Latinx students are at greater risk for school exclusion after accounting for school level demographics and behaviors (Anyon et al., 2014). For this reason, I selected South School District as the site for research to explore disproportionality in the suspensions of African American girls. South School District is an anomaly in this southwestern state given the demographics of its students, teachers, and administrators. During the 2015–2016 school year, there were six elementary schools, three middle schools, and one high school. African American principals led 98% of the schools in this school district, which is 9 times the state average. South School District served 9,716 students; 77% of the student population was African American, 5 times the state average, and 66% of the teachers were African American, 6.5 times the state average. In addition, South School District is one of the 27 school districts, representing only 2% of school districts in this southwestern state, led by an African American superintendent. The percentage of special education and gifted and talented students within the district exceed the state average.

Ninety percent of the disciplinary reasons reported to the state education agency from South School District that resulted in the assignment of disciplinary consequences to students were due to violations of the local school code of conduct. Worthy of notice in this district are discipline data that indicate that African American students were the only demographic group in this district disproportionately represented in disciplinary assignments:

- 85% of all students in this school district assigned a Disciplinary Alternative Education Placement (DAEP) were African American.
- 87% of all students in this school district assigned Out of School Suspensions (OSS) were African American.
- 86% of all students in this school district assigned In School Suspensions (ISS) were African American.

Disciplinary Policies in South School District

In South School District, administrator responses to disciplinary infractions by students are either mandatory or discretionary. Mandatory responses are those where state law requires the penalty. By contrast, discretionary responses permit a school district to adopt local policy in response to the requirements of the state education code. More specifically, the state education code requires school districts to define misconduct that may result in a range of specific disciplinary consequences, including removal from a regular classroom or campus, suspension (both in and out of school), placement in DAEP, or expulsion from school. The school district's Student Code of Conduct (SCOC) must clearly describe all disciplinary infractions with corresponding consequences. Mandatory disciplinary consequences as determined by state laws require school districts either to expel students or to assign them to an alternative education program. Police officers arresting students or charging them with a felony offense are examples of infractions that may result in a DAEP placement.

To provide context for this research, I present comparative student, teacher, and school demographic data for the three middle schools selected for this study in Tables 10.1 and 10.2.

Data Sources

Quantitative data sources examined for this research contained disciplinary data for female students for the 2015–2016 school year provided to the researcher by special request from the state education agency. The disciplinary data included ethnicity, gender, grade level, school enrolled, type of infraction, disciplinary consequence assigned and number of days assigned an exclusionary disciplinary consequence.

I had two qualitative data sources for this research: semi-structured interviews and the school district code of conduct. I conducted interviews with each of the three middle school principals over the course of one month. The interviews consisted of 21 semi-structured interview questions (See Appendix). I emailed the interview protocol to each principal in advance, so

TABLE 10.1 Student Demographics of Middle Schools Located in South School District Compared to State Level Data

Student Demographics	State Avg.	Martin	Williams	Everly
African American	12.6%	72.5%	84.6%	81.3%
Hispanic	52.2%	23.2%	11.2%	16.2%
White	28.5%	2.7%	2.2%	1.5%
American Indian	0.4%	0.0%	0.1%	0.0%
Asian	4.0%	0.2%	0.7%	0.0%
Pacific Islander	0.1%	0.0%	0.1%	0.3%
Two or More Races	2.1%	1.4%	1.1%	0.7%
Economically Disadvantaged	59.0%	74.7%	66.0%	76.2%
ELL	18.5%	8.4%	3.4%	4.5%
At Risk	50.1%	58.9%	58.0%	57.9%
Mobility	16.5%	19.6%	14.5%	19.1%

TABLE 10.2 Teacher Demographics of Middle Schools Located in South School District Compared to State Level Data

Teacher Demographics	State Avg.	Martin	Williams	Everly
African American	10.1%	74.2%	76.2%	78.2%
Hispanic	26.0%	3.5%	2.0%	3.0%
White	60.8%	18.8%	18.0%	16.5%
American Indian	0.4%	1.7%	0.0%	0.0%
Asian	1.5%	0.0%	0.0%	0.0%
Pacific Islander	0.2%	0.0%	0.0%	0.0%
Two or More	1.1%	1.7%	3.9%	2.3%
Male	23.5%	29.7%	37.2%	32.6%
Female	76.5%	70.3%	62.8%	67.4%
First Year Teacher	8.1%	3.5%	23.0%	16.1%
1–5 years	27.3%	21.0%	21.5%	37.0%
6–10 years	21.7%	26.0%	21.7%	30.3%
11–20 years	27.3%	37.9%	27.3%	8.4%
20+ years	15.7%	11.6%	15.7%	8.3%

they could review the questions prior to the scheduled interview. I audio-taped the three principal interviews and immediately transcribed them with all personally identifiable information removed. I assigned numeric codes to Principal 1 (Williams Middle), Principal 2 (Martin Middle), and Principal 3 (Everly Middle). To mask the identity of the respondents, I also assigned each school a pseudonym. Each interview was approximately 90 minutes. I analyzed the District Code of Conduct to identify institutional policies and practices that may contribute to the disproportionality in the assignment of disciplinary consequences to African American girls in middle school.

I achieved trustworthiness via the accurate capturing and portrayal of the data provided by the school principals. I enhanced this through the triangulation of interview findings with data from the student code of conduct handbook and discipline data provided from the state education agency.

Data Analysis

I collected data for this research and analyzed it in two phases: Phase I—Quantitative and Phase II—Qualitative.

Phase I—Quantitative

I analyzed disciplinary records for South School District to determine if disproportionality existed for African American students in the assignment of disciplinary consequences. I used Relative Risk Ratio (RRR) to assess disproportionality because the measure is at the incident level, i.e., In School Suspension (ISS) and Out of School Suspension (OSS) episodes, taking into consideration multiple occurrences, and thus providing for a more insightful metric for understanding disproportionalities. A Relative Risk Ratio (RRR) of 1 means there is an equal risk of classification, while a risk of larger than 1 indicates greater risk, and a RRR of less than 1 means a smaller risk (Bollmer, Bethel, Garrison-Mogren, & Brauen, 2007; Hosp & Reschly, 2003; Lewis, Butler, Bonner, Fred, & Joubert, 2010; MacMillan & Reschly, 1998; Porowski, O'Connor, & Passa, 2014). I calculated the Risk Index (RI) and RRR for this research using the following formulas.

Risk Index (RI)

$$\frac{\text{Total \# of Disciplinary Assignments for African American Students}}{\text{Total \# of African American Students}}$$

Relative Risk Ratio (RRR)

$$\frac{\text{RI African American Students (Target Group)}}{\text{RI Ethnic Group (Comparison Group)}}$$

Next, I reviewed disciplinary records for all girls enrolled in each of the middle schools in South School District during the 2015–2016 school year to examine trends in the type of disciplinary consequences assigned in response to violations of the student code of conduct. In addition, I compared the number of days assigned for exclusionary disciplinary consequences to African American girls to their similarly gendered peers to identify trends in the disproportionate assignment of disciplinary consequences.

Phase II—Qualitative

I audiotaped open-ended semi-structured interviews of the principals and shortly thereafter transcribed verbatim. Then, I read the transcribed interviews several times to identify major ideas, which I recorded via memos (Corbin & Strauss, 2008; Miles, Huberman, & Saldaña, 2014). The next phase in the analysis was the actual coding of the open-ended interviews that occurred in two coding cycles (Miles et al., 2014). For the first cycle, I engaged in values coding to assign individual codes to respondents' stated attitudes, beliefs, and values about policies, practices, and school structures that they attributed to the disproportionality in the assignment of disciplinary consequences for African American girls in middle school. Codes assigned when analyzing respondents' interviews were: (V) for values, (A) for attitudes and (B) for beliefs (Miles et al., 2014).

1. School to Prison Pipeline (attitudes/beliefs)
2. School Pushout of Girls/Disproportionality in Suspensions (attitudes/beliefs)
3. Zero Tolerance Disciplinary Policies (attitudes/beliefs)
4. In School Suspension (ISS)—(attitudes/beliefs)
5. Out of School Suspension (OSS—(attitudes/beliefs)
6. Discipline Code Violations and Consequences (attitudes/beliefs)
7. Cultural Competence of Teachers and Administrators (attitudes/beliefs)
8. School Leader and Teacher Perceptions of African American Girls (attitudes/beliefs)
9. Mitigating Factors (values/attitudes/beliefs)
10. Principal Actions (values/attitudes/beliefs)
11. Teacher Actions (values/attitudes/beliefs)
12. Research to Inform Practice (values/beliefs)

Figure 10.2 Pattern codes created during data analysis.

The second cycle of coding consisted of grouping individual value codes into pattern codes creating a smaller number of categories to identify themes, causes and explanations for factors that may help to understand better African American girls' assignment of disciplinary consequences from the perspective of middle school leaders. I listed identified codes for this research in Figure 10.2.

RESULTS

The following sections include the results of both phases of this mixed method study. Phase I focuses on the quantitative findings and Phase II the qualitative.

Phase I—Quantitative

Quantitative findings of discipline trends are reported at the state level, school district level, and individually at each of the three middle schools. Findings indicate that across all categories African American students were disproportionately disciplined with exclusionary practices at a higher level than most of their peers.

Discipline Trends at the State Level

In this Southwestern state, schools are 2.4 to 14.8 times more likely to assign an exclusionary disciplinary consequence to African American students than their non-African American peers are. I present the data representing these findings in Table 10.3.

TABLE 10.3   Relative Risk Ratio of Disciplinary Consequences for African American Students When Compared to Other Ethnic Groups in the State

Ethnicity	RRR
Asian	14.8*
White	3.4*
Pacific Islander	2.7*
American Indian	2.6*
Hispanic	2.4*
Two or More Races	2.3*

* Disproportionality

Discipline Trends at the School District Level

South School District assigns African American students disciplinary consequences at a rate of 1.44 to 7.62 times the rate of their non-African American peers except for their Native Hawaiian peers. Disproportionality in the assignment of *alternative educational placements* was observed for African American students when compared to their Hispanic, White, and multi-ethnic peers. Disproportionality in the assignment of out *of school suspensions* were observed for African American students when compared to their Asian, Hispanic, White, and multi-ethnic peers. Similarly, disproportionality in the assignment of in *school suspensions* was noted for African American students when compared to their American Indian, Hispanic, Native Hawaiian, White, and multi-ethnic peers. I present data representing these findings in Table 10.4.

Discipline Trends at Williams Middle School, South School District

School personnel assigned African American girls attending Williams Middle School more days on average per student for DAEP, OSS, and ISS

TABLE 10.4   Relative Risk Ratio of Disciplinary Consequences for African American Students When Compared to Other Ethnic Groups in the South School District

Demographic	All Disciplinary Consequences	RRR DAEP	RRR OSS	RRR ISS
American Indian	1.44*	NA	0.91	2.45*
Asian	7.62*	NA	3.37*	NA
Hispanic	2.09*	1.76*	2.20*	2.04*
Native Hawaiian	0.99	NA	0.87	1.01*
Two or More Races	1.99*	2.04*	1.74*	2.28*
White	1.48*	1.82*	1.70*	1.31*

* Disproportionality

than their non-African American female peers who received the same disciplinary consequence. I present data supporting these findings in Table 10.5.

Discipline Trends at Martin Middle School, South School District

African American female students enrolled in Martin Middle School received on average more days per student for ISS and OSS than their non-African American female peers who received the same disciplinary consequence. I present data supporting these findings in Table 10.6.

TABLE 10.5 Williams Middle School Disciplinary Assignment by Consequence, Ethnicity and Number of Days Assigned for African American Girls

Consequence	Ethnicity	Student Count	Days Assigned	Average
DAEP	Black or AA	9	334	37.11
DAEP	Hispanic/Latina	3	3	1.00
ISS	Black or AA	26	54	2.08
ISS	Hispanic/Latina	3	3	1.00
ISS	White	3	3	1.00
OSS	Black or AA	64	267	4.17
OSS	Hispanic/Latina	7	26	3.71
OSS	Two or more races	3	3	1.00
OSS	White	3	3	1.00
OSS	American Indian/Alaska	3	3	1.00

TABLE 10.6 Martin Middle School Disciplinary Assignment by Consequence, Ethnicity and Number of Days Assigned for African American Girls

Consequence	Ethnicity	Student Count	Days Assigned	Average
DAEP	Black or AA	3	3	1
DAEP	Hispanic/Latina	3	3	1
DAEP	Two or more races	3	3	1
DAEP	White	3	3	1
ISS	Black or AA	81	321	3.96
ISS	Hispanic/Latina	10	36	3.60
ISS	Two or more races	3	3	1.00
ISS	White	5	22	4.40
OSS	Black or AA	60	245	4.083
OSS	Hispanic/Latina	14	59	4.214
OSS	Two or more races	3	3	1.000
OSS	White	3	3	1.000

TABLE 10.7 Everly Middle School Disciplinary Assignment by Consequence, Ethnicity and Number of Days Assigned for African American Girls

Consequence	Ethnicity	Student Count	Days Assigned	Average
DAEP	Black or AA	5	150	30
ISS	Black or AA	52	115	2.21
ISS	Hispanic/Latina	7	12	1.71
ISS	Native Hawaiian	3	3	1.00
ISS	Two or more races	3	3	1.00
ISS	White	3	3	1.00
OSS	Black or AA	88	405	4.60
OSS	Hispanic/Latina	10	32	3.20
OSS	Native Hawaiian	3	3	1.00
OSS	White	3	3	1.00

Discipline Trends at Everly Middle School, South School District

African American female students attending Everly Middle School received on average more days per student for ISS and OSS than their non-African American female peers who received the same disciplinary consequence. I present data supporting these findings in Table 10.7.

Phase II—Qualitative

I identified three major themes in relation to the middle school principals' perceptions, beliefs, and attitudes that may contribute to the disproportionality in the assignment of exclusionary disciplinary consequences to middle school African American girls in South School District. These themes include:

1. Lack of leader awareness of disproportionality in the assignment of exclusionary disciplinary consequences to African American girls;
2. School leader understanding of institutional practices that contribute to the disproportionality in the assignment of disciplinary consequences to African American girls; and
3. School principal understanding of best practices to reduce the disproportionate assignment of disciplinary consequences to African American girls.

Lack of Leader Awareness

Prior to participation in this research, the respondents were not aware that African American girls were represented disproportionately in the assignment of disciplinary consequences. Further, none of the respondents was able to define the concept of the STPP. The principal of Williams Middle provided an often cited but incorrect definition of STPP, "I am aware of the research data that states that the 3rd grade students' population and how they perform on test scores will determine how many beds are needed for prison." The principal of Everly Middle acknowledged the STPP but did not expound on the definition, "Yes I am aware of it. I believe that it is real. Not so much for our young ladies as it is for the boys." The final respondent, the principal of Martin Middle, indicated that he had read books on the topic; however, he failed to make connections to school practices. He reported:

> I am aware of it. I have read several books about STPP um it is a true concept but as an educator we should not be the ones that are succumbing to that...we must figure out a way to change that mindset of no matter if it's girls or boys especially as African Americans.

All three principals indicated that within the last school year they attended numerous professional development opportunities sponsored by their respective school district and state education agency where professional developers discussed discipline. In many instances, workshop presenters discussed the disproportionality in the assignment of disciplinary consequences to African American youth, particularly in those workshops that focused on restorative justice. However, workshop presenters did not discuss the disproportionate assignment of exclusionary disciplinary consequences pertaining to African American girls in any of the professional development opportunities attended by the principals.

Institutional Practices and Policies

Paramount to dismantling the STTP is the understanding of how school policies and practices contribute to the funneling of students through this pipeline. None of the principals was able to articulate the connection of school and district institutional practices clearly such as zero tolerance disciplinary policies, exclusionary disciplinary assignments (i.e., ISS, OSS) or teacher bias as possible causes for the funneling of students through the school to prison pipeline in their schools.

Although none of the principals made a connection between zero tolerance practices and the school to prison pipeline, all three principals believed that zero tolerance was not an effective policy. The principal of Williams Middle responded, "connotation of zero tolerance itself is a misnomer—up to the execution level. Zero Tolerance...we address the issue at hand. We are still in control of the consequences for the students' actions." The principal of Everly Middle shared, "Well they eliminate the grey area, and zero tolerance um I look at this by a case by case basis and when you go zero tolerance it takes away that." The principal of Martin Middle expounded on zero tolerance and its implications for students, saying:

> Well, I feel that there are certain things that are not going to be zero toler-
> ance and you have to figure out what really is the root cause before we make
> a rash decision... uh we want to kinda want to look at before we decide this is
> what needs to happen... there may be some other circumstances that we truly
> investigate before we say you are gone.

Nonetheless, all three principals believed that ISS assignments were effective in providing a temporary holding space for students to calm down
and ultimately to return to their regular classroom. However, only one principal associated the quality of instruction for students in ISS as compared to
instruction provided in their regular classroom.

> In ISS, we are able to keep the students in school and yet out of contributing
> to what could be a distraction to the learning environment... but as far as the
> instruction goes, they are not getting the same instruction as they would from
> a normal classroom teacher.

Two out of the three principals believed that OSS is only effective if parents work with students to ensure that students do not view missed time
from school as a free or fun time away from school. The principal of Williams Middle shared, "We learn a lot of that [effectiveness] depends on parent follow up." The principal of Martin Middle School had similar thoughts:

> Nowadays... it does help. Because if the parent is not there to support or
> back up the discipline piece then the kids are just at home with free time.
> They are home with free time and they are missing out on academics.

The principal of Williams Middle concurred with the principal of Martin
Middle in terms of the negative relationship between OSS and instructional
time, "In terms of OSS... it's not always the very best thing for education
because when they do come back in they are three days behind and they
have lost instructional time."

Specifically looking at school practices that impacted African American
girls directly, all three principals agreed on the reasons why school personnel assigned African American girls disciplinary consequences. They cited
defiance such as talking back, failure to complete assignments, and violations of the dress/grooming codes as major reasons for assignments of
African American female students to ISS. The principal of Everly Middle
cited a frequent violation of the district dress code that often resulted in
school personnel assigning African American female students to ISS more
frequently than non-African American girls.

Putting a lot of vibrant colored hair weave in their hair is a violation of the district grooming policy. This policy affects African American girls more so than White or Latina girls. The district policy states that the school only permits natural hair color and that is to keep the students as professional as possible.

The principals also proffered examples of teacher bias to explain the disproportionate assignment of disciplinary consequences to African American girls. Two of the three principals responded that they believed that a "class" mismatch existed and not a cultural "mismatch" between the teachers and students. The principal of Martin Middle responded, "Cultural mismatch—that is hodgepodge—depends on the pockets where you are—perhaps 'middle-classism"—middle class teachers making middle class salaries teaching in a poor community—mismatch of values."

The principal of Everly expounded on the issue of middle-classism:

I have to remind teachers that because we see these fine brick homes around the campus, we are a Title I school, that means that the majority of our kids are on free and reduced lunch . . . so that shifts the whole connotation . . . that means serving low income students and which a lot of them are foster care . . . low income or from the trailer park.

The principal from Williams shared a different perspective. "If the teacher does not have a cultural awareness to where they understand African American girls' attitudes and sassiness and all of that and not where it comes from, then it could be a mismatch."

Another key example provided by the principals to help explain the impact of bias was the discussion about societal perceptions. The principal of Martin Middle shared that he noticed differing levels of aggressiveness among the girls. He stated:

I do see our African American girls doing a bit more aggressive behavior than Anglo girls. Not to say that Anglo girls don't do . . . there is a way that it happens . . . I can think it has to do with our African American girls having to prove something to show a person that they are not weak. In terms of aggressiveness between my African American and Latina girls.

Two of the three principals indicated that they have girls in their respective schools of whom negative stereotypes portrayed in society of African American women are applicable. By the same token, both administrators did acknowledge the fact that stereotypes can adversely impact how teachers and administrators interact and assign disciplinary consequences to African American girls. The principal of Williams Middle shared:

I believe some of our African American girls are more outspoken than their White or Latina counterparts. A lot of it is...it depends on the home instruction as well as the images that are portrayed on television and radio as to what is acceptable to our young ladies.

The principal of Everly Middle shared:

I can see that perception from teachers and administrators...I look at some of the young ladies that I come in contact with...I see this but at the same time we have to take a step back and go what is going on with that kid...what is missing... a lot of times there is a cry out because the father is not there or the mother is not there. I have seen in both instances where there has been a parent missing and it impacts that child...aggression comes out. They are also seeking approval.

The remaining principal presented an opposing position. The principal of Williams Middle stated, "I do not go there with that pre-notion—I do not make that grand narrative that this how all young ladies act."

A point often overlooked in the assignment in disciplinary consequences is mitigating factors. All responding principals presented mitigating factors that teachers should consider when assessing behaviors that may lead to disciplinary consequences. They presented two starkly divergent positions. The principal of Williams believed that the teacher should check their own pulse and gauge their relationship with girls when responding to misbehaviors that may result in a disciplinary consequence. The principal of Everly believed that responses are situational and that teachers and administrators should acknowledge and understand the challenges that students come to school with. The principal provided the following example:

Some of the students come with baggage...uh in the mornings or whatever it may be...time of the month, it's situational and if it is something with a student that a conversation can curtail then the conversation should occur.

Principal Perceptions of Best Practices

School policies, as well as teacher and administrator beliefs and actions criminalize African American girls and push them out of schools. The first step in countering the criminalization of African American girls is to understand what "their" criminalization looks like (Morris, 2016). All three principals identified district discipline policies that they believed school personnel should modify to reduce suspensions. Two of the three principals indicated that they would prohibit students from bringing cellphones to school. The principal of Everly provided an example:

A lot of the "drama" begins on social media...we can contain our students here but when they get home or outside on their cell phones, arguments and beef pours over into the school which in turn causes us to have to implement discipline for whatever reason.

The remaining principal indicated that that he would institute an honor code for all students so that they would be more accountable for their misbehaviors.

Additionally, principals from Williams and Everly Middle stated that to reduce disproportionality in their schools, they would review the discipline data to identify trends. The principal of Williams Middle was the only respondent who provided a programmatic solution to reduce the amount of instructional time missed by African American girls due to disciplinary consequences.

Another practice shared by all three principals centered on teacher preparation. While all three principals stated that they did not believe that there would be value in requiring aspiring teachers to take a class focused on discipline, they did believe it would be beneficial to aspiring teachers to learn as much about classroom management and how to engage effectively with students of varying ethnicities and socioeconomic status. The principal of Martin Middle succinctly captured his peers' thinking on this issue.

Not necessarily discipline but I would talk more about classroom management, classroom philosophies because your beliefs about children affects what you are doing with management...so if you got those two things you won't have any discipline problems. I think we just think about discipline, it takes that connotation I am the ruler and I have to be...it's a culture in that classroom and how do you create that culture.

Likewise, all three principals believed a course on discipline would be beneficial in assisting aspiring principals with understanding laws and policies in terms of implementing discipline for students.

DISCUSSION

Both quantitative and qualitative data collected and analyzed for this research were instructive in helping to understand possible factors that contributed to the disproportionate assignment of consequences to African American female students in South School District. The in-depth interviews were particularly informative in providing valuable insight into the phenomena under study from a middle school administrator perspective. During the interviews, the respondents were very much engaged in the conversation pertaining to the disproportionality in the assignment of disciplinary consequences to African American girls. Each principal provided numerous examples of how they advocated for African American girls in their respective schools. For example, respondents described how they intentionally met with African American girls, particularly those who appeared to violate school rules to mentor them and to check on their wellbeing.

Additionally, school leaders encouraged fathers to spend more time with their daughters engaged in meaningful conversations. School leaders believed it was important for dads or father figures to provide validation consistently to their daughters of their self-value and worth. It was clear that each principal developed positive, meaningful relationships with their students, particularly African American girls who needed guidance and support.

Despite the well intentions of each school leader and their desire for all students to be successful, both academically and socially, the discipline data indicated disproportionality in the assignment of disciplinary consequences in all three middle schools studied for this research. More specifically, school personnel assigned African American girls more days on average for each disciplinary assignment (i.e., DAEP, ISS, and OSS) when compared to their non-African American peers in Williams and Everly Middle Schools. Martin Middle assigned African American female students on average more days in an exclusionary disciplinary assignment for ISS only.

Disproportionality in the assignment of disciplinary consequences to African American female students is not an anomaly in the school district or the state. In fact, the trends that I identified in the middle schools located in South School District align with research reports on this issue throughout this southwestern state and the nation. We have learned from existing research that teachers and school leaders may differentially select African American students for disciplinary consequences because of societal stereotypes, implicit bias, or cultural mismatch between teachers and African American students (Gregory et al., 2010; Tyler Boykin, & Walton, 2006; Weinstein, Gregory, & Strambler, 2004). Educators and school leaders subjectively characterize African American girls' behaviors as "unladylike" or "ghetto" because perceptions of their actions are a deviation from socially accepted views of femininity that are based on White middle class values. Thus, Black girls are subject to more criminalizing behaviors such as suspension than their White, Asian, or Latina peers are (Morris, 2012).

Given the large percentages of African American teachers in each middle school, participants reported that they could possibly attribute the disproportionate assignment of disciplinary consequences in their respective schools to class issues but certainly not due to race or bias, therefore discounting the possibility of cultural mismatches. However, each principal failed to recognize that a class mismatch could result in a cultural mismatch between teachers and students. Cultural mismatch between teachers and students can contribute to mis-understandings (Gregory et al., 2010; Tyler et al., 2006; Weinstein et al., 2004), thereby resulting in increased numbers of disciplinary assignments.

I observed a lack of understanding of the implications for African American female students who school personnel assigned discretionary discipline by the middle school principals who participated in this study. More specifically, their individual lack of understanding of the specific institutional practices that criminalize African American female students for minor nonviolent misbehaviors may help to explain the disproportionality found in each of the middle schools in this research despite the principals' stated well intentions. School leaders have yet to realize that to make systemic change for marginalized students they must first understand their own biases, acknowledge their own deficit thinking, and engage in ongoing critical reflection of their beliefs of oppression and social justice. Thus, becoming aware of the cultural influences in school settings and their own biases that perpetuate the inequitable practices within schools (Bustamante, Nelson, & Onwuegbuzie, 2009; Kemp-Graham, 2014; Miller & Martin, 2015) would be paramount in reducing the overrepresentation of African American female students' involvement in exclusionary disciplinary actions.

For example, principals in this research were not able to articulate the meaning of STPP; however, all agreed that zero tolerance policies are ineffective. Conversely, the principals did not oppose the assignment of OSS and ISS despite decades of research that states that exclusionary disciplinary assignments do more harm to students than good. Furthermore, when asked to make a recommendation to revise a discipline policy that would reduce the number disciplinary assignment for African American students, the recommendations provided by the school leaders did not align to the very disciplinary infractions that principals identified as the main reasons they disciplined African American female middle school students more frequently, such as the dress code, defiance, or insubordination.

Respondents did not believe the inclusion of school discipline coursework in principal and teacher preparation programs would be beneficial for aspiring teachers and administrators in terms of understanding of root cases in the disproportionate assignment of disciplinary consequences to African American girls. However, research continues to inform us that to prepare 21st century schools leaders effectively to lead 21st century schools, principal preparation programs must include in their curriculum ongoing opportunities for students to connect the important aspects of school leadership and cultural competence (Hernandez & Kose, 2012). Issues that principal preparation programs should emphasize are diversity, self-awareness, and reflection, facilitating discussions on privilege, inequities, racism, and the importance of raising expectation for all students, and advocating for and understanding the backgrounds of traditionally marginalized students (Miller & Martin, 2015).

Finally, Morris (2016) passionately argued that school policies and teacher and administrator beliefs and actions criminalize African American girls and push them out of schools and that the first step in countering the criminalization of African American girls is to understand what "their" criminalization looks like. The principals in this research did not understand district and school level practices and policies that criminalize African American female students within their own respective schools. Their lack of understanding of these practices and policies may account for the disproportionality evidenced in each school.

Limitations

There are several limitations that readers should take into consideration when considering the findings from this research. The first limitation is that there were only three middle school principals interviewed. Even though researchers using case study methodology intend to provide rich descriptions and insight into the phenomena they are studying, the reader should take care in determining how they apply the results to other middle school principals. The second limitation is that I did not collect data about the perspectives of middle school teachers and students who are truly on the frontline; and thus, their perspectives could provide valuable insight into the phenomena studied for this research. The third limitation is that this study was contextually bound to three middle schools located within one school district. The assignment of disciplinary consequences to students, particularly those due to infractions of local school codes (i.e., student code of conduct), are specific to local school administrator and teacher interpretations of school and district discipline policies. Although the findings from this research may provide invaluable insight about factors that contribute to the disproportionality in the assignment of disciplinary consequences to middle school students, the reader must also take care in the applicability to other middle schools. Finally, the statistical power of the data presented in this research relied very heavily on the accuracy of the discipline data that was publicly available.

CONCLUSION

Researchers since the early 1970s have documented the inequities in how public schools mete out disciplinary consequences to students along racial lines (Edelman, Beck, & Smith, 1975; Gregory et al., 2010; Losen & Gillespie, 2012; Smith & Harper, 2015; Wallace, Goodkind, Wallace, & Bachman, 2008). Unfortunately, empirical research often left out African

American *girls* when they considered factors of race and gender. Researchers rarely capture and report the narratives and experiences of being African American and female, more directly, being "pushed out" of school with the same rigor as African American males in the research literature on school discipline in the United States (Blake et al., 2011; George, 2015; Morris, 2012, 2016; Rollock, 2007; Wun, 2015). As evidenced in this research, major research and policy conversations have not only omitted this phenomenon, but it appears that schools and districts are not having this essential conversation.

Teachers' and school leaders' over reliance on zero tolerance policies to address nonviolent minor offenses are the systemic institutional practices that "push out" African American girls from schools directly into the SSTP. Schools must systematically address these at all levels of the education system. Within middle level education, student-teacher relationships are vital in creating prime conditions for learning. Adolescents benefit both socially and academically when they "experience supportive relationships with their teachers" (Davis, 2006, p. 194).

Every middle school student deserves and desires to have at least one adult, if not more, unconditionally support them and want the best for them (Balkus, 2006). The implementation of effective advisory programs in middle schools can provide such a structure. Effective advisory programs ensure that students connect to at least one adult who can serve as an advocate for the student (National Middle School Association, 2010). Students need support from adults to navigate academic, personal, and family problems successfully.

At high-performing middle schools, administrators keep the needs of the students at center of all decision making and in addition uses data to drive instructional decisions (L'Esperance, Lenker, Bullock, Lockamy, & Mason, 2013). The leader sets the tone and culture of the school. The principal is the one who models the behavior that they expect for the students and staff, is the foundation of support for teachers, and their actions have a direct correlation with the teachers' satisfaction, cohesion, and commitment (Anfara & Mertens, 2012). School accountability has changed and the principal is ultimately responsible for everything that occurs on the campus, especially the delivery of instruction to meet the needs of all learners. "The role of leadership is to create conditions that support continuous professional learning that results in improved classroom practice" (Teague & Anfara, 2012, p. 62).

To address the disproportionality in the assignment of disciplinary consequences to African American girls and the corresponding dismantling of the STPP, schools will need school leaders who are committed to leading with a social justice perspective. Rivera-McCutchen (2014) argued that social justice leadership is a mindset that requires action to right what is wrong. Social justice leaders actively work to improve teaching and learning so that all students have equitable opportunities to learn and excel.

To provide this level of leadership and to serve as a role model in establishing and maintaining a positive school culture that guarantees all students an equal opportunity for success, middle school administrators must have a firm understanding of institutional practices and policies that directly or indirectly catapult African American female students through the School to Prison Pipeline. School leaders have the power and authority to ensure that disproportionality in disciplinary assignments are not present in their schools. School leaders can review discipline data regularly with their teachers to identify and address inequities in the assignment of discipline. Leaders can schedule ongoing professional development for all staff to help them work effectively with student populations who are different from them. Finally, school leaders can identify subjective school disciplinary policies that are harmful to students and recommend that their schools revise them.

APPENDIX
Interview Protocol for the Administrators

The proposed qualitative research will provide insight beyond the "discipline data" to tell the narratives of middle school teachers and school leaders who are curiously juxtaposed between working with adolescent African American girls and enforcing school discipline policies. Suspension data tell only one side of the story; this research will explore mitigating factors that may account for the disproportionality experienced by African American girls and school discipline from the perspectives of the teachers and administrators.

1. How many years have you been an administrator?
2. How many years were you a teacher?
3. Have you ever worked in an elementary or high school as an administrator before? If yes
   ■ Where, when and for how long?
   ■ Do you believe there are differences in the frequency by which you have had to assign ISS/OSS to African American girls? Please be descriptive.
4. What are your thoughts about Zero Tolerance Discipline policies?
5. On a weekly basis, how frequently do you send African American girls to ISS? OSS?
   ■ For those African American girls that you have assigned a disciplinary consequence of ISS/OSS, what were the top three reasons?
6. Could you share with me, how discipline is handled in your school. For example, when a student is sent to you for discipline, what do you do?
7. Nationwide, African American[1] girls have the highest suspension rates among all racial and ethnic groups and are the most severely and most disproportionately affected by school discipline policies and practices when compared to other girl (Smith & Harper, 2015).
   ■ What are your thoughts about this?
   ■ Can you identify a school/district policy in your school that may contribute to African American girls being assigned an

---

1. Throughout this interview students will be referred to as African-American, while African- American refers to people of African descent who reside in the United States, "Black" is a larger umbrella representing individuals throughout the African Diaspora (Morris, 2012). In this document, the reference to African American students includes both African American and Black students, as discipline data and research findings use both terms interchangeably.

out of the classroom disciplinary consequence more frequently than their White or Latino peers.

8. Researchers have presented strong evidence that suggest that there is a relationship in how African American girls are viewed by mainstream society and the negative perceptions held by many teachers and school leaders (Archer-Banks & Behar-Horenstein, 2012; Farinde & Allen, 2013). A number of studies have shown that African American female students are often stereotyped as sassy, hostile, or angry (Cooper, 2015; Evans-Winters & Esposito, 2010; E. W. Morris, 2007) and that these perceptions and biases may impact decision making in terms of the assignment of disciplinary consequences by school leaders (Murphy, Acosta, & Kennedy-Lewis, 2013).

   - Do you believe that there is merit in what the researchers have reported as possible reasons why African American girls are disproportionately represented in disciplinary action?
   - Do you believe on average the characterization of African American girls as being sassy, hostile or angry are correct? Why or why not?
   - Have you ever experienced these type of behaviors from African American female students that resulted in you assigning them a disciplinary consequence? If so, could you provide details of the incident—please do not include the name of the student or students.

9. Are you aware of the School to Prison pipeline? What are your thoughts about it?

10. Have you noticed trends in behaviors or reasons why African American girls in your school are recommended for disciplinary consequences that differ from boys? White girls? Latino girls?

11. What are your thoughts about ISS? What purpose does ISS serve in your opinion? Is it effective? Why or why not?

12. What are your thoughts about OSS? What purpose does OSS serve in your opinion? Is it effective? Why or why not?

13. If you were told that your school had the highest suspension rate of African American girls in your district, what would your response be? Would there be some things that you would do differently? Please be very descriptive.

14. If you could revise the discipline policy in your school, what would be the first policy that you would change? Why?

15. If you could suggest to Teacher Preparation Programs course recommendations, would you recommend a course on Discipline? If yes, what would that course look like?

16. If you could suggest to Principal Preparation Programs course recommendations, would you recommend a course on Discipline? If yes, what would that course look like?

17. Some researchers have suggested that there is a cultural mismatch between teachers and students that may account for the high rate of suspension of African American girls, what are your thoughts on this theory?
    - Do believe that cultural mismatch between your teachers and your students have resulted in students being sent out of your class for disciplinary action? Could you please describe this in detail.
    - Do believe that cultural mismatch can exist between school administrator and students that may result in disciplinary action been assigned to African American girls? Have you experienced this? Please describe in detail.

18. Please think back to the most recent African American female student that you assigned a disciplinary consequence.
    - Can you describe in detail what happened?
    - Was there an alternative other than a disciplinary consequence? If yes, what and why was that not an option for this student?

19. Please think back to the most recent situation where you had to reprimand an African American female student, describe the incident.
    - Are there some things that you would do differently?
    - Are there some things that you wished the student had done differently?

20. Can you provide one reason why African American girls on average are disproportionately represented in disciplinary action?
    - Is this a problem you have experienced? If yes, please provide details.
    - Is this an issue in your school/district? If yes, please provide details

21. Have you attended professional development/staff development workshops on Discipline? If yes,
    - When and can you provide the name of the PD.
    - Was disproportionality in suspensions discussed?
    - Were discipline and African American girls addressed specifically?
    - Was the PD effective in helping you to better discipline your students?

22. What are some factors teachers should consider when sending students out of the classroom for disciplinary consequences. Why?

23. What are some factors school administrators should consider when sending students out of the classroom for disciplinary consequences. Why?

24. Do you believe that there are mitigating factors that should be considered when explaining the disproportionate representation of African American girls in disciplinary consequences? Please be as detailed as possible.

25. Is there anything else that you want add that would help researchers understand school administrators' perspectives on disciplining of African American girls.

This concludes the interview. Thank you very much.

REFERENCES

Akos, P., Lineberry, C., & Queen, J. A. (2015). *Promoting a successful transition to middle school.* New York, NY: Routledge.

American Academy of Pediatrics. (2003). Out-of-school suspension and expulsion. *Pediatrics, 112*(5), 1206–1209.

American Psychological Association Zero Tolerance Task Force. (2008). Are zero tolerance policies effective in the schools?: An evidentiary review and recommendations. *The American Psychologist, 63*(9), 852–862.

Anfara, V. A., Jr., & Mertens, S. B. (2012). Capacity building is a key to the radical transformation of middle grades schools. *Middle School Journal, 43*(3), 58–64.

Anyon, Y., Jenson, J. M., Altschul, I., Farrar, J., McQueen, J., Greer, E., ... Simmons, J. (2014). The persistent effect of race and the promise of alternatives to suspension in school discipline outcomes. *Children and Youth Services Review, 44,* 379–386.

Archer-Banks, D. A., & Behar-Horenstein, L. S. (2012). Ogbu revisited unpacking high-achieving African American girls' high school experiences. *Urban Education, 47*(1), 198–223.

Arcia, E. (2007). A comparison of elementary/K–8 and middle schools' suspension rates. *Urban Education, 42*(5), 456–469.

Bailey, G., Giles, R. M., & Rogers, S. E. (2015). An investigation of the concerns of fifth graders transitioning to middle school. *Research in Middle Level Education Online, 38*(5), 1–12.

Balfanz, R. (2009). *Putting middle grades students on the graduation path: A policy and practice brief.* Westerville, OH: National Middle School Association. Retrieved from http://www.amle.org/portals/0/pdf/articles/Policy_Brief_Balfanz.pdf

Balkus, B. (2006). An advocate for every student at Millard Central Middle School. *Middle School Journal, 38*(2), 4–12.

Blake, J. J., Butler, B. R., Lewis, C. W., & Darensbourg, A. (2011). Unmasking the inequitable discipline experiences of urban Black girls: Implications for urban educational stakeholders. *The Urban Review, 43*(1), 90–106.

Bollmer, J., Bethel, J., Garrison-Mogren, R., & Brauen, M. (2007). Using the risk ratio to assess racial/ethnic disproportionality in special education at the school-district level. *The Journal of Special Education, 41*(3), 186–198.

Bustamante, R., Nelson, J. A., & Onwuegbuzie, A. J. (2009). Assessing schoolwide cultural competence: Implications for school leadership preparation. *Education Administration Quarterly, 45*(5), 793–827.

Carter, E. W., Clark, N. M., Cushing, L. S., & Kennedy, C. H. (2005). Moving from elementary to middle school. Supporting a smooth transition for students with severe disabilities. *Teaching Exceptional Children, 37*(3), 8–14.

Clark, M., Flower, K., Walton, J., & Oakley, E. (2008). Tackling male underachievement: Enhancing a strengths-based learning environment for middle school boys. *Professional School Counseling, 12*(2), 127–132.

Cooper, K. J. (2015). Black girls matter. *Diverse Issues in Higher Education, 32*(4), 16–17.

Corbin, J., & Strauss, A. (2008). *Basics of qualitative research: Techniques and procedures for developing grounded theory.* Thousand Oaks, CA: SAGE.

Crenshaw, K. W., Ocen, P., & Nanda, J. (2015). *Black girls matter: Pushed out, overpoliced and underprotected.* New York, NY: Center for Intersectionality & Social Policy.

Creswell, J.W. (2009). *Research design: Qualitative, quantitative, and mixed methods research.* Thousand Oaks, CA: SAGE.

Davis, H. A. (2006). Exploring the contexts of relationship quality between middle school students and teachers. *The Elementary School Journal, 106*(3), 193–223.

Eccles, J. S., Midgley, C., Wigfield, A., Buchanan, C.M., Rueman, D., Flanagan, C., & Mac Iver, D. (1993). Development during adolescence: The impact of stage-environment fit on young adolescents' experiences in schools and in families. *American Psychologist, 48*(2), 90–101.

Edelman, M., Beck, R., & Smith, P. (1975). *School suspensions: Are they helping children?* Cambridge, MA: Children's Defense Fund.

Elias, M. J. (2002). Transitioning to middle school. *The Education Digest, 67*(8), 41–43.

Evans-Winters, V. E., & Esposito, J. (2010). Other people's daughters: Critical race feminism and Black girls' education. *The Journal of Educational Foundations, 24*(1–2), 11–24.

Farinde, A. A., & Allen, A. (2013). Cultural dissonance: Exploring the relationship between White female teachers' perception and urban Black female students' disciplinary infractions. *The National Journal of Urban Education & Practice, 7*(2), 142–155.

Fenning, P., & Rose, J. (2007). Overrepresentation of African American students in exclusionary discipline the role of school policy. *Urban Education, 42*(6), 536–559.

George, J. A. (2015). Stereotype and school pushout: Race, gender and discipline disparities. *Arkansas Law Review, 68,* 101–130.

Gregory, A., & Mosely, P. M. (2004). The discipline gap: Teachers' views on the overrepresentation of African American students in the discipline system. *Equity & Excellence in Education, 37*(1), 18–30.

Gregory, A., Skiba, R. J., & Noguera, P. A. (2010). The achievement gap and the discipline gap: Two sides of the same coin? *Educational Researcher, 39*(1), 59–68.

Gutman, L. M., & Midgley, C. (2000). The role of protective factors in supporting the academic achievement of poor African American students during middle school transition. *Journal of Youth and Adolescence, 29*(2), 223–249.

Hernandez, F., & Kose, B. W. (2012). The developmental model of intercultural sensitivity A tool for understanding principals' cultural competence. *Education and Urban Society, 44*(4), 512–530.

Hosp, J. L., & Reschly, D. J. (2003). Referral rates for intervention or assessment a meta-analysis of racial differences. *The Journal of Special Education, 37*(2), 67–80.

Ivankova, N. V., Creswell, J. W., & Stick, S. L. (2006). Using mixed-methods sequential explanatory design: From theory to practice. *Field Methods, 18*(1), 3–20.

Kemp-Graham, K. (2014). To thine own self be true: Culturally competent and globally aware. In S. Harris & J. Mixon (Eds.), *Building cultural community through global educational leadership* (pp. 99–129). Ypsilanti, MI: National Council of Professors of Education Administration.

Kemp-Graham, K., & Templeton, N. (2016). The discipline gap in Texas: An exploratory analysis of the discretionary assignment of disciplinary consequences of Black students and White students in Texas who violated local school codes. *The Journal of Texas Alliance of Black School Educators, 2*(2), 1–25.

L'Esperance, M. E., Lenker, E., Bullock, A., Lockamy, B., & Mason, C. (2013). Creating a middle grades environment that significantly improves student achievement. *Middle School Journal, 44*(5), 32–39.

Lewis, C. W., Butler, B. R., Bonner, I., Fred, A., & Joubert, M. (2010). African American male discipline patterns and school district responses resulting impact on academic achievement: Implications for urban educators and policy makers. *Journal of African American Males in Education, 1*(1), 7–25.

Losen, D. J., Hodson, C., Keith, M. A., II, Morrison, K., & Belway, S. (2015). *Are we closing the school discipline gap?* Los Angeles, CA: Center for Civil Rights Remedies. Retrieved from https://www.civilrightsproject.ucla.edu/resources/projects/center-for-civil-rights-remedies/school-to-prison-folder/federal-reports/are-we-closing-the-school-discipline-gap.

Losen, D. J., & Gillespie, J. (2012). *Opportunities suspended: The disparate impact of disciplinary exclusion from school.* Los Angeles, CA: The Center for Civil Rights Remedies.

MacMillan, D. L., & Reschly, D. J. (1998). Overrepresentation of minority students the case for greater specificity or reconsideration of the variables examined. *The Journal of Special Education, 32*(1), 15–24.

Miles, M. B., Huberman, A. M., & Saldaña, J. (2014). *Qualitative data analysis: A methods sourcebook.* Thousand Oaks, CA: SAGE.

Miller, C. M., & Martin, B. N. (2015). Principal preparedness for leading in demographically changing schools: Where is the social justice training? *Educational Management Administration & Leadership, 43*(1), 129–151.

Monroe, C. R., & Obidah, J. E. (2004). The influence of cultural synchronization on a teacher's perceptions of disruption: A case study of an African American middle-school classroom. *Journal of Teacher Education, 55*(3), 256–268.

Morris, E. W. (2007). "Ladies" or "loudies"? Perceptions and experiences of Black girls in classrooms. *Youth & Society, 38*(4), 490–515.

Morris, M. W. (2012). *Race, gender, and the school-to-prison pipeline: Expanding our discussion to include Black girls.* New York, NY: African American Policy Forum.

Morris, M. W. (2014). Representing the educational experiences of Black girls in a juvenile court school. *Journal of Applied Research on Children, 5*(2), 1–28.

Morris, M. W. (2016). *Pushout: The criminalization of Black girls in schools.* New York, NY: The New Press.

Murphy, A. S., Acosta, M. A., & Kennedy-Lewis, B. L. (2013). "I'm not running around with my pants sagging, so how am I not acting like a lady?": Intersections of race and gender in the experiences of female middle school troublemakers. *The Urban Review, 45*(5), 586–610.

National Middle School Association. (2010). *This we believe: Keys to educating young adolescents.* Westerville, OH: Author.

Parker, A. K. (2009). Elementary organizational structures and young adolescents' self-concept and classroom environment perceptions across the transition to middle school. *Journal of Research in Childhood Education, 23*(3), 325–339.

Porowski, A., O'Connor, R., & Passa, A. (2014). *Disproportionality in school discipline: An assessment of trends in Maryland, 2009–12.* Washington, DC: Regional Educational Laboratory Mid-Atlantic.

Raffaele-Mendez, L. M. (2003). Predictors of suspension and negative school outcomes: A longitudinal investigation. *New Directions for Youth Development, 2003*(99), 17–33.

Rivera-McCutchen, R. L. (2014). The moral imperative of social justice leadership: A critical component of effective practice. *The Urban Review, 46*(4), 747–763.

Rollock, N. (2007). Why Black girls don't matter: Exploring how race and gender shape academic success in an inner city school. *Support for Learning, 22*(4), 197–202.

Smith-Evans, L., George, J., Graves, F., Kaufmann, L., & Frohlich, L. (2014). *Unlocking opportunity for African American girls: A call to action for educational equity.* Washington, DC: National Women's Law Center.

Smith, E. J., & Harper, S. R. (2015). *Disproportionate impact of K–12 school suspension and expulsion on Black students in Southern States.* Philadelphia: University of Pennsylvania, Center for the Study of Race and Equity in Education.

Spaulding, S. A., Irvin, L. K., Horner, R. H., May, S. L., Emeldi, M., Tobin, T. J., & Sugai, G. (2010). Schoolwide social-behavioral climate, student problem behavior, and related administrative decisions empirical patterns from 1,510 schools nationwide. *Journal of Positive Behavior Interventions, 12*(2), 69–85.

Teague, G. M., & Anfara, V. A., Jr. (2012). Professional learning communities create sustainable change through collaboration. *Middle School Journal, 44*(2), 58–64.

Theriot, M. T., & Dupper, D. R. (2010). Student discipline problems and the transition from elementary to middle school. *Education and Urban Society, 42*(2), 205–222.

Tyler, K. M., Boykin, A. W., & Walton, T. R. (2006). Cultural considerations in teachers' perceptions of student classroom behavior and achievement. *Teaching and Teacher Education, 22*(8), 998–1005.

U.S. Department of Education Office for Civil Rights. (2014). *Civil rights data collection data snapshot: School discipline.* Washington, DC: Author.

U.S. Department of Education Office for Civil Rights. (2016). *2013–14 Civil rights data collection a first look: Key data highlights on equity and opportunity gaps in our nation's public schools.* Washington, DC: Author.

Wallace, J. M., Jr., Goodkind, S., Wallace, C. M., & Bachman, J. G. (2008). Racial, ethnic, and gender differences in school discipline among U.S. high school students: 1991–2005. *The Negro Educational Review, 59*(1–2), 47–62.

Weinstein, R. S., Gregory, A., & Strambler, M. J. (2004). Intractable self-fulfilling prophecies fifty years after Brown v. Board of Education. *American Psychologist, 59*(6), 511–520.

Wilson, H. (2014). Turning off the school-to-prison pipeline. *Reclaiming Children and Youth, 23*(1), 49–53.

Wun, C. (2015). Against captivity black girls and school discipline policies in the afterlife of slavery. *Educational Policy, 30*(1), 171–196.

Yin, R. K. (2013). *Case study research: Design and methods.* Thousand Oaks, CA: SAGE.

CHAPTER 11

EDUCATORS' PRACTICE FOR ENGLISH LANGUAGE LEARNERS' CRITICAL CONSCIOUSNESS

From Marginalized Identities to Active Agents

Bogum Yoon
State University of New York at Binghamton

Christine Uliassi
State University of New York at Binghamton

ABSTRACT

The purpose of this chapter is to provide middle grade educators with practical suggestions on how to support English language learners' (ELLs) identities and their development of critical consciousness through critical practice in the classroom. Given that ELLs' identities are integral parts of their language and literacy learning, middle grade educators' attention to finding

Equity & Cultural Responsiveness in the Middle Grades, pages 239–253
Copyright © 2019 by Information Age Publishing
All rights of reproduction in any form reserved.

ways to support them is important. We base the practical suggestions on the synthesis of the existing findings of the first author's qualitative studies conducted in middle schools and an extensive literature review on this topic. This chapter provides insights into how middle grade educators can respond to social and political issues that ELLs encounter in the mainstream context and support the students' identities as active agents, not as marginalized passive learners.

Young adolescents are in the process of forming and developing their identities (Erikson, 1993). The phenomenon of identity development is a dynamic, often tension-filled process influenced by culture and interactions in society (Freire, 1998). This concept applies to adolescent English language learners (ELLs) who increasingly populate U.S. middle school classrooms as they study both in mainstream and English as a Second Language (ESL) classrooms. They are in a unique situation in that they are acquiring English as a new language while they are in the stage of identity formation and development in a new context. At this stage, middle school ELLs may notice that they live in the social and political context where the power of the mainstream culture operates.

Studies over decades (e.g., Cummins, 1989; Pappamihiel, 2002; Yoon, 2008) have shown that ELLs tend to have marginalized identities in the dominant culture and they acquire English as an assimilation process into the dominant culture. In this assimilation process, educators often focus on ELLs' linguistic needs. When educators focus solely on students' linguistic needs, they can ignore students' cultural and social needs that are crucial for students' successful learning. This focus neglects students' cultural and social identities, which can help ELLs to become learners who see themselves as confident and capable of enacting change in their lives and the world.

Numerous scholars noted the importance of cultural and social identities for ELLs' learning (e.g., Block, 2007; Cummins, 1989; Duff, 2012; Kramsch, 2009; Norton, 2000; Pavlenko & Blackledge, 2004; Yoon, 2015). Freire (1998) cautioned that often identity develops from *differences* and dominant groups' tendencies to position what is different as inferior. This positioning might lead to marginalized identities for ELLs in the mainstream context where students interact with their peers and teachers. Given that ELLs' cultural and social identities are integral parts of their language and literacy learning, middle grade educators' attention to support these identities is crucial. However, the question of *how* remains. Freire's (1998) concept of critical consciousness is useful to address the question. He asserted that developing critical consciousness through critical practice is a way to deepen the learner's understanding by uncovering and discussing the oppressive realities in the world.

Despite the importance of supporting ELLs' cultural and social identities and critical consciousness, there is little discussion on how and in what ways middle grade educators can assist students. To address the gap, we, as literacy scholars, provide middle grade educators with practical suggestions on working with ELLs to support their cultural and social identities and promote critical consciousness through critical practice. We particularly focus on what social and political issues middle school ELLs encounter on a daily basis and how teachers can respond to these issues. We describe how using diverse strategies and materials enable educators to support the students' identities and help them become active agents in the mainstream context.

Within this chapter, we first provide the theoretical framework that guides this chapter, drawn from Freire's (1970) critical consciousness and Janks' (2010, 2014) "little p" politics concept. Then, we summarize practical suggestions based on the first author's studies in middle school settings with several examples that highlight teachers' instructional practices that promote ELLs' identities and critical consciousness. Finally, we provide the implications drawn from these studies for the field of middle grades education. In this chapter, we define critical literacy broadly as an instructional practice designed to support ELLs' reading of the world as a text, with the world being their situated reality that they encounter on a daily basis (Yoon, 2015).

THEORETICAL PERSPECTIVES

Both Freire's (1970, 1998) critical consciousness and Janks' (2010, 2014) "little p" politics concepts serve as a guiding lens for our focus on the consideration of middle grade ELLs' identities and critical consciousness in the mainstream context to act as socially and culturally active human beings. More specifically, Freire (1970) underscored that a teacher's broader role is to empower students through the active process of critical consciousness, or *conscientization*, which he first used in his seminal work, *Pedagogy of the Oppressed*. A fundamental component in engaging in critical practice arises from the process of praxis—one that refers to an individual's reflection on social and political realities and action. Freire stressed that students cannot develop this critical consciousness unless educators give them opportunities to explore existing knowledge about the world around them. Freire's pedagogy focused on liberating individuals from oppression by developing their critical consciousness to challenge the status quo. Freire asserted that active participation by the oppressed is crucial in the revolutionary process necessary to transform the world.

Nurturing middle grade ELLs' critical consciousness through critical literacy practice matters to the students. Critical scholars use Freire's (1970) concept of critical consciousness to express the importance of students' awareness of the realities of the world. For instance, Shor (1992) described critical consciousness as "the way we see ourselves in relation to knowledge and power in society, to the way we use and study language, and to the way we act in school and daily life to reproduce or transform our conditions" (p. 128). In short, critical consciousness facilitates the students' agency, *motivation for being in action* (Johnston, 2004), and it is a necessary process for ELLs' identity as active agents.

Another theoretical construct that guides this chapter is Janks' (2010, 2014) notion of the little p politics. Macro-level politics (Big P) refer to issues involving government, social movements, or global concerns (e.g., climate change, linguistic imperialism, capitalism). More large-scale economic, social, and political issues and events are involved in Big P. Yet, Janks believed that in addition to these types of macro-level politics, micro-level politics (little p) are also important to understand text and the world. Micro-level politics include middle grade ELLs' daily life experiences that operate under power structures while interacting with individuals in the dominant culture. Micro-level politics also include everyday texts that students encounter like advertisements, photographs, or school posters (Janks, 2014). These little p texts send important messages to educators that they need to invite students to critically analyze everyday texts and to understand them in the context of Big P issues and discourse.

Middle grades educators can engage learners in little p politics through the politics of identity and place (Janks, 2010). The politics of identity and place include decisions about how people treat others based on who they are and what power they hold in their everyday circumstance. According to Janks (2014), the various groups and communities that "we move through during our lives" (p. 36), shape our identity. Moje and Luke (2009) posited identity as a socially mediated process by stating, "One sees identity less as an interpretation of the person who has the identity and more dependent on other people's recognitions of a person" (p. 418). This implies that identity is a social construct developed in the social context where power operates. Research shows examples of middle school teachers bringing current identity issues into classroom lessons for ELLs, allowing them to explore their realities and the politics of identity and place (little p) by rewriting bully incidents (Lau, 2012) or discussing a feeling of mistreatment in a mainstream classroom (Harman & Varga-Dobai, 2012). Middle grade ELLs might not see some of these everyday classroom issues as "politics," but educators can guide them to see how these issues relate to power.

Understanding this power structure through critical consciousness is a key component of critical literacy. According to Luke (2004), critical literacy helps us see how the dynamic text, world, and situation "use power over us, over others, on whose behalf, in whose interests" (p. 4). Given that one of the main purposes of critical literacy practice is to empower students to be active agents in the mainstream context, Freire's (1970) concept of critical consciousness and Janks' (2010, 2014) construct of little p are helpful to understand teachers' instructional practice and young adolescent ELLs' micro-politics of daily life. The current literature shows how middle grade ELLs can benefit from critical practice that allows them to position themselves as socially and culturally conscious human beings.

PRACTICAL SUGGESTIONS
FOR MIDDLE GRADE EDUCATORS

As noted earlier, we base our suggestions on studies conducted by the first author in middle school settings and relevant literature review. The author conducted her qualitative case studies in both mainstream classrooms and ESL classrooms to understand how middle school ELLs interacted with English language arts teachers and ESL teachers through classroom activities and how these interactions with teachers and classmates influences their identities as ELLs. In this section, we present examples and findings drawn from these studies to support the suggestions (see Yoon, 2007, 2008, 2015). We consider this chapter a synthesis of studies that discuss middle grade ELLs' language and literacy learning.

To promote ELLs' identities as active agents and build their critical consciousness, middle grades educators might consider the following four suggestions: (a) build up ELLs' confidence by considering them as cultural, social, and linguistic assets; (b) provide more opportunities to share ELLs' own stories; (c) integrate identities development into curriculum with cultural pluralism; and (d) implement multimodal approaches.

Suggestion 1: Develop ELLs' Confidence as Cultural, Social, and Linguistic Assets

Our research synthesis suggests that teachers need to build ELLs' confidence by positioning them as cultural, social, and linguistic assets who can bring diverse interpretations and cultural references to class. In this process, ELLs become active participants in learning activities in the mainstream context. For example, in a qualitative case study in middle school settings, Yoon (2007) compared the regular education classrooms of Mrs. Young and Mr. Brown (pseudonyms), who were sixth grade English language arts teachers. In Mr. Brown's classroom, where American cultural references (e.g., American football, products, television shows) were common, he did not offer opportunities for ELLs to participate in learning activities. The ELLs "did not interact well with their mainstream peers, who held a sort of "hidden power" over the ELLs and resisted working with them" (Yoon, 2007, p. 216). The finding implies that when little p politics operated in the mainstream context (Janks, 2010, 2014), ELLs tended to withdraw from their learning activities.

However, in Mrs. Young's classroom, the teacher continuously positioned her ELLs as cultural and linguistic assets by inviting them to bring their own knowledge about their home culture and native language. The students who were quiet most of the time earlier in the semester actively interacted with their peers and participated in learning activities. The ELLs in Mrs. Young's classroom shared in their interviews that Mrs. Young accepted their different backgrounds and they felt confident. The results of this study implied that middle school teachers could ask what each student brings to the classroom and use cultural, social, and linguistic assets as a basis for instruction. Otherwise, if teachers view cultural differences as deficits, both ELLs and other students may not have opportunities to realize how differences can expand their ways of thinking and enhance their lives.

A similar idea within this category is for middle grade educators to consider incorporating students' backgrounds into everyday lessons and interactions. Curtin (2006) studied six middle school ELLs from Mexico and found that students felt supported and valued by teachers who integrated their Mexican origin into the classroom and curriculum. For example, the teachers infused Spanish vocabulary into science lessons and used Mexican climate and landforms as topics in science units. This approach allowed students to participate in sharing their unique knowledge and viewpoints in lessons. Middle school teachers' validation of ELLs' cultural and linguistic assets can contribute to deeper awareness and confidence.

Building ELLs' cultural pride through implementing community walks with asset mapping is another way to promote the students' identities and critical consciousness. Choudhury and Share (2012) found that a sixth-grade ESL teacher supported ELLs' confidence when he engaged learners in projects that focused on seeking out the positive aspects of their diverse working-class community. The teacher, Mohammed, noted that the class needed this shift because of the students' deficit-oriented views of their own community, which often aligned with the media's biased depiction. On these organized community walks, the ELLs took photographs and interacted with a variety of community members, documenting resources and assets. In this process, they were able to develop critical awareness of the realities of the community around them. They were able to highlight the strong work ethic and diversity of many community businesses, including several ELLs' family members' positive influences. Mohammad empowered students to address some of the issues in the community through advocacy and action. Teachers who focus on cultural and community assets with activities such as community walks and asset mapping can improve ELLs' confidence, self-esteem, and pride in their culture and community.

A related way for teachers to build up ELLs' confidence in their cultural and linguistic assets is by guiding them to write family and community member profiles. Werderich (2008) suggested middle school teachers design lessons that guide students through the process of learning about the genre of profile and assist them with the literacy skills needed to produce one (i.e., reading and critiquing biographies, conducting interviews). These profiles show the value of the everyday experiences of diverse family and community members and can highlight their talents and assets. One of the objectives of these profiles, according to Werderich, is for students to "compare the life experiences of community members from different cultures" (p. 36). Werderich explained how these profiles exemplify the approach of *funds of knowledge* (Moll, Amanti, Neff, & Gonzalez, 1992), which is when teachers tap into the skills of minority families or community members. Family and community member profiles can lead to ELLs' critical awareness of the contributions of diverse individuals in their everyday world.

In sum, several studies that we reviewed support the notion that building up ELLs' confidence by using their differences as assets is a fundamental practice to develop their identities and critical consciousness in a new context.

Suggestion 2: Provide Opportunities to Share ELLs' Stories

Research also shows that more educators need to provide opportunities for ELLs to talk about their lived experiences inside and outside the classroom. This practice helps develop their identities as active agents likely to participate in learning activities. Kramsch (2009) noted that ELLs' experiences and stories matter for their learning. It is important for middle grades educators to listen to ELLs' experiences inside and outside the classroom and use their stories in the practice of critical literacy.

More specifically, Lau's (2012) study showed the importance of using ELLs' narratives and lived experiences as critical literacy curriculum. Lau explained how she, as researcher, and the ESL teacher (Grades 7 and 8) shifted their literacy readings and discussions to bullying after many of the ELLs in the class began complaining about classmates teasing them for their language and accents. The teachers recognized that these bullying stories were important and needed deeper exploration. One activity involved the students writing a bullying incident they experienced or observed. As a class, they analyzed the incidents and then the teacher gave them the task of "rewriting" the stories and showing how they would handle the issue if it occurred again. Then, they created anti-bullying posters for the school and shared their personal experiences in a PowerPoint for teachers and staff, opening the possibilities for critical discussions about bullying. The teachers' focus on student stories led to ELLs feeling empowered to speak up for themselves.

A contrasting teacher response shown in Yoon's (2015) study indicated the importance of inviting ELLs to share their stories and experiences in the classroom. Yoon shared how middle grade ELLs attempted to share their discrimination issues outside of the classroom (e.g., "*A boy called me a "nigger," "hey, Russian"*), but the ESL teacher unintentionally closed the students' discussion about their experiences and no further discussion went on. The teacher took a rather neutral stance by expressing a general statement (e.g., "kids are nasty"). If the teacher engaged in conversations to use as a critical literacy practice to help the ELLs understand the political world (little p) and develop their critical consciousness, the ELLs' participation and sense of agency might have been different.

These two studies' contrasting teacher practices illustrated the importance of middle school teachers' roles in creating a safe space for storytelling where students know teachers and peers will not shut their stories down. One possibility for a safe space outside of the classroom is an afterschool story club to engage ELLs and their peers with poetry, drama, and narratives based on their lives. Enciso (2011) described story club as a space where middle school immigrant students and their native-speaking peers shared stories that were either real or fictionalized tales of bigotry or advocacy. The walls between the two groups soon came down, as story club became a space of collective storytelling where students told, retold, and elaborated on their stories. Students critiqued, questioned, and challenged each other's stories. Themes developed in the stories included struggles with power, representation, and knowledge. The ELLs in the group were able to gain voice and mobilize their stories, all while learning about literacy skills such as writing narratives.

A related suggestion for middle school teachers is to invite students to share their personal stories through arts-based critical literacy activities. Harman and Varga-Dobai (2012) created a safe space for storytelling in the ESL classroom. Three times a week, this English for Speakers of Other Languages (ESOL) classroom became an alternative space where no one shut English language learners' stories down. Students depicted and even reimagined their lived experiences as readers' theater scripts. One of the readers' theater scripts the students performed drew from one student's experience in her mainstream classroom during an English test. She and her classmates enacted the frustration she felt during the test when she struggled with the content and was unable to get the attention of the teacher. In this safe space for creative storytelling, students deconstructed power in schools and in the larger social context of immigration.

Suggestion 3: Integrate Identities Development Into Curriculum for Cultural Pluralism

Middle grades educators should consider ELLs' language and literacy learning as a part of the identity formation and development process, but not as a separate and isolated curriculum. Several studies (e.g., Danzak, 2011; Landt, 2007) supported the idea that ELLs can make connections to their own lives and struggles when texts are culturally relevant and pluralistic. In this way, middle grade ELLs can better understand the realities that they encounter in the social and political world, which ultimately helps them develop their critical consciousness, language learning, and identities.

Specifically, research indicated that educators could support ELLs' identity formation and critical consciousness by selecting read aloud books that stimulate conversation about identity issues that relate to typical teenage struggles as well as cultural identity conflicts. Landt (2007) suggested engaging students in the book, *Cuba 15*, by Nancy Osa. In this story, Violet who has a Cuban background struggles with her Abuela's plans for her quinceañera, traditional coming of age ceremony for girls in Cuba. Violet initially feels too "American" to partake in this Cuban tradition but negotiates her Cuban and American identities as the story evolves. ELLs could connect with this text because of the focus on their complex identity development: striving to fit in America but having connection to another homeland. Violet is also struggling with common teen issues like friendships and self-image to which many students can relate. Reading aloud texts in the classroom can provide opportunities for critical conversations about cultural pluralism and identity to promote ELLs' critical consciousness.

Middle grades educators can also support ELLs' identity development and critical consciousness by designing lessons related to their families' immigration experiences. Danzak (2011) suggested inviting ELLs to narrate their immigration stories in graphic (comic) form, creating authentic, meaningful, multicultural texts. Danzak described a middle school project entitled "Graphic Journeys" that educators could use as a model for other teachers who recognize the importance of narrative in identity construction and reconstruction. First, the teacher made sure the students were quite familiar with the genre of graphic novels and comics. ELLs researched their family immigration stories; they recorded their narratives in a journal, interviewed family members, and gathered photographs and artifacts. The class incorporated technology into their graphic novels to create the images and texts for their comic. The students shared their final published graphic novels at a culminating event with families. Danzak (2011) argued how this was a powerful experience elevated the voices of students who were frequently silenced. Danzak described these immigration narratives as a tool to "affirm and reaffirm the students' own individual and group identities" (p. 188). Because immigration is a sensitive subject, the teacher in this study protected the students' right to confidentiality and gave students uncomfortable sharing their immigration story a writing option related to culture and identity.

The literature review and first author's qualitative studies also suggested that teachers promoted ELLs' identities and critical consciousness when they utilized and designed instructional materials that promoted cultural pluralism, not mono-culturalism. For instance, a study on analyzing multicultural literature by Yoon, Simpson, and Haag (2010) showed that some multicultural literature was not truly "multicultural." Rather than supporting cultural pluralism, some multicultural books appeared to communicate "mono-cultural" concepts to the reader. For instance, the storylines focused on diverse individuals' assimilation to the dominant culture, rather than celebrating cultural pluralism, which values individuals' native language and culture. Thus, middle grade educators need to examine closely how books respect both ELLs' native cultures and the host culture. It is important to pay attention to the ending message that multicultural books deliver, rather than simply picking up the book because the cover shows minority groups.

Suggestion 4: Utilize Multimodal Literacy to Engage ELLs

Our final suggestion based on the synthesis of the literature review and the first author's studies is to include alternative forms of literacy, including multimodal (visual, spoken, written, gestural) and multimedia (advertisements, photographs, videos, graphics) to benefit ELLs' identities and critical consciousness development. Traditional practices for ELLs create a "divide between learning and everyday reality of their lives" (Choudhury & Share, 2012, p. 40). Middle school learners are at the age to negotiate new media and technology to develop awareness of issues in the world around them. They are often adept at using technology including social media, presentation tools, and applications. Teachers can capitalize on their abilities and interests, providing new modes for students to learn and communicate.

Moreover, middle school teachers can design lessons that allow English language learners to be critical consumers of multimodal texts, such as advertisements. Ajayi (2009) described a project in which educators encouraged adolescent ELLs to use multimodal literacies to interpret advertisements for phones. To begin, the teacher activated students' background knowledge on the role of advertising in their lives and society. The students worked in groups to use critical skills to analyze meaning and power in advertisements using visual (symbols) and verbal texts. This project demonstrated how fostering multimodal literacy promoted critical literacy practices. Educators offered ELLs opportunities to create products that represented their viewpoint and challenged practices that marginalized them. As Ajayi (2009) explained, "Multimodal literacy has the potential to help English learners create new worlds, take on different identities, and challenge the taken-for-granted views about their worlds" (p. 591).

Another way to promote ELLs' identities and critical consciousness is to create assignments using a social media platform with multimodal communication tools where ELLs and their peers can engage in literacy activities. Hughes and Morrison (2014) found that ELLs were able to express themselves creatively—both their identities and their ideas—with the help of multimodal functions and the comfort and ease of the social media platform. In their sixth-grade unit on poetry, students analyzed and created poems with the assistance of multimedia tools like iMovie and Glogster and shared their work on the social media platform. With the multimodal tools, ELLs were able to move beyond traditional language skills to convey their ideas with pictures, videos, and sounds. The authors noted that the ELLs developed confidence, showed engagement, and improved their English skills during the poetry unit. They noted that the collaborative and interactive nature of social media enhanced the class community and gave ELLs a safe space to share work representative of their diverse identities.

In short, our research synthesis shows that educators can promote middle grade ELLs' identities and critical consciousness through a multimodal literacy approach because these non-traditional literacy forms and approaches allowed ELLs more opportunities to share their strengths.

CONCLUSION

Through our research synthesis, we uncovered how middle school educators could develop ELLs' cultural and social identities and critical consciousness. The gap (see Kubota & Lin, 2009) in the middle grades educational field on this topic motivated us to write this chapter. Freire's (1970, 1998) concept of critical consciousness and Janks' (2010, 2014) idea of little p politics provided an excellent lens to examine the studies. We hope this synthesis of existing studies contributes to the middle grades field with insightful suggestions and open conversation for further research and practice for English language learners.

As shown in the synthesis, a successful approach to supporting ELLs as they build identities and critical awareness was using culturally relevant materials and strategies to which ELLs could connect. The literature also suggested how teachers need to provide students with literacy opportunities to explore the realities of their worlds and the larger world around them, taking into consideration their diverse perspectives, cultural identities, and language backgrounds (Ajayi, 2009). Middle school teachers can and should provide students with critical literacy experiences that lead to critical consciousness about the world and their role in it. As Erikson (1993) noted, young adolescents are in the process of forming and developing their identities, and ELLs are additionally developing the language needed to express themselves fully. Therefore, middle school teachers have the potential to teach students during a period of dynamic change and growth.

Middle grades educators' attention to ELLs' critical consciousness as a literacy process is more important in this neoliberal, market-driven society. Developing critical consciousness is an inseparable process from developing language and literacy learning. According to Sleeter (2014), people often blame neoliberal economic and social forces for social inequalities, including inequities in school. People see neoliberalism in school reforms, including standardization of teaching practices, as a threat to empowered learning that is responsive to students' cultural identities (Sleeter, 2014). In this aspect, middle grades teachers' endeavor to empower students is important because empowerment allows them to "exercise the kind of courage needed to change the social order where necessary" (McLaren, 2009, p. 74).

Our position throughout this chapter was consistent: Young adolescent ELLs need more opportunities to develop their identities and critical consciousness through critical literacy practice. Middle school ELLs' learning and life experiences are more complex than students in elementary school are (Genesee, Lindholm-Leary, Saunders, & Christian, 2005). They are more conscious of peer pressure and identity than very young children are (Brown, 1987), and they "undergo distinctive changes from the ways of their earlier childhood" (Stevenson & Bishop, 2012, p. 41). In this aspect, middle grade educators' implementation of critical practice is fundamental for ELLs who can act as active agents when they utilize their primary language and culture as "cultural capital" (Bourdieu, 1977, 1986). Cultural capital, defined as "instruments for the appropriation of symbolic wealth socially designated as worthy of being sought and possessed" (Bourdieu, 1977, p. 488), implies that ELLs can utilize their primary language and culture as valuable tools and instruments to develop their learning in a new hosting culture.

In conclusion, it is important for middle grade educators to support ELLs' cultural and social identities together with their critical consciousness. In this way, students are able to shift their marginalized identities to active agents in this political mainstream context. Developing ELLs' identities, coupled with critical consciousness, are integral components for ELLs' learning. We invite middle grade educators to pay more attention to ELLs' cultural and social identities for them to analyze critically the world and to define themselves as capable agents in this complex world.

REFERENCES

Ajayi, L. (2009). English as a second language learners' exploration of multimodal texts in junior high school. *Journal of Adolescent & Adult Literacy, 52*(7), 585–595.

Block, D. (2007). The rise of identity in SLA research, post Firth and Wagner (1997). *The Modern Language Journal, 91,* 863–876.

Bourdieu, P. (1977). Cultural reproduction and social reproduction. In J. Karabel & A. H. Halsey (Eds.), *Power and ideology in education* (pp. 487–511). New York, NY: Oxford University Press.

Bourdieu, P. (1986). The forms of capital. In J. G. Richardson (Ed.), *Handbook of theory and research for the sociology of education* (pp. 241–258). New York, NY: Greenwood Press.

Brown, H. D. (1987). *Principles of language learning and teaching.* Englewood Cliffs, NJ: Prentice-Hall.

Choudhury, M., & Share, J. (2012). Critical media literacy: A pedagogy for new literacies and urban youth. *Voices from the Middle, 19*(4), 39–44.

Cummins, J. (1989). *Empowering minority students.* Sacramento, CA: California Association for Bilingual Education.

Curtin, E. M. (2006). Lessons on effective teaching from middle school ESL students. *Middle School Journal, 37*(3), 38–45.

Danzak, R. (2011). Defining identities through multiliteracies: EL teens narrate their immigration experiences as graphic stories. *Journal of Adolescent & Adult Literacy, 55*(3), 187–196.

Duff, P. (2012). Identity, agency, and second language acquisition. In S. M. Gass & A. Mackey (Eds.), *The Routledge handbook of second language acquisition* (pp. 410–426). New York, NY: Routledge.

Enciso, P. (2011). Storytelling in critical literacy pedagogy: Removing the walls between immigrant and non-immigrant youth. *English Teaching: Practice and Critique, 10*(1), 21–40.

Erikson, E. H. (1993). *Childhood and society.* New York, NY: Norton.

Freire, P. (1970). *Pedagogy of the oppressed.* New York, NY: Continuum.

Freire, P. (1998). *Teachers as cultural workers: Letters to those who dare teach.* Boulder, CO: Westview Press.

Genesee, F., Lindholm-Leary, K., Saunders, W., & Christian, D. (2005). English language learners in U.S. schools: An overview of research findings. *Journal of Education for Students Placed at Risk, 10*(4), 363–385.

Harman, R., & Varga-Dobai, K. (2012). Critical performative pedagogy: Emergent bilingual learners challenge local immigration issues. *International Journal of Multicultural Education, 14*(2), 1–17.

Hughes, J., & Morrison, L. (2014). The impact of social networking and a multiliteracies pedagogy on English language learners' writer identities. *Writing & Pedagogy, 6*(3), 607–631.

Janks, H. (2010). *Literacy and power.* New York, NY: Routledge.

Janks, H. (2014). *Doing critical literacy: Texts and activities for students and teachers.* New York, NY: Routledge.

Johnston, P. (2004). *Choice words.* Portland, ME: Stenhouse.

Kramsch, C. (2009). *The multilingual subject. What language learners say about their experience and why it matters.* Oxford, England: Oxford University Press.

Kubota, R., & Lin, A. (Eds.). (2009). *Race, culture, and identity in second language education: Exploring critically engaged practice.* New York, NY: Routledge.

Landt, S. (2007). Weaving multicultural literature into middle school curricula. *Middle School Journal, 39*(2), 19–24.

Lau, S. M. C. (2012). Reconceptualizing critical literacy teaching in ESL classrooms. *The Reading Teacher, 65*(5), 325–329.

Luke, A. (2004). Foreword. In M. McLaughlin, & G. Devoogd (Eds.), *Critical literacy: Enhancing students' comprehension of text* (pp. 4–5). New York, NY: Scholastic.

McLaren, P. (2009). Critical pedagogy: A look at major concepts. In A. Darder, M. P. Baltodano, & R. D. Torres (Eds.), *The critical pedagogy reader* (pp. 61–83). New York, NY: Routledge.

Moje, E., & Luke, A. (2009). Literacy and identity: Examining the metaphors in history and contemporary research. *Reading Research Quarterly, 44*(4), 415–437.

Moll, L., Amanti, C., Neff, D., & Gonzalez, N. (1992). Funds of knowledge for teaching: Using a qualitative approach to connect homes and classrooms. *Theory Into Practice, 31*(2), 132–141.

Norton, B. (2000). *Identity and language learning: Gender, ethnicity and educational change.* New York, NY: Longman.

Osa, N. (2003). *Cuba 15.* New York, NY: Delacourte Press.

Pappamihiel, N. E. (2002). English as a second language students and English language anxiety: Issues in the mainstream classroom. *Research in the Teaching of English, 36*(3), 327–355.

Pavlenko, A., & Blackledge, A. (Eds.). (2004). *Negotiation of identities in multilingual contexts.* Clevedon, England: Multilingual Matters.

Shor, I. (1992). *Empowering education: Critical teaching for social change.* Chicago, IL: University of Chicago Press.

Sleeter, C. E. (2014). Multiculturalism and education for citizenship in a context of neoliberalism. *Intercultural Education, 25*(2), 85–94.

Stevenson, C., & Bishop, P. A. (2012). Challenging curriculum: Curriculum is challenging, exploratory, and relevant. In *This we believe in action: Implementing successful middle level schools* (pp. 29–46). Westerville, OH: Association for Middle Level Education.

Werderich, D. E. (2008). Bringing family and community into the writing curriculum. *Middle School Journal, 39*(3), 34–39.

Yoon, B. (2007). Offering or limiting opportunities: Teachers' roles and approaches to English language learners' participation in literacy activities. *The Reading Teacher, 61*(3), 216–225.

Yoon, B. (2008). Uninvited guests: The influence of teachers' roles and pedagogies on the positioning of English language learners in regular classrooms. *American Educational Research Journal, 45*(2), 495–522.

Yoon, B. (2015). Complexities of critical practice: The conflict between the teacher's ideological stance and the students' critical stance. In B. Yoon & R. Sharif (Eds.), *Critical literacy practice: Applications of critical theory in diverse settings* (pp. 79–93). Singapore: Springer.

Yoon, B., Simpson, A., & Haag, C. (2010). Assimilation ideology: Critically examining underlying messages in multicultural literature. *Journal of Adolescent and Adult Literacy, 54*(2), 109–118.

SECTION IV

EMPOWERING MIDDLE LEVEL EDUCATORS TO WORK
WITH YOUTH WITH MARGINALIZED IDENTITIES

CHAPTER 12

ENACTING CULTURALLY RESPONSIVE PEDAGOGIES

A Multicase Study of Middle Level Teachers in Urban, Priority Schools

M. Shelley Thomas
University of Louisville

Penny B. Howell
University of Louisville

ABSTRACT

In this study, we explored four middle school teachers' enactment of culturally responsive pedagogies as well as their processes developing those pedagogies across three years. Using a multicase approach, we analyzed data using a complexity framework informed by sociocultural theory. Three core elements of culturally responsive pedagogies emerged: centering middle level learners in recognition of all their identities, the development of teaching stances characterized by high help and high perfectionism, and a push for critical consciousness. Teachers' processed culturally responsive pedagogies in nonlinear ways prompted by disequilibrium. Further, they embedded cul-

Equity & Cultural Responsiveness in the Middle Grades, pages 257–288
Copyright © 2019 by Information Age Publishing
All rights of reproduction in any form reserved.

257

turally responsive pedagogies within their teaching and interactions with events, agents, and circumstances. The findings of this multi-year study suggest ways middle level teachers can enact more culturally and developmentally responsive pedagogies.

As our nation's middle schools grow ethnically, linguistically, and culturally diverse, critical attention to cultural responsiveness is essential to ensure young adolescents, particularly those from marginalized communities, receive developmentally and culturally affirming instruction. Teacher education is an important means to that end. Researchers in teacher education have called for preparation experiences that help candidates "think pedagogically about diversity" to provide instruction for all students that is rigorous and responsive to their needs as learners (Banks et al., 2005, p. 245).

Enactment of developmentally and culturally responsive instruction requires exploring students' cultures and other identities (Banks et al., 2005). Furthermore, development of cultural responsiveness is a career long process, and knowledge, skills, and attitudes are foundational tools to conceptualize and enact culturally responsive practices (Gay, 2000). The Association for Middle Level Education (AMLE) (2012) identified specific knowledge and skills for the preparation of a culturally responsive middle level teacher. AMLE Teacher Preparation Standard 1, element b, calls for candidates to "demonstrate their understanding of the implications of diversity on the development of young adolescents." Enactment requires candidates to "implement curriculum and instruction that is responsive to young adolescents' local, national, and international histories, language/dialects, and individual identities (e.g., race, ethnicity, culture, age, appearance, ability, sexual orientation, socioeconomic status, family composition)" (AMLE, 2012, S1Eb).

Teacher preparation programs have attempted two approaches to ensure that the overwhelmingly White, middle class, female candidates enrolled in their programs are prepared to teach diverse learners (Hollins & Guzman, 2005). Some create stand-alone courses focused on developing a broad understanding of culturally responsive and sustaining pedagogies. Others embed readings, activities, and field experiences across coursework. While a large body of work considers candidates' processes (e.g., Bartolomé, 2004; Bronkhorst, Koster, Meijer, Woldman, & Vermunt, 2014; Gay & Kirkland, 2003), little research examines how practicing middle level teachers understand and enact developmentally appropriate, culturally responsive pedagogies.

Locally, a dean in Arts and Sciences (A&S) at the University of Louisville initiated conversations with the superintendent of public schools about working with the district to develop those skills in teachers intentionally, later including faculty in A&S and in the College of Education (COE). As a result, and in response to the need for cultural competence and responsiveness across professions, these individuals created an interdisciplinary, advanced certificate in diversity literacy. A&S faculty designed the Diversity Literacy Certificate (DLC) "to enhance ... knowledge and skills of the theory and practice of inclusion and equity, including what diversity means, what its personal and social effects are, and how it shapes lives, workplaces, and pedagogy" (Department of Philosophy, n.d.). Soon after, A&S and COE faculty and the local district created a program including the DLC within a graduate education degree. This exploratory study describes the development of culturally responsive pedagogies and perspectives among five middle school teachers enrolled in the aforementioned program. Two questions guided our work:

1. How did middle level teachers in an advanced degree program enact culturally responsive pedagogies?
2. How did middle level teachers in an advanced degree program process their learning of these pedagogies?

We draw on literature around the enactment of culturally responsive pedagogies, and the development of middle level learners to explore these questions.

ENACTMENT OF CULTURALLY RESPONSIVE PEDAGOGIES

Gay's (2000) assertion that the academic achievement of students from diverse backgrounds improves when educators ensure instruction is responsive and reflective of students' cultures undergirds culturally responsive pedagogies. Teaching that is culturally responsive is a continuum of behaviors and beliefs that empower students to examine critically both educational content and processes using students' cultures to create meaning and help them understand the world. In a culturally responsive classroom, teachers emphasize academic, social, and cultural success and consider the appropriateness and effectiveness of curriculum and pedagogy (Ladson-Billings, 1995).

Because this work necessitates locating the enactment of culturally responsive pedagogies, we operationalize these and clarify what they are not. In her critique of "faulty and simplistic" (Sleeter, 2012, p. 562) notions of culturally responsive pedagogy, Sleeter (2012) described a range of factors, problematic practices, as well as limited and limiting frameworks. Her discussion is pertinent to this study because participants grappled with these and other issues as they processed their experiences. Furthermore, in our argument for culturally responsive pedagogies as an explicit piece of middle level teacher preparation, we include intentionality around raising critical consciousness as a necessary component. We draw on Freire

(1972) as we describe critical consciousness as engagement with the world to transform it. Further, we attend to Gay and Kirkland's (2003) argument to include ongoing processes of reflection, awareness, and action toward change, specifically around race and racism, and cultural difference and discrimination, among others. Thus, attention to documented struggles is relevant and essential.

Sleeter's (2012) specific critiques included positioning cultural celebration as an end, absent discussions of power and connections to student learning, "trivialization" or reduction of culturally responsive pedagogies to "checklists" and strategies, "essentializing culture" or "assuming fixed and homogenous" attributes to members, and "substituting cultural for political analysis of inequalities" through the omission of investigation and discussion of oppressions (p. 568). Because teachers are capable, deliberate decision-makers who enact, not implement curriculum (Zumwalt, 1988), attention to teachers' critical consciousness is a fundamental element of culturally responsive pedagogies. Alternatively, the enactment of culturally responsive pedagogies and becoming culturally responsive is an ongoing, transformational process. By looking at the process of enactment through the lens of complexity theory, we describe typical events and experiences of teachers' lives (e.g., lesson planning, content acquisition, engagement with families, completion of their own coursework) along with their human lives (as community members, employees, and advocates) as occasions that fostered conditions for disequilibrium and creative states (Zellermayer & Margolin, 2005), "reflecting the way the world works" (Larsen-Freeman, 2016, p. 377) that contributed to critical consciousness.

THE DEVELOPMENT OF MIDDLE LEVEL LEARNERS

AMLE (2018) defined middle level learners as students who are 10-15 years old. Advocates recognize this period as early adolescence and define educational approaches responsive to the developmental needs of these learners (Jackson & Davis, 2000). As Beane (2005) noted, physiological characteristics of the physical, social, emotional, and intellectual development of young adolescents are often the focus of educational efforts. While these are critical and impactful within educational settings, little discussion in the literature has problematized these socially constructed views of 10 to 15-year-old students and limits the discussion to what is appropriate given their physiological traits. This has led to a narrow view of the possibilities for students who are more complex and diverse than the "so called 'characteristics of early adolescence'" (Beane, 2005, p. xiii) and has marginalized students of color by neglecting to incorporate a holistic view of development that considers the political contexts in which development occurs.

Gay (1994) acknowledged the dearth of middle grades literature encompassing ethnic or cultural diversity and suggested that "factors of race and ethnicity" (p. 149) for young adolescents of color bring additional dimensions to developmentally responsive curriculum that educators must understand and enact. Including responsiveness to ethnic identity development of young adolescents is essential to creating middle schools that are truly developmentally responsive (Gay, 1994; Manning, 1999). Gay repositioned identity formation as "developmental, multifarious, of paramount importance during adolescence" (p. 152). A student's perception of ethnicity influences social interactions, emotional wellbeing, self-confidence, and intellectual engagement (Phinney, 1990). To expand developmental responsiveness, Gay suggested that teachers *and* students need to understand development to include the evolution of self and of racial, cultural, and ethnic identities.

Manning (1999) identified three characteristics that create a more inclusive view of developmental responsiveness: Young adolescents: (a) form cultural identities; (b) form close friends, social networks, and opinions of others' similarities and differences; and (c) develop a sense of justice, a perception of fairness, and an overall sense of how to treat people. When educators honor and respond to these characteristics by enacting developmentally appropriate, culturally responsive pedagogies, they affect young adolescents' attitudes. Manning suggested, "As society grows more diverse, middle school educators will be challenged to promote students' positive feelings toward diversity" (p. 87). Thus, developmentally appropriate, culturally responsive pedagogies support young adolescents' perceptions of their own evolution.

THEORETICAL FRAMEWORK

Given the limitations of professional learning and teacher education research as process-product oriented and focused on isolated, specific processes (Opfer & Pedder, 2011) as well as linear and reductionist (Cochran-Smith, Ell, Ludlow, Grundnoff, & Aitken, 2014), we framed this study with complexity theory to "account for the fact that teachers' learning is deeply embedded in their professional lives and in the working conditions of their schools" (Cochran-Smith et al., 2014, p. 11). Larsen-Freeman (2016) contended that examining teaching and learning from a complexity framework is useful to stimulate conversations about enactment. This framework recognizes interdependence, relations, and learning as "recursive, iterative, ongoing adaptations to a dynamic world that must be understood within systems of evolving relationships" (Zuiker, Anderson, Jordan, & Stewart, 2016, p. 83). Tenants of complexity theory include multiple interactions, non-linearity, disequilibrium, and the self-producing and self-reproducing state of emergence (Larsen-Freeman, 2013).

To hone in further on processes, we draw from Ball's (2009) description of change as generative, influenced by learning, and "self-perpetuating...influenced by the instructional approaches and theory that he or she is exposed to...making connections with his or her students' knowledge and needs and begins planning" (p. 48). Additionally, given the intent of the program to foster transformation, we also grounded this study in sociocultural perspectives. Sociocultural theory makes explicit the dialogic nature of human thought, language, and learning, emphasizing human development in the context of social and cultural interaction (John-Steiner & Mahn, 1996). Teachers' learning and enactment occur within social contexts and interactions; furthermore, their curricular decisions are expressions of their sociocultural epistemologies and reflections of political decisions (Kliebard, 1995).

In this study, teachers adapted to changing conditions within their classrooms, schools, and district and responded to the needs of diverse learners. Thus, sociocultural theory, in our analyses, highlighted how the teachers, who learned through processes embedded in their work with adolescents, operationalized course content within their contexts across the program and emphasized how these processes contributed to their positionalities as leaders and advocates.

METHODOLOGY

Consideration of the complex system of interacting elements is essential and includes several components nested within and intersecting with one another. Because in complexity theory the whole is greater than the sum of the parts, we do not evaluate the components of the process against one another; rather, we examine how these interacted and intersected, creating feedback loops (Cochran-Smith et al., 2014). We selected a multicase study design (Stake, 2006) to attend to local circumstances and conditions within each case as well as to go beyond a single case to look more deeply at research questions that address common conditions across cases. In a multicase study, a collection of individual cases shares a common concern. The single cases allow understandings of the quintain, or collection of cases (Stake, 2006). For this study, individual cases also enabled understanding of enactment across the different contexts that comprise the quintain and attention to specific experiences and activity (the enactment of culturally responsive pedagogies) within particular situations while also attending to experiences and learning. Importantly, there is no assumption of generalizability, as "the power of case study is its attention to the local situation" (Stake, 2006, p. 8).

We also recognized that becoming culturally responsive is an ongoing, recursive process, and furthermore the context and experiences of these teachers were interdependent and overlapping rather than independent and distinct. Complexity as a theoretical lens informed analysis and understandings of these events, interactions, and reactions. Rather than determining which pieces were effective and which were ineffective, we considered how the teachers, individually and collectively, (a) engaged with these processes; (b) engaged with the events in their schools, classrooms, and coursework; (c) interacted with students, colleagues, instructors, and one another; and (d) reacted to all of these within the sociopolitical context, to determine patterns, opportunities for their development, and the emergence of critical consciousness.

Context

As part of school turnaround efforts within our state, teachers from a large, urban district received foundation funding to enroll in the DLC while completing an M.Ed. in Teacher Leadership (TL). Stated goals for the program included improving teacher practices, increasing understandings of the sociopolitical and historical contexts of inequities, and most critically, retaining experienced teachers who were successful with diverse students, while building their capacities as leaders and advocates.

At the time of this study, all participants were teaching in ethnically, linguistically, and culturally diverse middle schools situated in an urban context. The Kentucky Department of Education designated each school as a *Persistently Low Achieving* or "priority" school by indicating consistent failure to meet Adequate Yearly Progress goals of the state assessment system. The five teachers enrolled in the program viewed it as a means of preparing them to support diverse young adolescent students, providing them intellectual stimulation, and supporting their professional growth. The study spanned three years to include the entire two-year program and a post completion retrospective.

Participants

This multicase study (Stake, 2006; Yin, 2009) included a purposeful sample of the aforementioned teachers: two each in language arts and social studies, and one math teacher. All are female, and two taught at the same school. One identified as African Caribbean, and the remaining four identified as White. Years of experience varied from one to 10 years.

Each also experienced unique local school conditions and selected different courses for the DLC component. Courses included the following graduate level studies: Theories and Issues, Religions of the African Diaspora, and Advanced African American Studies from the department of Pan African Studies; Women's Personal Narratives, Women and Medicine, Queer Performance, and Black Women's Voices from the department of Women's and Gender Studies; Perspectives on Urban Poverty in Political Science, a seminar on Toni Morrison in English, and both a Fundamentals of Diversity course and a capstone course in the Philosophy Department.

Data Sources

Data source triangulation (Yin, 2009) determined consistency across data sources, time, and in different situations over the three-year period. For the first research question, "How did teachers enact culturally responsive pedagogies," data included observation field notes, a walkthrough protocol designed by district personnel, and any lesson design materials provided by each teacher. The walkthrough served as an observation guide to determine when the teachers used culturally responsive pedagogies. As researchers, we consulted with the designer and cross-walked the instrument with the literature to address concerns that it reduced culturally responsive pedagogies to a checklist. We also used correspondence as data to provide context. Semi-structured interviews followed each observation. Because of time constraints in the school day, there were no pre-observation conferences. For the second research question, "How did participants process their learning of these pedagogies," data included interview rubrics and other materials submitted for application to the program, essays and lesson plans submitted for both TL and DLC courses across the two years of coursework, as well as planning documents and e-mail correspondence among the key personnel[1] and from participants. We used Hallmark Assessment Tasks (HATs), designed by instructors as authentic to teaching tasks, and aligned to professional standards (Danielson, 2014) as data for each of the TL courses. Teachers participated in focus groups conducted a year after the program in the final stage of data collection.

Data Collection and Analysis

The three-year study was bounded by time to include the application process in the summer of 2013 and concluded with focus groups in the spring of 2016. Data collection and analysis spanned the two-year program and an additional year. During the first year and second semester of the program, we observed each teacher twice. That year, the unusual number of snow days affected instruction and observation schedules. Though schools made up most of these at the end, state law canceled several days. As a result, teachers refer to these circumstances in the data.

Concepts of complexity theory include the distinction between transformation as "an internal... intentional process" and change as "an internal procedure that deals with policies, structure, or practices" (Zellermayer & Margolin, 2005, p. 1278). In addition, the notion of disequilibrium as inherent to complex systems is relevant to this study, particularly Cochran-Smith et al.'s (2014), explanation of disequilibrium as a "constant flow of interactions and information (that) creates energy... to keep the system operating..." (p. 8). Components of complexity as a "relational theory" (Larsen-Freeman, 2016, p. 379) include agents (the teachers in this study), the physical environment (diverse middle school classrooms), and elements (the respective COE and DL coursework).

First cycle, eclectic coding occurred throughout and served to explore the diverse processes of the participants over time (Saldaña, 2016). During second cycle coding, we further triangulated data within and across cycles and analyzed using directed content analysis (Hsieh & Shannon, 2005), a form of analysis using existing theory to initiate coding. These "two... different coding methods capture[d] the complex... processes in the data" (Saldaña, 2016, p. 69). We used tenants of complexity theory (i.e., disequilibrium, instability, non-linearity) to describe how participants processed their coursework and enacted culturally responsive practices. Additionally, concepts of and components in complexity theory served to complement or complicate the initial analytic concepts identified during first cycle analysis. Analytic notes served to document and refine these recursive processes.

FINDINGS

We drew findings from different focal levels. To address the question, "How do teachers enact culturally responsive pedagogies," we used the aforementioned agents (i.e., the teachers) as the focal level and discuss the context and conditions in which the agents are nested (Larsen-Freeman, 2016) drawing from autobiographical text in their applications and coursework. To address the question, "How do teachers process their learning of culturally responsive pedagogies," we drew from across the quintain to describe disequilibrium and the emergence of critical consciousness.

Enacting Culturally Responsive Pedagogies in the Middle Grades

Enactment of culturally responsive pedagogies centered on relationships between students and their peers and students and their teachers.

Furthermore, teachers connected subject matter to students' experiences and worlds. In the next section, illustrative cases using field notes and interview responses hone in on content and pedagogical decisions and actions. Biographical information and perspectives from application materials and coursework frame each case.

Sheba: Off Script in the Name of Engagement and Learning

Sheba's early experiences "being of African origin and growing up in the Barbadian culture" influenced her emerging sense of diversity as it expanded from "human physical and mental differences rather than cultural" to a more extensive view, influenced by her encounters with other cultures and ethnicities. Radio broadcasts introduced her to a range of religious perspectives and musical genres and school "kept [her] abreast of world cultures through literature, art, geography, and history." Sheba explained how her identity and experiences influenced why she is committed to diversity literacy.

> First, to help those considered different...feel accepted and second, to inform those who react negatively to such differences...I acknowledge and celebrate cultural factors among my students because my culture predisposed me to knowing the pain of having one's appearance or cultural practices derided....It is the bias toward total self-acceptance that I aim to nurture in my students. Classroom procedures are informed by this belief in self-efficacy. It impacts my discipline, for instead of sending students to isolation for minor infractions and off-task behavior, I conference with them and push them to find their inner sense of self-respect and/or family honor that requires more appropriate behavior or greater academic effort. Respect for culture (and) also sense of acceptance and belonging in my class. For example, I persuade Spanish speakers not to be embarrassed by their language but to honor it and contribute Spanish words or structures to supplement and enhance my explanation of English words and structures. These measures help students feel more accepted and comfortable enough to speak up in class and seek assistance when necessary...and make connections to lessons from their cultures.

Sheba's enactment of these practices in her seventh grade language arts classroom affirms these expressed beliefs and stances.

Sheba's students studied novels and poetry to identify theme in two poems, "I Know Why the Caged Bird Sings" by Maya Angelou (1971), and "Sympathy" by Paul Laurence Dunbar (1913). In response to the name Maya Angelou, a student called out, "She just died. My mom told me." Without missing a beat, Sheba called out "Phenomenal Woman" (Angelou, 1978). Do you remember...Have you heard of it?" Another student remarked that the poem hung in their kitchen. "It's been in your kitchen. Have you read it? With that, Sheba pulled up the poem from the internet.

"I will try to read it. I need four girls to read. Listen up! See what this says, think about your mothers, sisters, daughters, yourselves-read it with attitude!" Sheba read a few lines modeling attitude before remarking, "this was not on my plan...You are going to think on it. You can't leave out any words." Students continued reading the poem to the end. Sheba followed up, "You've got alliteration, what does it mean? Did she mention 'success?' what do people see in her beyond pride?" Each question provoked discussions about the meaning of the poem.

Later, Sheba asked, "Can men be phenomenal men? What is a phenomenal man, what does it mean?" When students expressed some confusion, Sheba responded with another question and explored the root word phenomenon with her students, providing examples and soliciting others from students. After some excited responses, Sheba directed the class back to their study of "I Know Why the Caged Bird Sings" (Angelou, 1971).

Sheba's enactment of culturally responsive pedagogies within this 25-minute episode occurred in the context of a whole group discussion. She provided students with access to the developmentally and culturally appropriate content; furthermore, she increased accessibility through her focus on vocabulary. She provided opportunities for learning and engagement through her insistence that students talk and actively contribute to discussions. "If they resist and they don't readily volunteer I make sure I call them—not call them out—but I call them and wait until they have a response." Further, she demonstrated use of families' experiences and funds of knowledge (Moll, Amanti, Neff, & Gonzalez, 1992) by going "off script," responding in the moment to a student's comment that their mother acknowledged the passing of Maya Angelou, and later when another shared that "Phenomenal Woman" was on display in their kitchen.

In a later lesson, students connected back to "I Know Why the Caged Bird Sings" (Angelou, 1971) and "Sympathy" as extensions to *Sarny* by Gary Paulsen (1997). During this lesson, students took notes on their interpretations and connections to those texts. Reflecting on that lesson, Sheba explored connections among diversity and families' lives' and funds of knowledge as texts. She also highlighted a more inclusive definition of text, "...the text—well, the diversification of texts. Cause if the text is anywhere information is shared, it means that what goes on in their house is text." Sheba's perspectives on text sources built on students' knowledge, experiences, and backgrounds to incorporate and authentically connect the content to their lives.

The Mexican (students) and we have an Argentinean (student), and they come from different parts of Mexico with different experiences, I don't assume that all Mexicans are alike. And then we do the Native American because some of the Black students and some of the Mexican students have Native American ancestry so we go there, and of course, the—we have information about how they were treated by the Americans, so we discuss that as part of the history... All of their connections become our texts. And those who have connections with Scotland, Ireland, Germany, they might make a reference to something... "Oh my grandmother used to say that" then their grandmother's story becomes part of our class text.

Explorations of familiar texts as culturally responsive practices and perspectives provided a safe space for Sheba's students to explore their cultural backgrounds and experiences as they learned content. Personal connections to the content helped students feel valued and respected.

In addition to the use of texts for authentic content connections, Sheba described how she modeled interactions, which in turn, strengthened relationships. She explained:

I banter with them, I slip into informal language with them, and I move back to formal language. So, by doing that, you know they have a sense, ok it's safe in this class to share ideas, it's safe to say that or joke with her and it's ok.... And they know up to what level they can actually joke with me. So, given that, I think we have a really good relationship.

Sheba also utilized classroom conversations to support students' social and academic development. While the interactions reveal her friendly demeanor toward students, they include a deliberate focus on academic achievement, "... every so often we banter to give them a chance to use the language in terms, in a social way, as well as they banter in terms of pushing them to a high academic standard."

Sheba exhibited her understanding and effective enactment of developmentally appropriate, culturally responsive pedagogies through content, relationships, and high expectations that included developing middle schoolers' critical stance toward their worlds. She engaged students' lived experiences as texts and allowed all students to hear the perspectives of others through conversation, discussion, and friendly banter.

Alice and (Productive) Struggle

Alice described her educational experiences as "a student who struggled mightily with K–12 schooling." As she reflected on her decisions to become a teacher, she provided insights on how she processed the systems of schooling, teacher education, and teaching within which she worked, lived, and learned.

Eventually, I came to see my difficulties in school as an asset, a perspective that other teachers may not have, and heeded the call to teach. In my teaching program (redacted) I threw myself into the study of Culturally Responsive Teaching. Being recognized as one of (redacted) Most Outstanding Student

Teachers while teaching at one of our district's most diverse, low income schools surely prepared me to be a culturally responsive teacher! I was humbled as a rookie teacher this year to find that when I analyzed my data, there was that "achievement gap" I surely thought would not be in *my* class. I was naively surprised that though I saw myself as "different" due to my school struggles and socio-economic background, that my students saw me as just another "White teacher." With some reflection, I see that further growth in diversity literacy is what I need to help my students achieve: to respectfully help them navigate the world around them…

Alice entered the DLC program following her first year of teaching. In a paper written during the first semester, she elaborated on her struggles with school, describing "nearly daily visits with administrators or counselors at school, lots of course recovery for failed classes, and an eventual placement in an alternative school." She recognized how these experiences informed the way she sees kids. In addition, Alice believed that because she is White, students see her as her skin color, motivating her to "…critically evaluate my interaction with students, and work towards equitable discipline, an inclusive and social justice oriented curriculum, and building the relationships that will show rather than tell that I care and value all students."

When Alice responded to the invitation to schedule observations for research, she requested the visit take place during her most difficult class.

You can observe my 4th period…I am really struggling with this group. Many of the student's (sic) are our team's lowest readers and discipline plan frequent flyers. Their assessment average as a class is significantly lower than my other classes. I would appreciate any feedback with them!!

At the beginning of that lesson, Alice revisited the overarching goals for students to complete an overview of the regions of Africa and better understand how geography influences culture. She next reviewed expectations regarding voice levels and movement, and then directed students to small groups. She continued to check in with students, attending specifically to their understanding of the vocabulary in different resources. Recognizing students were struggling with a key vocabulary word, Alice shifted to address the whole class. "How many of you don't know what topography is?" Alice directed a student to look up the definition and read it to the class, and then asked another to share an example. Though the student, Abdi, declined, Alice offered to read it, and he agreed. When Alice reflected later on Abdi's decision, she said, "…I think sometimes the speaking thing; they don't want to do the speaking…" Though Abdi chose not to speak, and Alice respected his choice, she later shared an instance when he chose to share.

Alice explained that the 17 students who engaged in group work to explore regions in contemporary Africa included those from Somalia, the

Congo, Cuba, Puerto Rico, and Mexico as well as those identifying as African American, Biracial, and White. For their project, each member collected specific information for their group's assigned region. She also noted that she co-designed the project with another sixth grade teaching partner with students' strengths and needs in mind. Alice detailed her rationale for the activities:

> They enjoy fact finding... and I think they like the independence and the autonomy of being able to do like a web search on their own. So, the content is required, the proficiency (test) is pretty heavy on geography, knowing basic physical features of Africa. They need to do that rather than just kind of watching a documentary or read it straight out of the text. We said 'let's do a modified jigsaw, let's let them become an expert on a region and share that out... they love kind of being the researcher... they are getting better at note taking and saying things in their own words, so that's a skill we worked on all year long is the paraphrasing.

Alice selected students' resources for accessibility and interest, using what she had learned in her coursework about activating English language learners' prior knowledge and creating connections rather than assuming background knowledge. She explained further, "I think I am mindful of that... because I don't assume... And I try to get a lot of the kids to share out what they do know and then we kind of address it, whether it's accurate or whether it's a stereotype... a lot of the stuff we talked about... were stereotypes." Alice explained how Abdi, the student referenced earlier, shared his story, creating an opportunity for connections and learning.

> Abdi was a shepherd, and he has talked to kids about that, and he was actually arguing with (another student)... The student was like, "I was in charge of like, 20 sheep" and Abdi's like, "Are you kidding me man?" cause (the other student) lived in a pretty urban or suburban area, but Abdi lived out in the country. "I have 200 sheep!" I was like, "how old were you?" and he was like, "eight" and I was like "what did you do to control the sheep?" and he goes, "a whistle and a stick." And he whistled, and the kids are like, "daaaang" and so they're interested, and I said, "tell them what you did" and someone raised their hand..., "why are you telling the sheep to go places?"... "I gotta keep them safe," and they were like, "from what?" "Lions." And the kids were like, "nuh-uh." And he's like, "uh-huh."

As Alice developed relationships with students and learned about their backgrounds, she recognized the rich and powerful lived experiences of students from the continent of Africa as opportunities to deepen perspectives and challenge stereotypes within the geography content required by state mandated curriculum. Because several of her students' home countries are on the African continent, this class discussion revealed the value she placed on her students' backgrounds and cultures while attending to the scope and sequence of the curriculum.

Furthermore, Alice was clear about her intent to incorporate her students' prior experiences and funds of knowledge authentically. Alice not only prompted students like Abdi to share, she provided opportunities and resources to support them to do so. In discussing Abdi, she illustrated how she planned for enactment of culturally responsive and sustaining pedagogies and considers how she can support Abdi and his classmates as they share their stories.

> I've asked Abdi and I've asked [another student], who is from the Congo, um, by way of Tanzania, and another couple kids if they would talk about, uh, their experience in Africa. And some have said, "yes, I definitely wanna do it" and they are gonna come up with like a powerpoint, and some have said "I don't know if I feel comfortable." So, we've talked about options, and I'm going to talk to their language—their ESL teacher and see if maybe even she could help them come up with a voc-key.

Alice's lesson also incorporated developmentally appropriate elements based on her knowledge of students' needs providing choice, opportunities for exploratory and collaborative work, and student autonomy.

Anne: Figuring Out What is Best for Kids in Light of Accountability

Anne described her educational experiences as a rural, working class student who, as the first person in her family to attend college, left her community to "escape" and explore the more diverse, larger city of the university. After completing a master's degree, she became a teacher at one of the city's middle schools. As she reflected on her own background, Anne described how she built relationships with students by sharing her past with them.

> My own culture is rooted in growing up in a rural area, which is not as different as you imagine from the urban students I teach...When I hear them make fun of what someone is wearing, I am open with them about the fact that I had to wear 'hand me downs' to school that belonged to another little girl in my grade at school and everyone knew. I have had more than one student loosen up with me after hearing that, knowing that I can relate to their situation.

Anne's seventh grade social studies students included those who were recent arrivals from Kenya, Haiti, Iraq, and Russia, along with their Black, White, and biracial peers. As a teacher at a school designated *Persistently Low Achieving* by the state, Anne's instructional decisions reflected her reactions to that designation coupled with her intentions to engage students with the content and with one another.

One lesson, designed to support students to meet state assessment demands, was part of a larger exploration of the elements of culture and included primary and secondary sources with different perspectives of Genghis Khan and the Mongols. Students watched a purposefully selected, content-dense video detailing the life and "exploits" of Genghis Khan. To support their learning, Anne's instruction included graphic organizers and discussions with peers. As they watched, students completed a t-chart, identifying positive and negative "things" about Genghis Khan in preparation for a collaborative group activity later. Anne used scaffolding and feedback throughout the lesson to keep students engaged and ensured they were on track while encouraging them to work together, "We are going to help each other. It's OK."

After about nine minutes of intense, scaffolded note taking, Anne stopped the video and reviewed the learning target that she projected as a PowerPoint slide, *I can use primary and secondary sources to describe and explain different perspectives concerning Genghis Khan and the Mongols.* She directed students to consider different perspectives as they worked collaboratively on their RAFTs, a literacy strategy requiring the author to write about an event from a specific perspective. After a few reminders about the structure of RAFT, she connected the students back to the learning target. She sent them back to work with a promise to help as needed and encouraged them to get others' thoughts, "Use your group mates as a sounding board." Anne circulated the room to encourage students who were not writing by asking questions to stimulate their thinking.

Anne later explained that her instructional and curricular choices first considered how to engage students with the history. In addition to engaging students, she also noted the importance of selecting content that would address state standards and peak students' interests. Anne described the video as a "crash course," a result of a last-minute lesson modification because of a schedule change. The schedule change occurred in response to another accountability mandate. That week, teachers had to use class time for students to complete Individual Learning Plans, a state requirement to ensure all students complete school—college and career ready,[2] requiring her to condense material. Anne's instructional choices reveal her willingness, in spite of making cuts, to maintain student-talk in the lesson, intending students to meet learning targets *and* engage in conversations to hear others' perspectives by ensuring the shortened lesson included discussion.

A little over a week later, the class continued their study of the elements of culture and perspectives, but the focus shifted to Central and South America as they compared the Mayan, Aztec, and Incan cultures. Anne designed a lesson with content including the system of roads the Incas built. The class worked in teams across the school parking lot to simulate the messaging system. As Anne had anticipated, students mixed up the instructions, became confused, and lost the message. Still outside, she called the class together to share aloud the difficulties they encountered. They responded, "I couldn't remember!" "It's cold!" and "People are not listening!" Anne appreciated students' struggles and experiences as learning opportunities, then redirected them to what they learned about the messaging system. Before wrapping up, students reflected on what they learned and shared their perspectives about the advantages and disadvantages the Incas faced with the road system.

Later, Anne explained, though this was the first time she had done the activity, she was pleased with the results. Again, because of scheduling issues related to school district demands as well as missed snow days, Ann had to reduce the study of the Incas into one lesson. While she knew it was impossible to consider an entire culture in one day, she determined that the priority was for students to understand Incan communications over large distances and difficult terrain.

Anne enhanced students' learning in the classroom by creating a focus of providing, listening to, and understanding perspectives of people and experiences. Her lessons required the students to communicate and listen to one another in various mediums. These culturally and developmentally responsive practices supported students' needs as young adolescents. They all had a voice, a role, and a perspective that was important to the community of the classroom as well as essential to learn the content. While Anne felt the pressures of state mandated testing and regulations, she prioritized lessons and activities that would incorporate students' voices and perspectives while attending to the required scope and sequence.

Olyvia: Community in Support of Mathematical Thinking

In reflecting on her educational experiences, Olyvia described herself as a "little White girl" who attended Catholic school until high school. She detailed the "bubble" where she was "the little White girl in my little White world at the Catholic school with my Catholic friends and our Catholic ways." As the only member of her class to switch to public school, Olyvia explained that her Catholic school friends "ditched" her, and she was on her own. However, as a high school athlete, Olyvia made new friends, many of whom were African American, and several who lived in public housing and relied on food stamps. She described her reaction to these circumstances by saying, "My mind was blown! How could some of my new friends be so poor, but so normal?"

Prior to teaching, Olyvia worked as an emergency medical technician. This job took her to every part of the city and required her to interact with diverse families across the suburbs and the urban area. In spite of those experiences and a personal sense that she understood diversity, she was surprised by how the diversity in the middle school "...opened my eyes to the depths of culture and new ways of learning that I never expected." Olyvia also recognized the critical need for mathematics to be relevant to students' lives. "This is not saying I need to use different names in word problems, but really pick up on their cultural practices and interests and include that in my everyday lessons."

Olyvia's eighth grade mathematics intervention classroom included 19 diverse students who identified as Black, White, and biracial along with classmates who were refugees from African nations. Olyvia estimated that approximately half were almost two grade levels behind in math, based on district proficiency assessments; consequently, another teacher taught their regular math class while Olyvia provided additional support. Because the state testing window was a few days away, they were preparing for the tests, graphing equations by matching graphs to the correct equation. On their handouts, students had two different graphs and two different problems, but similar looking equations. Their task was to match the graphs with the equations just as they would do on the test. As the whole class looked at examples of graphs and equations using the document camera, Olyvia conducted a think aloud, reasoning through appropriate test-taking strategies such as eliminating options and making the best choice. After completing an example question, matching an equation to a graph, Olyvia displayed the next set of instructions on a PowerPoint slide. These explicitly listed expectations that students were to work together; they were to use their notes; and they could only talk to their partners. As students worked, Olyvia circulated, checking answers. When the pairs finished, Olyvia transitioned back to the whole group. She asked students to project their answers using the document camera and to describe their reasoning. In some cases, she prompted for specific information, "How do you know slope?" When a student struggled, she instructed him to look at the equation piece by piece. "A lot of people get this mixed up. If you would like assistance you may ask someone with their hand up." Olyvia coached students through each step to match the equations with the graphs, and as they worked, she prompted them to use language and mathematical terms to explain. Several students took their turns solving problems and explaining how and why they made decisions. At the end of the period, Olyvia recognized their accomplishments, "A lot of you were getting it. You know this. We will talk more about this."

Olyvia explained that the state testing format influences her use of matching as an assessment. She recognized that students needed experience with matching, so she used it with a graphing task. Olyvia attributed her commitment to engage students in collaborative group work to broader goals around community building influenced by the DLC coursework. Further, she believed her intentionality and students' experiences working together positively influenced students' relationships with her and one another.

The following week, and the day before the state performance test, students graphed real life scenarios, created a data table, and used their tables and graphs to answer questions. The lesson began with students completing a multi-step problem with time limits to simulate the testing situation as a warm up. As they completed the problems, Olyvia utilized a question-response-evaluate method to guide the students through an analysis of their answers to promote good test taking strategies. Later, she explained her intentions:

> I feel like they learn ... doing activities ... let's try it this way as well. Now you try it by yourself. Now talk to your friend about it. And then let's all share our ideas together so that we can see how we each thought about this task and how we each approached it.

Olyvia also described her focused attention to community building through student-talk during each lesson.

> We talked about how important you know each student is and how everyone can bring something to the table we talked about that ... in the beginning and then I like to try to reiterate it ... we need to respect this person while they're speaking, because you never know what they might bring to the table, just little things, you know, to keep 'em responsible and respectful to each other.

Olyvia's consistent and persistent community building encouraged students to interact with mathematics and one another. She viewed student-talk about mathematical thinking as a necessary instructional decision to support students assigned to an intervention classroom. Thus, her reactions to upcoming state assessments were to address content and skills directly within classroom structures and instructional decisions that recognized difference and used it as learning opportunities.

Veda: Representation and Student Voice

When Veda described her early educational experiences, she defined herself as a perpetual learner. Furthermore, she explained that as a teacher she learns constantly, and that "there is not a single day that goes by that I do not learn something interesting or inspiring from my students." Her goals for the program included "grow(ing) in perceptions, privilege and access and inclusive curriculum design."

Veda also related how her experiences shaped her advocacy for diverse texts. She explained how, as a middle schooler, she did not see herself or her family represented in the curriculum, "We primarily spoke English, but I was constantly being spoken to in Portuguese, French, Greek, and Albanian ... I never felt like the stories we read or the students in textbooks looked or acted like me or my family." Veda revisited her sense of exclusion when she elaborated on her feelings of cultural disconnect as a middle schooler because the curricula did not reflect her background and contributed to her disengagement. As a result, she is "very particular about the types of texts we read." She added that she also recognizes her positionality as a White woman, and how that influences relationships with students.

Veda's enactment of culturally responsive pedagogies demonstrated her attention to texts as well as her intentionality to provide students multiple perspectives drawing from their diverse outlooks and interests. Veda's language arts classroom of 21 sixth graders including Black, White, biracial, and Mexican students began their study of how events and experiences influence an author's perspective by reading Langston Hughes' (1926) poem, "I, too, sing America." The activities for "I, too, sing America" would prepare them to use what they learned about connections between experience and perspectives to write claim poetry, a concept prioritized in the state mandated curriculum. To begin, students turned to their elbow partners and discussed what they needed to know about an author's background to understand why that author selected a specific topic. Veda circulated, listening to discussions and reviewing notes. "I saw people write 'Background' what does that mean? That's what we want to focus on." Veda next pointed to the poster of Langston Hughes in the classroom, "We have his picture up, but never talked about him. Now we will."

Students prepared to watch a short video clip on Langston Hughes and take notes on a graphic organizer. Veda circulated, reading students' notes and redirecting those off task. She then instructed students to work with elbow partners to fill in missing information as she continued to move around. "What do you have? Keep in mind 'he died of cancer' is not really what we are looking for. What did we learn about his perspectives?" Later, she asked students to share responses, then transitioned to identifying claims and perspectives in "I, Too." Their handout was another organizer with the poem, separated by stanza on the left and question prompts with each stanza along the right side. The questions asked *what does it mean to "sing America?" What does it mean to be the "darker brother? Who is "they"? What is the conflict here? What does this stanza (section) tell you about Hughes' hopes for the future,* and *Why will people be ashamed?* As students worked, Veda continued to circulate, give feedback, and answer questions. Her feedback focused heavily on evidence, another important concept in the writing curriculum for the state. "You are making claims and you are not supporting them." After 10 minutes of work, Veda directed the students to provide evidence. "Here is an example of what we are doing and what we need to do. What is missing?" When a student replied, evidence, Veda responded, "Perfect!" What can I annotate to show me this is true? Ask yourself, does anybody have to believe me? We need to give evidence. Do I have evidence?"

By reading Langston Hughes (1926), Veda's lesson intentionally included content that reflected many of her middle school students while addressing the concepts prioritized in the state mandated curriculum. However, she described the challenge of finding texts that reflect students' cultures.

> Finding texts that students can see themselves in. Um, a lot of the times, the texts are—like we just took a diagnostic yesterday—all of the texts were about, like, they all had White characters, they all had specifically White events, like the Gold Rush and things like that. So I know that they're getting that in they're probably getting that in most of their classes. So like, talking about Langston Hughes, like, that's not in the textbook.

Veda explained that though it takes time to locate supplemental texts because the textbooks are not diverse, students are more engaged when they see themselves in the curriculum.

In another lesson, Veda again engaged students in an exploration of theme in a text through a reading of *The Sneetches* by Dr. Seuss (1961). After students read the text, they watched a brief video and collaborated to respond to questions on a handout. Questions included comprehension checks and asked for the theme: *I think this poem is meant to teach me. . . . Because. . . .* While students worked, Veda circulated, reading and reacting to student work, clarifying for one student the vocabulary in the question, *how is the language different for plain and star-bellied sneetches,* "language is how you express things" and then affirming that student when they responded, "Exactly, good way to put it." Veda reminded students to stay on task and encouraged a student to check a response, "I hear what you are saying, but I'm not sure we have enough evidence."

Veda reviewed responses, encouraging all to share and affirming their efforts. She next transitioned into an independent, task that required personal reflections (i.e., What feelings did you have during the class activity and why, what makes you feel like a Plain-Belly Sneetch, a Star-Belly Sneetch, what lessons did you learn?) and a commitment to action (List three actions you will take to help everyone feel like they belong). For their exit slip, Veda explained that they were going to connect a famous quote: *An eye for an eye would make the whole world blind,* and connect it to the theme of *The Sneetches* (Seuss, 1961). Students wrote independently then submitted their exit slips before leaving.

Veda explained that the lesson was based on a plan she found in *Teaching Tolerance,* and reflected her recognition that her students' need a more student-centered approach with a collaborative activity in response to off task behavior. She recognized that by working together on a structured, engaging task, they were making connections through substantive conversations, "You could hear, 'This is racist, this is messed up' . . . I knew that this would be something that they would be comfortable talking to each other about and that would get them involved." She engaged sixth graders in dialogue, reflection, and action and critically considered curriculum to identify and rectify omissions. Using talk, formative assessments, and supportive feedback, Veda pushed students through something that they cared about-discussions of race and equity.

The Complex Process of Teacher Learning: Disequilibrium as Generative

As described earlier, we drew findings for the research question, how did teachers process their learning of culturally responsive pedagogies from across the quintain and discussed together with reference to specific data. All five teachers recognized the elements of the program experiences and opportunities as "generative" (Mason, 2008, p. 39), exposing teachers to information and theories they connected to their teaching; in sum, for pushing them to support their diverse middle level learners. That said, each also struggled with internal and external conflicts, encountering disequilibrium with personal and professional growth best described as cumulative rather than incremental. The volume and nature of the readings, in addition to their everyday responsibilities as teachers and school leaders, their other roles in communities as well as in their families also led to frustration and anxiety. One explained during the first semester that she never gave up on anything, but "for once I am perilously close to doing so." The same teacher reflected on how her state of mind contributed to her advocacy when two years later she mused, "I sometimes have a sense of helplessness because there is so much to be done, but I am not in a position to do it in a large scale." As she continued, she disclosed that her sense of helplessness did not prevent her from acting on behalf of students, "So I think as a result I become more passionate-and more irritable-to my students. (in terms of behavior), I don't let anything slip. Often I have at-the-door conferences... I've become more vigilant."

Teachers also pushed back on coursework and instructor expectations. For example, one minimized the privilege and systems language as "jargon" and several struggled with the process of writing thesis-defense essays. They frequently submitted assignments late and/or rewrote them because of inadequate performance. However, by the end of the coursework and in the follow-up focus group, each articulated specific examples of how their knowledge base expanded and their teaching repertoires increased. "I feel like now I'm just, I feel more confident, taking the class we took (on urban poverty), I feel more well read. And I'm more equipped to teach." When asked about how she thought differently now, she explained that because of the DLC experiences, she had a more holistic understanding of the sociopolitical context that shapes students' learning, and she reflected that in her instructional decisions.

Importantly, from these complex experiences, the teachers often emerged with an increasing sense of critical consciousness, and corresponding commitment to teaching their middle level learners. In an explicit example, one teacher, who minimized examinations of structural inequities, wrote this response to an assignment question that asked how the project will synthesize the content of the DLC courses, "I have never had to think more deeply... I have never had to look at myself with a more critical lens and I think that had originally prohibited me from being the best teacher I can be." Though she often resisted, she recognized that what she learned changed the way she viewed herself and her students.

Across the TL and DLC courses and assignments, different content resonated with each teacher. Furthermore, the teachers' ability to embed what they learned into contexts played a critical role in how they scaffolded experiences. TL course assignments provided them a routine and familiar structure that was authentic to their work as teachers and increased their efficacy. Importantly, DLC courses provided distinctive opportunities and scaffolds. Each teacher struggled at some point with DLC courses. Struggles were distinctive from those associated with the TL courses and included existential discomfort and disequilibrium as well as the capacity to meet less explicit assessment criteria, larger reading loads, and different expectations of performance compared to TL courses. For example, they preferred the assessment style of the TL courses, with their consistent and authentic formats, because they were familiar and easily adapted to their classrooms. Eventually, Veda, Anne, and Olyvia navigated these differences by intentionally engaging with the DLC courses through their lenses as middle school teachers and negotiated the format of their DLC assessments.

DLC courses provided the experiences, interactions, and content for teachers' ongoing processes of "sociocultural consciousness" (Villegas & Lucas, 2001, p. 33). For example, Anne, who enrolled in several courses in Pan African Studies, indicated she selected those to support her students, and, in a philosophy course, connected Black feminism to critical thinking, arguing that Black feminism is critical by its very nature. It is thus an opportunity to explore more inclusion of Black women's voices to teach critical thinking.

Teachers also described the instabilities they experienced with administrators who did not value culturally responsive pedagogies to the same extent they did, and colleagues who disregarded their mentorship or advice on how to support diverse students. In contrast, when colleagues and administrators recognized their capacities and sought out their input, the teachers felt validated and competent. Anne was involved in a school wide cultural competence committee and a smaller professional learning community that designed professional development and deliberated over issues of diversity and how, for example, these should inform homework policies. She describes an instance, "it was a very heated discussion between one of our teachers and the ELL teacher about the issues and we kind of helped—I helped to, um, you know, mediate that, and work out a solution." Sheba acknowledged that the DLC courses pushed her thinking. She described a hallway conversation she had with a colleague while a struggling student stood nearby. A course on gender studies inspired Sheba's advocacy:

> The teacher, she said, "this girl writes really well but she wouldn't stay in class and she wouldn't do the work." And the girl says, "I am not a girl, I told you, I'm a boy," and I said, my next comment was, "Well if his work is that good, then you know, I should read it sometime" or whatever. And then the teacher started saying, "but he" whatever, so he automatically changed gender...he began to use the male pronoun, I thought that that little interaction was part of me sharing what I'd learned in the course and was better than saying, "oh I learned this in a course on Gender Studies."

Importantly, teachers also described the significance of continuously immersing themselves in cycles of enactment of culturally responsive pedagogies, reflection, and feedback as essential. They sought opportunities to engage in learning and enactment, creating states of emergence during classes at the university and through their teaching and reflections. Characteristics that were common among their choices for learning opportunities were the focus on enactment of culturally responsive pedagogies, reflection, and coaching or feedback from others.

DISCUSSION AND IMPLICATIONS

Each of the teachers enacted culturally responsive pedagogies through their relationships with students and the selection of content to engage and reflect them. Additionally, they demonstrated what Nieto and Bode (2012) referred to as high help and high perfectionism. We saw high help where the teachers expressed their strong desire to "help when [students were] confused or making mistakes" (p. 258), as well as high perfectionism when they stressed accuracy and high standards (Ferguson, 2008). Further, this supports Nieto's (2005) perspectives of caring and committed teachers. When Nieto asked teachers for the reasons they teach, she was able to develop a nuanced, complex understanding of their caring relationships with students. Nieto and Bode (2012) specifically defined these as "a sense of mission; solidarity with and empathy for students; the courage to challenge mainstream knowledge; improvisation; and a passion for social justice" (p. 256). Across the data, we found that teachers operationalized this notion of caring, translating their sense of mission, empathy, ability to improvise and passion for social justice into their daily practices.

To advocate for culturally responsive pedagogies, middle level teacher educators must consider the political factors that push against such a stance and prepare teachers to respond to these. Indeed, though each stated they valued culturally responsive pedagogies when they began the program, throughout the study, teachers also described barriers and pushback from administrators and colleagues. They described time pressures related to the structures of schooling in an urban priority school. They also struggled with colleagues' deficit views of students and those unwilling to teach something new and "outside their comfort zone." One lamented that she had no avenues to demonstrate leadership in culturally responsive pedagogies or create change. She elaborated the school was in "crisis mode" without a long-term plan or vision. Another shared that colleagues disregarded discussions about more culturally responsive content in favor of those about management. That said, each sought others with whom to collaborate. Likewise, they sought spaces beyond the program, including additional professional development, which created interactions and feedback loops. In spite of their willingness to seek out sustaining spaces, the barriers and pushback had consequences. All expressed misgivings about their school environments; one changed schools.

Centering Middle Level Learners with Attention to All Their Identities

Centering diverse middle level learners means that teachers should obtain cultural knowledge, connect culture to classroom practice, and reject deficit conceptions of students (Pang & Park, 2011). The teachers participated in advanced coursework in diversity literacy and often sought out courses to obtain cultural knowledge. Experts who were scholars in fields such as sociology, philosophy, English, urban studies, anthropology, and Pan African Studies taught the courses. We acknowledge these circumstances would be difficult to replicate; rather, we recommend attention to the conditions that prompted disequilibrium and the emergence of new insights and perspectives for teachers.

First, effective instructors were well versed in their subject areas and taught at a level appropriate for graduate, adult learners without assuming large amounts of prior knowledge on a topic. Second, the diversity literacy content focused heavily on deep structural issues and implications. Olyvia's insights from the Anthropology of Refugees enabled her to support refugee students. Pang and Park (2011) advocated for this type of deep knowledge about students because of the possibilities for connecting learning to their lives and experiences. Third, because teachers learned and processed content through assignments and readings, they had opportunities to engage in discussion and receive feedback that in turn challenged deficit perspectives by providing grounded and substantiated counter evidence fostering creative states (Zellermayer & Margolin, 2005). Assignments such as the lesson plans, work samples, and rationales submitted in the COE courses and papers written for the DLC courses required the teachers to apply, articulate and reflect.

Developing a Teaching Stance that Includes High Help and High Perfectionism

As explained previously, high help and high perfectionism support student learning. In combination, these actions are particularly effective with students of color because students are both encouraged and supported to persist. In contrast, Ferguson (2008) described that in diverse classrooms where high help is present but high perfectionism is not, achievement falls, and with low help and high perfectionism, student behavior is more problematic.

To support development of a teaching stance that cultivates high help and high perfectionism with middle school students, we direct teachers to examine their decision-making at each phase-before, during, and after the act of teaching. Hollins (2012) described the act of teaching as an interpretive process that allows teachers to plan, enact, interpret, and then translate practice for future learning. Enactment includes (a) sociocultural knowledge of students; and (b) how students interact with the curricular materials, with each other, and with the teacher (Hollins, 2012). Thus, planning that includes culturally responsive pedagogies for middle level learners must go beyond posing questions or adjusting an assignment. Instead, teachers should make careful and deliberate observations of students at work and in social settings, consider their previous work, and engage them in strategic discussions to provide insight about students' connectedness or disconnectedness to the knowledge, experience, skill, and the task (Hollins, 2008). Each of the teachers in this study expected and welcomed students' questions and reactions. Anne, for instance, asked students for feedback, stressed the importance of listening to students, and appreciated and used their input.

Veda's persistence that students provide credible evidence in their writing while she provided them examples and opportunities, and Sheba's insistence that students build their vocabularies through conversations, reading, and writing were powerful examples of high perfectionism that tapped into the respective teachers' sociocultural knowledge of students and of how students interacted. In addition to their determination that students meet expectations, both Veda and Sheba used guided practice, feedback, and scaffolding to enable success.

Pushing Teachers Toward Critical Consciousness

Critical consciousness is essential to the development of teacher lenses in support of diverse students. However, teaching and teacher education literature are replete with counterexamples of critical consciousness (e.g., Garrett & Segall, 2013; Gay & Kirkland, 2003; Haviland, 2008; Thomas & Vanderhaar, 2008). Each of these counterexamples requires explicit, yet complex responses in the interest of developing critical consciousness. Research on the development of culturally responsive pedagogies in preservice teachers demonstrates that they frequently lack socio-historical knowledge about race and racism (Brown, 2011) and possess simplistic notions of culture. Responses to these underdeveloped knowledge bases include frameworks where they are involved in actively recognizing and rectifying knowledge gaps.

Practicing teachers need similar experiences. Research on practicing teachers' conceptions of critical consciousness found that professional development experiences include miseducative content that perpetuate rather than eliminate deficit views (Bomer, Dworin, May, & Semingson, 2008). Deficit perspectives are views that individuals and their cultural backgrounds are lacking, inadequate, or inferior. The consequences of deficit thinking include the reinforcement of stereotypes, blaming the victim, and the dismissal of structural explanations of individuals' experiences (Nieto & Bode, 2012). Thus, middle level teachers must replace deficit notions of students and their families with supportive, realistic understandings of their circumstances and strengths, using, for example, social class sensitive pedagogy (Jones & Vagle, 2013). Teachers engaging a social class sensitive pedagogy apply a class sensitive lens to school policies and classroom practices (Jones & Vagle, 2013).

Finally, recognizing teachers as adult learners interacting within complex systems, it is important to consider how to transform (rather than change) their thinking continually, with opportunities for them to situate new learning. The middle school teachers enacted culturally responsive pedagogies as agents (i.e., person who takes an active role) who positioned middle school students as agents. Importantly, each of the teachers recognized their continuing need for growth in developing culturally responsive pedagogies and critical consciousness. In some instances, we included quotes from the teachers that have elements that require additional deconstruction and critique. For example, we included but did not critique Alice's references to students as discipline plan "frequent flyers" and Sheba's reduction of gender to binaries in discussing "phenomenal women" and "phenomenal men." Likewise, others currently seem unproblematic, but in a different context might be more complicated. Sheba and Veda both, for example, engaged students in discussions of race that seemed to them, under the historical and political contexts at the time, to be inclusive and productive for the particular students in their classrooms at that point. That said, we must consider how more recent events and the shifting political context affect these conversations with and among middle level learners. Ultimately, we all must engage in self-critique and consciousness raising.

CONCLUSIONS

As middle level teacher education aspires to prepare teachers who are responsive to young adolescents' multiple identities, (AMLE, 2012), it is essential they provide an expanded view of developmental responsiveness (Gay, 1994, 2000; Manning, 1999). Gay (1994) suggested that inclusive developmental responsiveness means teachers *and* students have opportunities to explore the evolution of self and of racial, cultural, and ethnic identities.

In this study, the enactment of culturally responsive pedagogies positioned young adolescents to take an active role in the exploration of themselves—socially, intellectually, and culturally. Teachers encouraged cultural identity development through close friendships in classroom communities where students developed social networks and opinions of others' similarities and differences. Teachers also positioned students to develop a sense of justice, a perception of fairness, and a sense of how to treat people (Manning, 1999). Returning to Gay's (1994) charge, teachers should explore notions of justice and fairness as well. Teachers participating in this study had such an opportunity through the DLC coursework. Beyond those explorations, and as a next step, how did the teachers develop the knowledge and skills to "think pedagogically about diversity" (Banks et al., 2005, p. 245)? How did they enact those pedagogies as well process what they learned along the way?

By using a complexity framework and attending to teachers' thoughts, language and learning within sociocultural contexts, findings identified three core elements for teachers' enactment of culturally responsive pedagogies: centering middle level learners in ways that recognize all their identities, the development of teaching stances characterized by high help and high perfectionism, and a push for critical consciousness. Furthermore, they processed, or entered and remained in "creative states" (Zellermayer & Margolin, 2005, p. 1279) that they maintained long enough to work through challenges including their own doubts. Events, interactions, and tensions had "catalytic power" (Zellermayer & Margolin, 2005, p. 1279) and transformative results. The results as well as the processes contain lessons on how middle level teachers can enact more culturally and developmentally responsive pedagogies. Further exploration will likely expand on those lessons.

NOTES

1. Key personnel included the district administrators who made funding and admissions decisions as well as the DLC and TL advisors.
2. See https://education.ky.gov/educational/compschcouns/ILP/Pages/default .aspx

REFERENCES

Angelou, M. (1978). Phenomenal woman. In *And still I rise* (pp. 8–10). New York, NY: Random House.

Angelou, M. (1971). *I know why the caged bird sings.* New York, NY: Bantam.

Association for Middle Level Education. (2012). *Association for Middle Level Education middle level teacher preparation standards with rubrics and supporting explanations.* Westerville, OH: Author. Retrieved from http://www.amle.org/aboutamle/professionalpreparation/amlestandards.aspx

Association for Middle Level Education. (2018). *AMLE at a glance.* Retrieved from http://www.amle.org/AboutAMLE/AMLEataGlance/tabid/122/Default .aspx

Ball, A. F. (2009). Toward a theory of generative change in culturally and linguistically complex classrooms. *American Educational Research Journal, 46*(1), 45–72.

Banks, J., Cochran-Smith, M., Moll, L., Richert, A., Zeichner, K., LePage, P. . . . Duffy, H. (2005). Teaching diverse learners. In L. Darling-Hammond & J. Bransford (Eds.), *Preparing teachers for a changing world: What teachers should learn and be able to do* (pp. 232–274). San Francisco, CA: Jossey-Bass.

Bartolomé, L. I. (2004). Critical pedagogy and teacher education: Radicalizing prospective teachers. *Teacher Education Quarterly, 31*(1), 97–112.

Beane, J. (2005). Foreword. In E. Brown & K. Saltman (Eds.), *The critical middle school reader* (pp. xi–xv). New York, NY: Taylor & Francis.

Bomer, R., Dworin, J., May, L., & Semingson, P. (2008). Miseducating teachers about the poor: A critical analysis of Ruby Payne's claims about poverty. *Teachers College Record, 110*(12) 2497–2531.

Bronkhorst, L. H., Koster, B., Meijer, P. C., Woldman, N., & Vermunt, J. D. (2014). Exploring student teachers' resistance to teacher education pedagogies. *Teaching and Teacher Education, 40,* 73–82.

Brown, K. D. (2011). Breaking the cycle of Sisyphus: Social education and the acquisition of critical sociocultural knowledge about race and racism in the United States. *The Social Studies 102*(6), 249–255.

Cochran-Smith, M., Ell, F., Ludlow, L., Grundnoff, L., & Aitken, G. (2014). The challenge and promise of complexity theory for teacher education research. *Teachers College Record, 116*(5), 1–38.

Danielson, C. (2014). *Framework for teaching: Adapted for Kentucky*. Retrieved from https://www.nctq.org/dmsView/Kentucky_Framework_for_Teaching

Department of Philosophy. (n. d.). *Diversity literacy certificate*. Retrieved from https://louisville.edu/philosophy/academics/graduate/diversity-literacy-certificate/

Dunbar, P. L. (1913). Sympathy. In *The complete poems of Paul Laurence Dunbar* (p. 102). New York, NY: Dodd, Mead, & Co.

Ferguson, R. F. (2008). Helping students of color meet high standards. In M. Pollock (Ed.), *Everyday antiracism: Getting real about race in school* (pp. 78–81). New York, NY: New Press.

Freire, P. (1972). *Pedagogy of the oppressed* (30th ed.). (M. Ramos, Trans.). London, England: Continuum.

Garrett, H. J., & Segall, A. (2013). (Re) considerations of ignorance and resistance in teacher education. *Journal of Teacher Education, 64*(4), 294–304.

Gay, G. (1994). Coming of age ethnically: Teaching young adolescents of color. *Theory Into Practice, 33*(3), 149–155.

Gay, G. (2000). *Culturally responsive teaching: Theory, research, and practice*. New York, NY: Teachers College Press.

Gay, G., & Kirkland, K. (2003). Developing cultural critical consciousness and self-reflection in preservice teacher education. *Theory Into Practice, 42*(3), 181–187.

Haviland, V. S. (2008). Things get glossed over: Rearticulating the silencing power of whiteness in education. *Journal of Teacher Education, 59*(1), 40–54.

Hsieh, H., & Shannon, S. E. (2005). Three approaches to qualitative content analysis. *Qualitative Health Research, 15*(9), 1277–1288.

Hollins, E. R. (2008). *Culture in school learning: Revealing the deep meaning* (2nd ed.). New York, NY: Routledge.

Hollins, E. R. (2012). *Learning to teach in urban schools*. New York, NY: Routledge.

Hollins, E., & Guzman, M. T. (2005). Research on preparing teachers for diverse populations. In M. Cochran-Smith, & K. Zeichner (Eds.), *Studying teacher education: The report of the AERA panel on research and teacher education* (pp. 477–548). Mahwah, NJ: Erlbaum.

Hughes, L. (1926). I, too, sing America. In *The weary blues* (p. 46). New York, NY: Knopf.

Jackson, A., & Davis, G. A. (2000). *Turning points 2000: Educating adolescents in the 21st century*. New York, NY: Teachers College Press.

Jones, S., & Vagle, M. D. (2013). Living contradictions and working for change: Toward a theory of social class sensitive pedagogy. *Educational Researcher, 42*(3), 129–141.

John-Steiner, V., & Mahn, H. (1996). Sociocultural approaches to learning and development: A Vygotskian framework. *Educational Psychologist, 31*(3), 191–206.

Kliebard, H. M. (1995). *The struggle for the American curriculum: 1893–1958* (2nd ed.). New York, NY: Routledge.

Ladson-Billings, G. (1995). Toward a theory of culturally relevant pedagogy. *American Education Research Journal, 332*(3), 465–491.

Larsen-Freeman, D. (2013). Complexity theory: A new way to think. *Revista Brasileira de Linguística Aplicada, 13*(2), 369–373. doi:10.1590/S1984-63982013000200002

Larsen-Freeman, D. (2016). Classroom-oriented research from a complex systems perspective. *Studies in Second Language Learning and Teaching, 6*(3), 377–393. doi:10.14746/ssllt.2016.6.3.2

Manning, L. (1999). Developmentally responsive multicultural education for young adolescents. *Childhood Education, 7*(2), 82–87.

Mason, M. (2008). What is complexity theory and what are its implications for educational change? *Educational Philosophy and Theory, 40*(1), 35–49. doi:10.1111/j.1469-5812.2007.00413.x

Moll, L. C., Amanti, C., Neff, D., & Gonzalez, N. (1992). Funds of knowledge for teaching: Using a qualitative approach to connect homes and classrooms. *Theory Into Practice, 31*(2), 32–141.

Nieto, S. (2005). *Why we teach.* New York, NY: Teachers College Press.

Nieto, S., & Bode, P. (2012). *Affirming diversity: The socio-political context of multicultural education* (6th ed.). Boston, MA: Pearson.

Opfer, V. D., & Pedder, D. (2011). Conceptualizing teacher professional learning. *Review of Educational Research, 81*(3), 376–407.

Pang, V. O., & Park, C. D. (2011). Creating interdisciplinary multicultural teacher education: Courageous leadership is crucial. In A. F. Ball & C. A. Tyson (Eds.), *Studying diversity in teacher education,* (pp. 63–80). Boston, MA: Rowan and Littlefield.

Paulsen, G. (1997). *Sarny, a life remembered.* New York, NY: Delacorte.

Phinney, J. (1990). Ethnic identity in adolescence and adulthood: A review of research. *Psychological Bulletin, 108*(3), 499–514.

Saldaña, J. (2016). *The coding manual for qualitative researchers* (3rd ed.). Los Angeles, CA: SAGE.

Seuss, Dr. (1961). *The Sneetches and other stories.* New York, NY: Random House.

Sleeter, C. E. (2012). Confronting the marginalization of culturally responsive pedagogy. *Urban Education, 47*(3), 562–584. doi.org/10.1177/0042085911431472

Stake, R. (2006). *Multiple case study analysis.* New York, NY: Guilford Press.

Thomas, S., & Vanderhaar, J. (2008). Negotiating resistance to multiculturalism in a teacher education curriculum: A case study. *Teacher Educator, 43*, 173–197. doi:10.1080/08878730802055057

Villegas, A., & Lucas, T. (2001). *Educating culturally responsive teachers: A coherent approach.* Albany: State University of New York Press.

Yin, R. K. (2009). *Case study research: Design and methods* (4th ed.). Los Angeles, CA: SAGE.

Zellermayer, M., & Margolin, I. (2005). Teacher educators' professional learning described through the lens of complexity theory. *Teachers College Record, 107*(6), 1275–1304.

Zuiker, S. J., Anderson, K. T., Jordan, M. E., & Stewart, O. G. (2016). Complementary lenses: Using theories of situativity and complexity to understand collaborative learning as systems-level social activity. *Learning, Culture and Social Interaction, 9*, 80–94. doi.org/10.1016/j.lcsi.2016.02.003

Zumwalt, K. (1988). Are we improving or undermining teaching? In L. Tanner (Ed.), *Critical issues in curriculum. Eighty-seventh yearbook of the national society for the study of education* (pp. 148–174). Chicago, IL: University of Chicago Press.

CHAPTER 13

PREPARING CULTURALLY RESPONSIVE MIDDLE LEVEL EDUCATORS TO ENGAGE IN CRITICAL CONVERSATIONS

Preservice Teachers Learning in an Integrated Curriculum Course

Toni M. Williams
University of South Carolina

ABSTRACT

Creating a safe space for middle level teacher candidates to explore their identities as they recognize community and cultural knowledge from young adolescents vastly different from theirs is essential. All young adolescents bring various backgrounds and experiences into the classroom with them, and culturally relevant pedagogy gives teachers an opportunity to share counter-stories and display the importance of community. This chapter focuses on the clinical practices and methods used in an integrated curriculum course to stimulate conversations among middle level teacher candidates about cultur-

Equity & Cultural Responsiveness in the Middle Grades, pages 289–309
Copyright © 2019 by Information Age Publishing

al diversity. Teacher education does not always explore and delve into the issues facing marginalized students and what makes learning happen for them, thus I challenged my middle level teacher candidates to examine their identities through class discussion and activities centered on diversity and culture.

> *Educators who understand these young people and the cultural context in which they grow to maturity will make informed decisions about the kinds of schools and learning experiences that young adolescents need.*
> —National Middle School Association [NMSA], 2010, p. 9

The Association for Middle Level Education (AMLE) is committed to supporting teachers in providing guidance and advocacy for young adolescents who are growing up within and navigating societal changes every day. As middle level teacher educators, we too must prepare our students—teacher candidates—to take on societal and cultural issues in the context of school and learning (NMSA, 2010). We know that teacher candidates will not be able to support young adolescents from diverse backgrounds if they do not first engage in experiences that mirror the kind of teaching we hope they will offer when they are teachers (Shevalier & McKenzie, 2012). We know that they will not be able to support young adolescents as critical thinkers if they do not learn to be critical thinkers themselves. This chapter shares findings and implications from a study of teacher candidates. It illuminates the clinical practices and methods used to stimulate conversations about cultural diversity in an integrated curriculum class and the candidates' responses to them. The goal was to prepare teacher candidates to engage in similar interactions with their young adolescent students, preparing both for success within a diverse society. I grounded these practices in culturally responsive/relevant teaching, defined as that which honors and builds from students' diverse backgrounds, teaches students to engage with the world critically, and positively impacts student development and achievement (Gay, 2000; Ladson-Billings, 1995). Given this backdrop, this chapter highlights teacher candidate reactions and insights gained when using teaching approaches and strategies that supported them in:

- Beginning to understand diversity by examining themselves;
- Learning to engage in critical conversations and using those experiences to engage young adolescent students in similar critical talk;
- Connecting theory to practice while working with adolescents from backgrounds different from their own.

A focus of the course was on supporting teacher candidates in discussing issues of race, although the course also addressed other forms of discrimination and oppression (e.g., sexuality, gender, immigration, language, class).

I focused heavily on race because, as Milner (2015) wrote, "While race may be difficult to address among educators, it may be one of the most important issues to consider, particularly in schools where students of color are grossly underserved" (p. 9). In this chapter, I share findings and implications from a study that asked the following two research questions: (a) What insights can I gain about effective practices; and (b) How do teacher candidates respond to a course designed to teach culturally relevant pedagogy and a critical consciousness through a focus on integrated curriculum?

SIGNIFICANCE

NMSA (2010) maintained that well prepared middle level teacher candidates demonstrate their understanding of how young adolescents grow and develop, as they understand the multiple influences on them. Furthermore, successful middle level teacher preparation programs help middle level teacher candidates to overcome the stereotypes that are prevalent among young adolescents (AMLE, 2012). AMLE's (2012) preparation guidelines are among the key reasons why this study is important. When the nation's most influential middle level professional organization insists that we prepare teachers for a diverse society by supporting teacher candidates to not only overcome stereotypes but to examine their own biases to consider when they might be projecting stereotypes on their students, teacher educators have an important role to play.

Alexander (2012) called this the age of the new Jim Crow as the micro- and macro-aggressions that persons of color have experienced for centuries are now more visible to all citizens through the increased use of social media. Microaggressions are subtle, everyday acts of covert racism sent to people of color, while macroaggressions are more blatant and glaring (Donovan, Galban, Grace, Bennett, & Felicie, 2012). As hate crimes are committed across the United States in growing rates (Southern Poverty Law Center, 2016), young adolescents, through social media, learn about current events that involve the stereotyping and profiling of people of color. Thus, they are aware of issues regarding race, whether they are victims of it, perpetrators of it, or observers of it. Therefore, it is essential that teacher candidates learn how to engage young adolescents in critical conversations.

Consequently, Love (2017) wrote about how the murdering of students' spirits in schools is as lethal as murders in the streets. This is evident in the form of lower expectations for students of color (Howard, 2014), inequitable enforcement of discipline (Morris, 2016), over-referral of students of color to special needs programs and under-referral to gifted programs (Ford & Milner, 2005), and neglecting to draw on students' community cultures of wealth (Yosso, 2005) to create curriculum that reflects meaningful knowledge. As a result, many students of color encounter tension within classrooms due to a lack of culturally responsive teaching and continuous stereotyping. Consequently, students become disengaged and, in some instances, disengage from school and the education system altogether (Davis, 2003; Polite & Davis, 1999).

Because teacher candidates and their students see or experience systemic racism everywhere, it is important that educators engage them in critical conversations so that they can understand and learn to address them in their own and others' lives. Challenging social injustices within a diverse society while teaching and modeling for young adolescents to do the same is essential for survival of novice teachers in today's world.

THEORETICAL FRAMEWORK AND REVIEW OF LITERATURE

In the case of transforming schools to meet the needs of Black children,
educators will have to relinquish aspects of white privilege or internalized racism
in order to retool and transform their teaching.
—Boutte, 2015, p. 3

The theoretical framework guiding this self-study (Billough & Pinnegar, 2001) draws from bodies of work that underlie critical conversations in middle level and preservice teacher education. It focuses on the importance of teachers examining themselves and their own biases before they can teach in culturally relevant ways. This is a part of the retooling that Boutte wrote about as necessary if we are to teach every child successfully.

Boutte (2015) suggested that educators need to examine and adjust the following: (a) knowledge bases, various frameworks for thinking about teaching, and engaging African American students; (b) dispositions; (c) instructional strategies; and (d) curriculum so that it is relevant to African American students. Examining dispositions is especially important in this discussion because it is where educators must consider how they view themselves in relation to those around them and is at the heart of critical conversations.

To understand these issues, I draw from Milner's (2017) description of culture as "a dynamic concept that encompasses, among other areas, racial and ethnic identity, class, language, economic status, and gender" (p. 6). This informs me as I endeavor to learn more about my teacher candidates and the various ideologies they bring to class. In turn, I try to push them to seek understanding of young adolescents, so that they can better appreciate the varied ways that culture affects how we believe, think, learn, and process. My theoretical frame is primarily from two bodies of literature that inform this study: culturally responsive teaching (Gay, 2010b), and critical conversations in preservice teacher education (Gay, 2010a; Sleeter, 2012, 2017).

Culturally Relevant and Responsive Teaching

Culturally relevant and responsive teaching is committed to developing students' cultural competence, academic success, and critical consciousness, using content and literacy knowledge and skills to inform, access information, and analyze and challenge injustices with the social order (Ladson-Billings, 1995). Key to this definition is a focus on teaching that draws on students' prior experiences, frames of reference, and cultural knowledge to make learning relevant (Gay, 2010b). "Utilizing students' culture as a vehicle for learning" (Ladson-Billings, 1995, p. 61) supports students in choosing academic excellence while maintaining cultural integrity of their heritage and history as well as appreciating the cultural heritage of every other student. This is just as important for the education of teacher candidates as it is for their work with students in schools. This means creating university experiences that build on the assets and strengths of teacher candidates just as we want them to build curriculum from young adolescents' communities and heritage.

My definition of culturally relevant pedagogy also draws from a strength- or asset-based approach. Milner (2015, 2017) challenged us to teach in culturally relevant ways by considering the effects that our understandings of students' cultural backgrounds as assets can have on their success in school. This means requiring teacher candidates to examine biases they may hold about young adolescents from backgrounds different from their own, so they can recognize adolescents' strengths rather than focus on deficits grounded in bias. Teacher candidates often bring with them a lifetime of implicit bias that often affects their ability to identify and appreciate the strengths of students from backgrounds other than their own (López-Robertson, Long, & Nash, 2010). This leads to the second body of literature that undergirds my theoretical frame that points out the need for critical conversations in teacher education.

The Need for Critical Conversations in Teacher Education

Research documents how teacher educators find it difficult to engage in critical conversations particularly when the topic is race and racism. In a study of preservice teachers, Hill (2012) contended, "Many candidates were uncomfortable with diversity and were not appropriately prepared for the realities of cultural and social justice issues manifest in urban and diverse schooling contexts" (p. 420). Milner (2017) wrote, "Teachers from any racial and ethnic background could be successful with any racial group of students when they possess or developed the knowledge, attitudes, dispositions, beliefs, skills, and practices necessary to meet student needs" (p. 2).

Culturally relevant teaching involves the engagement of teacher candidates in critical conversations, as described in the previous section, to be fundamental in meeting that goal.

Milner (2017) also wrote that the focus of culturally relevant pedagogy on developing a critical consciousness needs more attention, as we work to maintain the integrity of the original framework. A focus on critical conversations, while fundamental to the definition of culturally relevant teaching, is often missing from its actualization. This is where critical conversations with teacher candidates are important to building their understandings of culturally relevant teaching. Educators across the country face the need to support students' reflection on and ability to act against injustices witnessed every day. In response to this need, scholars emphasize the importance of critical conversations through which students ask and answer questions about power, privilege, voice, marginalization, invisibilization, and oppression (Gay, 2010a; Howard & Rodriguez-Minkoff, 2017; Sleeter, 2012, 2017).

The notion of cultural modeling (Lee, Spencer, & Harpalani, 2003) also factors into understanding the need for critical conversations in middle level education and teacher preparation programs. Lee, Spencer, and Harpalani (2003) wrote that critical talk about "cultural context is often neglected in the study of human development and education" (p. 3). They provided the notion of cultural modeling—or building academic proficiency by drawing on students' home and community funds of knowledge (Moll & Whitmore, 1993) as a framework to look at everyday practices in families and peer social networks as they might inform curriculum and practice in schools. This inherently requires critical thought as teachers and students consider issues of power and privilege that determine whose cultural models dominate schooling and where they can make changes to create more equitable and supportive teaching for all students.

METHODOLOGY

I conducted an action research study (Mills, 2014) described in this chapter over a four-month period. I took an interpretive approach in which I looked at meanings participants made over time in specific social settings (Schensul, Schensul, & LeCompte, 1999). In this action-based study, where I collected data while actively teaching and supervising teacher candidates, I sought not only to engage in critical conversations with them, but also to understand the meaning of these experiences in relation to their internship, the course they were taking with me, and their work with young adolescent students. While action research was the basis of the work, I also drew from self-study methodology for its focus on research that will "provoke, challenge, and illuminate rather than confirm and settle" (Billough

& Pinnegar, 2001, p. 20). I describe the context, participants, and methodology used to collect and analyze data in the following sections.

Context

I collected data in the context of a university course taught to middle level teacher candidates onsite at an urban emergent middle school. Milner (2012) described an urban emergent middle school as, "schools which are typically located in large cities but not as large as the major cities in the urban intensive category" (p. 559). The school served approximately 345 students, 98% of whom were African American and more than 90% of whom were eligible for free or reduced-price lunch. I was the course instructor. I also previously conducted professional development workshops focused on culturally relevant teaching for faculty and staff at the school. I taught the course onsite at this school for five years prior to this study. As a result, I developed a close and collaborative relationship with the school faculty and staff.

The Course

Integrated Curriculum was the title of the course in which I collected data. It was a three-credit hour requirement in the undergraduate program for candidates studying to become middle level educators. Teacher candidates took the course in conjunction with their methods courses and a yearlong residency in a school. The course required candidates to design an integrated unit to include the four content areas: math, science, social studies, and English language arts. The required text used to guide class discussion was Sleeter's (2005) *Un-Standardizing Curriculum: Multicultural Teaching in the Standards-Based Classroom.* I chose the book because it included the major tenets of culturally relevant teaching through its focus on multicultural curriculum design while encouraging candidates to think critically about the kind of knowledge that enters the classroom and who owns it. It drew me to its emphasis on the way that it undergirded transformative knowledge by critical consciousness and the way that the author urged educators to reflect on themselves and their ideologies.

Course Emphasis

While the course focused on a range of issues, the primary emphasis was on supporting teacher candidates' growth in being able to: (a) provide adolescents with multiple opportunities to learn in integrated ways; and (b) teach in ways that encourage young adolescents to observe, question, and interpret knowledge and ideas from diverse perspectives and with a critical eye. I anchored the course in the belief that teacher candidates should be reflective, responsive teacher-leaders who effectively address the inequities of policies, practices, and achievement related to race, gender, class, and linguistic differences. Furthermore, I encouraged teacher candidates to interweave knowledge of standards, assessment, pedagogy, and their unique population to create dynamic and engaging academic learning environments that ensure high levels of achievement for all young adolescents. Within the course, we also explored the relationships between curriculum and the community and how school curriculum can support young adolescents' critical learning about the community and the world in which they live. The class provided teacher candidates with a safe space to explore various ways in which they can become informed advocates.

The course also included a study of issues of social equity and a goal was to empower "teachers to build their own research capacities" (Lazar, Edwards, & McMillan, 2012, p. 11) for the success of all their students. I teach the teacher candidates in a diverse school community where they can observe, reflect, and discuss in a safe space to explore the challenges, barriers, and successes to teaching in such an environment. Teacher education candidates met once a week in the enrichment room of the middle school where they became involved in the community of the school by attending various functions and engaging with young adolescents in classrooms. They observed teachers in the school and noted how they utilized culturally responsive practices in their classrooms. Candidates took notes and brought them back for discussion. Throughout the semester, the principal and teachers enhanced my students' learning when they visited the class to engage teacher candidates in conversations about culturally responsive practices and what they look like throughout the school. In small and whole group discussion, we explored how to plan engaging content area lessons by drawing on adolescents' backgrounds. There were thorough discussions about how young adolescents and schools are increasingly diverse and how young adolescents learn from and through their communities. Through on-site observations of teachers implementing culturally relevant practices and reading the text described earlier, teacher education candidates began to contextualize their home and school experiences along with their internship experiences.

Discussions and Engagements

Each week, I required teacher candidates to respond to leading questions or quotes from the Sleeter (2005) text to open class. For example:

- What is meant by cultural mismatch in schools?
- What kinds of things must we unlearn to create socially just classrooms inclusive of high academic expectations and achievements?

During class discussions, I asked questions like those that follow to drive critical conversations. I used strategies like asking teacher candidates to turn and talk in pairs or in small groups or to respond using written exit slips (end-of-class reflections) or via Twitter to help them reflect on our critical conversations and connect them to their work with young adolescent students. I asked, based on any given class session that today, their thoughts about:

- Who determines knowledge?
- What three learnings will you bring to your classroom?
- What two things worry you about teaching middle school?
- What is one goal you have for the semester?
- Your vision statement for the school year?
- What you believe about student learning?
- How your beliefs about student learning impact how you teach students who differ from you culturally and socioeconomically?

Other activities included Take a Stand and The Stereotype Gallery Walk, designed to encourage candidates to begin to question their own assumptions to create a critical consciousness as novice teachers. I designed these activities to encourage my candidates to talk about feelings on issues of race, diversity, and culture that they may have previously thought about, but not confronted.

During the Take a Stand engagement, I presented candidates with a quote or statement focused on an issue of diversity, race, or culture in education. Two examples include: "Even teachers whose work is closely defined by content standards and testing can find spaces for adapting, modifying or developing intellectually rich multicultural curriculum" (Sleeter, 2005, p. 8); and "But it is the targeted identities that hold our attention and the dominant identities that often go unexamined" (Tatum, 2000, p. 6). I asked teacher candidates to take a stand and decide whether they agreed, strongly agreed, disagreed, strongly disagreed with the statements. Candidates had to form an opinion for this engagement because there was no option of a "Neutral" corner in this activity. Next, they moved into the corner with their peers, selecting the same option to engage in a short discussion about why they felt as they did. Each group then explained why they chose agree, strongly agree, disagree, or strongly disagree to the entire class. As candidates listened to the various rationales and explanations, they were free to move from corner (agree) to corner (disagree) as the discussion progressed.

The Stereotype Gallery Walk allowed candidates to walk silently around the room and place sticky notes with their thoughts and beliefs about various groups of people (e.g., Southerners, Northerners, Christians, men, women, gay/lesbian) on sheets of poster paper. There were rounds for candidates to walk and write, walk and read, walk and reflect, and finally question and discuss. At the end of the walk, we discussed each topic and the stereotypes associated with it and then literally tore up the pieces of paper to symbolize tearing down stereotypes that we were working to unlearn. At the end of each class session, teacher candidates often used Twitter to share closing thoughts, and some of them continued the conversation through class reflection assignments.

Participants

Teacher Candidates

The participants in this self-study included 18 White, middle class teacher candidates who were in their senior fall semester enrolled in an integrated curriculum course. Twelve teacher candidates were females and six were males.

Teachers

The school had a staff and faculty of 60 people. The five teachers involved in this study were those who supported the teacher candidates by speaking in our class and by welcoming and supporting them in their classrooms. All teachers participated in the professional development on culturally relevant teaching that I provided for the school. I listed teacher participants in Table 13.1.

Administrators

The administrator who participated in this study was a Black woman who had been principal at the school for two years at the time of the study. She came to visit my class to welcome the teacher candidates and provide them with a historical overview of the school.

TABLE 13.1 Teacher Positions and Experience	
Position	Years Experience
Curriculum resource teacher	15
Character education teacher	12
Eighth grade math teacher	5
Parent liaison (counseling background)	12
School resource officer	9
Principal	15

Data Collection and Analysis

I collected data weekly during class meetings over a four-month period, as I recorded notes during class and between class sessions through tweeted reflections, texts, and emails. Further data included my weekly teaching plans, PowerPoints, and teaching outlines. I organized data into electronic files according to the data source: Twitter, email, in-class reflection, lesson plan, and so on. I analyzed the data using qualitative pattern analysis procedures (Jansen & Peshkin, 1992) and grounded theory (Corbin & Strauss 2008). I reviewed all data sets several times and, as a result, constructed categories that helped me organize findings according to major insights. I established trustworthiness through triangulation of the data. "Collecting information using a variety of sources and methods is one aspect of what is called triangulation" (Maxwell, 2005, p. 95). I used three different types of data (i.e., tweeted reflections, emails, class notes) to protect the integrity of the study.

FINDINGS

In this self-study, it was clear that teaching onsite within a school community context provided teacher candidates with real world examples of young adolescents from diverse backgrounds receiving quality teaching and learning at a middle school. Working with teachers and administrators who valued a critical perspective and using a course text that supported it, I was able to engage teacher candidates in the important work of critical talk as a foundation to understanding culturally relevant teaching. Teaching the course at the school in the community allowed teacher education candidates to interact with young adolescents and teachers. In the process, they were able to practice skills they were learning through their own critical conversations and had opportunities to examine their identities, dispositions, and biases. Specific findings about elements of the experience reflect characteristics of engagement in critical conversations. I discuss these in the following sections.

Making Time and Space to Talk, Reflect, and Grow

Time and space to reflect was an essential element of my work with teacher candidates throughout this course. Given space and time dedicated to reflection, candidates often discussed their internship experiences in class and connections they made from theory to practice. Consequently, they often asked questions about diversity and equity as they planned units. There were discussions regarding the importance of knowing students and the challenges that they faced daily. Teacher education candidates commented in reflections and class conversations that they needed a safe environment to address these issues just as young adolescents needed to have a safe learning environment and positive attitudes from their teachers. Creating such a space for future teachers to talk with their peers about how to be culturally responsive while negotiating issues of equity and diversity was critical to the success of this course. While they read about social justice issues and issues of voice, privilege, and oppression in texts, it was not until teacher candidates had time to reflect on their own way of learning and teaching from their internship experiences that they were able to digest the material and draw conclusions from it. One teacher candidate shared through a final reflection:

> This class has helped me conceptualize the need for reflective and reflexive skills. I never thought about the practice of reflecting in past courses but maybe that is because deep down we all feel obligated to be right all the time. I think that I have I have become more of a reflective practitioner because I need to know the answer to my entire Why? questions. Why did this work? Why didn't this strategy work? Reflection forces us to show humility and admit, regardless of the outcome, that we need work as teachers...The desire to be better for my future students has helped me become a more reflective individual. Recognizing my mistakes and my victories are vital to me becoming an effective reflective educator.

Many times, during the semester, teacher candidates reflected on their own cultural identities and experiences by reading and responding to quotes through discussions. It was during these discussions and activities that teacher candidates began to confront the issues of diversity, power, and privilege within the school community and when designing curriculum. Throughout the semester, teacher candidates began to explore diversity through their reflections, which helped to make them aware of the importance of making better connections with the diversity of young adolescents in their individual internship placements. Reflecting on personal cultural identities both challenged and empowered the teacher candidates to take an active role in the lives of their young adolescent students.

Furthermore, teacher candidates began to share more of their internship teaching experiences and challenges during class discussions. Time to reflect, opportunities to seek counter-stories, and immersion in a critical school community all had an impact on the teacher candidates' willingness to confront their own biases and often led to epiphanies or ah-ha moments. Teacher candidates revealed this in exit slips, tweets, and final reflections. In a final reflection, one candidate wrote, "This course has helped me develop a reflexive practice by understanding how I, along with others, construct realities and identities. The realities that have been presented to me have been extremely eye opening and have altered my dispositions." Another expressed in a final reflection:

> This class has exposed me to the brutal reality that we do not serve an equal and just system. It is easy to verbalize my feelings and my future plans about having a classroom that serves and values each precious heart in the room but what is not easy is realizing that I have deeply rooted connotations that I did not realize I had before stepping into Dr. William's class. Battling these preexisting thoughts about race, culture, and honestly anyone who is not exactly like me is a challenge. With that said, it is a welcomed challenge because I believe that people grow others remove them from their comfort zones.

Sometimes confronting bias meant that teacher candidates revealed to their peers a biased past that was a surprise to some. In one example, a candidate who had gone to high school with another candidate expressed surprise at her peer's expression of epiphany regarding issues of racism or racial inequity in a class reflection.

> My classmate stood up and claimed that as she was growing up she had never thought about these debates. I think that it should be noted that [she] attended the same school as me as a child. However, contrary to [her] standing, these were issues that ran through my head regularly as a high school student. Though it would seem that I was different than [her] in this regard, we still remained similar because neither of us ever brought it up [in high school]. In fact, no one spoke about it. The diversity and obvious social justice issues present at our school remained under the rug for the entire duration.

Teacher candidates made connections between their experiences as learners and what it could mean to them as teachers preparing to encounter similar issues in their classrooms.

Immersion in the School's Community

Twice during the semester teacher candidates spent time in various classrooms throughout the school. Teacher candidates were able to learn from the community by being a part of it each week for class and by observing teachers in the school. There were also guest speakers from the school (i.e., school resource officer, third year teacher, character education teacher, curriculum coordinator, principal) who came to speak with teacher candidates about their experiences teaching adolescents with marginalized identities. Teacher candidates learned about the resources and programs that the school provided such as, S.T.E.A.M (Science, Technology, Engineering, Arts, and Math) programming, Saturday school, after school tutoring, Parent University (monthly workshops for parents on ways to support students), Freedom school (summer program), and Gateway to Technology program (aerospace class).

Following an observation in a class, one student noted the relationship the teacher had with her students. The student stated during class, "The teacher had a strong relationship with her students and I could tell that they all respected her and she connected with them." While this was not explicit in pointing out culturally relevant teaching or critical pedagogies, it demonstrates one way that the teacher candidates learned important elements of a culturally relevant classroom because of the immersion experience.

Opportunities provided through course activities to seek counter-stories to dominant narratives about marginalized students supported teacher candidates in expressing a desire to continue seeking and constructing such stories in the future. Whether or not candidates carry through with this goal once they become teachers is an important question for a follow-up study, but at the point of completing the course, many of them exhibited a dedication to continue pursuing multiple stories and perspectives. For example, one student wrote in an exit slip that she would "open [herself] up to students' culture to subconsciously stretch [her] limits," while another wrote:

> I think one of the most important ways to identify my cultural limits is to learn about other cultures and embrace the difference each culture had to offer. It is important to be mindful and open to what other students bring to the classroom.

Another student shared in her final reflection about the importance of asking questions to understand counterstories based on a class conversation:

> In a previous class discussion, we were talking about the Tatum article, which is about the "Complexity of Identity." We were all offering insight on what is what like to be a part of a minority group when someone asked the White-men in the class what it was like to basically be the majority of the majority. I think as a future educator, this class discussion was one of the biggest take-aways of the semester because no one knows what it is like to be in another person's shoes unless you ask and try to understand.

The counternarratives that the school provided for teacher candidates helped them to expand their knowledge of diversity and connect to young adolescents as they framed their own understandings of teaching and learning.

Beginning to Develop the Critical Habit

We know that teacher candidates are learning to become open to discussing issues that are going on around them inside and outside of the classroom. As a result of some of the conversations on equity, teacher candidates left demonstrating that they had taken the plunge into developing a critical habit and utilizing it to construct curriculum in the lives of their own students. For example, one candidate wrote at the end of the semester, "We must unlearn the idea of fairness and learn that of equity." Another commented, "I constantly reflect, and think about how I can grow in social justice and equity in the classroom." And yet another candidate's comment revealed growing knowledge about the existence of bias and the need to confront it when they stated, "We must unlearn any prejudices and/or stereotypes we have due to [our] upbringing or experiences to create social justice in our classroom."

Constructing a course in which I supported teacher candidates in using their voices to learn, share, and grow provided a space for those not comfortable bringing their voices forward in the past to do so. A representative comment came from one candidate who had been particularly silent in other contexts but felt that she could use her voice to engage in discussions in our class. She exclaimed, "THANK YOU! THANK YOU! I truly mean it when I say that this has been possible with all of you support, guidance and help! Thank you for helping me find my voice and confidence."

In classrooms, cultural clashes will occur; however, as teacher candidates continued to engage in our class discussions, they began to feel empowered to use their voices to generate knowledge and learning opportunities for the candidates at their internship sites.

As a foundation for culturally relevant teaching, teacher candidates in this course seemed to leave with a dedication to seeking knowledge about and building curriculum from adolescents' cultural backgrounds and expertise. Quotes from exit slips and end of semester reflections demonstrated this reality as candidates made comments such as, "It is important that my teaching materials mirror the lives of my students."

Simply learning that young adolescent students needed to be participants in the curricular planning process was new to the teacher candidates. Candidates exhibited this growth when they identified their learning in comments such as, "We must unlearn the idea that teachers do all of the planning. Students should participate in the process." This was an important foundation to being able to build practice from young adolescents' background experiences.

Finally, our critical conversations during the university course directly impacted the candidates' ability and desire to engage young adolescents in the same way. For example, a unit plan that one of the candidates submitted included the following questions designed to encourage adolescents to think critically about the notion of community:

- What does "community" mean to you?
- When you think of the word community, do you think about your home environment, people that make up your neighborhood, your school community, or your church?
- Are there important people in your community that you find yourselves thinking about? Are there leaders and followers or does everyone work together?

Another candidate described how one of her students reacted to the election results of 2016. As a result, I pushed the teacher candidate to think critically about her need to (a) understand more about her students' perspectives, and (b) learn how to engage middle level students in important discussions about bias and silencing. The candidate explained:

> I overheard one of my students say to another student "How is Donald Trump going to be my president; he doesn't like people who look like me?" As a white, privileged young woman, I was stunned and had to ask my coaching teacher how to discuss it with my students.

Teacher candidates began to frame their own understandings of teaching and learning as they listened to the lived experiences of their students.

Getting to Know Teacher Candidates as a Model for Middle Level Teaching

Just as I wanted the teacher candidates to get to know their own students, I needed to get to know the candidates. I could not ignore the fact that society shaped the way I (we) think about others, and that I might hold mindsets I would need to reject to understand my candidates. I needed to develop the same kind of student-centered environment that I hoped they would develop in middle level classrooms. I needed to get to know teacher candidates on both academic and personal levels so that differences between us would not be a roadblock, but the solid foundation to learning something greater together. I learned about the teacher candidates by:

- Showing a genuine interest in them and what their needs were during the course. I talked to them individually, expressed interest in their lives, families, fears, joys;
- Providing space for them to vent about their concerns and frustrations while still leaving the class on a positive note and with hope for the future; often this was during our class time or as I visited them in their classrooms or met with them after school;

- Making myself available to candidates outside of class to talk with them as needed, something that candidates mentioned in my course evaluations about how I was always available and responsive to them.

Teacher candidates revealed that these experiences impressed on them the importance of knowing their own young adolescent students. Because I committed to knowing and appreciating them, they began emphasizing that they would commit to knowing their own students. They wanted to create classroom communities that made every student feel included. The students represented this through exit slip comments such as, "We cannot have equitable classrooms for social justice until we truly know our students;" "[I need to be] mindful of the culture that each one of my students has a value that diversity as a resource in the classroom;" and "One thing I learned from class today is how crucial it is to establish an inclusive inviting classroom community."

IMPLICATIONS

In *This We Believe,* NMSA (2010) contended that people talk positively about a joyful community that promotes in-depth learning and enhances young adolescents' physical and emotional well-being and the essence of a happy, healthy school. This is the kind of atmosphere I tried to create with teacher candidates in a middle level course taught onsite at a local middle school. However, joyful does not mean that the community experience is without struggles and difficulties. The findings of this study outline the varied elements of the experiences that, interwoven with each other, created a joyful, dedicated community in which we pushed each other, learned from each other, and grew in the company of educators committed to young adolescents.

These findings lead me to offer insights and implications for teacher education in the preparation of middle level teachers. These implications include:

- A commitment to understanding culturally relevant teaching and how to support critical conversations; I could not have supported the teacher candidates or the teachers and administrators (who ultimately supported the teacher candidates) if I had not developed my own expertise in the areas I hoped they would come to understand and appreciate.
- Engagement while teaching onsite in a local school can make all the difference, but teacher educators must also pay attention to the professional development of teachers and administrators in the school.

- Teacher candidates need time for to discuss issues of equity and diversity in an atmosphere in which they feel safe. Teacher educators can develop such as atmosphere when they follow tenets of culturally relevant pedagogy in their own teaching, particularly getting to know the teacher candidates and drawing on their cultural backgrounds as teaching resources.
- Space and time to get to know teacher candidates well, to allow them to vent about issues in their lives and their teaching and feel safe and supported doing so.

LIMITATIONS

While the study provides outcomes that challenge teacher educators to have critical conversations with teacher candidates, there were some limitations. One limitation of the study is that it centered on 18 White, middle class male and female teacher candidates who were historically, a non-diverse, homogeneous group. Another limitation is that of the school site which was 98% African American and did not provide a diverse group of young adolescent students. The study did not capture the voices of young adolescent students, which would be a key starting point for future research. Finally, time was a limitation because the structure of the middle school day sometimes cut our observations short.

CONCLUSION

Lee et al. (2003) outlined three dimensions of cultural modeling that informed and paralleled my own findings; the importance of focusing on (a) family and community spaces, (b) academic disciplines, and (c) classroom practices with classrooms understood to be sites of co-constructed knowledge. This is what I worked to access in the integrative methods course, endeavoring to create a space where teacher candidates co-constructed knowledge based on questions, observations, evaluations, and concerns as they progressed throughout the semester and grew as student teachers.

Villegas and Lucas (2002) wrote, "Teacher educators must first articulate a vision of teaching and learning within the diverse society we have become" (p. 21). For me, this vision involves the ability to support teacher candidates and young adolescent students in being able to think critically, communicate effectively, analyze problems and formulate solutions, collaborate with colleagues, illustrate a sense of creativity, and become globally aware. These were further elements of the environment I sought to provide. Throughout this study, the reality that all students bring rich backgrounds and experiences to the classroom continues to inspire me. Culturally relevant pedagogy and critical conversations give us opportunities to share and learn counter-stories teacher candidates may bring as we learn together how to interact and discuss within a diverse world. If the teacher educator is willing to put forth the time and the effort, her teacher candidates will reward her with their confidence in themselves and their potential to impact the lives of young adolescent students more positively.

REFERENCES

Alexander, M. (2012). *The new Jim Crow: Mass incarceration in the age of colorblindness.* New York, NY: The New Press.

Association for Middle Level Education. (2012). *Association for Middle Level Education middle level teacher preparation standards with rubrics and supporting explanations.* Retrieved from http://www.amle.org/aboutamle/professionalpreparation/amlestandards.aspx

Billough, R. V., Jr., & Pinnegar, S. (2001). Guidelines for quality in autobiographical forms of self-study research. *Educational Researcher, 30*(3), 13–21.

Boutte, G. S. (2015). *Educating African American students: And how are the children?* New York, NY: Routledge.

Corbin, J. M., & Strauss, A. L. (2008). *Basics of qualitative research: Techniques and procedures for developing grounded theory.* Thousand Oaks, CA: SAGE.

Davis, J. E. (2003). Early schooling and academic achievement of African American males. *Urban Education, 38*(5), 515–537.

Donovan, R. A., Galban, D. J., Grace, R. K., Bennett, J. K., & Felicie, S. Z. (2012). Impact of racial macro- and microaggressions in Black women's lives: A preliminary analysis. *Journal of Black Psychology, 39*(2), 185–196.

Ford, D. Y., & Milner, H. R. (2005). *Teaching culturally diverse gifted students.* Waco, TX: Prufrock Press.

Gay, G. (2000). Curriculum theory and multicultural education. In J. A. Banks & C. A. McGee Banks (Eds.), *Handbook of research on multicultural education* (pp. 30–49). San Francisco, CA: Jossey-Bass.

Gay, G. (2010a). Acting on beliefs in teacher education for cultural diversity. *Journal of Teacher Education, 61*(1–2), 143–152.

Gay, G. (2010b). *Culturally responsive teaching: Theory, research, and practice* (2nd ed.). New York, NY: Teachers College Press.

Gay, G., & Kirkland, K. (2003). Developing cultural critical consciousness and self-reflection in preservice teacher education. *Theory Into Practice, 42*(3), 181–187.

Hill, K. D. (2012). We're actually comfortable with diversity: Affirming teacher candidates for culturally relevant reading pedagogy in urban practicum. *Action in Teacher Education, 34*(5–6) 420–432.

Howard, T. (2014). *Why race and cultural matter in schools: Closing the achievement gap in America's classrooms.* New York, NY: Teachers College Press.

Howard, T. C., & Rodriguez-Minkoff, A. C. (2017). Culturally relevant pedagogy 20 years later: Progress or pontificating? What have we learned, and where do we go? *Teachers College Record, 119*(1), 1–32.

Jansen, G., & Peshkin, A. (1992). Subjectivity in qualitative research. In M. D. LeCompte, W. L. Millroy, & J. Priessle (Eds.), *The handbook of qualitative research in education* (pp. 681–725). San Diego, CA: Academic Press.

Ladson-Billings, G. (1995). Toward a theory of culturally relevant pedagogy. *American Educational Research Journal, 32*(3), 465–491.

Lazar, A. M., Edwards, P. A., & McMillan, G. T. (2012). Bridging literacy and equity: The essential guide to social equity teaching. *International Journal of Multicultural Education, 16*(1), 62–65.

Lee, C. D., Spencer, M. B., & Harpalani, V. (2003). "Every shut eye ain't sleep": Studying how people live culturally. *Educational Researcher, 32*(5), 6–13.

López-Robertson, J., Long, S, & Nash, K. (2010). First steps in constructing counter narratives of young children and their families. *Language Arts, 88*(2), 93–103.

Love, B. (2017). Difficult knowledge: When a Black feminist educator was too afraid to #SayHerName. *English Education, 49*(2), 17–208.

Maxwell, J. (2005). *Qualitative research design: An interactive approach.* Thousand Oaks, CA: SAGE.

Mills, G. E. (2014). *Action research: A guide for the teacher researcher* (5th ed.). Upper Saddle River, NJ: Merrill/Prentice Hall.

Milner, H. R. (2012). But what is urban education? *Urban Education, 47*(3), 556–561.

Milner, H. R. (2015). *Rac(e)ing to class: Confronting poverty and race in schools and classrooms.* Cambridge, MA: Harvard Education Press.

Milner, H. R. (2017). Where's the race in culturally relevant pedagogy?. *Teachers College Record, 119*(1), 1–32.

Moll, L. C., & Whitmore, K. F. (1993). Vygotsky in classroom practice: Moving from individual transmission to social transaction. In E. A. Forman, N. Minick, & C. A. Stone (Eds.), *Contexts for learning: Sociocultural dynamics in children's development* (pp. 19–42). New York, NY: Oxford University Press.

Morris, M. (2016). *Pushout: The criminalization of Black girls in schools.* New York, NY: The New Press.

National Middle School Association. (2010). *This we believe: Keys to educating young adolescents.* Westerville, OH: Author.

Polite, V. C., & Davis, J. E. (Eds.). (1999). *African American males in school and society: Practices and policies for effective education.* New York, NY: Teachers College Press.

Schensul, S. L., Schensul, J. J., & LeCompte, M. D. (1999). Semistructured interviewing. In S. L. Schensul, J. J. Schensul, & M. D. LeCompte (Eds.), *Essential ethnographic methods: Observations, interview, and questionnaires* (pp. 149–164). Walnut Creek, CA: AltaMira Press.

Shevalier, R., & McKenzie, B.A. (2012). Culturally responsive teaching as an ethics-and care-based approach to urban education. *Urban Education, 47*(6), 1086–1105.

Sleeter, C. (2005). *Un-standardizing curriculum: Multicultural teaching in the standards-based classroom.* New York, NY: Teachers College Press.

Sleeter, C. (2012). Confronting the marginalization of culturally responsive pedagogy. *Urban Education, 47*(3), 562–584.

Sleeter, C. (2017). Critical race theory and the whiteness of teacher education. *Urban Education, 52*(2), 155–169.

Southern Poverty Law Center. (2016). *Ten ways to fight hate: A community response guide.* Retrieved from https://www.splcenter.org/20170814/ten-ways-fight-hate -community-response-guide

Tatum, B. D. (2000). The complexity of identity: Who am I? In S. M. Adam, W. J. Blumenfeld, R. Castaneda, H. W. Hackman, M. L. Peters, & X. Zuniga (Eds.), *Readings for diversity and social justice* (pp. 681–725). New York, NY: Routledge.

Villegas, A., & Lucas, A. (2002). *Educating culturally responsive teachers: A coherent approach.* Albany: State University of New York Press.

Yosso, T. J. (2005). Whose culture has capital? A critical race theory discussion of community cultural wealth. *Race Ethnicity and Education, 8*(1), 69–91.

CHAPTER 14

PREPARING TEACHERS TO PREVENT CLASSROOM MANAGEMENT CHALLENGES USING CULTURALLY RESPONSIVE CLASSROOM PRACTICES

Amy S. Murphy
University of Georgia

Brianna L. Kennedy
Utrecht University

ABSTRACT

Situating classroom management in a sociocultural context, this chapter provides an overview of how teacher educators can prepare preservice teachers (PSTs) to use culturally responsive practices to support students from culturally and linguistically diverse backgrounds. In particular, we explore how teacher educators can help PSTs learn how to prevent classroom management chal-

Equity & Cultural Responsiveness in the Middle Grades, pages 311–334
Copyright © 2019 by Information Age Publishing

lenges by attending to three interconnected domains of culturally responsive practice: (a) student-teacher relationships based in culturally relevant, critical teacher care; (b) culturally relevant pedagogy; and (c) culturally responsive classroom management. We suggest that preparing preservice teachers for this work requires that they both critically reflect on their own cultural biases and learn how to use their students' diverse backgrounds as assets in the classroom. Throughout the chapter, we highlight promising practices teacher educators can use in coursework and field placements for cultivating these dispositions and pedagogies with middle grades preservice teachers.

Disparities between the educational experiences and outcomes of White students and their culturally diverse peers highlight a critical focus of teacher preparation. In her reconceptualization of the discourse around the achievement gap, Ladson-Billings (2007) argued that the United States has accumulated an "education debt" in which poor children and Black and Latinx children bear the brunt of historical, political, and economic injustices. These disparities arise in part from a wide opportunity gap in which students from wealthier and Whiter areas receive access to resources such as high-quality teachers, advanced courses, technology and lab equipment, and safe schools. Opportunity gaps widen when schools disproportionately exclude ethnically diverse students from the learning environment due to disciplinary measures such as in-school suspension and out-of-school suspension. According to the U.S. Department of Education's Office for Civil Rights (U.S. DOE, 2016), schools are nearly two times more likely to expel Black students as White students, and Black students are 3.8 times more likely to receive an out-of-school suspension. American Indian or Alaska Native, Latinx, Native Hawaiian or other Pacific Islander, and multiracial boys also experience disproportionate suspension rates. Whereas they represent 15% of K–12 students in the United States, they receive 19% of out-of-school suspensions. The discipline gap widens in southern states where schools suspend Black students at least five times more than their representation in the population in more than 125 school districts (Smith & Harper, 2015). Adequate preparation can help teachers think critically about these inequalities and gain the beliefs, dispositions, and skills necessary to make a difference. To support preservice teachers (PSTs) in this development, teacher educators need to infuse their programs with a focus on the role culture plays in classroom management challenges and how educators can curtail inequitable discipline practices in their middle grades classrooms.

Classroom management challenges often communicate that educators are not meeting students' relational, pedagogical, or behavioral needs. Young adolescents need to have personal connections with adults who care for them, to learn in classrooms that challenge them to think critically about the world around them and to know their teachers will treat them equitably and with respect (National Middle School Association, 2010). For young adolescents from marginalized backgrounds, these needs include culturally responsive practices that affirm and integrate their cultural identities in the classroom. When these needs go unmet, student resistance may result. Toshalis (2015) argued that educators should not only expect students to resist these conditions but should view student resistance as a resource from which we can learn.

> Just as nations demand sovereignty, so too do students demand agency, and rightfully so. Students need their learning to be theirs; they need behavioral expectations to be negotiated; they need school-based relationships to be collaborative. Resistance is a signal that those experiences may be lacking, that a change in the terms of engagement may be needed. (p. 49)

Situating classroom practices in a sociocultural context, we propose that changing the terms of engagement necessitates that teachers attend to three interconnected domains of culturally responsive practice to meet the needs of marginalized youth and prevent classroom management challenges: student-teacher relationships based in culturally relevant, critical teacher care (Roberts, 2010); culturally relevant pedagogy (Ladson-Billings, 1995); and culturally responsive classroom management (Weinstein, Curran, & Tomlinson-Clarke, 2003). Developing culturally responsive practices begins with helping PSTs critically reflect on their own cultural backgrounds and biases and learn how to use their students' cultural backgrounds as assets in the classroom. Throughout this chapter, we offer promising practices teacher educators can use in coursework and field experiences to help PSTs develop these dispositions and pedagogies. To begin, we examine the power teachers have in the classroom to change the terms of engagement and intervene in the discipline gap that disproportionately affects culturally diverse students by considering the experiences of one new middle grades teacher, "Emily." We created this composite character's narrative based on our experiences with many preservice and novice teachers.

TYPICAL CHALLENGES OF A FIRST-YEAR TEACHER: EXAMINING HOW EMILY'S DILEMMAS ILLUSTRATE THE IMPORTANCE OF THE THREE DOMAINS OF TEACHING PRACTICE

Emily always knew she wanted to be a teacher. Excited about her first position as an eighth-grade science teacher, she readied herself for the school year by decorating her classroom and studying the district's instructional pacing guide. When she was honest with herself she admitted being a little scared about how to connect with students whose backgrounds were so different from hers. The Title I school, with its large Dominican and African American population of students, differed from the schools she attended, where the students, like herself, were predominantly White and middle class. A bright learner and teacher pleaser, Emily's teachers tracked her early for honors courses and she rarely shared classes with students who did not look and act like her. Nevertheless, she was eager for her first teaching position, believing that her future students needed teachers such as herself to help them value education and learning.

To follow the pacing guide, Emily started the first few days of school by jumping into content; there was no time to waste on practicing routines and community building activities. She poured hours into preparing her lectures and labs, leaving no time to accept her students' invitations to attend their basketball games and events at the Dominican Community Center. Caught between the advice to "not smile until winter break" and wanting to be liked by her students, she let them pick their own seats and lab groups, warning students that she'd let them work with whomever they wanted "unless they can't handle it."

Two months into the school year, though, even she was getting tired of the note taking and lab routine. Not only were both Emily and her students bored, her classroom was out of control. Students called out answers during her lectures, talked with their friends during individual work time, misused lab materials, and talked back when she admonished them for not being able to handle the freedom she gave them. Colleagues advised Emily to double down on her rules and to show students she meant business by writing discipline referrals for any inappropriate behaviors. She worried this was going to be a very long year.

Many educators would classify a number of challenges in Emily's classroom as classroom management dilemmas. While Emily certainly needed to address student behaviors in her classroom, dealing only with classroom management would produce an inadequate response because management strategies comprise only one of the three interdependent aspects of classroom dynamics. The other two include relationships and curriculum and instruction. The successful resolution of Emily's biggest dilemmas lies at the nexus of these three domains of practice.

The breakdown at the intersection of these three domains of practice (i.e., classroom management, student-teacher relationships, curriculum, and instruction) led to Emily's problems. Emily's primary focus on content left her little time to build a classroom community and to get to know students' lives outside of school. By not attending students' extracurricular events, she missed opportunities to make connections with families and to learn about students' cultures and interests, information she could have used to design curriculum and activities that reflected her students' lives and engaged them in learning. Emily's repetitive direct instructional style also failed to respond to the social learning needs of the students in her classes, as young adolescents learn best in classrooms characterized by active learning, challenging and exploratory curricula, and social interaction (NMSA, 2010). Further, her inconsistent management style conveyed to students a lack of control. Thus, what appeared as classroom management pitfalls actually resulted from a combination of issues related to weak student-teacher relationships, irrelevant curriculum and instruction, and inconsistent classroom management techniques.

PREPARING PRESERVICE TEACHERS TO WORK WITH MARGINALIZED POPULATIONS

Emily's challenges are all too common as beginning teachers often cite classroom management as a chief concern (Melnick & Meister, 2008; Moore, 2003; Rosas & West, 2009). Milner and Tenore (2010) suggested that these concerns become "exacerbated in urban settings, where students' languages, experiences, ethnicities, religions, and abilities may be highly diverse and may or may not be shared by the teacher" (p. 561). With this in mind, teacher educators have the opportunity to prepare PSTs to overcome challenges by openly interrogating the role of culture in teaching and learning, a process that begins by helping PSTs recognize how their own cultural backgrounds shape their behaviors, beliefs, and biases. This reflective work of understanding one's own cultural influences dovetails with the need for teachers to enact culturally responsive teaching, which Gay (2010) described as using "the cultural knowledge, prior experiences, frames of reference, and performance styles of ethnically diverse students to make learning encounters more relevant to and effective for them" (p. 31). Because students from marginalized backgrounds benefit when teachers both recognize their own cultural biases and implement culturally responsive practices (Howard, 2003; Milner & Tenore, 2010; Villegas & Lucas, 2002), teacher educators should design their programs to pair critical reflection with a focus on student-teacher relationships, culturally relevant pedagogy, and culturally relevant classroom management.

Developing Preservice Teachers' Critical Consciousness as a Prerequisite to Culturally Responsive Practices

One of the central tasks of teacher preparation involves helping PSTs analyze their beliefs and form new visions (Feiman-Nemser, 2001).

Accordingly, it is incumbent upon teacher educators to facilitate critical reflection in which PSTs look inward and recognize that educators' cultural backgrounds and historical legacies impact their dispositions and beliefs, notions of appropriate behavior, and what they consider worthy to learn in the curriculum (Gay, 2010; Howard, 2003). An essential prerequisite to critical reflection is understanding that all individuals, students, and teachers alike, filter information and experiences through their own cultural lenses. Culturally responsive teachers should not only acknowledge cultural differences, but should also make allowances for them in the classroom (Nieto & Bode, 2012). Further, equity-focused teacher education requires that PSTs develop critical consciousness, an ongoing process by which one becomes aware of the systems of power and privilege that (re)produce inequities (Freire, 1970). Teacher educators can support the development of preservice teachers' critical consciousness through texts and learning experiences that require PSTs to question their tacit assumptions and critique oppressive power structures in society and schools.

Such critical reflection may be a problematic proposition for PSTs who come to the field believing that they can achieve equity through colorblindness and that anyone can be successful if they work hard enough (Sleeter, 2008; Villegas & Lucas, 2002). Because many PSTs have not had authentic experiences in communities similar to those in which they will teach, they may position students who are different from them as "other." White teachers in particular may not see themselves as cultural beings, and thus hold their beliefs and expectations as normative, creating a standard against which they judge students who are different from them. While many teachers may not realize that they view culturally diverse students and their families through this narrow lens, Gay (2010) suggested that nevertheless some teachers may be "cultural hegemonists [who] expect all students to behave according to the school's cultural standards of normality. When students of color fail to comply, teachers find them unlovable, problematic, and difficult to honor or embrace without equivocation" (pp. 48—49). These beliefs reflect a deficit perspective in which educators view students' behaviors and challenges as inherent in the child, family, or community rather than acknowledging the ecological factors in the classroom, school, or society at large that impact the child (Weiner, 2006). So, for example, rather than trying to understand why a student from an historically oppressed group might disengage in school, a teacher might assume that the student and his parents undervalue learning, that the student struggles with learning problems, or that he lacks awareness of how to behave in a classroom. Teacher educators can help PSTs uncover their perspectives about students and communities and help them shift to an affirming perspective that considers the assets students bring with them to school.

To help PSTs develop a critical consciousness and learn how to reframe deficit thinking, we must infuse opportunities for critical reflection and dialogue throughout teacher education (Cochran-Smith, 2004; Gay & Kirkland, 2003; Hollins, 2011; Ladson-Billings, 2011; Nieto & McDonough, 2011; Villegas & Lucas, 2002). Howard (2003) suggested we attend to five key issues as we incorporate critical reflection into teacher education: (a) Make sure that we, as teacher educators, are adequately prepared to address the complexities of race, ethnicity, and culture; (b) Understand that reflection is an ongoing process that requires work; (c) Be specific about what teachers should reflect on; (d) Acknowledge that teaching is a political act; and (e) Avoid portraying culture in reductive ways. With Howard's guidelines in mind, we highlight "Snapshots in Practice" throughout this chapter, which teacher educators can use with PSTs as they embed critical reflection throughout equity-focused teacher preparation. Next, we explore three interrelated domains of culturally responsive practices that work together to prevent classroom management challenges.

Snapshots of Practice: Modeling and Practicing Critical Reflection

Teacher educators should provide models and guided frameworks to assist PSTs in applying a critical lens to their thinking about course readings and field experiences. One way teacher educators can model critical reflection in their courses is by structuring debriefing sessions in which they momentarily pause class discussions to analyze what PSTs are saying and how they are communicating their ideas (Gay & Kirkland, 2003). For example, if PSTs shared how students in their rural placements seem to lack motivation for completing work, teacher educators could stop the conversation and model for PSTs how to ask critical questions about the shared comments: How does the language we use to describe these students position them? What structural factors at the school and district levels may contribute to students' disengagement? Compare the services and resources this school receives to wealthier schools in the neighboring suburban district. How might that impact student motivation? How might the content and way educators deliver it affect the students' desires to work? Is the curriculum challenging or have the educators lowered it to "reach" these students? While teacher educators will initially lead and model how to ask critical questions such as these, eventually students should lead these debriefing discussions as they begin to develop their own critical consciousness.

Personal narratives and critical autobiographies can also help PSTs recognize how historical and institutional structures of power have affected their own lives (Cochran-Smith, 2004; Hammerness, Darling-Hammond,

Grossman, Rust, & Shulman, 2005; Lea, 2004; Nieto & McDonough, 2011; Villegas & Lucas, 2002). Teacher educators can scaffold students' thinking by asking direct questions that help students view their educational experiences through a critical lens such as: What is your family's economic status? Give specific indicators of how you identify this status. Do you or other members of your family speak another language fluently? If so, how did you learn it? In what ways is this an advantage or disadvantage for you? Did you share a cultural background with the majority of your teachers? How do you think this impacted your education? What was the typical demographic makeup of your K–12 classrooms? How was this an advantage or disadvantage for you? What was your academic track (e.g., general education, honors) and how do you think that impacted the quality of education you received? Questions such as these move the students' narratives beyond a surface retelling of their histories and instead help them understand how cultural and structural forces shaped their experiences. In our preservice education courses, we encourage students to share their autobiographies with one another to move the analysis beyond the individual level and to recognize patterns and differences across PSTs' experiences. To shed a critical light on the autobiographies, we ask students to note how issues of class, race, ethnicity, language, religion, gender, sexual orientation, geography, and so on have shaped their educational experiences as well as the connections and disconnections they noticed in their readings.

Because developing a critical consciousness oftentimes involves a resocialization about how one thinks and views the world, critical reflection may lead to resistance among some PSTs (Hollins, 2011; Lea, 2004; Sleeter, 2008). Resistant students may refuse to participate in class discussion, claiming they do not have enough experience with issues of power and inequities to contribute to the discussion. When using personal experiences to highlight inequities, students from privileged backgrounds may also demonstrate resistance by seeking out individual exceptions to group phenomena. For example, a White student might use her parents' ascension into the middle class as a justification for meritocracy, the idea that everyone can get ahead if they just work hard enough. To combat such resistance, teacher educators should be sure to couple reflections about personal experiences with an analysis of the ways in which historical, structural, and institutional structures of power contribute to one's histories (Cochran-Smith, 2004; Lea, 2004). Teacher educators can also require students to articulate how their new learning affects them as a teacher and as a learner. Scaffolding discussions and assignments in these ways helps PSTs develop a habit of questioning their tacit assumptions and critiquing the power structures in schools and society (Howard, 2003).

INTEGRATING THREE DOMAINS OF CULTURALLY RESPONSIVE PRACTICE

In this section, we provide concrete examples of what it looks like when teachers adopt culturally responsive practices and how the enactment of these practices may prevent potential classroom management challenges. Middle grades students from marginalized backgrounds benefit when teachers enact culturally responsive practices that include offering personal support for students, encouraging students' cultural identity development, recognizing culturally appropriate behaviors, and focusing on multicultural education (Kennedy, Brinegar, Hurd, & Harrison, 2016). In addressing these needs, we blend previous work on culturally relevant, critical teacher care (Roberts, 2010), culturally relevant pedagogy (Ladson-Billings, 1995, 2014), and culturally responsive classroom management (Weinstein et al., 2003) to capture students' simultaneous needs in the classroom. We propose that a teacher's overall success with students from marginalized backgrounds depends on the effective implementation of all three domains. Although we address each section separately, we illustrate throughout how each domain works in concert with one another to support equitable classrooms and prevent classroom management dilemmas.

Culturally Relevant, Critical Teacher Care

We begin by focusing on relationships because the ability of teachers to push students toward their educational potential and use classroom management strategies effectively rests on the strength of their relationships with students. In Emily's vignette, for example, we saw that her persistent focus on academic content came at the expense of dedicating time to getting to know her students and developing connections with them. Emily did not understand that she first had to build strong relationships with her students to motivate them to engage in academically rigorous work. As Delpit (2012) stated, "It is the quality of relationship that allows a teacher's push for excellence... [M]any of our children of color don't learn *from* a teacher, as much as *for* a teacher" (p. 86). Further, the adage that teachers must "connect before you correct" highlights the need for many students to experience care from teachers before students will respond to redirection or correction.

Many young adolescents experience competing needs in their relationships with adults, as they simultaneously desire independence and meaningful relationships (Cushman & Rogers, 2009; NMSA, 2010). To respond to this, middle level educators should be advocates who respect students' individual identity development while demonstrating care in their student-teacher relationships. Noddings' (1984) foundational work on the ethic of care emphasized that great teaching requires caring relationships and trust between the teacher and students. She noted that students must feel cared for and respected by the teacher; it is not enough for the teacher to profess care. For students from marginalized backgrounds, the connection between care and successful teaching is particularly important (Ladson-Billings, 1995; Roberts, 2010; Rolón-Dow, 2005). Based on her study of African American teachers' care towards their African American students, Roberts (2010) introduced the term *culturally relevant, critical teacher care,* which purposefully instills a political aspect to caring as it recognizes how historical, economic, and racial inequities impact the educational experiences of students from historically oppressed groups. Rolón-Dow (2005) explored similar ideas in her study of the connection between care and race/ethnicity in the experiences of Puerto Rican middle school girls. Although some teachers in her study communicated care for the girls' academic success, they spoke of the school's Latinx communities in deficit terms, blaming the communities themselves for issues of poverty and low parental school involvement rather than understanding the larger economic and societal structures that produced these conditions. For students from marginalized backgrounds, teacher care cannot be divorced from understanding how sociopolitical forces have shaped the communities in which they live. Rolón-Dow concluded that critical care begins by "acknowledging that, to care for students of color in the United States, we must seek to understand the role that race/ethnicity has played in shaping and defining the sociocultural and political conditions of their communities" (p. 104). Awareness of racism, poverty, and other systemic problems that negatively affect the schooling of students who belong to these groups is a prerequisite for culturally relevant, critical teacher care.

As we work to combat educational inequities, teachers have an obligation to provide nurturing and challenging classrooms that usher their students toward educational excellence (Corbett, Wilson, & Williams, 2002; Delpit, 2012). Pedagogy infused with "warm demanding" both insists on students' academic success and prioritizes positive student-teacher relationships. This term arose from Kleinfeld's (1975) work in Alaskan schools with Athabaskan Indian and Eskimo students where she found that teachers demonstrated both a warm demeanor towards students while commanding academic excellence. Since then, researchers have documented positive impacts of warm demander pedagogy with African American students (Bondy, Ross, Hambacher, & Acosta, 2012) and students in urban classrooms (Corbett et al., 2002).

Although they do not use the term "warm demeanor," Corbett, Wilson, and Williams (2002) also studied teachers who both demand excellence and provide support students need to be successful in urban classrooms. Described by the authors as "it's my job" teachers, the educators in their study demonstrated care with a "no excuses" approach in which they *cajoled, berated, praised, hounded, prodded,* and *stayed on* their students to ensure students completed high quality work. In a study of Chicago schools, researchers showed this simultaneous attention to academic press (e.g., having high expectations, holding students accountable for learning) and social support (e.g., positive and strong relationship between adults and students in the school) to be necessary to contribute to higher student achievement (Lee, Smith, Perry, & Smylie, 1999). When only one of these factors was present, student achievement lagged.

Middle grades students want to learn from teachers who clearly articulate their expectations and hold students accountable for meeting them (Cushman & Rogers, 2009). As a student in Corbett et al.'s (2002) study explained, an "it's my job" teacher, "[is] different from other teachers because she's not gonna sit there and let you do what you wanna do; you do what she said. In other classes, the teacher didn't care; they let us sit there" (p. 49). Students experience care when their teachers do not allow them to fail, when they provide the support they need to succeed, and when they hold students accountable for reaching high expectations. Teachers who enact care in this way understand the difference between being authoritative and an authoritarian, a distinction that can be challenging for some teachers, particularly novices. Some teachers, perhaps out of fear of others seeing them as domineering, provide unstructured, laid back environments for their students typified by low academic standards. They may believe that lowering expectations shows care because it reduces students' risk of failure or that this approach builds their relationship with students because others see them as being "cool" with the students (Cushman & Rogers, 2009). Teachers who enact culturally relevant, critical teacher care recognize that this "bargaining for compliance" (Toshalis, 2015, p. 285) further exacerbates educational inequities, as the teacher's laissez-faire demeanor allows students to fall behind.

Teacher care and classroom management overlap to prevent conflicts in this classroom. Being clear, fair, and consistent with students about academic and behavioral expectations is a way of showing students that the teacher cares too much about them to let them fail or to learn in a chaotic classroom environment. As the next section demonstrates, teachers also show care when they invest time in learning about their students' lives and cultures and use that knowledge to develop relevant curriculum and engaging instruction.

Culturally Relevant Pedagogy

Most teachers have experienced firsthand how students' interest in the content, instruction, and curricular materials can directly affect their engagement and behavior in class. As Kohn (2006) asserted, "*When students are 'off task,' our first response should be to ask, 'What's the task?'* (p. 19, emphasis in original). As we saw in Emily's experience, students exhibit a number of behaviors when educators do not engage them, behaviors that could possibly lead to disciplinary actions. Relevant curriculum and instruction are particularly essential for students from culturally and linguistically diverse backgrounds who oftentimes do not see themselves reflected in the curriculum nor their interaction styles integrated into the instruction. In order to engage young adolescents, teachers need to provide challenging and meaningful curriculum that spurs students to think critically about themselves, their community, and the world (NMSA, 2010).

Culturally relevant pedagogy focuses on ensuring that curriculum and instructional tasks make authentic connections between content and the experiences in students' lives (Ladson-Billings, 1995). Consistent with critical teacher care, culturally relevant pedagogy builds students' critical awareness about the world around them by engaging them in authentic inquiries about their communities as well as larger societal structures and inequities. Young adolescents want to wrestle with complex and exploratory learning tasks that matter to them (NMSA, 2010), thus it is perhaps unsurprising that a recent review of the literature on culturally relevant education across content areas shows a connection between culturally relevant pedagogy and students' motivation, interest in content, and perceptions of themselves as capable students (Aronson & Laughter, 2016). Extending Ladson-Billings's (1995) foundational work on culturally relevant pedagogy, Paris (2012) proposed that we need to enact culturally *sustaining* pedagogy to support "young people in sustaining the cultural and linguistic competence of their communities while simultaneously offering access to dominant cultural competence" (p. 95). This pedagogy recognizes the need for teachers to integrate their students' cultural knowledge and interactional styles into the classroom while at the same time teaching students from marginalized identities how the "culture of power" (Delpit, 1988, p. 282) operates so that they can both participate in it and critique it.

For teachers to design curriculum that builds on and sustains their students' cultural perspectives, they must first learn about their students' communities and cultures (Moll, Amandi, Neff, & Gonzalez, 1992). When designing lessons that integrate students' frames of reference, for example, teachers benefit from knowing where families purchase their groceries and what groceries they purchase, where students hang out after school, where they live, where their parents work. All this information creates a bank of resources and shared frames of reference upon which teachers can draw when designing curriculum. For example, rather than lecturing and giving notes on the human impact on ecosystems, students in Emily's class could complete a project-based investigation into the impact local chicken processing plants (where many of her students' parents work) have on the local agriculture and water supply. Teachers can also incorporate the communities' rich assets into the classroom by inviting adults who are important to the students to share their expertise on topics related to the curriculum (Ladson-Billings, 1995).

In addition to integrating students' communities and cultures into the curriculum, culturally relevant pedagogy uses instructional strategies that align with students' communication and performance styles. Emdin's (2016) work on reality pedagogy speaks to the need for teachers to adapt their instructional techniques to their students, for "while the teacher is the person charged with delivering the content, the student is the person who shapes how best to teach that content" (p. 27). For instance, instead of learning through direct instruction or individual work, students who come from collectivist cultures, which prioritize the good of the group over individual members' contributions, may excel in cooperative learning environments where they work with their peers to construct knowledge. Teachers should also encourage students' diverse communication styles in the classroom. Emdin explained that when students participate in higher order thinking and experience the joy of learning challenging content, teachers "must work purposefully to allow for disruptions in the traditional sanitized classroom by welcoming the often loud and irreverent responses indicating deep student engagement" (p. 148). Rather than curtailing students' initial enthusiasm for learning by requiring that they speak quietly or in academic language, teachers should expand their behavioral expectations and welcome students' diverse ways of communicating their content knowledge. Such culturally sustaining pedagogy (Paris, 2012) signals to students that the teacher prioritizes their learning and values their cultural interactional styles.

Curriculum that captures students' attention and instructional activities that productively harness young adolescents' energy work in tandem to minimize classroom management challenges. Hearkening back to Kohn's (2006) assertion, students are less likely to exhibit off-task behaviors when teachers design instructional tasks that integrate students' cultural backgrounds, frames of reference, and performance styles. Further, teachers' investment in learning about students' lives and communities illustrates their care and commitment to reaching young adolescents (Milner & Tenore, 2010). We finally turn to examine culturally responsive classroom management, the third domain of culturally responsive practice. In the next section, we examine the critical role it plays in ensuring equitable classrooms for all students, particularly those from marginalized identities.

Culturally Responsive Classroom Management

Throughout this chapter, we have suggested that classroom management challenges rarely exist in a vacuum; rather, they often result from a combination of issues related to deficits in student-teacher relationships, curriculum and instruction, and classroom management. Nevertheless, consistent, clear, and fair classroom management strategies are critical to the success of a classroom. Emily's class, for example, suffered from a lack of routines and a hands-off approach to classroom organization. By allowing students to select their own seats and then admonishing them for speaking with their neighbors, she unwittingly set up a situation in which she lacked control of the learning environment. Emily also did not understand how culture influences student behavior and her expectations of what appropriate behavior looks and sounds like (Weinstein et al., 2003). She considered it rude and disrespectful when her students called out answers during instruction because her cultural norms dictated that one person speaks at a time and that students should raise their hands to offer answers in class. Conversely, many of her African American students' responses reflected how they interacted at home and in their churches. This disconnect between her expectations and students' interactional styles further damaged her relationships with students and contributed to the classroom management challenges she faced.

Understanding the Role of Educators' Subjective Judgments of Student Behavior

For many students from culturally diverse backgrounds, teachers' subjective judgments of their behaviors lead to disproportionate disciplinary actions. Evidence suggests that racial disparities in discipline result not from differences in the severity of students' behavior, but from educators' implicit biases (Okonofua & Eberhardt, 2015; Skiba, Michael, Nardo, & Peterson, 2002). Skiba et al. (2002) explored three predominant theories frequently offered to explain disproportionate discipline rates between Black and White students: that the disparity is a result of faulty methodologies, that the core determinant is not race but social class, and that Black students' behavior is simply worse than White students' behavior. Their findings led them to theorize that the "discrepancies in school punishment for Black and White students are *an indicator of systematic and prevalent bias* [emphasis added] in the practice of school discipline" (p. 338). In short, Black students received more discipline not because they behaved worse than White students nor because of their social class. Rather, this study suggests that Black students received more discipline due to educators' unconscious beliefs and attitudes about student behavior. Similarly, Okonofua and Eberhardt (2015) found that teachers perceived Black students' misbehavior more severely than White students' misbehavior, even when students behaved in the same way.

Disentangling the reasons students from different racial groups receive disciplinary actions helps us get a fuller picture of how educators' implicit biases play a role in the discipline gap. White students most often receive punishment for objective infractions (e.g., smoking, skipping class, vandalism), whereas Black students predominantly receive punishment for subjective ones (e.g., defiance of school authority, disrespect, disruptiveness, excessive noise) (Mendez & Knoff, 2003; Skiba et al., 2002). By their nature, subjective infractions require an educator's judgment about what appropriate behavior looks like; ultimately, the teacher decides what constitutes disrespect, excessive volume, and disruptive behavior. An intersectional approach that addresses how factors such as race and gender converge in school discipline (Morris, 2007; Murphy, Acosta, & Kennedy-Lewis, 2013) revealed that Black boys receive suspensions most often, followed by Black girls and Latino males (Losen & Skiba, 2010; U.S. DOE, 2016). Studies on the experiences of persistently disciplined middle school Black girls have found these students receive messages from educators that they act "unladylike" for being loud, judgments rooted in cultural expectations of how young women should behave (Morris, 2007; Murphy et al., 2013). These studies reveal the role educators' implicit bias plays in perpetuating disproportionate discipline gaps.

While schools report discipline data in terms of in-school suspensions, out-of-school suspensions, and expulsions, these sanctions do not start with an administrator who doles out consequences. Instead, these institutionalized discipline measures often begin in the classroom when a teacher writes a discipline referral as the result of a classroom conflict. Although discipline events are co-constructed, with both the student and teacher impacting the course of events, teachers have the institutional power to control the situation in ways that have real consequences for students (Toshalis, 2015; Vavrus & Cole, 2002). When a teacher writes a referral because she feels disrespected or that a student is being too loud, for example, the teacher's subjective judgment about appropriate behavior takes precedence over the student's perceptions and the student ultimately bears the official consequences.

Enacting Culturally Responsive Classroom Management

Recognition that implicit bias plays a role in the disproportionate rates by which schools discipline many ethnically diverse students in the United States creates a moral imperative for equity-focused educators to address the cultural implications of classroom management dilemmas. To reduce classroom management challenges, particularly those that arise from cultural discontinuities, teachers need to be able to read their students' nonverbal cues, verbal responses, and frames of reference accurately so they can appropriately respond to students. Learning how to de-escalate conflicts is particularly important as young adolescents may try to test adults' boundaries and challenge authority (Caskey & Anfara, 2014). Moreover, because classroom conflicts often arise when there are disconnections in communication, it is important for teachers to recognize their own communication style and to learn their students' styles so they may interact with students in culturally consistent ways (Weinstein et al., 2003).

Heath's (1983) influential study of White working-class teachers and Black working-class families in the Piedmont Carolinas illustrated the cultural disconnections that can occur when teachers and students do not share the same communication styles. Through ethnographic observation, Heath noted that Black parents spoke to their children in direct and declarative sentences, whereas White teachers spoke to their own children using indirect and rhetorical questions. Bringing these approaches into the classroom, the incongruence in how White teachers spoke to their Black students and how the students' parents spoke to them at home created miscommunication when the students did not understand why the teachers asked what the students perceived as silly questions. In the context of culturally responsive classroom management, this study illustrates that effective communication in the classroom necessitates that teachers learn about and adjust for students' interactional styles. For example, teachers who work with predominantly Black students from working class households whose parents may speak to them with explicit directives at home should avoid redirecting off-task students with indirect questions (Bondy, Ross, Gallingane, & Hambacher, 2007; Delpit, 1988). Instead of redirecting by saying, "What should you be doing right now?," the teacher may make an explicit and direct statement such as, "You need to stop talking and get to work." For teachers who do not share this communication style, this may sound harsh or even rude. Spending time with students and their families during school and community events or conducting home visits can help teachers understand the nuances of communication that will benefit them in their interactions with students from cultural backgrounds different from their own.

Culturally responsive classroom teachers are explicit and clear with students regarding classroom expectations, especially when there are cultural differences between the teacher and students (Bondy et al., 2007; Weinstein et al., 2003). One cannot assume, for instance, that each person in a classroom community has the same understanding of what the rule "Be respectful" looks and sounds like. Issues potentially arise when educators do not explicitly explain, model, and provide a rationale for dictates such as these, for whereas some cultures show respect by making eye contact, members of other cultures demonstrate respect by casting their eyes downward and avoiding looking authority figures in the eye (Weinstein et al., 2003). Emdin's (2016) descriptions of attending Black church services illustrated the ways in which interactional styles are culturally mediated. He observed how the congregation responded to and with the preacher, which reflected not only a deep engagement with the preacher, but a respect for his teachings. When students use a similar style of communicating in classrooms by "calling out" when the teacher asks a question, the teacher could possibly admonish them if the teacher perceives this to be talking out of turn.

Rather than always expecting students to conform to the teachers' culturally based notions of behavior, culturally responsive teachers adjust the learning environment to best meet the needs of the particular students in their classroom. For example, a study of one Navajo middle school found a mismatch between teachers' classroom management system and the cultural norms of the Navajo students (McCarthy & Benally, 2003). To manage what the teachers perceived to be unruly student behavior, they relied on a program of individual incentives and consequences. However, this method ran counter to the Navajo culture in which students live in the present and prize the collective over the individual. To shift to more culturally responsive classroom management approaches, teachers sought professional development to learn about the cultural attributes of Navajo students.

Like the teachers in McCarthy and Benally's (2003) study, educators who enact culturally responsive classroom management examine their own expectations of student behavior and how culture influences these expectations. This critical reflection needs to begin in teacher education, as reflection is essential for PSTs as they examine their own implicit biases and how these may impact their subjective judgments of student behavior.

Snapshots of Practice: Field-Based Teacher Inquiries[1] About Classroom Management Dilemmas

Many PSTs need help navigating the theory-to-practice divide between what they learn in their teacher education programs and what they experience in their field placements. For novices, learning how to enact culturally responsive practices in the moment can be challenging, especially when faced with difficult student behaviors. Teacher educators can help PSTs develop habits of thinking that encourage them to respond to classroom management dilemmas from a position of inquiry rather than one of exasperation. Toshalis (2015) cautioned that if educators respond to student resistance "from frustration more than curiosity, if we use discipline more than inquiry, we squander one of the most precious insights our students give us. Resistance is a message that something is not right; an educator needs preparation, courage, and practice to hear that message and channel it into something productive" (p. 8).

Field-based teacher inquiries provide a structured opportunity for PSTs in full-time placements to hear the messages students may be sending when they resist in the classroom. In particular, this assignment encourages PSTs to recognize that a student's behavior may be a signal that the content is irrelevant or that the student does not yet trust the teacher.

In this form of teacher inquiry (Dana & Yendol-Hoppey, 2014), PSTs begin by identifying a management-related dilemma over which they have control and phrasing it in the form of a question (e.g., How can I build a strong relationship with a particular student to minimize negative classroom behaviors? How can I structure cooperative learning activities to maximize engagement and minimize off-task talk?). Students share their dilemmas with their peers to garner feedback based on the class readings (see list of suggested readings below) and each other's professional experiences. Importantly, when they introduce the context of the dilemma they begin by describing the student or class' assets and speculating about ways in which their own teaching methods or relationships with students may be contributing to the dilemma. Teacher educators should also prompt PSTs to consider how cultural dynamics may play a role in the dilemma.

Over the course of a few weeks, the PSTs implement one discrete strategy based on culturally responsive classroom practices to improve their classroom dilemmas (e.g., eating lunch with the student to get to know him better and using that knowledge to incorporate his interests into content delivery; modeling and practicing the procedures for a particular cooperative learning structure). During this time, they record observations and data to note changes in student learning and behavior, teacher behavior, and the classroom in general. The PSTs then write an analysis of their inquiries in which they use the course readings as a lens for understanding their dilemmas and what occurred in their intervention. Through focused inquiry, the Field-based Teacher Inquiry assignment helps PSTs understand how classroom management dilemmas can arise from issues related to their relationships with students, their curricular and instructional choices, and their management techniques and styles.

Snapshots of Practice: Reframing Student Behavior

When describing students' challenging behaviors, one might hear explanations that assign responsibility squarely on the adolescent. If a student refuses to do her work, we might hear, "She's lazy and only does her work if I'm standing right over her." Sometimes explanations for student behavior reside in the student's family or community: "I taught his siblings. They're all like that," or, "Her mom never comes to our parent-teacher conferences. She just doesn't care about education." These deficit-oriented explanations for student behavior reflect the "pervasive assumption that when students misbehave or achieve poorly, they must be 'fixed' because the problem inheres in the students or their families, not in the social ecology of the school, grade, or classroom" (Weiner, 2006, p. 42). An essential task of equity-focused teacher education involves helping PSTs recognize deficit thinking and reframe student behavior from an asset-based perspective. While classroom management largely refers to the order and organization of the classroom, "culturally responsive classroom management is a frame of mind as much as a set of strategies or practices" (Weinstein et al., 2003, p. 275). The Reframing Student Behavior assignment (developed by this chapter's second author) helps PSTs create habits of the mind that reframe deficit thinking to an asset-based perspective.

In this assignment, PSTs begin by finding posts related to classroom management dilemmas in online teaching forums, spaces where teachers post questions about their classrooms and get responses from other users. After finding an entry that reflects a deficit perspective, they then write an imitation response to the teacher in which they reframe the student behavior from a student-centered perspective. Their response must propose possible reasons for the student behavior and then propose solutions to the teacher based on our class materials. Below is an example of how a PST may respond to a teacher's online forum post:

> It sounds like you have already given up on this group. You say things like, "I despise this class," and, "I really, really hate this group," yet you seem surprised when they respond with hostility. They think that you hate them, and with good reason. So you must show interest in their lives and their abilities. It may be especially helpful if you learned more about their cultural backgrounds. Do they think that the material is irrelevant to their lives? Math is hard and it can seem pointless to young people, so trying to find real-life applications may help increase their interest in the material.

The PST might then propose practical solutions to repairing the damage done in terms of the relationships in the classroom and how the teacher could build on students' funds of knowledge (Moll et al., 1992) when creating curricula. Thus, while the Reframing Student Behavior assignment initially focuses on classroom management challenges, it requires PSTs to articulate how the simultaneous interaction of relationships, curriculum, and classroom management ultimately impact classroom dynamics. Further, the assignment gives PSTs practice at reframing dilemmas by understanding how students may be experiencing the classroom environment and instruction.

REIMAGINING EMILY'S FIRST-YEAR

Emily readied herself for the school year by learning as much as she could about the 8th grade science curriculum and exploring the school's surrounding communities, which were largely Dominican and African-American. Although she had not yet met her students, she gathered preliminary information about their communities by walking through their neighborhoods, shopping in their stores, and attending cultural events. These experiences provided examples she used in her first unit of the year, which focused on the processes of scientific inquiry.

Emily devoted the first days of school to developing a classroom community and establishing behavior expectations. She stated the rules, explained their rationale, and gave examples and non-examples, as well as modeled the routines that would make the class run smoothly. Because the school expected her to teach content right away, she paired the standards with community-building activities. For example, students brought in cultural artifacts from their homes and then made observations and inferences about each other's objects as well as each other's lives. As the school year went on, she learned more about students by attending their games and events at the Dominican Community Center and used this knowledge to design projects and activities that reflected their lives. When she encountered classroom management dilemmas, she thought critically about what may be at the root of the issue by considering her student-teacher interactions, what instructional task she had assigned when the conflict arose, and whether her expectations were inequitable or unclear. No first year is without challenges, but Emily loved her students and was thrilled to be teaching them.

Social justice-oriented teacher education programs can prepare first-year teachers like Emily to be culturally responsive educators who know how to prevent classroom management challenges. Constantly mindful of how culture and power influences classroom dynamics, culturally responsive teachers work to build relationships with students predicated on critical care, develop curriculum and instructional activities that relate to students' lives, and use management practices consistent with their students' cultures. Taken together, these interconnected domains embody a developmentally responsive, challenging, empowering, and equitable pedagogy essential to educating young adolescents (NMSA, 2010).

NOTE

1. This assignment is an adaptation of Try-It assignments developed by instructors in the School of Teaching and Learning at the University of Florida.

SUGGESTED READINGS FOR PRESERVICE TEACHERS

Bondy, E., & Ross, D. D. (2008). The teacher as warm demander. *Educational Leadership, 66*(1), 54–58.

Corbett, D., Wilson, B., & Williams, B. (2002). *Effort and excellence in urban classrooms.* New York, NY: Teachers College Press.

Curwin, R. L. (2010). *Meeting students where they live: Motivation in urban schools.* Alexandria, VA: Association for Supervision and Curriculum Development.

Cushman, K., & Rogers, L. (2009). *Fires in the middle school bathroom: Advice for teachers from middle schoolers.* New York, NY: The New Press.

Delpit, L. (2012). *"Multiplication is for White people": Raising expectations for other people's children.* New York, NY: The New Press.

Gorski, P. (2008). The myth of the "culture of poverty." *Educational Leadership, 65*(7), 32–36.

Greene, R. W. (2010). Calling all frequent flyers. *Educational Leadership, 68*(2), 28–34.

Haberman, M. (2010). The pedagogy of poverty versus good teaching. *Phi Delta Kappan, 92*(2), 81–87.

Kennedy, B. L. (2011). Teaching disaffected middle school students: How classroom dynamics shape students' experiences. *Middle School Journal, 42*(4), 32–42.

Ladson-Billings, G. (1995). But that's just good teaching! The case for culturally relevant pedagogy. *Theory Into Practice, 34*(3), 159–165.

Nieto, S., & Bode, P. (2012). *Affirming diversity: The sociopolitical context of multicultural education* (6th ed.). Boston, MA: Allyn & Bacon.

Ross, D., Kamman, M., & Coady, M. (2007). Accepting responsibility for the learning of all students: What does it mean? In M. S. Rosenburg, D. L. Westling, & J. McLeskey (Eds.), *Special education for today's teachers: An introduction* (pp. 52–81). Upper Saddle River, NJ: Prentice Hall.

Toshalis, E. (2015). *Make me! Understanding and engaging student resistance in school.* Cambridge, MA: Harvard Educational Press.

Valenzuela, A. (2010). *Subtractive schooling: US-Mexican youth and the politics of caring.* Albany: State University of New York Press.

Weiner, L. (2006). Challenging deficit thinking. *Educational Leadership, 64*(1), 42–45.

Weinstein, C., Curran, W., & Tomlinson-Clarke, S. (2003). Culturally responsive classroom management: Awareness into Action. *Theory Into Practice, 42*(4), 269–276.

Williams, B. (2007). What teacher behaviors encourage one at risk African-American boy to be a productive member of our classroom community? In C. Caro-Bruce, R. Flessner, M. Klehr, & K. Zeichner (Eds.), *Creating equitable classrooms through action research* (pp. 100–124). Thousand Oaks, CA: Corwin Press.

REFERENCES

Aronson, B., & Laughter, J. (2016). The theory and practice of culturally relevant education: A synthesis of research across content areas. *Review of Educational Research, 86*(1), 163–206.

Bondy, E., Ross, D. D., Gallingane, C., & Hambacher, E. (2007). Creating environments of success and resilience: Culturally responsive classroom management and more. *Urban Education, 42*(4), 326–348.

Bondy, E., Ross, D. D., Hambacher, E., & Acosta, M. (2012). Becoming warm demanders: Perspectives and practices of first year teachers. *Urban Education, 48*(3), 420–450.

Caskey, M. M., & Anfara, V. A., Jr. (2014). *Research summary: Developmental characteristics of young adolescents.* Westerville, OH: Association for Middle Level Education. Retrieved from http://www.amle.org/ServicesEvents/ResearchSummary/TabId/622/ArtMID/2112/ArticleID/455/Developmental-Characteristics-of-Young-Adolescents.aspx

Cochran-Smith, M. (2004). *Walking the road: Race, diversity, and social justice in teacher education.* New York, NY: Teachers College Press.

Corbett, D., Wilson, B., & Williams, B. (2002). *Effort and excellence in urban classrooms.* New York, NY: Teachers College Press.

Cushman, K., & Rogers, L. (2009). *Fires in the middle school bathroom: Advice for teachers from middle schoolers.* New York, NY: The New Press.

Dana, N. F., & Yendol-Hoppey, D. (2014). *The reflective educator's guide to classroom research* (3rd ed.). Thousand Oaks, CA: Corwin.

Delpit, L. (1988). The silenced dialogue: Power and pedagogy in educating other people's children. *Harvard Educational Review, 58*(3), 280–298.

Delpit, L. (2012). *"Multiplication is for White people": Raising expectations for other people's children.* New York, NY: The New Press.

Emdin, C. (2016). *For White folks who teach in the hood . . . and the rest of y'all too: Reality pedagogy and urban education.* Boston, MA: Beacon Press.

Feiman-Nemser, S. (2001). From preparation to practice: Designing a continuum to strengthen and sustain teaching. *Teachers College Record, 103*(6), 1013–1055.

Freire, P. (1970). *Pedagogy of the oppressed.* New York, NY: Continuum.

Gay, G. (2010). *Culturally responsive teaching: Theory, research, and practice.* New York, NY: Teachers College Press.

Gay, G., & Kirkland, K. (2003). Developing cultural critical consciousness and self-reflection in preservice teacher education. *Theory Into Practice, 42*(3), 181–187.

Hammerness, K., Darling-Hammond, D., Grossman, P., Rust, F., & Shulman, L. (2005). The design of teacher education programs. In L. Darling-Hammond & J. Bransford (Eds.), *Preparing teachers for a changing world: What teachers should learn and be able to do* (pp. 390–441). San Francisco, CA: Jossey-Bass.

Heath, S. B. (1983). *Ways with words: Language, life, and work in communities and classrooms.* New York, NY: Cambridge University Press.

Hollins, E. R. (2011). The meaning of culture in learning to teacher: The power of socialization and identity formation. In A. F. Ball & C. A. Tyson (Eds.), *Studying diversity in teacher education* (pp. 105–130). Lanham, MD: Rowman & Littlefield.

Howard, T. C. (2003). Culturally relevant pedagogy: Ingredients for critical teacher reflection. *Theory Into Practice, 42*(3), 195–202.

Kennedy, B. L., Brinegar, K., Hurd, E., & Harrison, L. (2016). Synthesizing middle grades research on cultural responsiveness: The importance of a shared conceptual framework. *Middle Grades Review, 2*(3), 1–20. Retrieved from https://

scholarworks.uvm.edu/cgi/viewcontent.cgi?referer=https://www.google.com/&httpsredir=1&article=1061&context=mgreview

Kleinfeld, J. (1975). Effective teachers of Eskimo and Indian students. *School Review*, *83*(2), 301–344.

Kohn, A. (2006). *Beyond discipline: From compliance to community.* Alexandria, VA: Association for Supervision and Curriculum Development.

Ladson-Billings, G. (1995). But that's just good teaching! The case for culturally relevant pedagogy. *Theory Into Practice, 34*(3), 159–165.

Ladson-Billings, G. (2007). From the achievement gap to the education debt: Understanding achievement in U.S. schools. *Educational Researcher, 35*(7), 3–12.

Ladson-Billings, G. (2011). Asking the right questions: A research agenda for studying diversity in teacher education. In A. F. Ball & C. A. Tyson (Eds.), *Studying diversity in teacher education* (pp. 385–398). Lanham, MD: Rowman & Littlefield.

Ladson-Billings, G. (2014). Culturally relevant pedagogy 2.0: aka the remix. *Harvard Educational Review, 84*(1), 74–84.

Lea, V. (2004). The reflective cultural portfolio: Identifying public cultural scripts in the private voices of White student teachers. *Journal of Teacher Education, 55*(2), 116–127.

Lee, V. E., Smith, J. B., Perry, T. E., & Smylie, M. A. (1999). *Social support, academic press, and student achievement: A view from the middle grades in Chicago. Improving Chicago's schools. A report of the Chicago Annenberg research project.* Chicago, IL: Consortium on Chicago School Research. Retrieved from https://consortium.uchicago.edu/sites/default/files/publications/p0e01.pdf

Losen, D. J., & Skiba, R. J. (2010). *Suspended education: Urban middle schools in crisis.* Los Angeles, CA: UCLA Civil Rights Project.

McCarthy, J., & Benally, J. (2003). Classroom management in a Navajo middle school. *Theory Into Practice, 42*(4), 296–304.

Melnick, S. A., & Meister, D. G. (2008). A comparison of beginning and experienced teachers' concerns. *Educational Research Quarterly, 31*(3), 39–56.

Mendez, L. R., & Knoff, H. M. (2003). Who gets suspended from school and why: A demographic analysis of schools and disciplinary infractions in a large school district. *Education and Treatment of Children, 26*(1), 30–52.

Milner, H. R., & Tenore, F. B. (2010). Classroom management in diverse classrooms. *Urban Education, 45*(5), 460–603.

Moll, L. C., Amanti, C., Neff, D., & Gonzalez, N. (1992). Funds of knowledge for teaching: Using a qualitative approach to connect homes and classrooms. *Theory Into Practice, 31*(2), 132–141.

Moore, R. (2003). Reexamining the field experiences of preservice teachers. *Journal of Teacher Education, 54*(1), 31–42.

Morris, E. W. (2007). "Ladies" or "loudies"? Perceptions and experiences of Black girls in classrooms. *Youth and Society, 38*(4), 490–515.

Murphy, A. S., Acosta, A., & Kennedy-Lewis, B. L. (2013). "I'm not running around with my pants sagging, so how am I not acting like a lady?": Intersections of race and gender in the experiences of middle school troublemakers. *The Urban Review, 45*(5), 586–610.

National Middle School Association. (2010). *This we believe: Keys to educating young adolescents.* Westerville, OH: Author.

Nieto, S., & Bode, P. (2012). *Affirming diversity: The sociopolitical context of multicultural education* (6th ed.). Boston, MA: Allyn & Bacon.

Nieto, S., & McDonough, K. (2011). "Placing equity front and center" revisited. In A. F. Ball & C. A. Tyson (Eds), *Studying diversity in education* (pp. 363–384). Lanham, MD: Rowman & Littlefield.

Noddings, N. (1984) *Caring: A feminine approach to ethics and education.* Berkeley: University of California Press.

Okonofua, J. A., & Eberhardt, J. L. (2015). Two strikes: Race and the disciplining of young students. *Psychological Science, 26*(5), 617–624.

Paris, D. (2012). Culturally sustaining pedagogy: A needed change in stance, terminology, and practice. *Educational Researcher, 41*(3), 93–97.

Roberts, M. A. (2010). Toward a theory of culturally relevant critical teacher care: African American teachers' definitions and perceptions of care for African American students. *Journal of Moral Education, 39*(4), 449–467.

Rolón-Dow, R. (2005). Critical care: A color(full) analysis of care narratives in the schooling experiences of Puerto Rican girls. *American Education Research Journal, 42*(1), 77–111.

Rosas, C., & West, M. (2009). Teachers' beliefs about classroom management: Preservice and inservice teachers' beliefs about classroom management. *International Journal of Applied Educational Studies, 5*(1), 54–61.

Skiba, R. J., Michael, R. S., Nardo, A. C., & Peterson, R. L. (2002). The color of discipline: Sources of racial and gender disproportionality in school punishment. *The Urban Review, 34*(4), 317–342.

Sleeter, C. E. (2008). Preparing White teachers for diverse students. In M. Cochran-Smith, S. Feiman-Nemser & D. J. McIntyre (Eds.), *Handbook of research on teacher education* (3rd ed., pp. 559–582). New York, NY: Routledge.

Smith, E. J., & Harper, S. R. (2015). *Disproportionate impact of K–12 school suspension and expulsion on Black students in southern states.* Philadelphia, PA: Center for the Study of Race and Equity in Education.

Toshalis, E. (2015). *Make me! Understanding and engaging student resistance in school.* Cambridge, MA: Harvard Education Press.

U.S. Department of Education Office for Civil Rights. (2016). *2013–14 Civil rights data collection a first look: Key data highlights on equity and opportunity gaps in our nation's public schools.* Washington, DC: U.S. Department of Education. Retrieved from http://www2.ed.gov/about/offices/list/ocr/docs/2013-14-first-look.pdf

Vavrus, F., & Cole, K. (2002). "I didn't do nothin'": The discursive construction of school discipline. *The Urban Review, 34*(2), 87–111.

Villegas, A. M., & Lucas, T. (2002). *Educating culturally responsive teachers: A coherent approach.* Albany: State University of New York Press.

Weiner, L. (2006). Challenging deficit thinking. *Educational Leadership, 64*(1), 42–45.

Weinstein, C., Curran, W., & Tomlinson-Clarke, S. (2003). Culturally responsive classroom management: Awareness into action. *Theory Into Practice, 42*(4), 269–276.

CHAPTER 15

ESTABLISHING A PEDAGOGY OF EQUITY AND CULTURALLY RESPONSIVENESS IN THE MIDDLE GRADES

Kathleen M. Brinegar
Northern Vermont University

Lisa M. Harrison
Ohio University

Ellis Hurd
Illinois State University

We created this Handbook as a call to action. It adds to the small but growing body of literature specifically related to young adolescents, marginalized identities, and equity (see Brinegar, Kennedy-Lewis, Harrison, & Hurd, 2016; Kennedy, Brinegar, Hurd, & Harrison, 2016). Its chapters demonstrate how the middle grades movement can no longer afford to be complicit in an educational system that oppresses and marginalizes those whose identities are not part of the mainstream culture. Educational leaders have

Equity & Cultural Responsiveness in the Middle Grades, pages 335–348
Copyright © 2019 by Information Age Publishing
All rights of reproduction in any form reserved.

publicly called for a greater focus on equity in education. In her 2006 AERA Presidential Address, Ladson-Billings asserted:

> We do not have an achievement gap...I am arguing that the historical, economic, sociopolitical, and moral decisions and policies that characterize our society have created an education debt...That debt service manifests itself in the distrust and suspicion about what schools can and will do in communities serving the poor and children of color. (pp. 5 & 9)

We have a responsibility as middle grades educators to acknowledge and own this debt by honoring young adolescents with marginalized identities who persist despite it and critically examining our role in creating and maintaining it. As Ladson-Billings stated in that same address, "On the face of it, we must address it because it is the equitable and just thing to do" (p. 9). And if that is not enough of a motivator, we must also address this debt if the middle grades movement is going to survive. At best, continuing in its current trajectory will lead the middle grades movement to its own demise as educators will need to turn outside of the field to support their young adolescent learners, particularly as the student population of the United States shifts to include more young adolescents of culturally and linguistically diverse backgrounds (Hussar & Bailey, 2017). At worse, systems of oppression operationalized by a lack of specific attention paid to the diversity of identities and experiences that young adolescent learners bring to their classrooms will continue to marginalize or render certain young adolescents invisible.

Hurd, Harrison, Brinegar, and Kennedy (2018) stated:

> Developing equity frameworks that fit in a middle grades context, critically rethinking our positions for ecologically-based spaces, and integrating the middle school concept as a means to support equitable practices, even disrupt marginalized and oppressive practices, are all efforts that lay the essential foundation for this important work. (pp. 31–32)

This concluding chapter builds on the suggestions above to outline six specific calls for action that, when combined, have the potential to transform the middle grades movement and reduce the educational debt for *every* young adolescent. For as Vagle and Hamel stated in their chapter (Chapter 2), "Part of being active agents in institutions that divide involves doing honest appraisal about ourselves and the institutions in which we participate" (p. 27).

EQUITIZING THE MIDDLE GRADES FRAMEWORK

Equity pedagogies and frameworks must become a part of the middle school lexicon, not add-ons to consider once the best schooling practices for White, middle class, young adolescents have been essentialized. After all, if the goal of any educational endeavor focused on the public good is not equity, what it is? We argue, and the research described in the chapters of this book demonstrates, that many equity frameworks do in fact align with the aims of the middle grades movement. Our first priority as middle grades researchers, educators, and advocates then should be to get to know equity frameworks, particularly as previous research focused on equity in the middle grades showed that 70% of articles in mainstream middle grades publications that focused on culture, power, and difference did not use an equity framework to ground their work (Hurd et al., 2018). In addition, the lack of definitions for the terms and frameworks that were used (Brinegar et al., 2016) prevented researchers from understanding how authors situated their subjects (Marsh & Willis, 2003).

One cannot possibly create frameworks for organizing middle schools, developing and implementing middle grades curriculum, supporting and educating middle school teachers, and fostering positive growth and development for young adolescents if equity is not at the center of the work. Thus, educators and researchers focused on supporting the development of young adolescents should be able to define and understand terms and concepts related to marginalized identities and equity. Such terms include, cultural competence (Martinez, 2014), culturally relevant pedagogy (Ladson-Billings, 1995, 2014), cultural responsiveness (Gay, 2000), funds of knowledge (Moll, Amanti, Neff, & Gonzalez, 1992), culturally sustaining pedagogy (Paris, 2012: Paris & Alim, 2017), intersectionality (Crenshaw, 1989, 1991), equity literacy (Gorski, 2013), reality pedagogy (Emdin, 2016), and critical consciousness (Freire, 1970).

Once we make equity a priority from within the movement and understand the research occurring outside of it, we can adapt it, add to it, and reframe it as warranted, using decades of work focused on young adolescents and schooling. For example, in their chapter, Beucher and Smith (Chapter 9) used research centered on culturally responsive pedagogy related to Native American youth to expand on the Association for Middle Level Education's (AMLE) *This We Believe's* (2010) notion of relationship building. They stressed, for example, that if getting to know one's students is an important aspect of middle grades schooling, then critical to that process is for teachers to not only get to know the students as they appear in their classrooms, but to also get to know the impact that decades of schooling focused on the elimination of their culture, including their family's heritage and identity, has had on students and families with indigenous identities.

Although Beucher and Smith's work demonstrated the compatibility and importance of using equity as the lens through which to explore schooling practices for young adolescents, until such an approach becomes mainstream in middle grades work, the middle grades movement will remain at odds with the greater vision of educational equity for everyone.

REDEFINING YOUNG ADOLESCENTS
IN CULTURALLY SUSTAINING WAYS

If we want to create a culturally responsive middle grades movement, we must stop trying to define what is normal or typical of young adolescents and as such, stating what is essential for them. If we continue to engage in this practice, there will be learners who are abnormal or atypical, at-risk or challenging, because our essentialized practices do not work for them. Such dichotomies serve only to "other" students who society already marginalizes for the color of their skin, religious beliefs, parental income, sexual orientation, or gender identity.

In the opening chapter, we presented arguments against developmentalism and make the case for a new approach to defining young adolescents that combines a recognition of the potential for shared experiences for this age group while acknowledging the vast differences in what it means to be a young adolescent. In practice, this means that we can, and should, commit to getting to know each one of our young adolescent learners, and we cannot pretend to know what is best or right for each one until we fully understand who they are as an individual. And that takes work. It would be much easier if we could say that if one does x, y, and z, young adolescent learners will be successful. The problem here is parallel to what makes the American Dream so problematic. It insinuates that if a person, or in our case a learner, is unsuccessful, the problem is inherent with the person, or the teachers and administrators who did not execute "it" correctly, not the "it" itself. Valencia (1997) described how deficit thinking portrays individuals with marginalized identities in terms of their shortcomings due to intelligence, language deficiencies, or cultural differences. In a schooling context, this leads to the development and use of strategies focused on modifying the behavior of the individual to "fit" what is acceptable instead of altering systems and structures that stem from unequal power dynamics. Such a model inevitably leads to assimilation. These deficit and pejorative ways of thinking are pervasive, even in middle grades research focused on equity or marginalized populations. In a review of middle grades research focused on equity, 27% of articles used a deficit-based lens (Hurd et al., 2018).

Conversely, utilizing an assets-based approach to getting to know young adolescents, combined with an acknowledgement of the way power has shaped them and framed their experiences, has the potential to better help identify and implement ways of structuring schools and educating learners that do not fix them, but instead in ways that see them, know them, accept them, and sustain them so that they may positively transform their own lives and the lives of others. As Vagle and Hamel stated in Chapter 2, "Young people are full of capacity to be agents of change in their lives and communities. The young people do not need adults to shape them, fix them, or change them. The young people need us to show up, as human-beings, offering opportunities for connection" (p. 41).

In a previous review of equity-based middle grades research, Hurd et al. (2018) identified the following assets-based practices and structures to support youth with marginalized identities:

- Encourage individual expression (student voice/choice) within and across content areas;
- Create spaces for active and stimulating learning tied to authentic assessments;
- Create non-White spaces for all marginalized and minoritized youth (e.g., content-rich library and media spaces with readings for all marginalized and minoritized youth);
- Scaffold connections to students' lives and identities;
- Provide for comprehensive discussions and curriculum surrounding race, moral issues, empathy, lesbian/gay/bisexual/transgender, anger, bullying and social aggression, social exclusion, poverty, low and high status individuals, etc.;
- Insist on safe, inclusive, gender-equitable, and non-discriminatory learning communities and environments that are not punitive or harmful to youth (e.g., Gay-Straight Alliance);
- Encourage genuine and high expectations against demands for competition and standardization;
- Organize school and community events for democratic service, social action, and restorative justice;
- Restructure teacher training, professional development, and school leadership for approaches that draw on total, ecological middle school concepts;
- Create innovative and sustainable partnerships with local community-based organizations and colleges and/or universities;
- Secure external funding to support democratic programs and equitable instruction;
- Educate and work with the community for equitable schooling practices, policies, and enhanced living spaces; and
- Avoid the "savior mentality" or idea that teachers are saving poor, marginalized youth to fix them. Instead, find ways to contribute and engage with the local youth and community. (p. 39)

Further research on and application of these strategies has the potential to lead to positive growth and development for young adolescents with marginalized identities.

In addition, the chapters contained in this volume provide further examples of assets-based approaches to teaching and learning with young adolescents. For example, Pacheco and Smith's (Chapter 5) use of codemeshing as a culturally sustaining practice provided an example of an assets-based approach to countering English-centric schooling experiences for linguistically diverse learners. They presented ways that bilingual students used their heritage languages in their academic work. According to Pacheco and Smith, the "varied uses of heritage languages within the composing process supported students in not only creating multilingual and multimodal texts, but in creating a multilingual classroom space" (p. 103). Such a classroom space empowered students, teachers, and families to view a part of identity usually banned from academic work as an asset to the school community instead of a hindrance. Yoon and Uliassi (Chapter 11) echoed this sentiment in their chapter, "Teachers need to build ELLs [English language learners] confidence by positioning them as cultural, social, and linguistic assets who can bring to classrooms diverse interpretations and cultural references" (p. 243). Middle grades research needs to further explore practices that have this same positive impact on students' academic, social, and emotional learning.

COUNTERACTING BIAS BY ACKNOWLEDGING, RESPECTING, AND CELEBRATING COUNTERNARRATIVES

Any inclusion of equity frameworks or reframing of the way we view young adolescents, would be for naught, if we do not do what Vagle and Hamel proposed in their chapter (Chapter 2), which is take a critical look at who has been privileged by middle grades research and thus who the current middle grades concept privileges. Beucher and Smith's chapter (Chapter 9) urged, "If we are to succeed in developing culturally responsive curriculum, we must be aware of our own cultural blind spots, lest we recreate the very systems we intend to disrupt" (pp. 184–185). We should do this on multiple levels within education. On an individual level, teachers should work towards developing cross cultural competencies fostered through reflective practices designed to gain a deeper understanding of teachers' own world view and confront their biases (McAllister & Irvine, 2000). Likewise, this work should occur on a systemic level to consider how the hidden curriculum impacts what we teach and what we do not teach in schools and whose voices and experiences we reflect and value within educational spaces (Apple, 2004).

Our introductory chapter presents ways that traditional developmentalist conceptions of physical, cognitive, and socioemotional development privilege White, middle class, heterosexual males through the limited and simplistic ways they describe typical young adolescent behavior due to the lack of attention paid to cultural influences on individuals. This echoes the work of Busey (2017) and Milne (2016) who previously criticized mainstream middle grades research for ignoring race as a construct that influences development. Within this Handbook, multiple authors presented ways that bias continues to marginalize specific identities, including Moulton (Chapter 4) in reference to homelessness, Kemp-Graham (Chapter 10) in the ways administrators discipline young adolescent African-American girls, Downing (Chapter 6) in relation to staff sanctioned bullying of LGBTQ+ youth, and Beucher and Smith (Chapter 9) in their discussion of creating empowering curriculum for indigenous youth.

The recognition of bias goes hand in hand with the acknowledgement that realities beyond those that we have experienced or have been introduced to exist. Thus, if promoters of the middle grades movement ground it in an inclusive philosophy that promotes equity, they must contribute to the voicing and sharing of narratives and counternarratives. Gibbs Grey (Chapter 7) wrote extensively about counternarratives in her chapter, stating:

> According to Solorzano and Yosso (2009), the counternarrative or counter-story is "a method of telling the stories of those people whose experiences are not often told (i.e., those on the margins of society) . . . and is a tool for exposing, analyzing, and challenging the majoritarian stories of racial privilege" (p. 138) . . . Furthermore, counternarratives seek to dispel myths about people of color and marginalized communities that are often present in dominant, majoritarian narratives. (p. 135)

As middle grades researchers we need to continue exposing counternarratives and sharing new narratives of marginalized youth so that educators can better understand their students through them. The chapters by Moulton (Chapter 4) and Beucher and Smith (Chapter 9) both provided examples of ways that school policies and curriculum created with incomplete narratives negatively influenced middle grades students with marginalized identities. Their examples demonstrate the importance of educators providing spaces in their schools and classrooms for students to voice their narratives. Gibbs Grey (Chapter 7), whose work encouraged Black youth to frame their college essays as counternarratives "that allowed them to speak about their lives on their own terms and from their own perspectives" (p. #), did just this. Providing such spaces gave students the opportunity to speak their truths and educators the chance to hear the lived experiences of their students.

REVISITING *THIS WE BELIEVE*

A critical examination of the middle grades movement and concept would be incomplete without utilizing the knowledge gleaned from the above calls of action to revisit its seminal works. Such works provide a public statement of the values and principles that guide middle grades research and frame the middle grades concept. Busey (2017)'s critical race discourse analysis of AMLE's *This We Believe* (NMSA, 2010) found the document to be problematic in a variety of ways. He stated, "the intersection of race, early adolescent development, and middle grades education is addressed, but couched in palatable euphemisms that ultimately negate the lived realities of students of color in middle schools" (p. 15) and "AMLE's *This We Believe* adopted a liberal colorblind ideology of culturally relevant pedagogy choosing to ignore the racial nuances undergirding the concept itself" (pp. 18–19). As such, he made three recommendations for statements to include in a revision of *This We Believe*, "we believe race is central to identity development...We believe smartness is a racialized construct; racial difference does not constitute a cognitive deficiency...We believe race matters in creating positive school environments and subsequently, positive socioemotional and psychological development" (pp. 24–28). While these suggestions provide an important first step in revisiting the underlying values of the movement and concept, they just begin to skim the surface of the development of a middle grades philosophy that is equitable and responsive to every young adolescent.

The research from these chapters presents further recommendations. Moulton's chapter (Chapter 4) specifically called for a reconsideration of AMLE's *This We Believe* (NMSA, 2010). He made the following recommendations:

> ...elements of the position paper were constricting and limiting with regards to students experiencing homelessness. Research described young adolescents as having a "heightened interest in personal grooming" (NMSA, 2010, p. 6) while simultaneously making unhealthy nutritional choices. *This We Believe* does not even allude to the possibility that young adolescents may not have access to healthier options given the effects of poverty. *This We Believe* stated, "Young adolescents also witness and experience the negative results of homelessness, racism, drug and alcohol abuse, crime, international terrorism, wars, domestic violence, and child abuse" (p. 9). This relegation to a position on a list does little to impact homelessness and the subsequent call for schools to "foster responsible, moral decision makers" (p. 9) almost seems to imply a lack of morality present within homelessness. (p. 86)

Other authors also specifically discussed gaps in *This We Believe* (NMSA, 2010). Beucher and Smith (Chapter 9) provided examples of curriculum development that combined culturally responsive pedagogy with three of *This We Believe*'s principles related to relationship building, "educators must understand the needs of middle school youth...all members of a classroom benefit from collaborative, engaged, active, and purposeful learning...[and] how these [school structures] should foster positive relationships among in-school stakeholders and the out-of-school community" (p. 193). As Beucher and Smith discussed each principle they reframed it from a culturally responsive lens. For example, in relation to fostering positive relationships among all educational stakeholders they shared:

> School systems must know their community in order to offer a learning environment that will honor youth's tribal customs and beliefs that offer, "American Indian students a sense of pride in their education" (Hudiberg, Mascher, Sagehorn, & Stidham, 2015, p. 138)...Critical consciousness as an organizing pedagogy is respective of youth by positioning them as intellectuals. The curriculum that we are designing intends to have students learn from community elders 7and members who visited Standing Rock and have knowledge of the cultural and ancestral practices that will acknowledge students' histories, perspectives, and viewpoints. (p. 194)

Examples of ways to expound upon how we can and should be responsive to young adolescents in middle grades seminal documents such as these are cited in nearly every chapter in this Handbook.

REEXAMINING THE MIDDLE GRADES CONCEPT

Once we reconsider the philosophy that undergirds middle grades education and the concept, we must do the same with what has come to be known as the middle grades concept. As we alluded to in the opening chapter of this book, the field of middle level education needs to examine current middle level practices that it holds sacred to the middle level movement. The field largely centers these practices around the following components; exploratory programs, integrated curriculum, transition programs, advisory, heterogeneous/multi-age grouping, interdisciplinary teaming, common planning time, and family-community connections (see Jackson & Davis, 2000 and NMSA, 2010). A re-examination of these practices in a critical way can serve to remake a middle grades concept that is relevant and meaningful into the future. Two questions to guide this work might include: Does the middle grades concept sustain all aspects of students' identities? And does it prepare students with dominant identities to be critically conscious? Given that its founders began the middle grades movement to create more equitable schooling experiences for young adolescents (Beane, 1997; Dickinson & Butler, 2001; Koos, 1927; Lounsbury, 1991; Lounsbury & Vars,

1978; NMSA, 1991, 2010), it is time to revisit those activist roots. If we want a middle grades concept that can provide guidance for those working to dismantle systems of oppression for young adolescents, the answers to both questions posed above need to be yes.

In a previous review of equity-based middle grades research, Hurd et al. (2018) found that there are some strong examples of middle grades research that show how to use the middle grades concept to create more equitable middle schools and experiences for diverse young adolescents. For example, Brown and Leaman (2007) showed how to use exploratory programs as a curricular space to support students' understanding of their ethnic identity and local community context. However, Hurd et al. concluded in their review of literature that researchers discussed the middle grades concept, even in equity-based research, in ways that were void of cultural context and therefore did not demonstrate how to use the middle grades concept to dismantle or disrupt educational or social inequities.

PREPARING FUTURE MIDDLE GRADES EDUCATORS WHO KNOW NO OTHER WAY TO TEACH THAN AN EQUITABLE ONE

Thomas and Howell's chapter (Chapter 12) reminds us that becoming culturally responsive is an ongoing, transformational process, thus it needs to begin as we prepare individuals to become middle grades educators. Collectively, the chapters in this book all echoed this by calling for educators to do the hard work, ideally before entering the profession. This hard work includes exploring one's positionality, becoming aware of one's cultural blind spots, focusing on assets-based as opposed to deficit-based thinking, and understanding the cultural characteristics and contributions of marginalized groups. While the idea of preparing teachers to work with diverse populations in equitable ways is not new (Cochran-Smith, 2010; Gorski & Swalwell, 2015; hooks, 1994; Jones & Hughes-Decatur, 2012; Ladson-Billings, 1995; Sleeter, 2012), what is missing from the research literature is a focus on equitable, social justice-oriented teacher education in support of young adolescents (Brinegar, 2015).

It is imperative then, for middle grades teacher educators to develop and infuse equity frameworks into their work with pre and in-service middle grades educators, as Ellerbrock and Vomvoridi-Ivanovic (Chapter 3) demonstrated in their chapter. It is equally as important for middle grades researchers to investigate teacher education practices that lead to the enactment of equitable and culturally responsive practices for young adolescents by their teacher candidates. For example, the focus of Thomas and Howell's chapter (Chapter 12) on the emergence of critical consciousness in graduate students has implications for pre-service teachers. They described the value of preparing middle grades educators who consistently enact cycles of culturally responsive practices, reflection, and feedback. They stressed the need for teachers who examine their decision-making within each phase of teaching. Likewise, Murphy and Kennedy (Chapter 14) stressed that, "Teacher educators have the opportunity to prepare PSTs to overcome challenges by openly interrogating the role of culture in teaching and learning, a process that begins by helping PSTs recognize how their own cultural backgrounds shape their behaviors, beliefs, and biases" (p. 315). They shared multiple research-based strategies for accomplishing this in a middle grades context. It is this middle grades context that makes the teacher education work in this book unique and critically important, and we hope the start of a greater focus on equity in work with middle grades pre-service teachers.

CONCLUSION

As stated previously, this book is a call to action. The research represented in this text is a small step in the work needed to ensure equitable and socially just educational outcomes for all young adolescents. As seen throughout the chapters of this volume:

> The young adolescents who populate the halls and classrooms of middle schools across the United States must have teachers who actively seek equity. Equity is not a prize that can be actualized and must be continuously sought in order to provide the most equitable environment for students. (Moulton, this volume, pp. 84–85)

It is therefore our responsibility as middle grades educators, researchers, and advocates to reexamine and reconsider our work to continuously seek equitable educational opportunities for all young adolescents, especially those with marginalized identities.

We would be remiss to not acknowledge that the focal point of the invaluable work and efforts toward equity and cultural responsiveness, reside with young adolescents themselves and their local communities. Young adolescents, especially those with marginalized identities, need to and should have a voice. They are in the daily throes of battle against inequity, subjugation, and oppressive teaching that traditionally caters mostly to White, middle class young adolescents. Likewise, members of the local community have a deep understanding of the socio-cultural context that impacts the lives of young adolescents and can serve as a resource to those who are trying to support student development. Therefore, who better to have at the center of that effort of equity and cultural responsiveness than the two most involved and impacted constituents for change? This is one necessary direction for future research that was not as prominent within this text.

We invite our readers to continue engaging in the work needed to: equitize the middle grades framework; redefine young adolescents in culturally sustaining ways; counteract bias by acknowledging, respecting, and celebrating counternarratives; revisit *This We Believe* and its 16 principles; reexamine the middle grades concept; prepare future middle grades educators who know no other way to teach than an equitable one; and identify further areas for research and action in support of young adolescents with marginalized identities. The future of our movement, but most importantly the future of young adolescents depends on it.

REFERENCES

Apple, M. W. (2004). *Ideology and curriculum* (3rd ed.). New York, NY: Routledge.

Beane, J. A. (1997). *Curriculum integration. Designing the core of democratic education.* New York, NY: Teachers College Press.

Brinegar, K. (2015). A content analysis of four peer-reviewed middle grades publications: Are we really paying attention to every young adolescent? *Middle Grades Review, 1*(1), 1–8. Retrieved from https://files.eric.ed.gov/fulltext/EJ1154860.pdf

Brinegar, K., Kennedy-Lewis, B., Harrison, L., & Hurd, E. (2016). Cultural responsiveness. In S.B. Mertens, M. M. Caskey, P. Bishop, N. Flowers, D. Strahan, D., G. Andrews, & L. Daniel (Eds.), *The MLER SIG Research Agenda* (pp. 4–6). Retrieved from http://mlersig.net/mler-sig-research-agenda-project/

Brown, D. F., & Leaman, H. L. (2007). Recognizing and responding to young adolescents' ethnic identity development. In S. B. Mertens, V. A. Anfara, & M. M. Caskey (Eds.), *The young adolescent and the middle school.* Charlotte, NC: Information Age.

Busey, C. (2017, April). *This who believes? A critical race discourse analysis of the Association for Middle Level Education's* This We Believe. Paper presented at the annual meeting of the American Educational Research Association, San Antonio, TX.

Cochran-Smith, M. (2010). Toward a theory of teacher education for social justice. In A. Hargreaves, A. Lieberman, M. Fullan, & D. Hopkins (Eds.), *Second international handbook of educational change* (pp. 445–467, Vol. 23). Dordrecht, Netherlands: Springer Science & Business.

Crenshaw, K. (1989). Demarginalizing the intersection of race and sex: A black feminist critique of antidiscrimination doctrine, feminist theory, and antiracist politics. *University of Chicago Legal Forum, 1*, 139–167. Retrieved from https://chicagounbound.uchicago.edu/cgi/viewcontent.cgi?article=1052&context=uclf

Crenshaw, K. (1991). Mapping the margins: Intersectionality, identity politics, and violence against women of color. *Stanford Law Review, 43*(6), 1241–1279.

Dickinson, T. S., & Butler, D. A. (2001). Reinventing the middle school: A proposal to counter arrested development. *Middle School Journal, 33*(1), 1–13.

Emdin, C. (2016). *For White folks who teach in the hood . . . and the rest of Y'all too: Reality pedagogy in urban education.* Boston, MA: Beacon Press.

Freire, P. (1970). *Pedagogy of the oppressed.* New York, NY: Continuum.

Gay, G. (2000). *Culturally responsive teaching: Theory, research, and practice.* New York, NY: Teachers College Press.

Gorski, P. C. (2013). *Reaching and teaching students in poverty: Strategies for erasing the opportunity gap.* New York, NY: Teachers College Press.

Gorski, P. C., & Swalwell, K. (2015). Equity literacy for all. *Educational Leadership, 72*(6), 34–40.

hooks, b. (1994). *Teaching to transgress: Education as the practice of freedom.* New York, NY: Routledge.

Hudiberg, M., Mascher, E., Sagehorn, A., & Stidham, J. (2015). Moving toward a culturally competent model of education: Preliminary results of a study of culturally responsive teaching in an American Indian Community. *School Libraries Worldwide, 21*(1), 137–148.

Hurd, E., Harrison, L., Brinegar, K., & Kennedy, B. L. (2018). Cultural responsiveness in the middle grades: A literature review. In S. B. Mertens & M. M. Caskey (Eds.), *Literature reviews in support of the Middle Level Education Research Agenda* (pp. 25–51). Charlotte, NC: Information Age.

Hussar, W. J., & Bailey, T. M. (2017). *Projections of education statistics to 2025 (NCES 2017-019).* Washington, DC: National Center for Education Statistics, Institute of Education Sciences, U.S. Department of Education. Retrieved from https://nces.ed.gov/pubs2017/2017019.pdf

Jackson, A. W., & Davis, G. A. (2000). *Turning points 2000: Educating adolescents in the 21stcentury.* New York, NY: Teacher's College Press.

Jones, S. R., & Hughes-Decatur, H. (2012). Speaking of bodies in justice-oriented, feminist teacher education. *Journal of Teacher Education, 63*(1), 51–61.

Kennedy, B. L., Brinegar, K., Hurd, E., & Harrison, L. (2016). Synthesizing middle grades research on cultural responsiveness: The importance of a shared conceptual framework. *Middle Grades Review, 2*(3), 1–20. Retrieved from http://scholarworks.uvm.edu/mgreview/vol2/iss3/2

Koos, L. V. (1927). *The junior high school.* Boston, MA: Ginn and Company.

Ladson-Billings, G. (1995). Toward a theory of culturally relevant pedagogy. *American Educational Research Journal, 32*(3), 465–491.

Ladson-Billings, G. (2006). From the achievement gap to the education debt: Understanding achievement in U.S. schools. *Educational Researcher, 35*(7), 3–12. Retrieved from https://doi.org/10.3102/0013189X035007003

Ladson-Billings, G. (2014) Culturally relevant pedagogy 2.0: A.K.A. the remix. *Harvard Educational Review, 84*(1), 74–84.

Lounsbury, J. H. (1991). *As I see it.* Columbus, OH: National Middle School Association.

Lounsbury. J. H., & Vars, G. F. (1978). *A curriculum for the middle school years.* New York, NY: Harper & Row.

Marsh, C., & Willis, G. (2003). *Curriculum: Alternative approaches, ongoing issues* (3rd ed.). Upper Saddle River, NJ: Merrill and Prentice Hall.

Martinez, D. E. (2014). Methodologies of social justice: Indigenous foundations and lessons. In G. Henson, & A. Wilson (Eds.), *Exploring social justice: Indigenous perspectives* (pp. 2–21). Vernon, British Columbia: J Charlton.

McAllister, G., & Irvine, J. J. (2000). Cross cultural competency and multicultural teacher education. *Review of Educational Research, 70*(1), 3–24. doi.org/10.3102/00346543070001003

Milne, A. (2016). Where am I in our schools' white spaces? Social justice for the learners we marginalise. *Middle Grades Review, 1*(3), 1–8. Retrieved from https://files.eric.ed.gov/fulltext/EJ1154894.pdf

Moll, L. C., Amanti, C., Neff, D., & Gonzalez, N. (1992). Funds of knowledge for teaching: Using a qualitative approach to connect homes and classrooms. *Theory Into Practice, 31*(2), 132–141.

National Middle School Association. (1991). *Professional certification and preparation for the middle level: A position paper of National Middle School Association.* Columbus, OH: Author.

National Middle School Association. (2010). *This we believe: Keys to educating young adolescents.* Westerville, OH: Author.

Paris, D. (2012). Culturally sustaining pedagogy: A needed change in stance, terminology, and practice. *Educational Researcher, 41*(3), 93–97.

Paris, D., & Alim, H. S. (Eds.). (2017). *Culturally sustaining pedagogies: Teaching and learning for justice in a changing world.* New York, NY: Teachers College Press.

Sleeter, C. E. (2012). Confronting the marginalization of culturally responsive pedagogy. *Urban Education, 47*(3), 562–584.

Solorzano, D. G, & Yosso, T. J. (2009). Critical race methodology: Counter-storytelling as an analytical framework for educational research. In E. Taylor, D. Gillborn, & G. Ladson-Billings. (Eds.), *Foundations of critical race theory in education* (pp. 131–147). New York, NY: Routledge.

Valencia, R. (Ed.). (1997). *The evolution of deficit thinking: Educational thought and practice.* Washington DC: Falmer Press.

ABOUT THE EDITORS

Kathleen M. Brinegar (she, her, hers) is associate academic dean and associate professor of education at Northern Vermont University where she serves as program director of the middle and secondary teacher education programs. Her research focuses on equity, cultural responsiveness, student engagement, and adolescent literacy. Kathleen is co-editor of *Middle School Journal* and vice chair of the Middle Level Education Research SIG of American Educational Research Association (AERA). E-mail: Kathleen.Brinegar@NorthernVermont.edu

Lisa M. Harrison (she, her, hers) is associate professor of middle childhood education (MCE) at Ohio University where she serves as the MCE program coordinator. Her research interest focuses on issues of equity and social justice in middle level education and teacher preparation. She also explores the lived experiences of Black girls. Lisa serves on the Board of Trustees for the Association for Middle Level Education (AMLE) and AMLE Professional Preparation Advisory Committee; she is co-editor of *Middle School Journal*. E-mail: harrisl1@ohio.edu

Ellis Hurd (he, him, his) is professor of middle level/bilingual education in the School of Teaching and Learning at Illinois State University. He has 20 years of teaching experience in diverse settings across two states. He has published on teacher, middle grades/bilingual, and urban education, equity and cultural responsiveness, and mixed identities. Ellis is as a member of the Association for Middle Level Education (AMLE) Program Review Board for the Council for the Accreditation of Educator Preparation (CAEP) and co-editor of *Middle School Journal*. E-mail: ehurd@ilstu.edu

ABOUT THE CONTRIBUTORS

William Andrews (he, him, his) is academic advisor and internship coordinator in the iLab at Winooski Middle and High School in Winooski, VT. William has taught middle and high school social studies for nearly 10 years and is a founding member of the iLab which is a student centered, project-based learning environment for middle and high school students. E-mail: wandrews@wsdschools.org

Becky Beucher (she, her, hers) is assistant professor of secondary literacy education in the School of Teaching and Learning at Illinois State University. She taught secondary English language arts for 6 years before pursuing a PhD in literacy education. Her research interests include investigating racialized youth's multiliteracy practices across middle and high school contexts. She has published on youths' multimodal storying processes. Becky collaboratively develops culturally responsive multiliteracies curriculum with practicing teachers. Email: rlbeuch@ilstu.edu

Brendan Downing (he, him, his) is a teacher education doctoral student and Albert Schweitzer Fellow at Ohio University. His research interests include LGBTQ youth education, specifically young adolescent victimization. Brendan seeks to bring transformative change to how young adolescent LGBTQ students are understood and treated in the education system. Brendan spent 7years in the K–12 system, 2 years teaching middle school technology, 4 years teaching high school technology and art and 1 year as a district STEM Coach. E-mail: bd184503@ohio.edu

Equity & Cultural Responsiveness in the Middle Grades, pages 351–355
Copyright © 2019 by Information Age Publishing
351

Cheryl R. Ellerbrock (she, her, hers) is associate professor of middle grades and general secondary education in the Department of Teaching and Learning at the University of South Florida. She publishes on the ways secondary schooling is responsive to the needs of adolescent learners, ways to foster a responsive middle-to-high-school transition, and ways to cultivate developmentally and culturally responsive teachers. Cheryl is program chair of the Middle Level Education Research SIG of American Educational Research Association (AERA) and member of Association for Middle Level Education's Research Advisory Council. Email: ellerbro@usf.edu

ThedaMarie Gibbs Grey (she, her, hers) is assistant professor of reading education in the Department of Teacher Education at the Ohio University, Patton College of Education. Her scholarship and practice focus on affirming the literacies and lives of Black youth. She possesses a commitment to preparing literacy educators to teach all students equitably and effectively. Her most recent research focuses on humanizing the voices of Black middle school girls through a yearlong ethnographic study and mentorship program. Email: gibbst1@ohio.edu

Tracy Hamel (she, her, hers) is a doctoral candidate in curriculum and instruction, elementary education at the University of Minnesota. She has elementary, middle, high school, undergraduate and graduate level teaching experience in diverse settings across two states. Tracy is working to complete her dissertation, a post-intentional phenomenological study of how critical consciousness takes shape for young people and adults through a process of youth participatory action research. Tracy works alongside high school students at a community based organization facilitating youth participatory action research projects. Tracy is the curriculum director for a community based organization serving elementary, middle, and high school students. E-mail: hamel061@umn.edu

Penny B. Howell (she, her, hers) is associate professor of middle level education at the University of Louisville. She is the liaison to the university's signature Partnership Middle School, and her research and teaching focus include middle level teacher education. She is currently the chair of the Middle Level Education Research SIG of American Educational Research Association (AERA), serves as chair of the Association for Middle Level Education (AMLE) Professional Preparation Advisory Committee and is a member of the AMLE Program Review Board. She is a former middle school teacher and literacy consultant. She received her master's and doctoral degrees from Teachers College, Columbia University. Email: penny.howell@louisville.edu

Kriss Y. Kemp-Graham (she, her, hers) is associate professor in the Educational Leadership Department at Texas A&M University-Commerce. She has more than two decades of experience working at the school and central office levels in New York and New Jersey. Dr. Kemp-Graham has published on school administrator cultural competence, social justice leadership, and disproportionality in the assignment of disciplinary consequences to African American students. She has also published two books: *Preparing for School Leadership in Texas: Mastering Principal Competencies and Challenges of 21st Century School Leadership* and *The Elephant in the Room: Urban School Reform.* Dr. Kemp-Graham is an active member of numerous state and national professional organizations. E-mail: kriss.kemp-graham@tamuc.edu

Brianna L. Kennedy (she, her, hers) is on the faculty of social and behavioral sciences at Utrecht University, the Netherlands. She adopts methodological plurality to conduct research centered on under-served K–12 students. She has published articles addressing the racial discipline gap in U.S. schools. Currently, she is developing projects regarding social justice issues in schools in the Global North. Before pursuing a PhD in urban education at the University of Southern California Los Angeles, Dr. Kennedy taught young adolescents in the Los Angeles Unified School District. E-mail: b.l.kennedy@uu.nl

Matthew J. Moulton (he, him, his) is assistant professor in the Department of Teaching and Learning at Indiana State University. He has worked with young adolescents across the country for more than 10 years in both formal and informal settings. Matt is a teacher educator whose research with and for young adolescents experiencing homelessness directly enhances his teaching. He has published manuscripts on teacher education, student homelessness, and the importance of community contexts in preparing future teachers. E-mail: matthew.moulton@indstate.edu

Amy S. Murphy (she, her, hers) is clinical assistant professor in the Department of Educational Theory and Practice at the University of Georgia (UGA). As part of UGA's Professional Development School District, she is professor-in-residence at a local middle school where she works with UGA middle grades program teacher candidates and facilitates job-embedded professional development with inservice teachers. She has published on culturally responsive classroom management, school discipline, and social justice teacher education. E-mail: asmurphy@uga.edu

James Nagle (he, him, his) is associate professor of education at Saint Michael's College in Colchester, VT. He teaches curriculum and instruction courses in the middle and secondary program. His research areas include the intersection of educational policies initiatives and teacher learning, and personalized learning and flexible pathways for English learners. James is also the co-editor of the *Middle Grades Review* and co-director of the Middle Grades Collaborative that offers professional development to middle school teachers and administrators. E-mail: jnagle2@smcvt.edu

Mark B. Pacheco (he, him, his) is assistant professor of ESOL/bilingual education in the College of Education at the University of Florida. His research focuses on the language and literacy practices of multilingual learners and how educators can support these practices. He has worked as a teacher and teacher educator in the United States and abroad. E-mail: mpacheco@coe.ufl.edu

Amy Smith (she, her, hers) is a doctoral student in the School of Teaching and Learning at Illinois State University, where her research interests include critical media literacy and equity and cultural responsiveness at the secondary level. She has more than 15 years of classroom and school administrative experience. Email: assmith3@ilstu.edu

Blaine E. Smith (she, her, hers) is assistant professor of new literacies and bi/multilingual immigrant learners in the Department of Teaching, Learning, and Sociocultural Studies at the University of Arizona. Her research focuses on the digital literacies of culturally and linguistically diverse adolescents across contexts, with special attention to their multimodal composing processes. Blaine's research has appeared in *Computers & Education, Journal of Second Language Writing, Written Communication,* and *Bilingual Research Journal.* Email: blainesmith@email.arizona.edu

Shelley Thomas (she, her, hers) is associate professor of middle and secondary education at the University of Louisville and a steering committee member of the Cooperative Consortium for Transdisciplinary Social Justice Research at the university. Her research includes social justice perspectives of teachers and teacher candidates and culturally responsive teaching in clinical teacher education. She is a former middle and high school social studies teacher. She received an M.A.T. from the University of Louisville and an EdD from Teachers College, Columbia University. E-mail: shelley.thomas@louisville.edu

Christine Uliassi (she, her, hers) is a doctoral candidate in State University of New York (SUNY) Binghamton's Graduate School of Education. Her research focus is critical teaching practices for English language learners. She has also published on intersectionality in children's books, artifactual literacies, and teacher preparation in literacy. She was an elementary and ESL educator in the Fairfax County Public Schools in Virginia for 12 years. She now supports teacher candidates. E-mail: culiass1@binghamton.edu

Mark Vagle (he, him, his), a former teacher (elementary and middle school) and middle school administrator, is professor of education at University of Minnesota. Mark is principal author and editor of *Not a Stage! A Critical Re-Conception of Young Adolescent Education.* This book and his numerous articles focus on the powerful ways moment-to-moment classroom interactions reveal broader systemic issues and concerns. His most current research examines the profound influence social class has on the ways in which teachers and students perceive and engage with one another and how particular social class-sensitive pedagogies can be enacted in classrooms. E-mail: mvagle@umn.edu

Eugenia Vomvoridi-Ivanovic (she, her, hers) is associate professor of mathematics education in the Department of Teaching and Learning at the University of South Florida. Her areas of experience and interest in research and teaching focus on improving mathematics education for students historically underrepresented and undereducated in the field of mathematics and whose linguistic and cultural backgrounds have not traditionally been recognized as being resources for academic learning. Email: eugeniav@usf.edu

Toni M. Williams (she, her, hers) is assistant professor in the middle level and language and literacy programs in the Department of Instruction and Teacher Education at the University of South Carolina. She supervises middle level preservice interns as they prepare for student teaching. She has published on culturally responsive education, Black males, and life histories of Black middle school teachers. She has 13 years of middle school experience dedicated to teaching and nurturing adolescents and preservice teachers. E-mail: tmwilli2@sc.edu

Bogum Yoon (she or Yoon) is associate professor of literacy education in the Department of Teaching, Learning, and Educational Leadership at the State University of New York at Binghamton. Her research areas include critical global literacies, cultural pluralism, positional identities and agency, and English language learners. Yoon is a series book editor of *Research in Second Language Learning* by Information Age Publishing, and column editor of critical global literacies for *English Journal* by National Council of Teachers of English. E-mail: byoon@binghamton.edu

CPSIA information can be obtained
at www.ICGtesting.com
Printed in the USA
BVHW042351050419
544783BV00006B/102/P